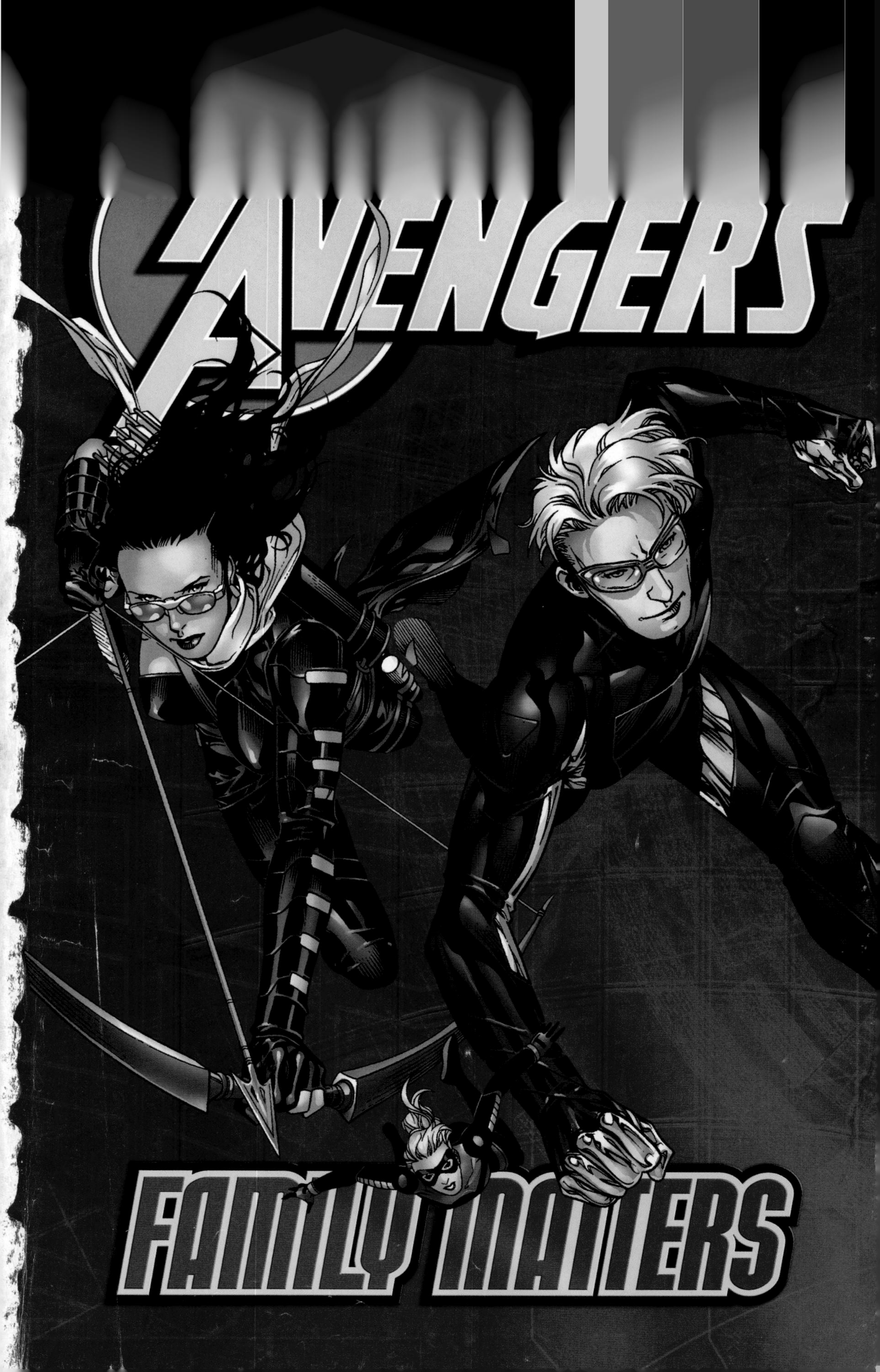
AVENGERS
FAMILY MATTERS

YOUNG AVENGERS VOL. 2: FAMILY MATTERS. Contains material originally published in magazine form as YOUNG AVENGERS #7-12 and YOUNG AVENGERS SPECIAL. First printing 2006. ISBN# 0-7851-2021-1. Published by MARVEL PUBLISHING, INC., a subsidiary of MARVEL ENTERTAINMENT, INC. OFFICE OF PUBLICATION: 417 5th Avenue, New York, NY 10016. Copyright © 2005 and 2006 Marvel Characters, Inc. All rights reserved. $22.99 per copy in the U.S. and $36.95 in Canada (GST #R127032852); Canadian Agreement #40668537. All characters featured in this issue and the distinctive names and likenesses thereof, and all related indicia are trademarks of Marvel Characters, Inc. No similarity between any of the names, characters, persons, and/or institutions in this magazine with those of any living or dead person or institution is intended, and any such similarity which may exist is purely coincidental. **Printed in the U.S.A.** ALAN FINE, President & CEO Of Marvel Toys and Marvel Publishing, Inc.; DAVID BOGART, VP Of Publishing Operations; DAN CARR, Executive Director of Publishing Technology; JUSTIN F. GABRIE, Managing Editor; STAN LEE, Chairman Emeritus. For information regarding advertising in Marvel Comics or on Marvel.com, please contact Joe Maimone, Advertising Director, at jmaimone@marvel.com or 212-576-8534.

YOUNG AVENGERS
FAMILY MATTERS

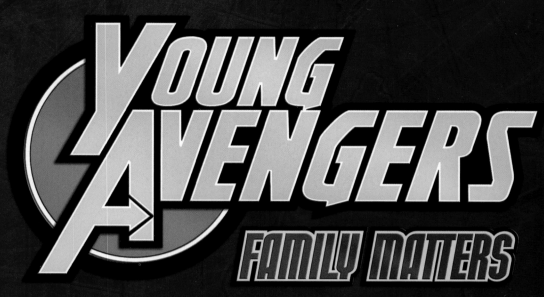

WRITER: ALLAN HEINBERG

PENCILERS: ANDREA DIVITO (ISSUES #7-8) & JIM CHEUNG

INKERS: DREW HENNESSY (ISSUES #7-8), DAVE MEIKIS, JOHN DELL, ROB STULL, DEXTER VINES, LIVESAY, JAY LEISTEN, MATT RYAN, JAIME MENDOZA, MARK MORALES & JIM CHEUNG

COLORIST: JUSTIN PONSOR

LETTERER: VIRTUAL CALLIGRAPHY'S CORY PETIT
COVER ART: JIM CHEUNG, JOHN DELL & JUSTIN PONSOR
ASSISTANT EDITORS: MOLLY LAZER & AUBREY SITTERSON
ASSOCIATE EDITOR: ANDY SCHMIDT
EDITOR: TOM BREVOORT

YOUNG AVENGERS CREATED BY ALLAN HEINBERG & JIM CHEUNG

YOUNG AVENGERS SPECIAL #1
PAGES 1, 2, 8, 9, 20, 21, 25, 26 & 34-36:
ARTIST: MICHAEL GAYDOS
COLORIST: JOSE VILLARRUBIA
PAGES 3-7:
ARTIST: NEAL ADAMS
COLORIST: JUSTIN PONSOR
PAGES 10-14:
ARTIST: GENE HA
COLORIST: ART LYON
PAGES: 15-19:
ARTIST: JAE LEE
COLORIST: JUNE CHUNG
PAGES 22-24:
ARTIST: BILL SIENKIEWICZ
COLORIST: JUSTIN PONSOR
PAGES: 27-33:
ARTIST: PASQUAL FERRY
COLORIST: DAVE MCCAIG

COLLECTION EDITOR: JENNIFER GRÜNWALD
ASSISTANT EDITOR: MICHAEL SHORT
ASSOCIATE EDITOR: MARK D. BEAZLEY
SENIOR EDITOR, SPECIAL PROJECTS: JEFF YOUNGQUIST
VICE PRESIDENT OF SALES: DAVID GABRIEL

PRODUCTION: JERRON QUALITY COLOR
VICE PRESIDENT OF CREATIVE: TOM MARVELLI

EDITOR IN CHIEF: JOE QUESADA
PUBLISHER: DAN BUCKLEY

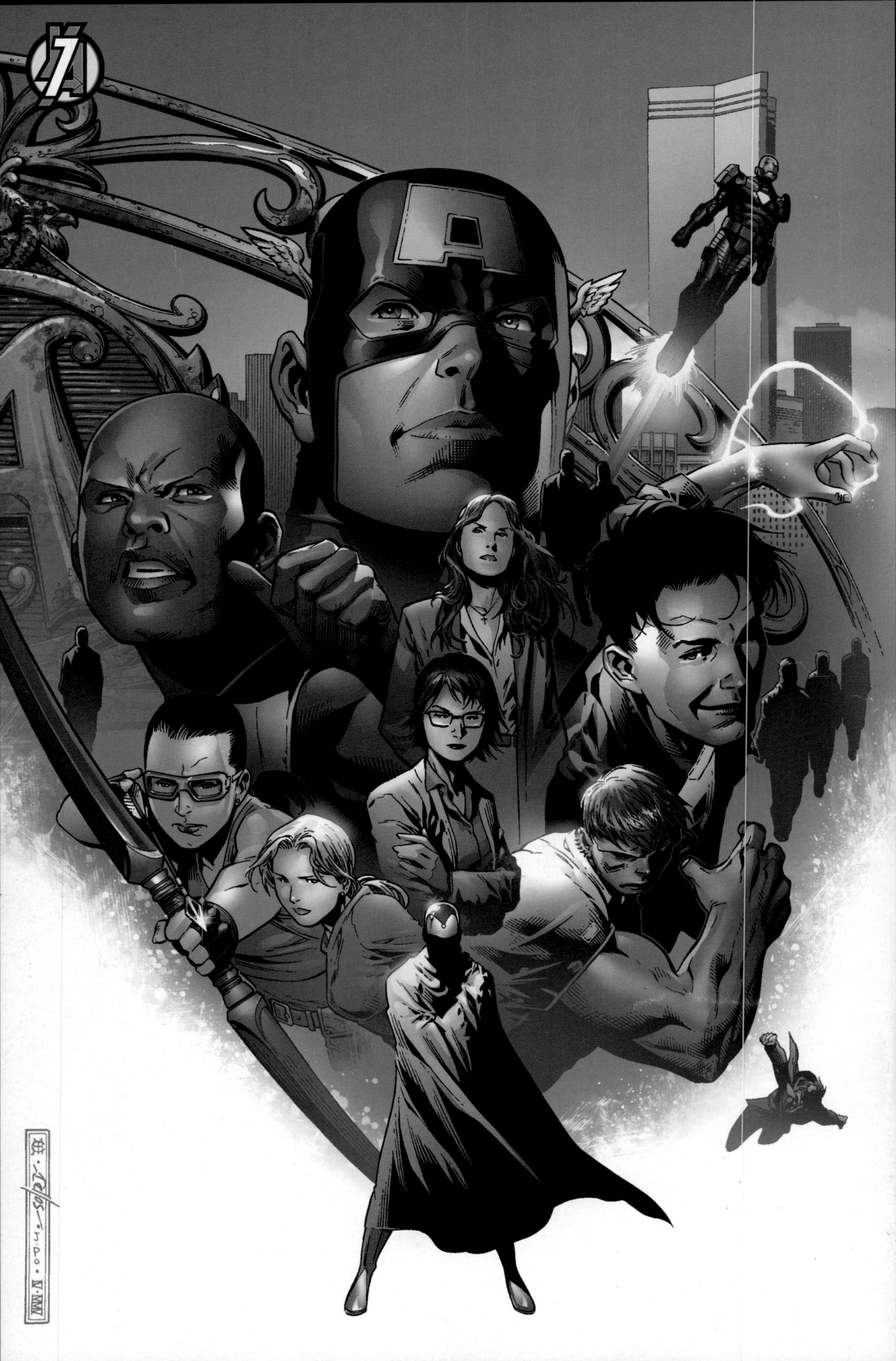

DAILY BUGLE

THE NEW YOUNG AVENGERS?

The reinvented supergroup brings a "shocking" end to attempt... ...st. The Young Avengers proudly display their quarry, The Shocker, am...
the fluttering evidence of his failure. One hundred percent of the... ...was recovered. The Shocker is currently in custody.
-Photo by Todd Cas...

> WHAT THE HELL DO THESE KIDS THINK THEY'RE DOING?

By Bugle Reporter Kat Farrell
Staff Writer

Dolor sit amet, consectetuer adipiscing elit, sed diam nonummy nibh euismod tincidunt ut laoreet dolore magna on aliquam erat volutpat. Ut wisi enim ad twe minim veniam, quis nostrud exerci tatio ullamcorper suscipit lobortis nisl ut ang.

Eliquip ex ea commodo consequat. Duis ... eum iriure dolor a hendrerit in

cumsan ... usto odio dignissim qui blandit praese... ...ptatum zzril delenit augue duis dolore... feugait nulla facilisi.

Ut w... enim ad minim veniam, quis nostrud ...erci tation ullamcorper suscipit lobor... nisl ut aliquip ex ea commodo con-seq... Duis autem vel eum iriure dolor in her... rerit in vulputate velit esse molestie co... sequat, vel illum dolore eu feugiat n... la facilisis at vero eros et accumsan et ...sto odio dignissim qui blandit praesent ...atum zzril delenit augue duis dolore te

drerit in vulputate velit esse molestie c... sequat, vel illum dolore eu feugiat nu... facilisis at vero eros et accumsan et i... odio dignissim qui blandit praesent lu... tum zzril delenit augue duis dolore te... feugait nulla facilisi.

Bolfang iktum dolor sit amet, fansta... adipiscing elit, sed diam nonummy euismod tincidunt ut laoreet dolore aliquam erat volutpat.

Duis autem vel eum iriure dolor in... drerit in vulputate velit esse moles...

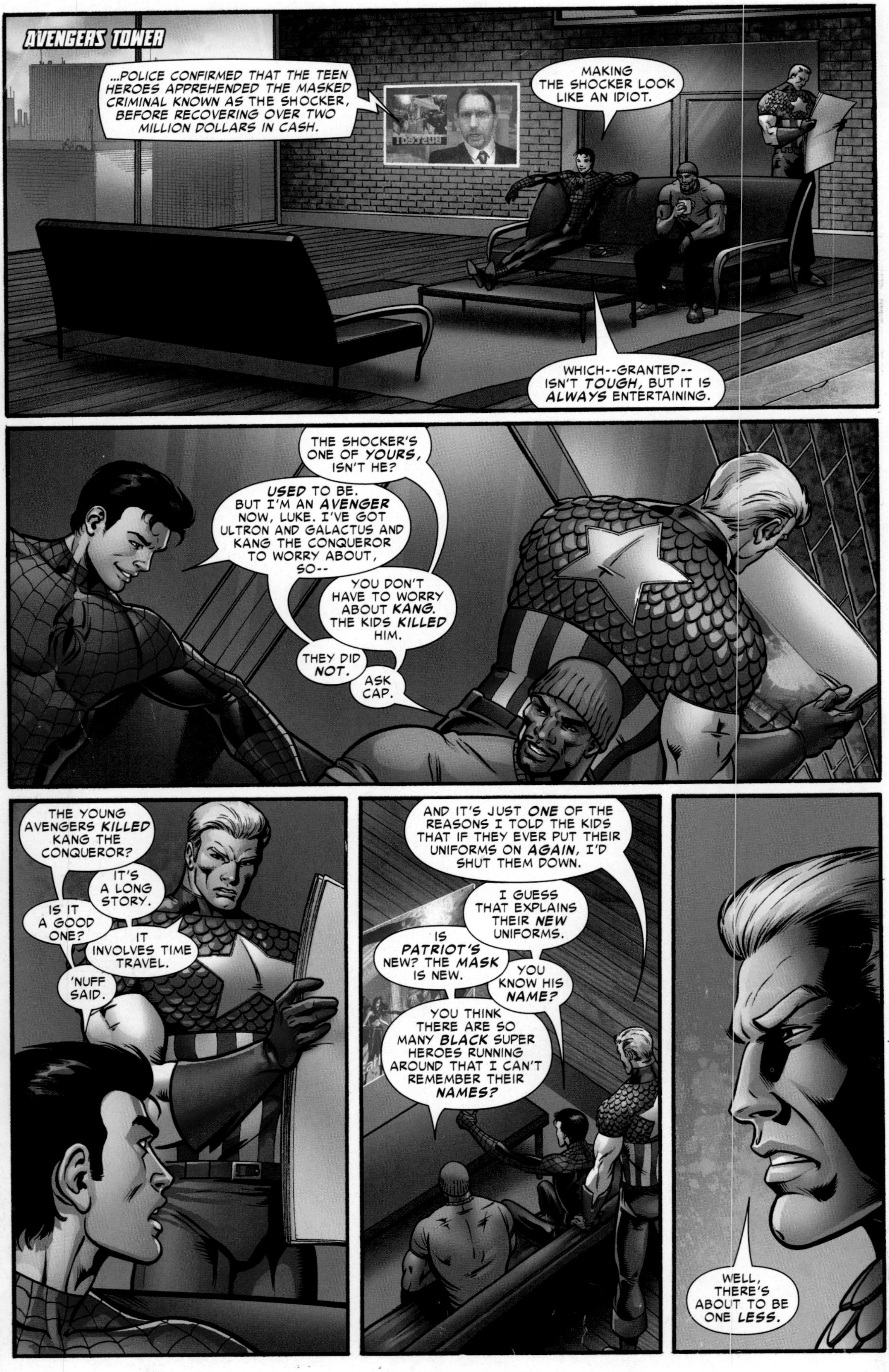
AVENGERS TOWER
...POLICE CONFIRMED THAT THE TEEN HEROES APPREHENDED THE MASKED CRIMINAL KNOWN AS THE SHOCKER, BEFORE RECOVERING OVER TWO MILLION DOLLARS IN CASH.
BUSTED!
MAKING THE SHOCKER LOOK LIKE AN IDIOT.
WHICH--GRANTED--ISN'T TOUGH, BUT IT IS ALWAYS ENTERTAINING.
THE SHOCKER'S ONE OF YOURS, ISN'T HE?
USED TO BE. BUT I'M AN AVENGER NOW, LUKE. I'VE GOT ULTRON AND GALACTUS AND KANG THE CONQUEROR TO WORRY ABOUT, SO--
YOU DON'T HAVE TO WORRY ABOUT KANG. THE KIDS KILLED HIM.
THEY DID NOT.
ASK CAP.
THE YOUNG AVENGERS KILLED KANG THE CONQUEROR?
IT'S A LONG STORY.
IS IT A GOOD ONE?
IT INVOLVES TIME TRAVEL.
'NUFF SAID.
AND IT'S JUST ONE OF THE REASONS I TOLD THE KIDS THAT IF THEY EVER PUT THEIR UNIFORMS ON AGAIN, I'D SHUT THEM DOWN.
I GUESS THAT EXPLAINS THEIR NEW UNIFORMS.
IS PATRIOT'S NEW? THE MASK IS NEW.
YOU KNOW HIS NAME?
YOU THINK THERE ARE SO MANY BLACK SUPER HEROES RUNNING AROUND THAT I CAN'T REMEMBER THEIR NAMES?
WELL, THERE'S ABOUT TO BE ONE LESS.

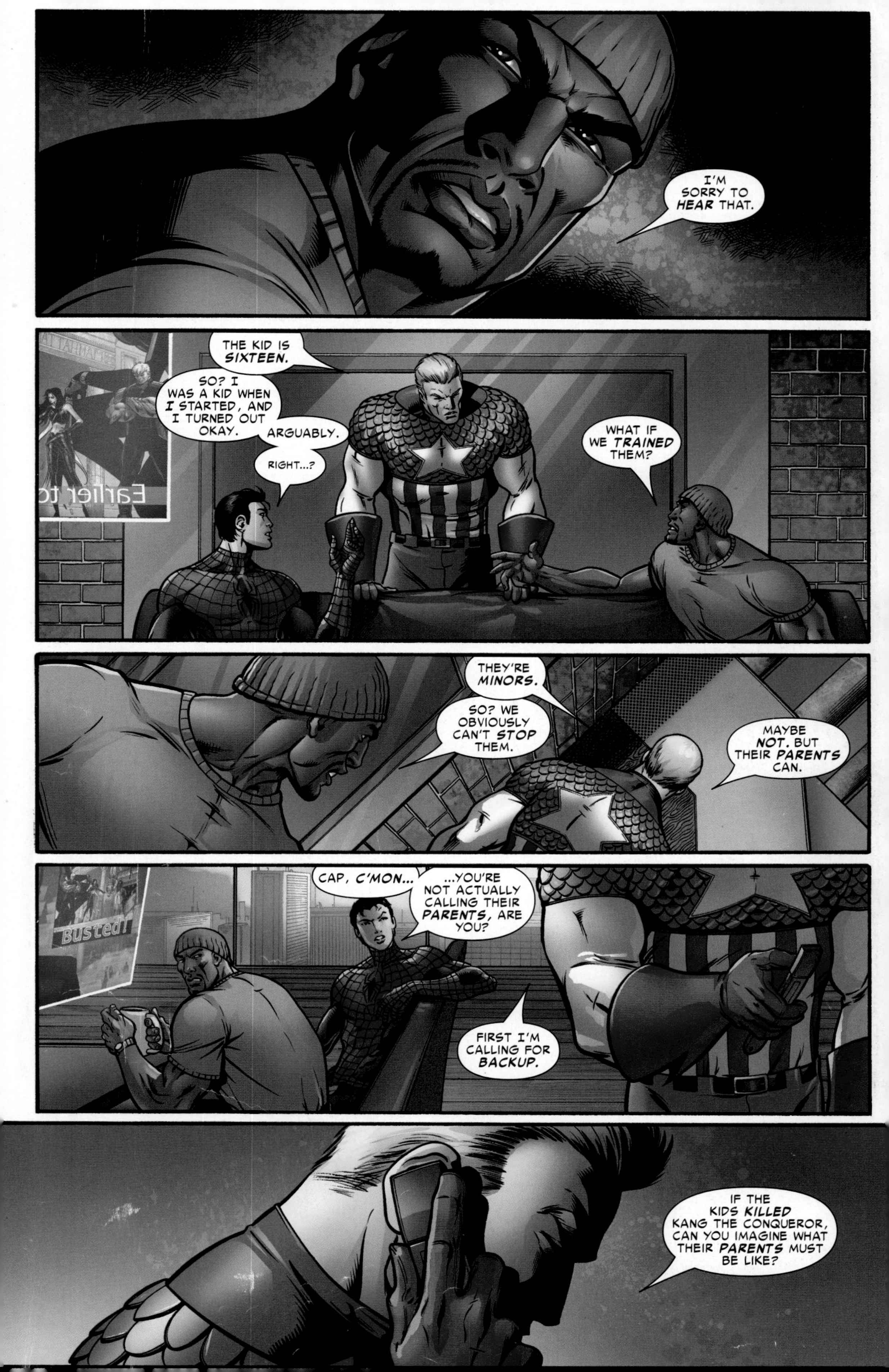
I'M SORRY TO HEAR THAT.
THE KID IS SIXTEEN.
SO? I WAS A KID WHEN I STARTED, AND I TURNED OUT OKAY.
ARGUABLY.
RIGHT...?
WHAT IF WE TRAINED THEM?
THEY'RE MINORS.
SO? WE OBVIOUSLY CAN'T STOP THEM.
MAYBE NOT. BUT THEIR PARENTS CAN.
Busted!
CAP, C'MON...
...YOU'RE NOT ACTUALLY CALLING THEIR PARENTS, ARE YOU?
FIRST I'M CALLING FOR BACKUP.
IF THE KIDS KILLED KANG THE CONQUEROR, CAN YOU IMAGINE WHAT THEIR PARENTS MUST BE LIKE?

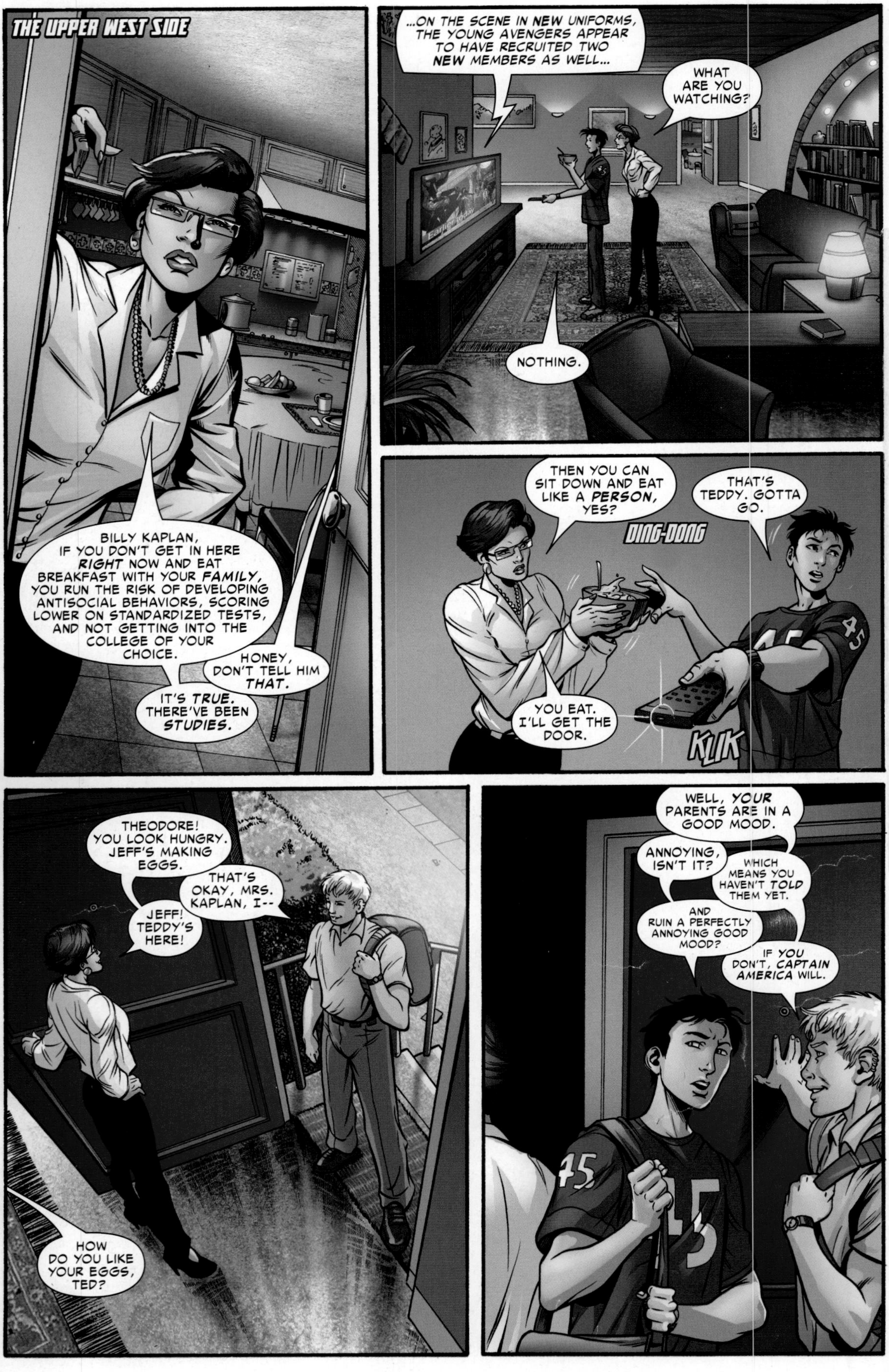
THE UPPER WEST SIDE
BILLY KAPLAN, IF YOU DON'T GET IN HERE RIGHT NOW AND EAT BREAKFAST WITH YOUR FAMILY, YOU RUN THE RISK OF DEVELOPING ANTISOCIAL BEHAVIORS, SCORING LOWER ON STANDARDIZED TESTS, AND NOT GETTING INTO THE COLLEGE OF YOUR CHOICE.
HONEY, DON'T TELL HIM THAT.
IT'S TRUE. THERE'VE BEEN STUDIES.
...ON THE SCENE IN NEW UNIFORMS, THE YOUNG AVENGERS APPEAR TO HAVE RECRUITED TWO NEW MEMBERS AS WELL...
WHAT ARE YOU WATCHING?
NOTHING.
THEN YOU CAN SIT DOWN AND EAT LIKE A PERSON, YES?
DING-DONG
THAT'S TEDDY. GOTTA GO.
YOU EAT. I'LL GET THE DOOR.
KLIK
THEODORE! YOU LOOK HUNGRY. JEFF'S MAKING EGGS.
THAT'S OKAY, MRS. KAPLAN, I--
JEFF! TEDDY'S HERE!
HOW DO YOU LIKE YOUR EGGS, TED?
WELL, YOUR PARENTS ARE IN A GOOD MOOD.
ANNOYING, ISN'T IT?
WHICH MEANS YOU HAVEN'T TOLD THEM YET.
AND RUIN A PERFECTLY ANNOYING GOOD MOOD?
IF YOU DON'T, CAPTAIN AMERICA WILL.

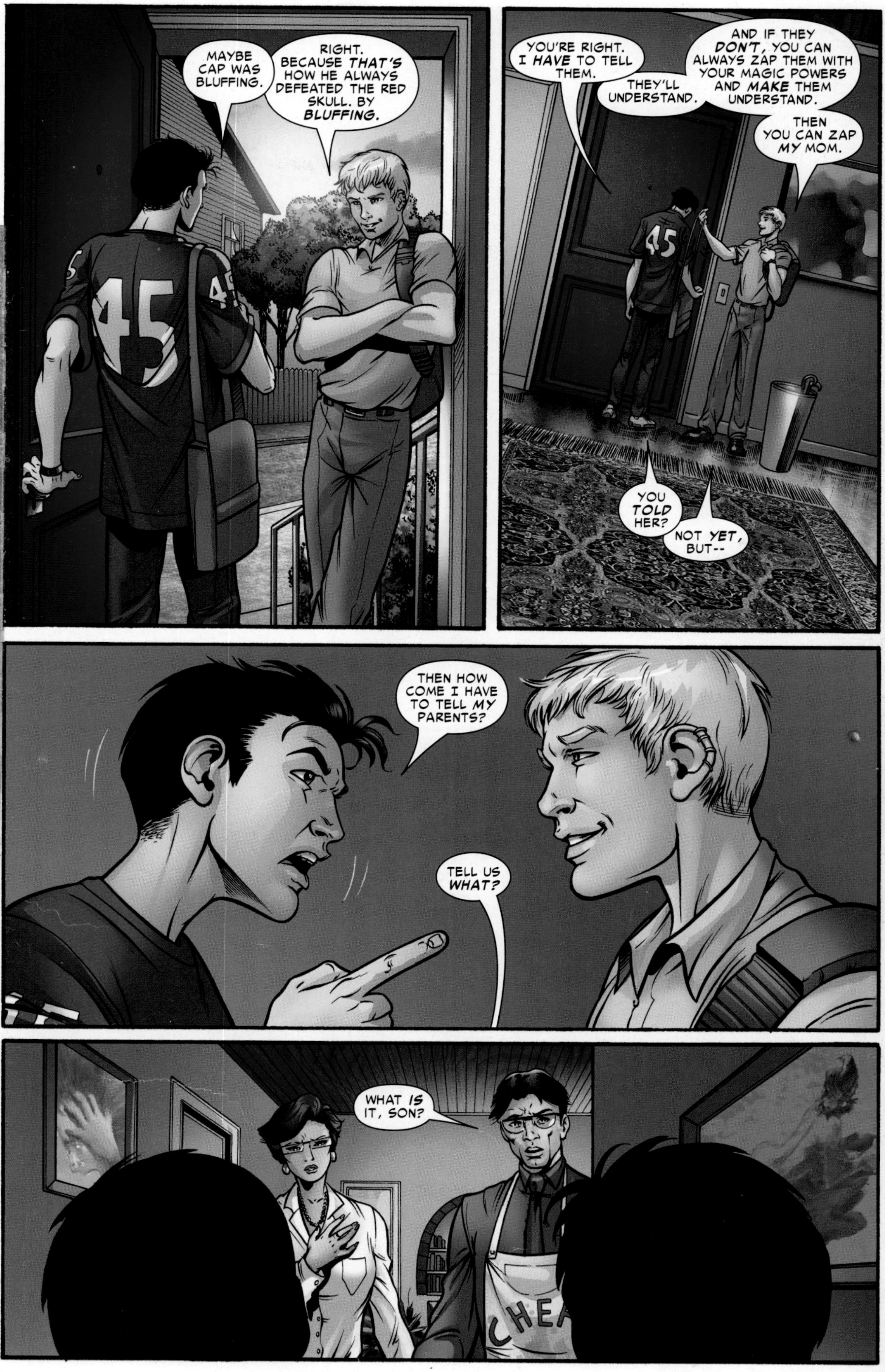

MAYBE CAP WAS BLUFFING.
RIGHT. BECAUSE *THAT'S* HOW HE ALWAYS DEFEATED THE RED SKULL. BY *BLUFFING*.
YOU'RE RIGHT. I *HAVE* TO TELL THEM.
THEY'LL UNDERSTAND.
AND IF THEY *DON'T*, YOU CAN ALWAYS ZAP THEM WITH YOUR MAGIC POWERS AND *MAKE* THEM UNDERSTAND.
THEN YOU CAN ZAP *MY* MOM.
YOU *TOLD* HER?
NOT *YET*, BUT--
THEN HOW COME I HAVE TO TELL *MY* PARENTS?
TELL US *WHAT?*
WHAT *IS* IT, SON?

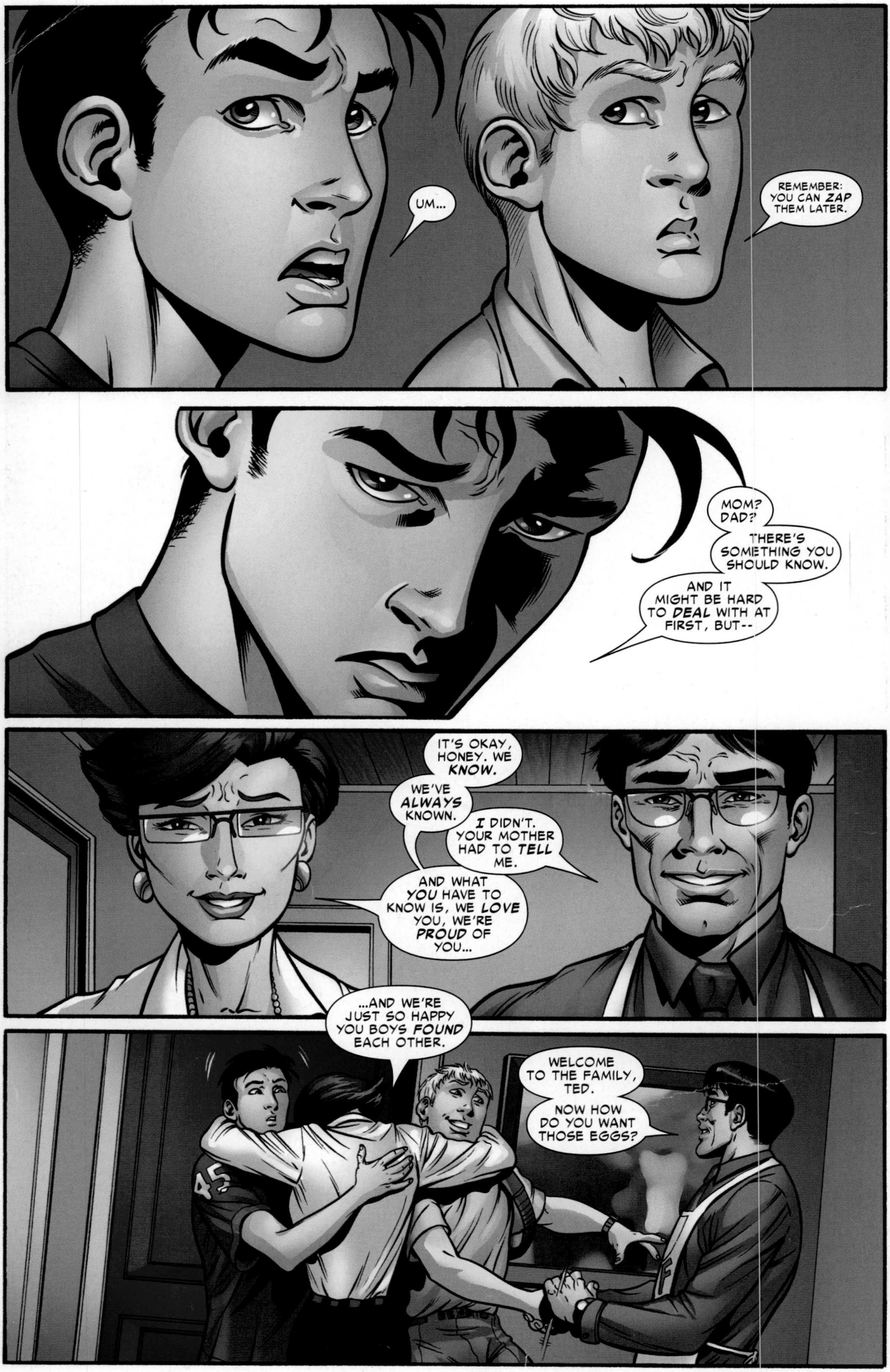
UM...
REMEMBER: YOU CAN ZAP THEM LATER.
MOM? DAD?
THERE'S SOMETHING YOU SHOULD KNOW.
AND IT MIGHT BE HARD TO DEAL WITH AT FIRST, BUT--
IT'S OKAY, HONEY. WE KNOW.
WE'VE ALWAYS KNOWN.
I DIDN'T. YOUR MOTHER HAD TO TELL ME.
AND WHAT YOU HAVE TO KNOW IS, WE LOVE YOU, WE'RE PROUD OF YOU...
...AND WE'RE JUST SO HAPPY YOU BOYS FOUND EACH OTHER.
WELCOME TO THE FAMILY, TED.
NOW HOW DO YOU WANT THOSE EGGS?

THE **GIANT** GIRL. YOU DON'T THINK--

PEGGY, C'MON...

I KNOW, BUT THE **COSTUME**, THE **HAIR**--

Earlier today

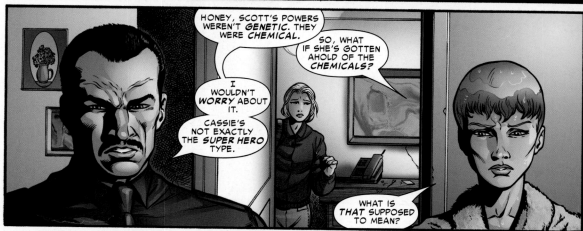

HONEY, SCOTT'S POWERS WEREN'T **GENETIC**. THEY WERE **CHEMICAL**.

SO, WHAT IF SHE'S GOTTEN AHOLD OF THE **CHEMICALS**?

I WOULDN'T **WORRY** ABOUT IT.

CASSIE'S NOT EXACTLY THE **SUPER HERO** TYPE.

WHAT IS **THAT** SUPPOSED TO MEAN?

IT MEANS SHE CAN BARELY **FOCUS** LONG ENOUGH TO DO HER **HOMEWORK**, LET ALONE CAPTURE THE SHOCKER.

BESIDES, CASSIE **KNOWS** HOW YOU FELT ABOUT HER DAD BEING ANT-MAN.

THERE'S NO WAY SHE'D PUT YOU THROUGH **THAT** AGAIN.

SHE **LOVES** YOU TOO MUCH.

WHAT ARE YOU *LOOKING* FOR, ELI?

NOTHING.

YOU GOT HOME *LATE* LAST NIGHT.

A COUPLE OF THE GUYS WANTED TO HANG OUT AFTER WORK.

SORRY, GRANDMA.

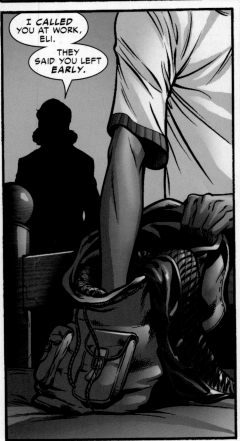

I CALLED YOU AT WORK, ELI.

THEY SAID YOU LEFT *EARLY*.

IS THERE SOMETHING YOU'D LIKE TO *TELL* ME?

I'M GONNA BE LATE FOR SCHOOL.

YOU MAKE SURE YOU SEE YOUR *GRANDFATHER* BEFORE YOU LEAVE.

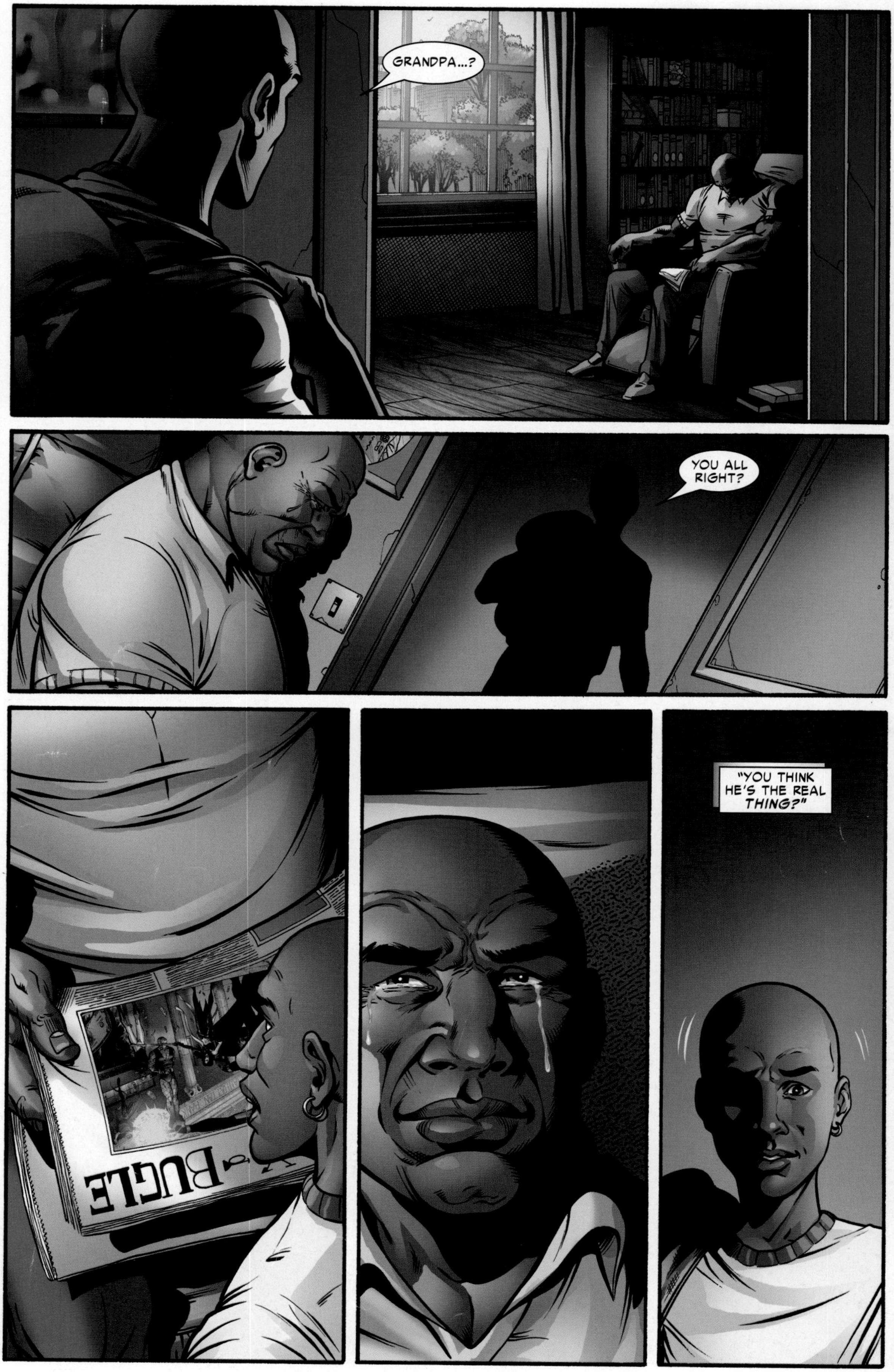
GRANDPA...?
YOU ALL RIGHT?
BUGLE
"YOU THINK HE'S THE REAL THING?"

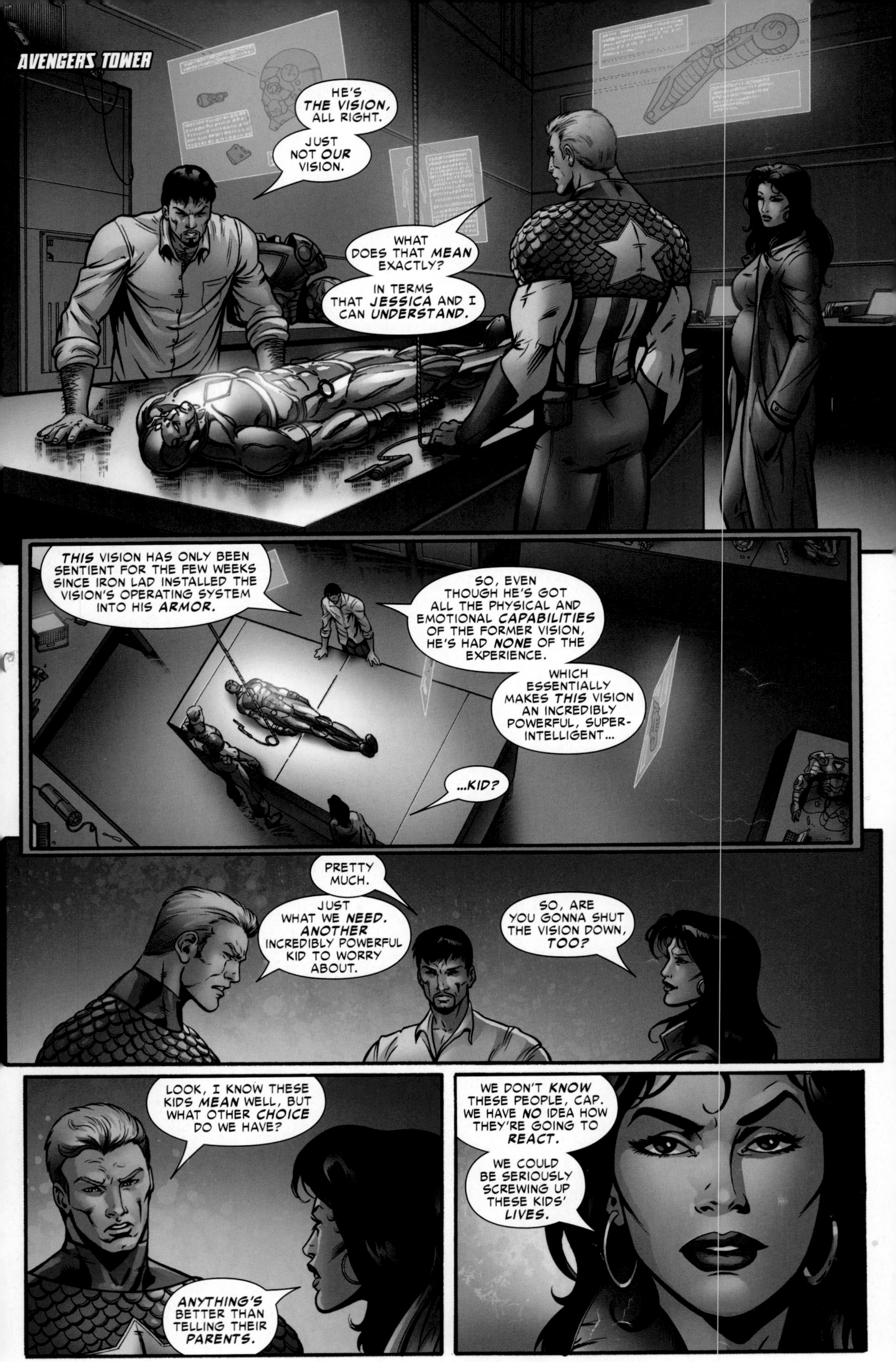
AVENGERS TOWER
HE'S THE VISION, ALL RIGHT.
JUST NOT OUR VISION.
WHAT DOES THAT MEAN EXACTLY?
IN TERMS THAT JESSICA AND I CAN UNDERSTAND.
THIS VISION HAS ONLY BEEN SENTIENT FOR THE FEW WEEKS SINCE IRON LAD INSTALLED THE VISION'S OPERATING SYSTEM INTO HIS ARMOR.
SO, EVEN THOUGH HE'S GOT ALL THE PHYSICAL AND EMOTIONAL CAPABILITIES OF THE FORMER VISION, HE'S HAD NONE OF THE EXPERIENCE.
WHICH ESSENTIALLY MAKES THIS VISION AN INCREDIBLY POWERFUL, SUPER-INTELLIGENT...
...KID?
PRETTY MUCH.
JUST WHAT WE NEED. ANOTHER INCREDIBLY POWERFUL KID TO WORRY ABOUT.
SO, ARE YOU GONNA SHUT THE VISION DOWN, TOO?
LOOK, I KNOW THESE KIDS MEAN WELL, BUT WHAT OTHER CHOICE DO WE HAVE?
ANYTHING'S BETTER THAN TELLING THEIR PARENTS.
WE DON'T KNOW THESE PEOPLE, CAP. WE HAVE NO IDEA HOW THEY'RE GOING TO REACT.
WE COULD BE SERIOUSLY SCREWING UP THESE KIDS' LIVES.

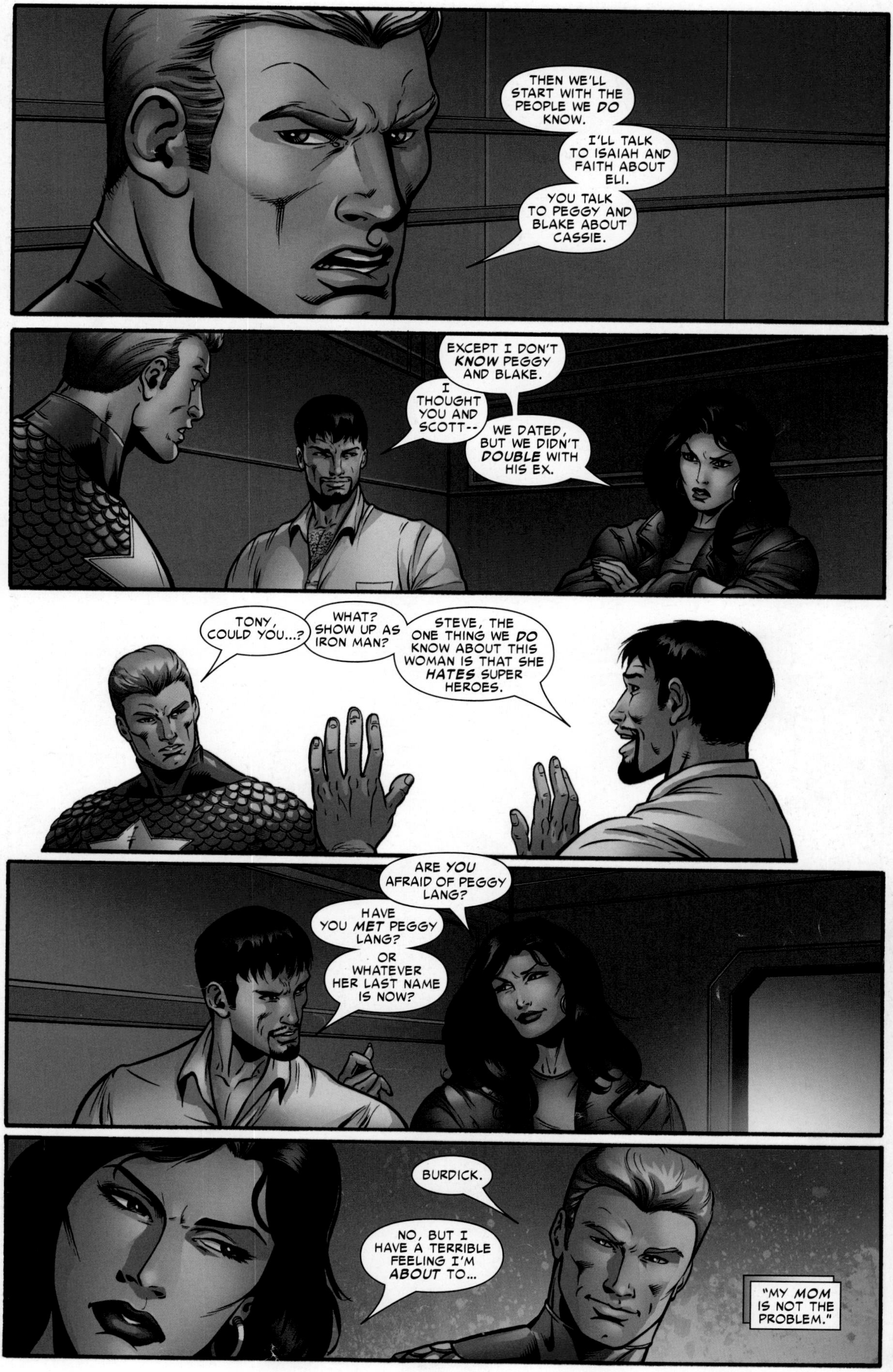

THEN WE'LL START WITH THE PEOPLE WE DO KNOW.
I'LL TALK TO ISAIAH AND FAITH ABOUT ELI.
YOU TALK TO PEGGY AND BLAKE ABOUT CASSIE.
EXCEPT I DON'T KNOW PEGGY AND BLAKE.
I THOUGHT YOU AND SCOTT--
WE DATED, BUT WE DIDN'T DOUBLE WITH HIS EX.
TONY, COULD YOU...?
WHAT? SHOW UP AS IRON MAN?
STEVE, THE ONE THING WE DO KNOW ABOUT THIS WOMAN IS THAT SHE HATES SUPER HEROES.
ARE YOU AFRAID OF PEGGY LANG?
HAVE YOU MET PEGGY LANG?
OR WHATEVER HER LAST NAME IS NOW?
BURDICK.
NO, BUT I HAVE A TERRIBLE FEELING I'M ABOUT TO...
"MY MOM IS NOT THE PROBLEM."

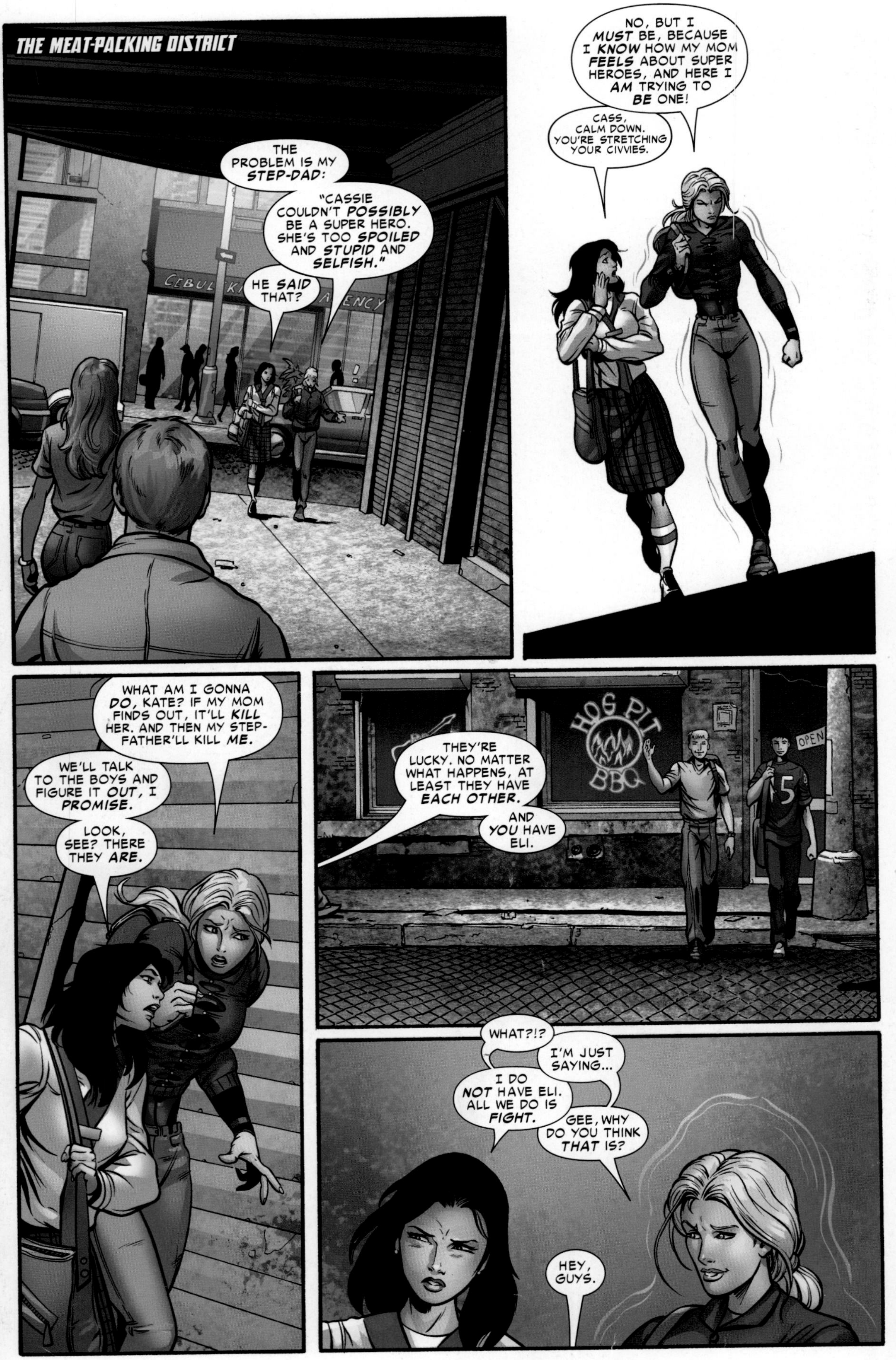
THE MEAT-PACKING DISTRICT
THE PROBLEM IS MY STEP-DAD:
"CASSIE COULDN'T POSSIBLY BE A SUPER HERO. SHE'S TOO SPOILED AND STUPID AND SELFISH."
HE SAID THAT?
NO, BUT I MUST BE, BECAUSE I KNOW HOW MY MOM FEELS ABOUT SUPER HEROES, AND HERE I AM TRYING TO BE ONE!
CASS, CALM DOWN. YOU'RE STRETCHING YOUR CIVVIES.
WHAT AM I GONNA DO, KATE? IF MY MOM FINDS OUT, IT'LL KILL HER. AND THEN MY STEP-FATHER'LL KILL ME.
WE'LL TALK TO THE BOYS AND FIGURE IT OUT, I PROMISE.
LOOK, SEE? THERE THEY ARE.
HOG PIT BBQ
OPEN
THEY'RE LUCKY. NO MATTER WHAT HAPPENS, AT LEAST THEY HAVE EACH OTHER.
AND YOU HAVE ELI.
WHAT?!?
I'M JUST SAYING...
I DO NOT HAVE ELI. ALL WE DO IS FIGHT.
GEE, WHY DO YOU THINK THAT IS?
HEY, GUYS.

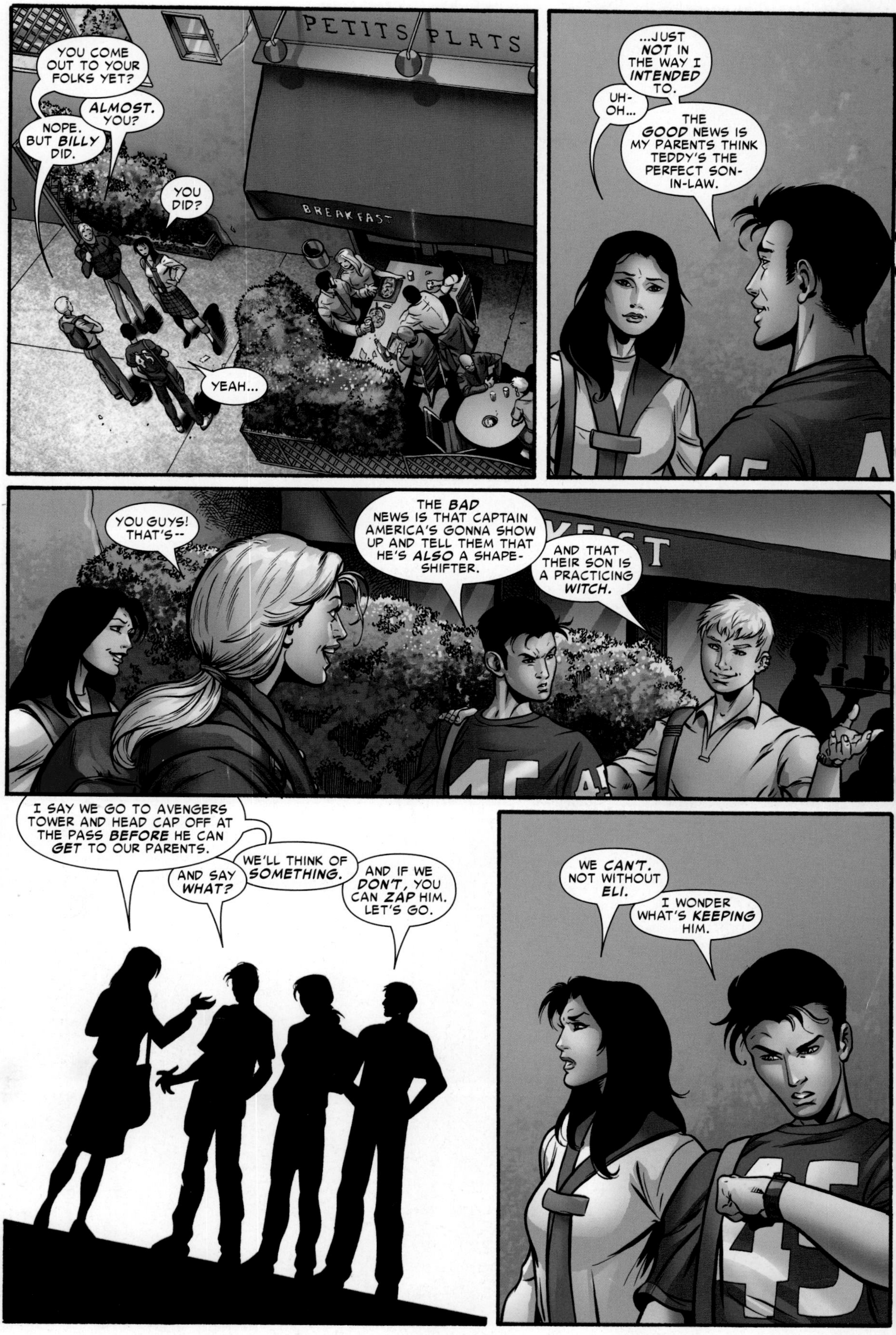
PETITS PLATS
YOU COME OUT TO YOUR FOLKS YET?
ALMOST. YOU?
NOPE. BUT BILLY DID.
YOU DID?
YEAH...
BREAKFAST
...JUST NOT IN THE WAY I INTENDED TO.
UH-OH...
THE GOOD NEWS IS MY PARENTS THINK TEDDY'S THE PERFECT SON-IN-LAW.
YOU GUYS! THAT'S--
THE BAD NEWS IS THAT CAPTAIN AMERICA'S GONNA SHOW UP AND TELL THEM THAT HE'S ALSO A SHAPE-SHIFTER.
AND THAT THEIR SON IS A PRACTICING WITCH.
I SAY WE GO TO AVENGERS TOWER AND HEAD CAP OFF AT THE PASS BEFORE HE CAN GET TO OUR PARENTS.
AND SAY WHAT?
WE'LL THINK OF SOMETHING.
AND IF WE DON'T, YOU CAN ZAP HIM. LET'S GO.
WE CAN'T. NOT WITHOUT ELI.
I WONDER WHAT'S KEEPING HIM.

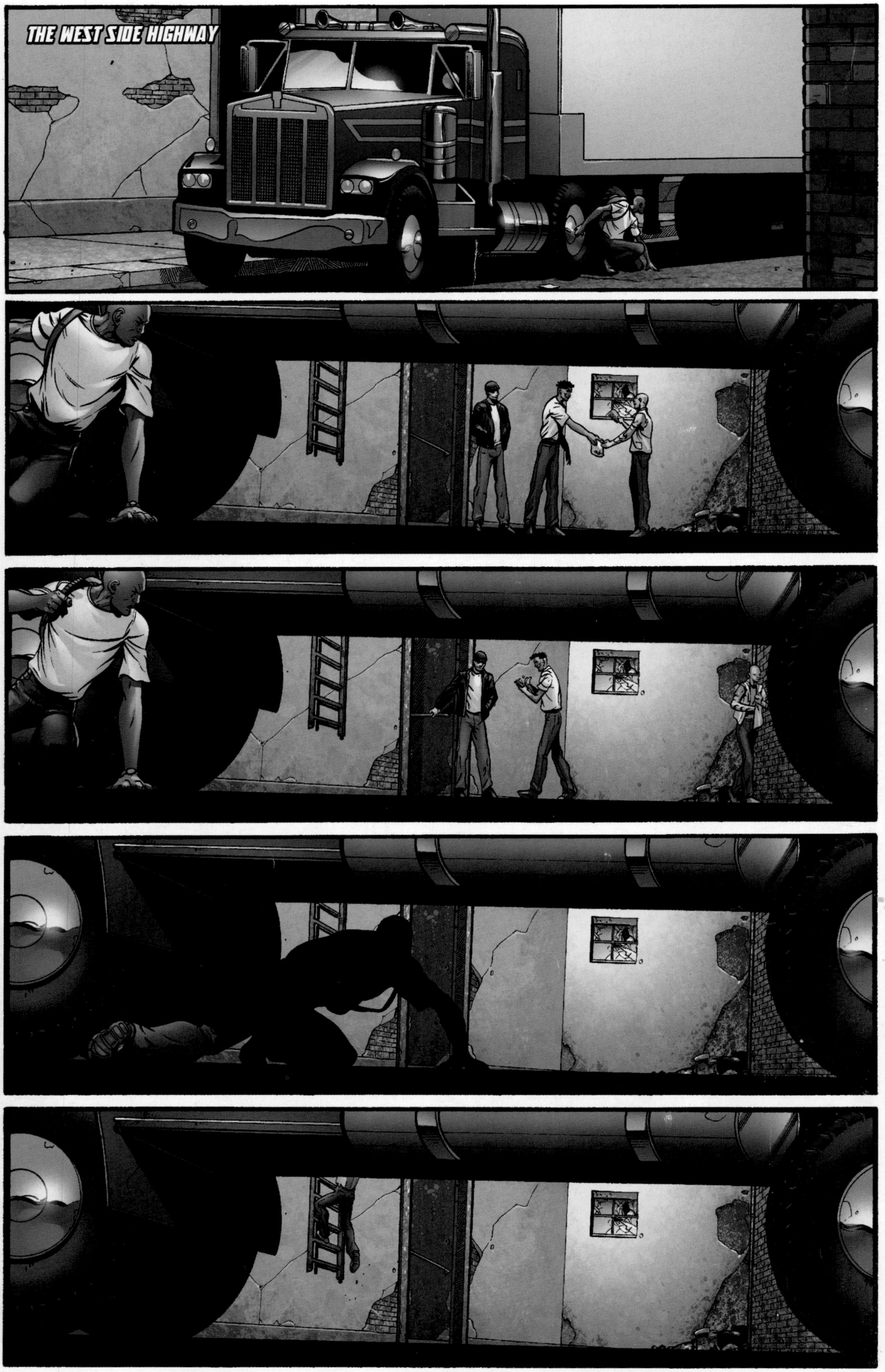
THE WEST SIDE HIGHWAY

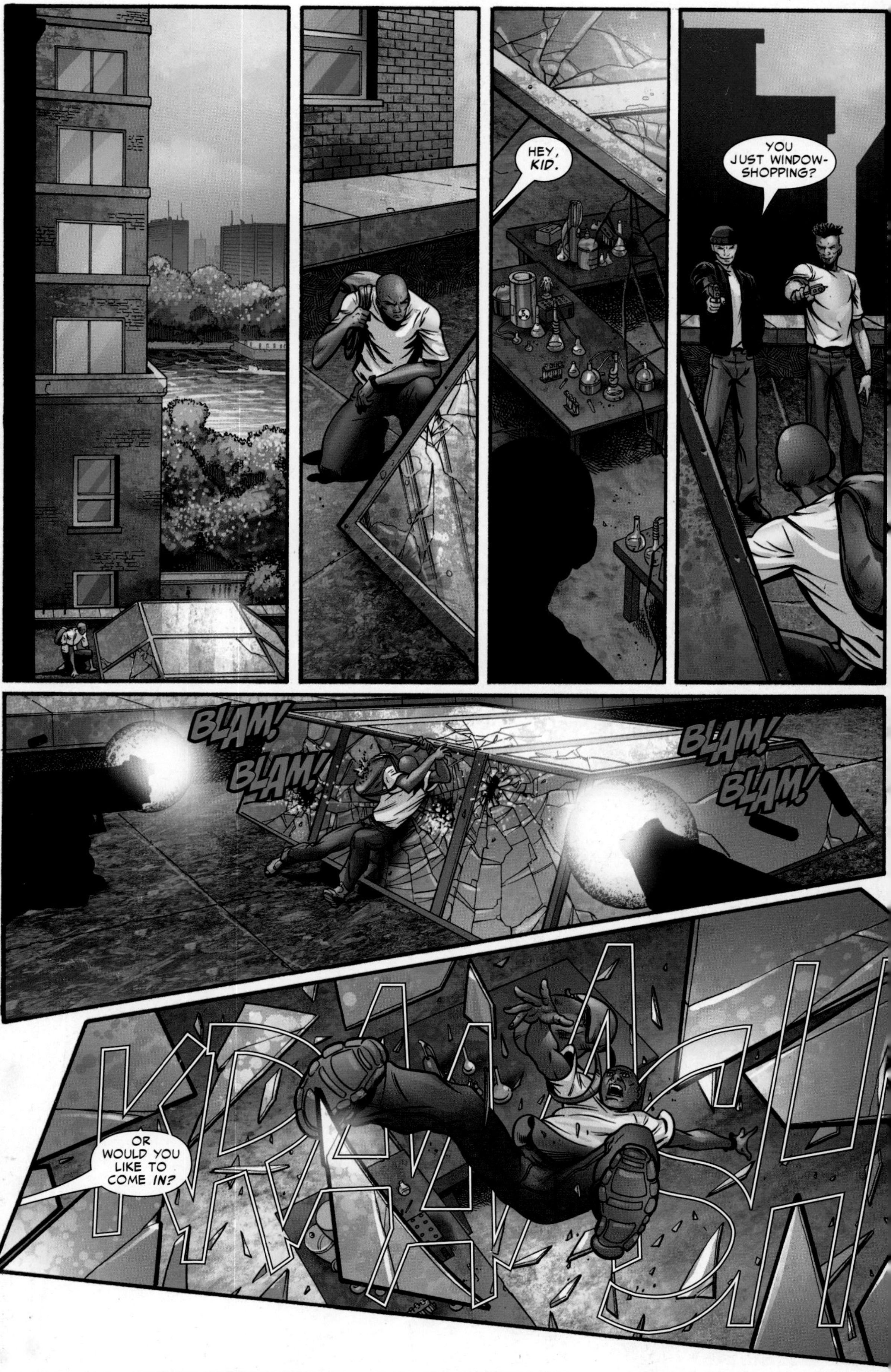
HEY, KID.
YOU JUST WINDOW-SHOPPING?
BLAM!
BLAM!
BLAM!
BLAM!
OR WOULD YOU LIKE TO COME IN?

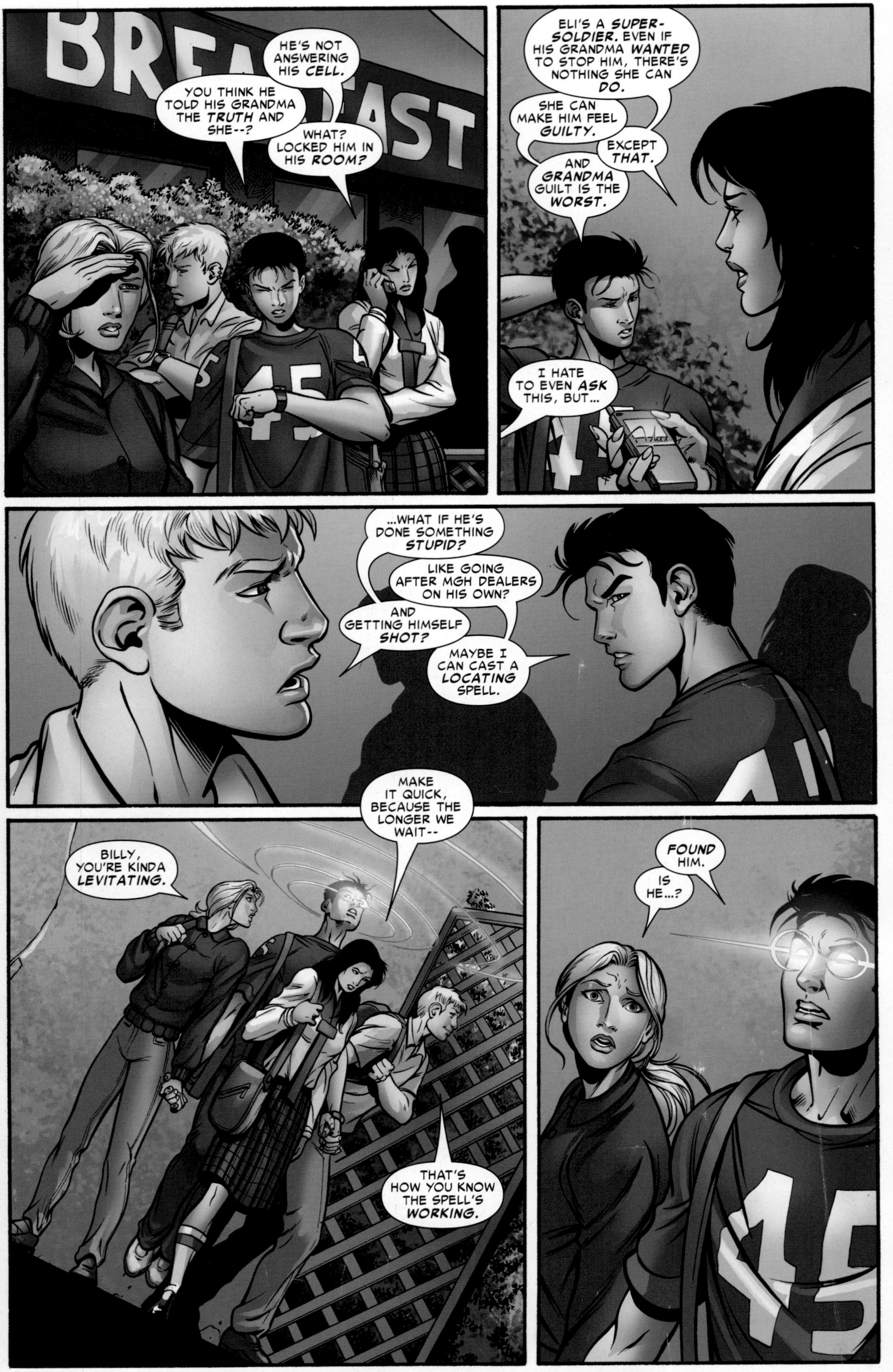
BREAKFAST
HE'S NOT ANSWERING HIS CELL.
YOU THINK HE TOLD HIS GRANDMA THE TRUTH AND SHE--?
WHAT? LOCKED HIM IN HIS ROOM?
ELI'S A SUPER-SOLDIER. EVEN IF HIS GRANDMA WANTED TO STOP HIM, THERE'S NOTHING SHE CAN DO.
SHE CAN MAKE HIM FEEL GUILTY.
EXCEPT THAT.
AND GRANDMA GUILT IS THE WORST.
I HATE TO EVEN ASK THIS, BUT...
...WHAT IF HE'S DONE SOMETHING STUPID?
LIKE GOING AFTER MGH DEALERS ON HIS OWN?
AND GETTING HIMSELF SHOT?
MAYBE I CAN CAST A LOCATING SPELL.
MAKE IT QUICK, BECAUSE THE LONGER WE WAIT--
BILLY, YOU'RE KINDA LEVITATING.
THAT'S HOW YOU KNOW THE SPELL'S WORKING.
FOUND HIM.
IS HE...?

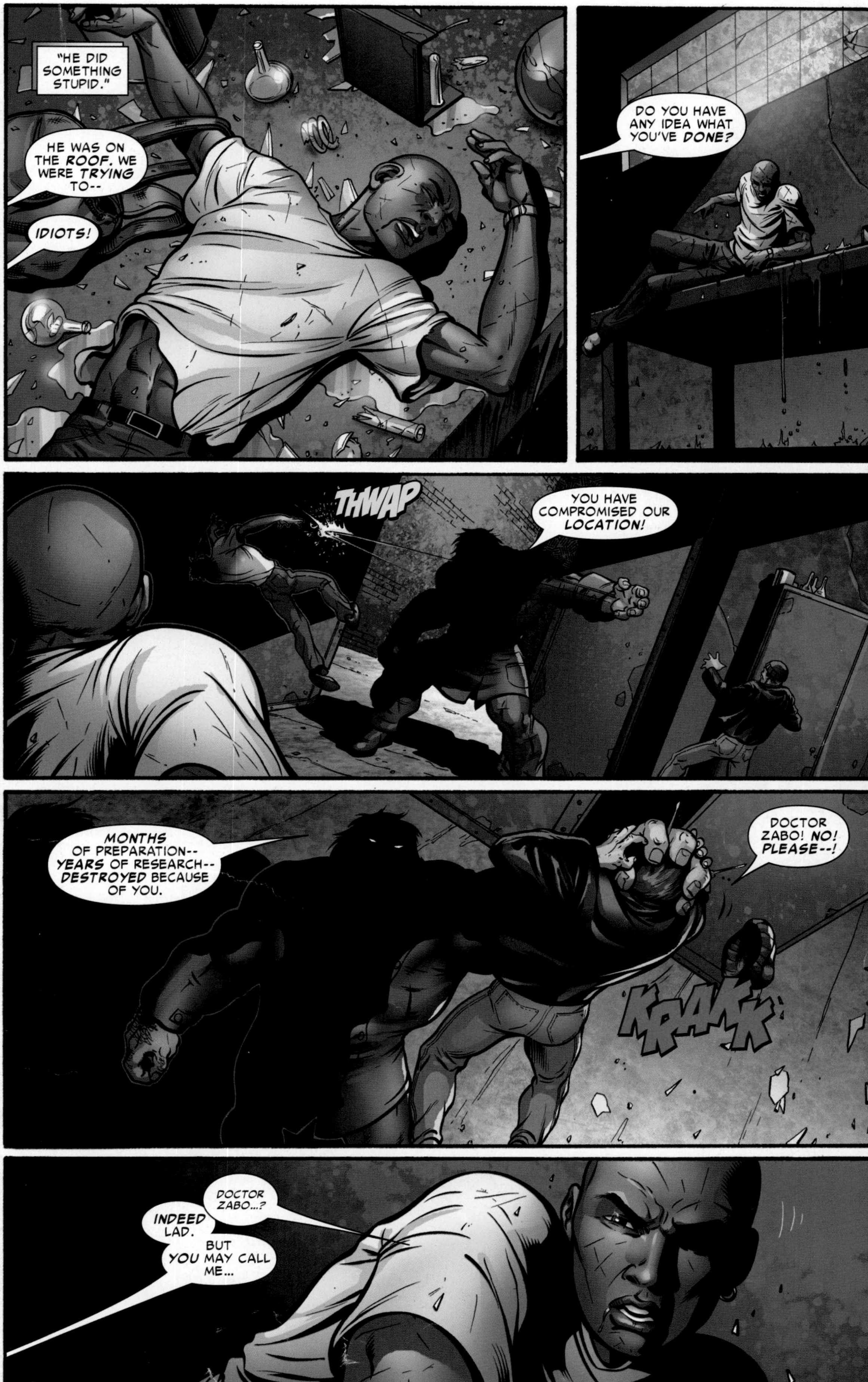
"HE DID SOMETHING STUPID."
HE WAS ON THE ROOF. WE WERE TRYING TO--
IDIOTS!
DO YOU HAVE ANY IDEA WHAT YOU'VE DONE?
THWAP
YOU HAVE COMPROMISED OUR LOCATION!
MONTHS OF PREPARATION-- YEARS OF RESEARCH-- DESTROYED BECAUSE OF YOU.
DOCTOR ZABO! NO! PLEASE--!
KRAKK
DOCTOR ZABO...?
INDEED LAD.
BUT YOU MAY CALL ME...

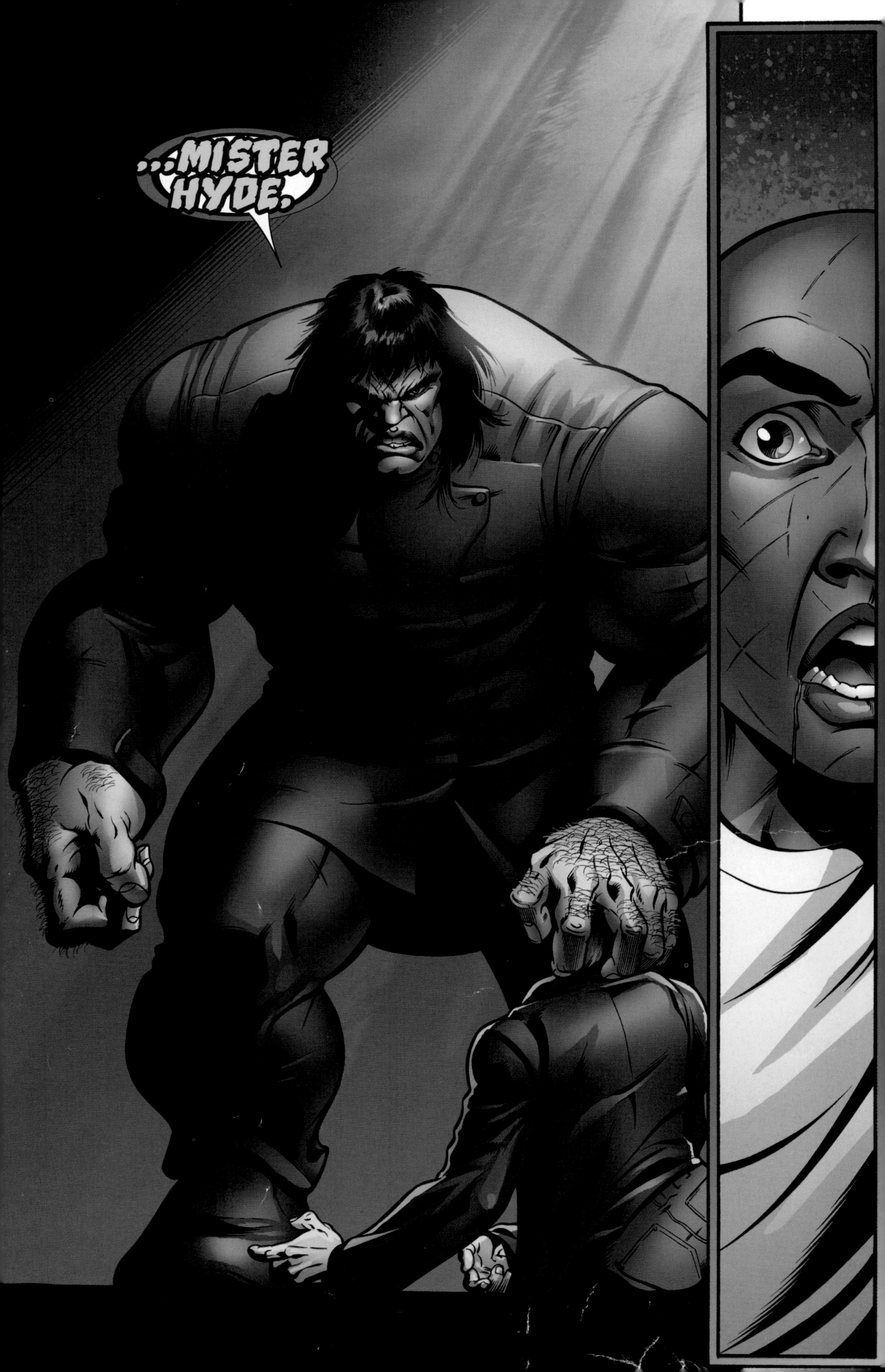
...MISTER HYDE.

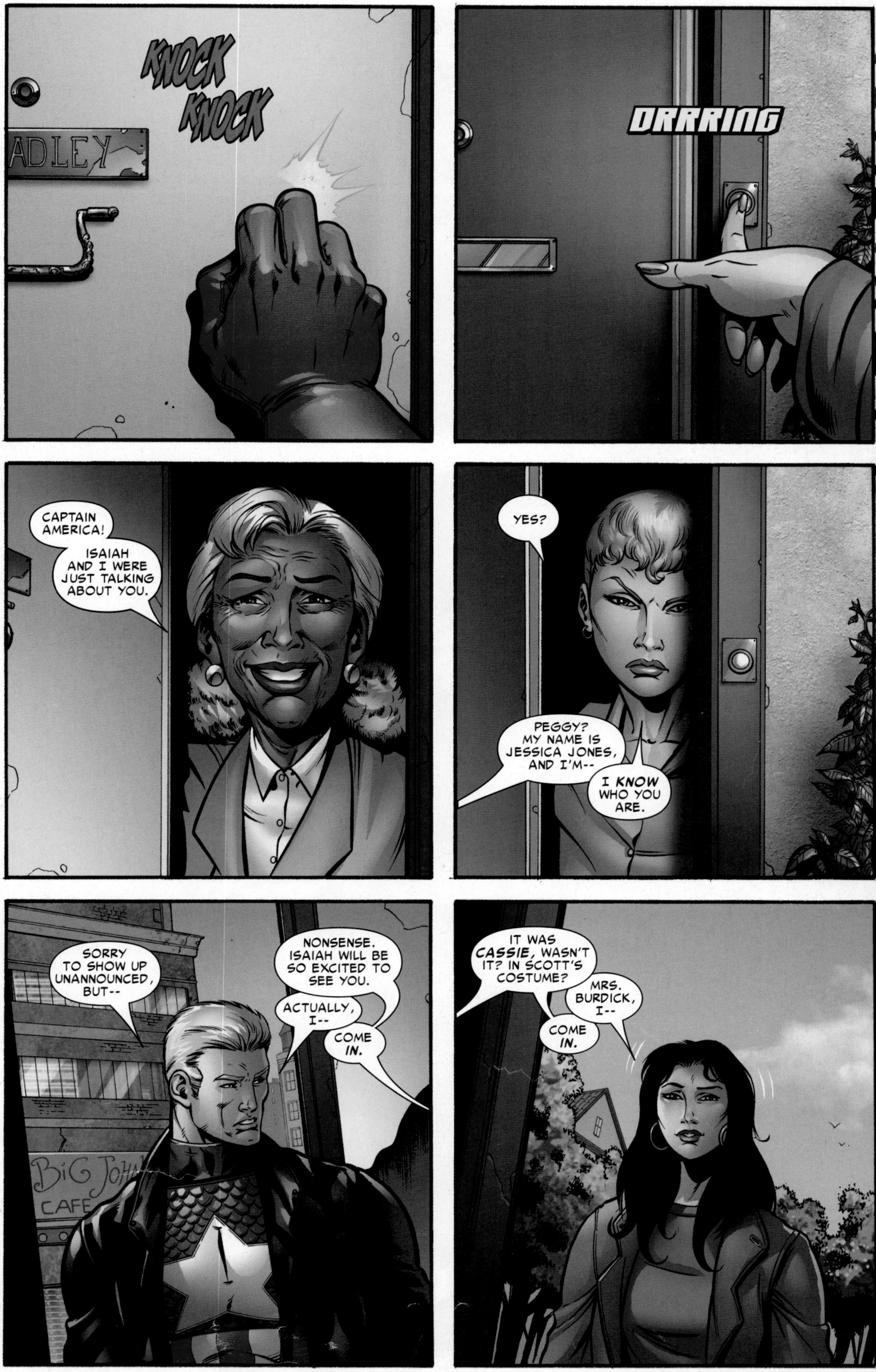

KNOCK KNOCK
ADLEY
DRRRING
CAPTAIN AMERICA!
ISAIAH AND I WERE JUST TALKING ABOUT YOU.
YES?
PEGGY? MY NAME IS JESSICA JONES, AND I'M--
I KNOW WHO YOU ARE.
SORRY TO SHOW UP UNANNOUNCED, BUT--
NONSENSE. ISAIAH WILL BE SO EXCITED TO SEE YOU.
ACTUALLY, I--
COME IN.
BIG JOHN
CAFE
IT WAS CASSIE, WASN'T IT? IN SCOTT'S COSTUME?
MRS. BURDICK, I--
COME IN.

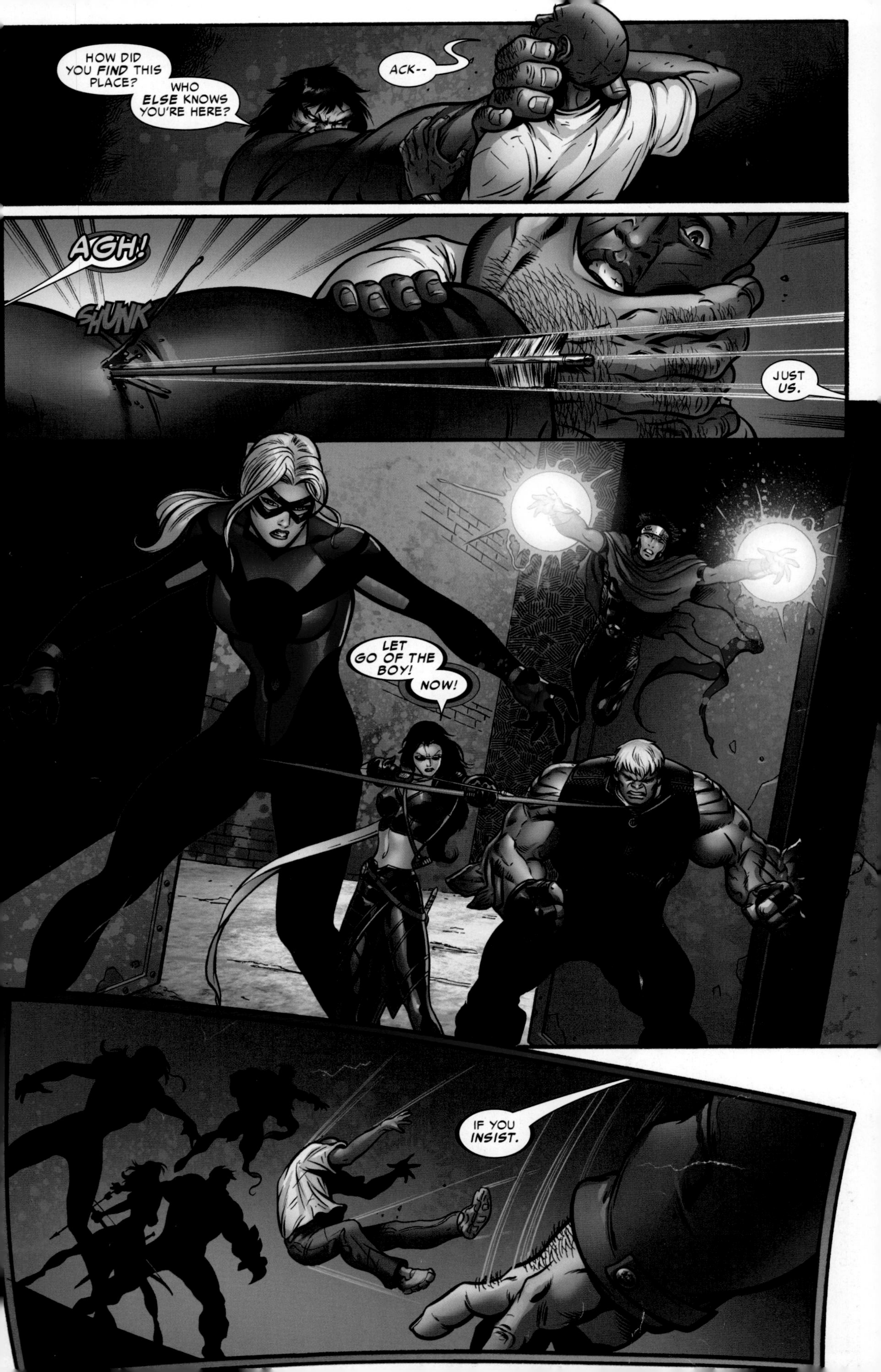
HOW DID YOU FIND THIS PLACE? WHO ELSE KNOWS YOU'RE HERE?
ACK--
AGH!
SHUNK
JUST US.
LET GO OF THE BOY! NOW!
IF YOU INSIST.

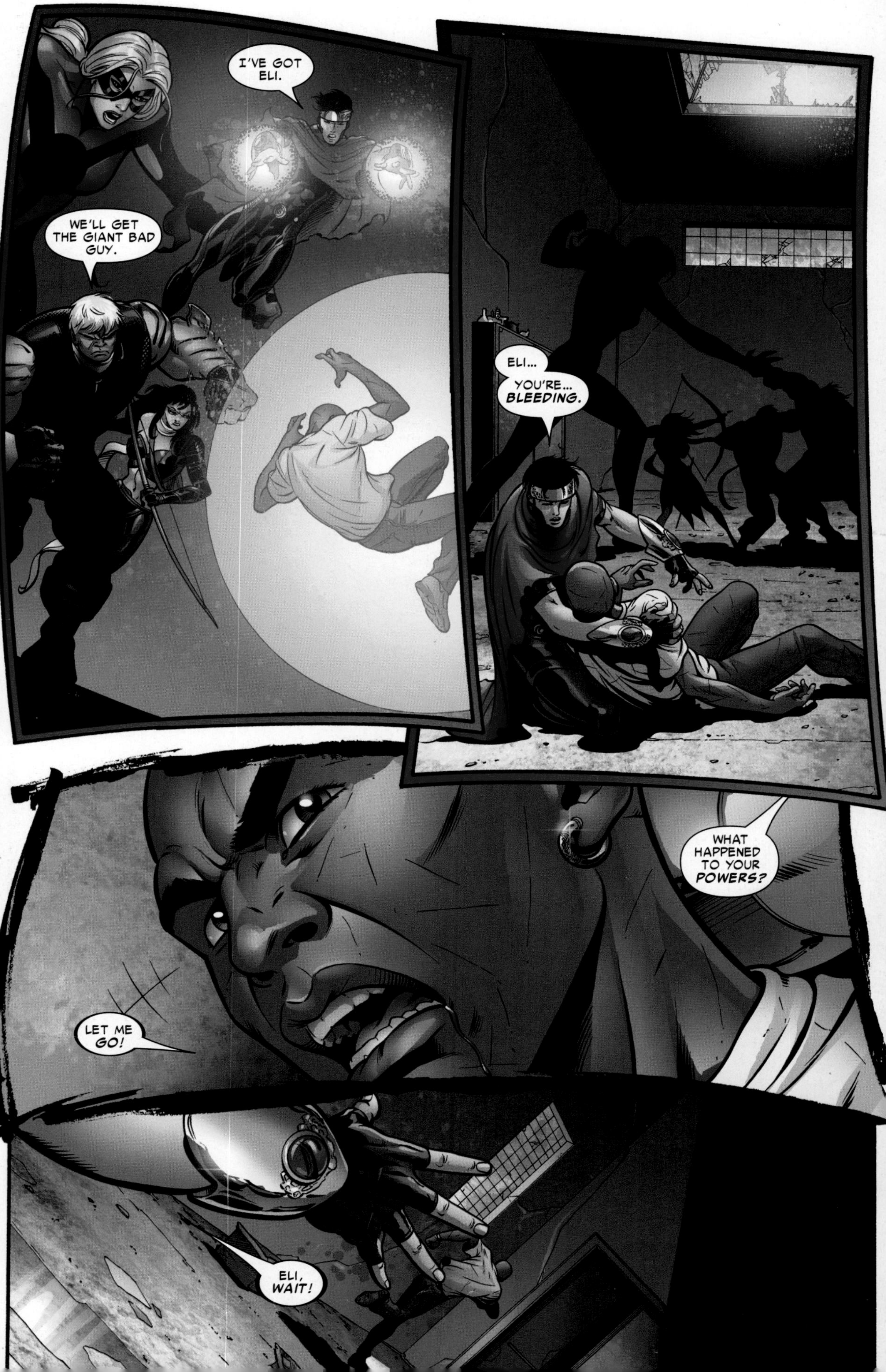
I'VE GOT ELI.
WE'LL GET THE GIANT BAD GUY.
ELI... YOU'RE... BLEEDING.
WHAT HAPPENED TO YOUR POWERS?
LET ME GO!
ELI, WAIT!

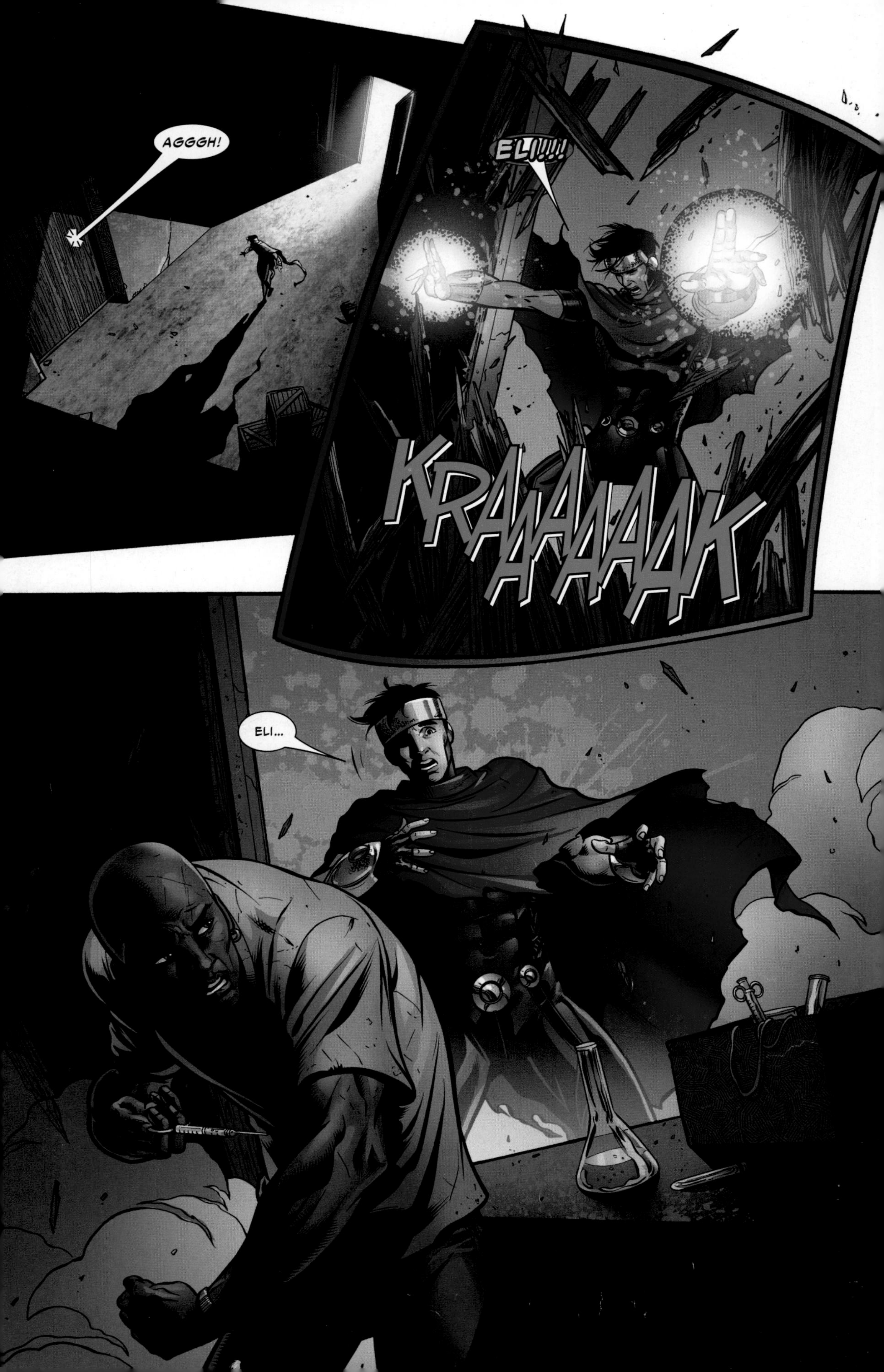

AGGGH!
ELI!!!!
KRAAAAAAK
ELI...

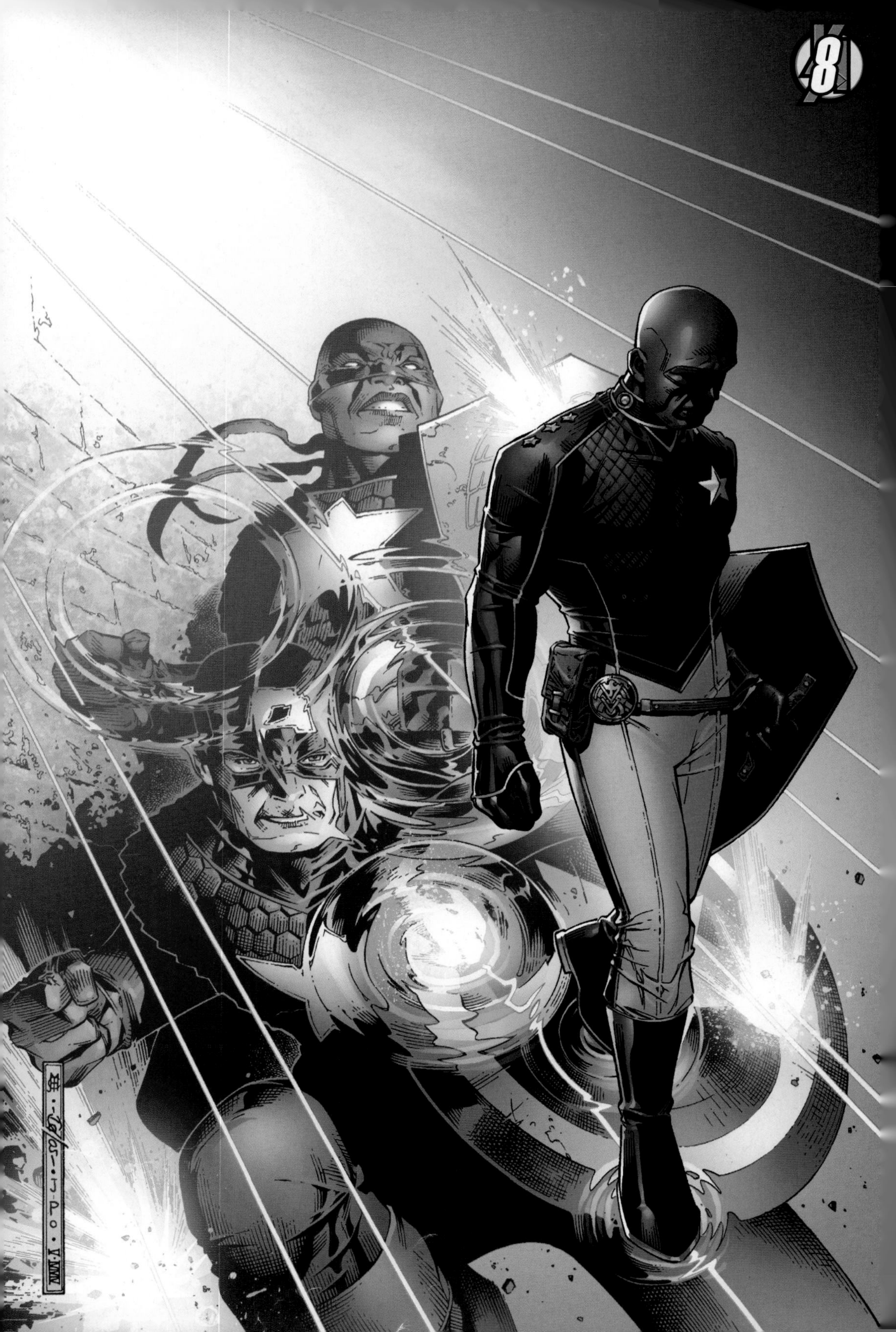

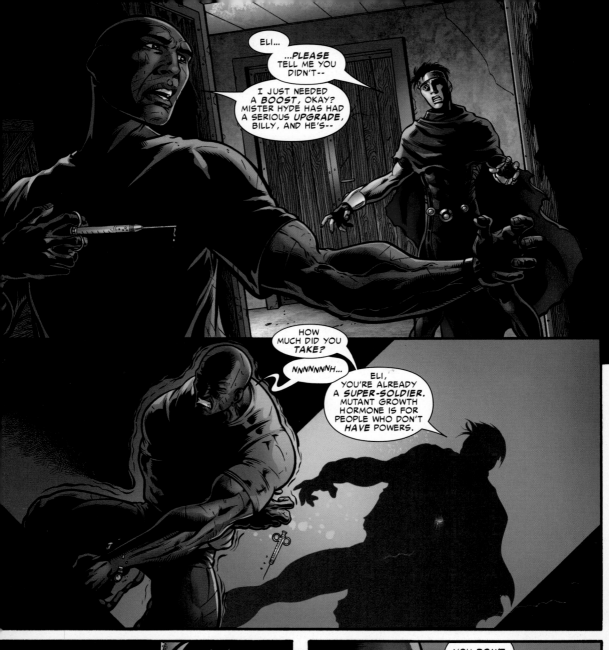

ELI...

...PLEASE TELL ME YOU DIDN'T--

I JUST NEEDED A *BOOST*, OKAY? MISTER HYDE HAS HAD A SERIOUS *UPGRADE*, BILLY, AND HE'S--

HOW MUCH DID YOU *TAKE?*

NNNNNNNH...

ELI, YOU'RE ALREADY A *SUPER-SOLDIER.* MUTANT GROWTH HORMONE IS FOR PEOPLE WHO DON'T *HAVE* POWERS.

OH, MY GOD.

YOU *DON'T* HAVE POWERS.

DO YOU, ELI?

BILLY, PLEASE...

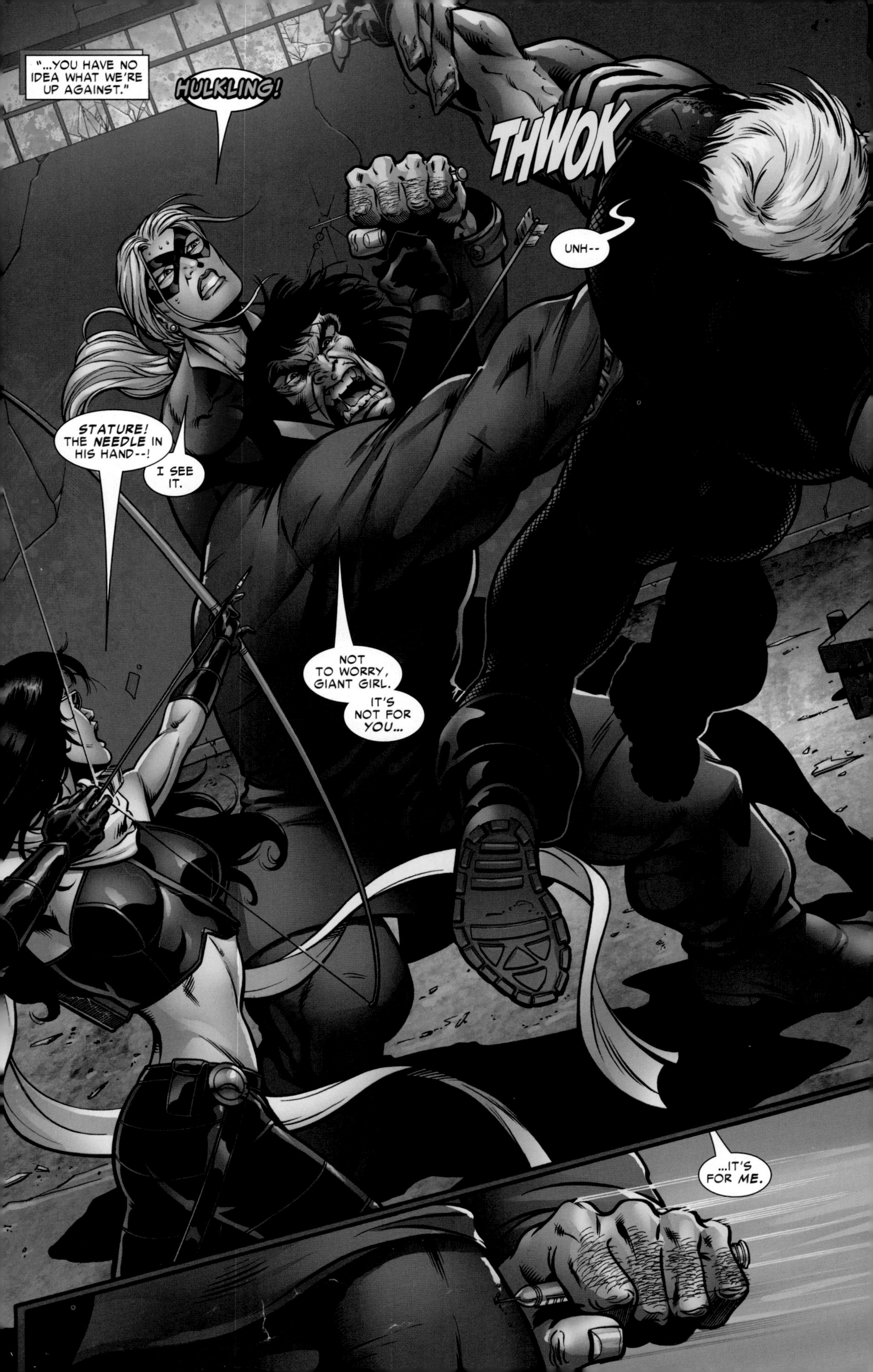
"...YOU HAVE NO IDEA WHAT WE'RE UP AGAINST."
HULKLING!
THWOK
UNH--
STATURE! THE NEEDLE IN HIS HAND--!
I SEE IT.
NOT TO WORRY, GIANT GIRL.
IT'S NOT FOR YOU...
...IT'S FOR ME.

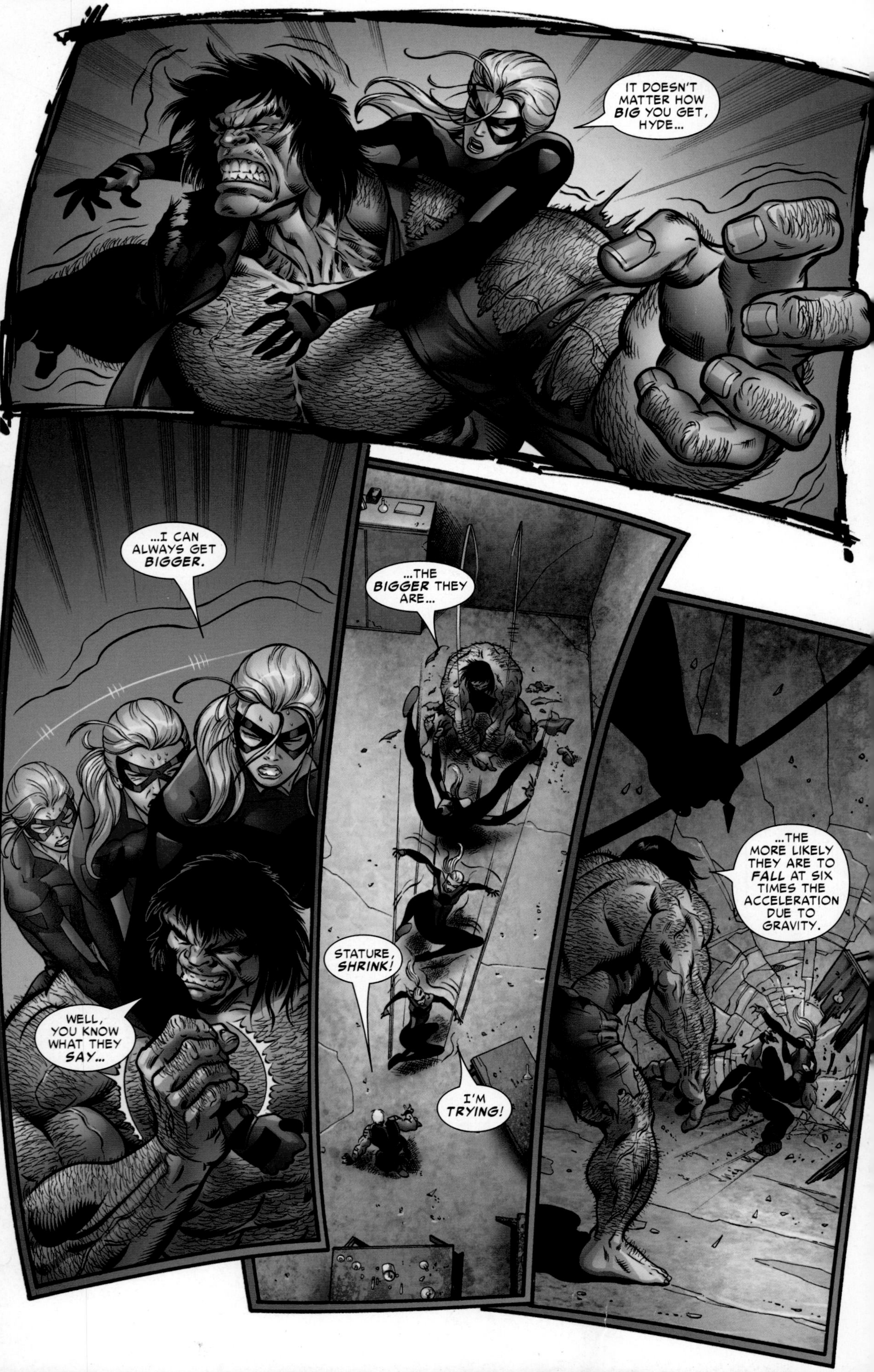
IT DOESN'T MATTER HOW BIG YOU GET, HYDE...
...I CAN ALWAYS GET BIGGER.
WELL, YOU KNOW WHAT THEY SAY...
...THE BIGGER THEY ARE...
STATURE, SHRINK!
I'M TRYING!
...THE MORE LIKELY THEY ARE TO FALL AT SIX TIMES THE ACCELERATION DUE TO GRAVITY.

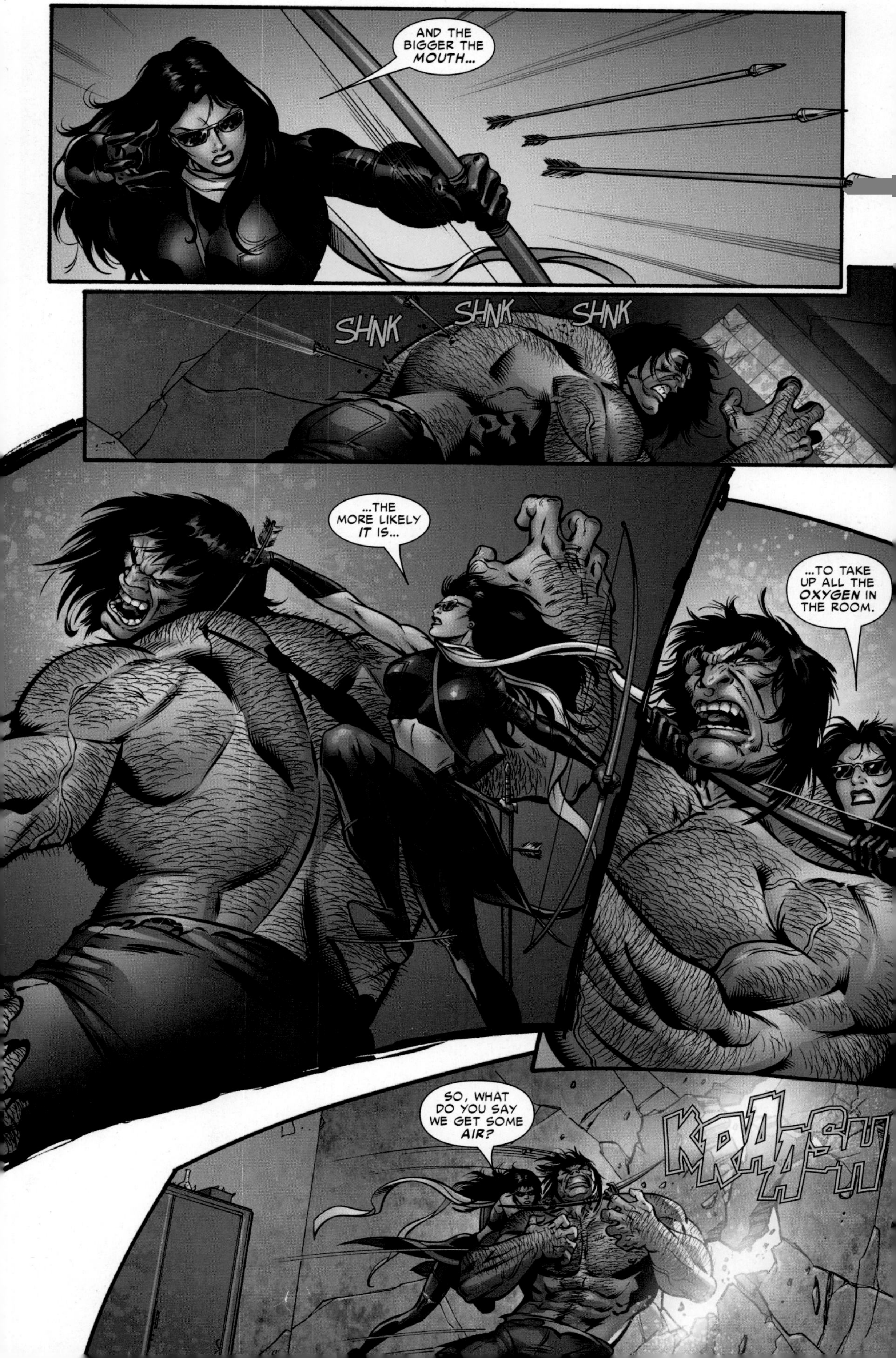
AND THE BIGGER THE MOUTH...
SHNK
SHNK
SHNK
...THE MORE LIKELY IT IS...
...TO TAKE UP ALL THE OXYGEN IN THE ROOM.
SO, WHAT DO YOU SAY WE GET SOME AIR?
KRAASH

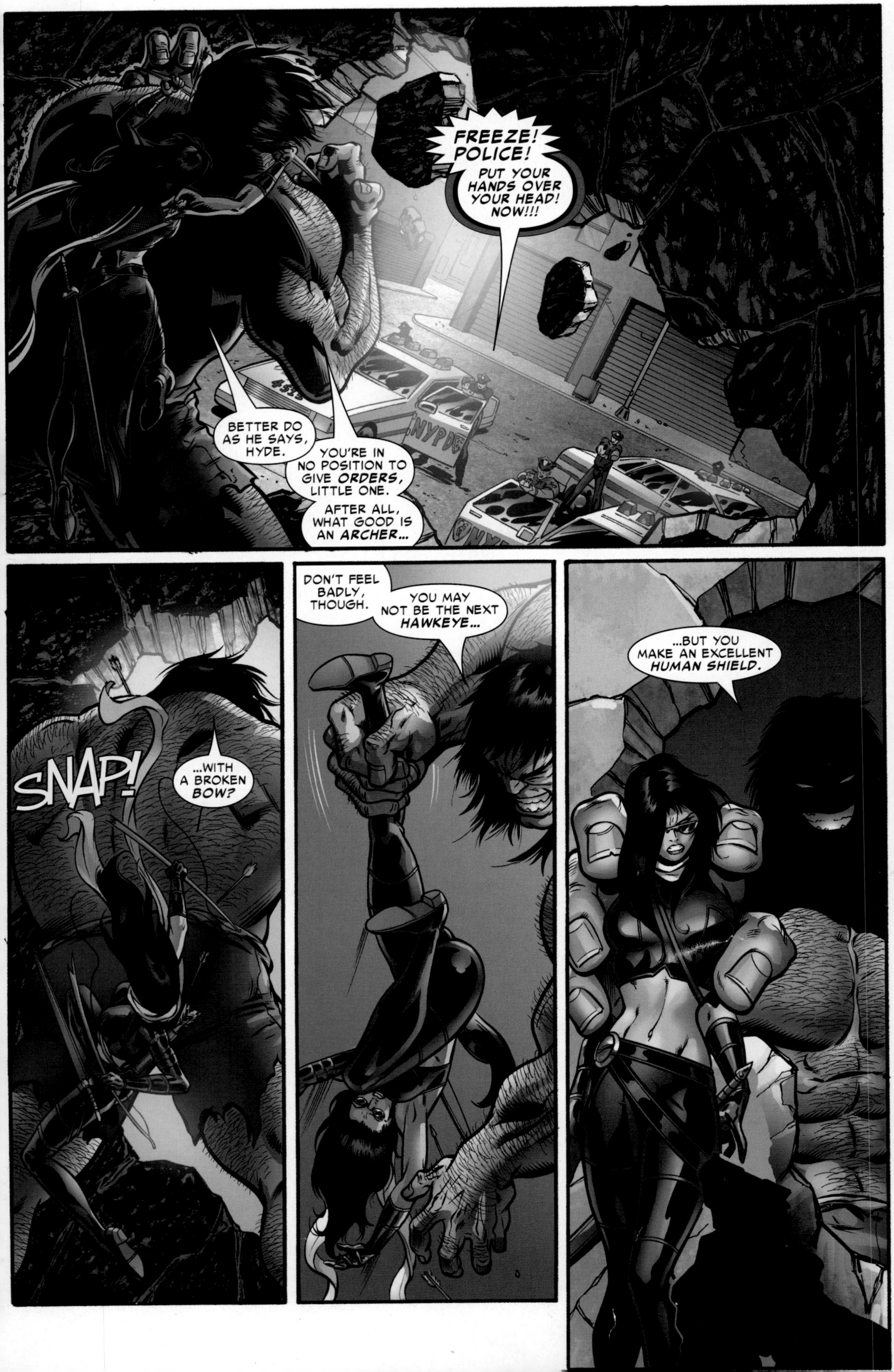

FREEZE! POLICE!
PUT YOUR HANDS OVER YOUR HEAD! NOW!!!
BETTER DO AS HE SAYS, HYDE.
YOU'RE IN NO POSITION TO GIVE ORDERS, LITTLE ONE.
AFTER ALL, WHAT GOOD IS AN ARCHER...
SNAP!
...WITH A BROKEN BOW?
DON'T FEEL BADLY, THOUGH.
YOU MAY NOT BE THE NEXT HAWKEYE...
...BUT YOU MAKE AN EXCELLENT HUMAN SHIELD.

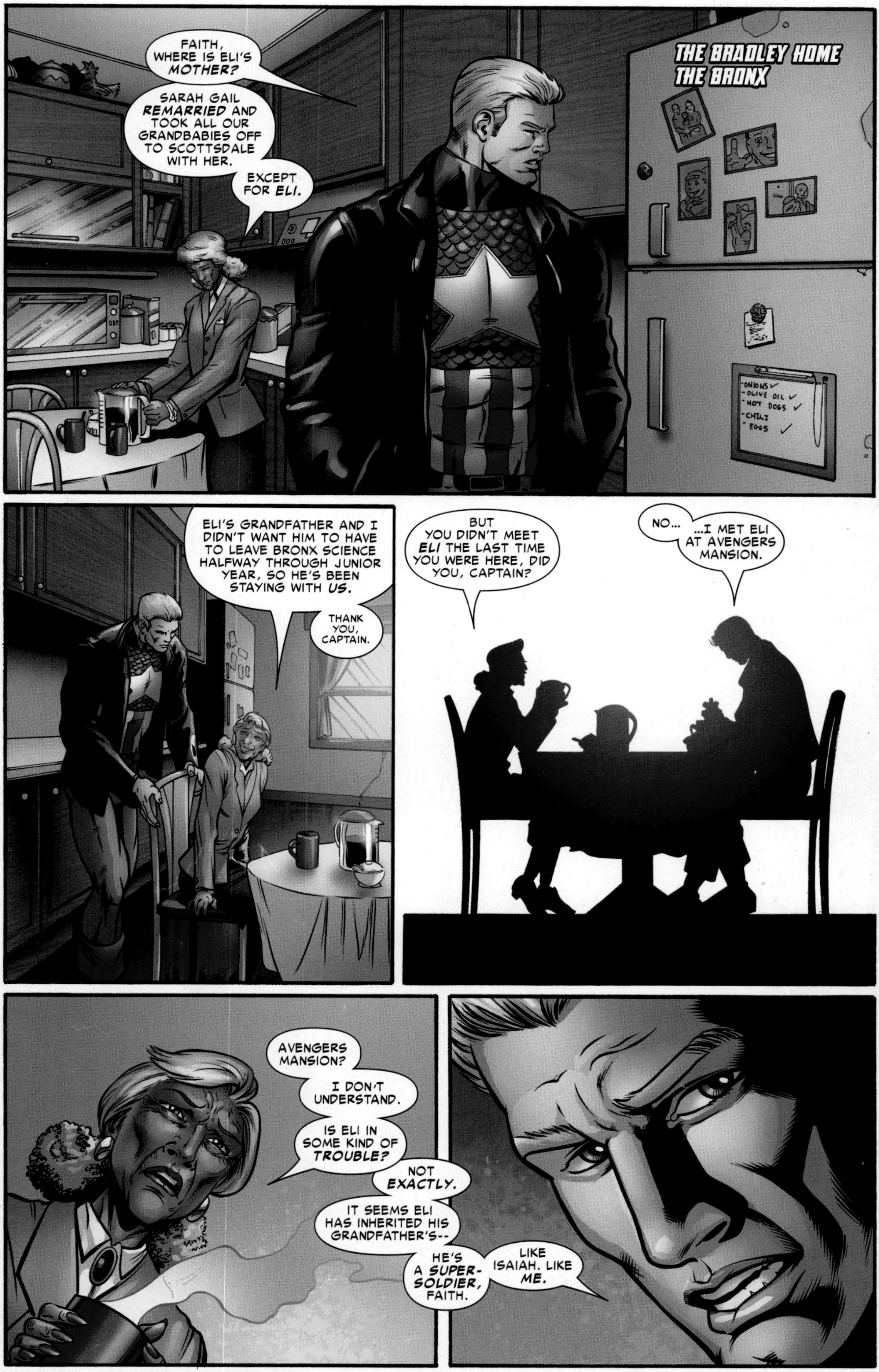
THE BRADLEY HOME
THE BRONX
FAITH, WHERE IS ELI'S MOTHER?
SARAH GAIL REMARRIED AND TOOK ALL OUR GRANDBABIES OFF TO SCOTTSDALE WITH HER.
EXCEPT FOR ELI.
ONIONS ✓
OLIVE OIL ✓
HOT DOGS ✓
CHILI
EGGS ✓
ELI'S GRANDFATHER AND I DIDN'T WANT HIM TO HAVE TO LEAVE BRONX SCIENCE HALFWAY THROUGH JUNIOR YEAR, SO HE'S BEEN STAYING WITH US.
THANK YOU, CAPTAIN.
BUT YOU DIDN'T MEET ELI THE LAST TIME YOU WERE HERE, DID YOU, CAPTAIN?
NO...
...I MET ELI AT AVENGERS MANSION.
AVENGERS MANSION?
I DON'T UNDERSTAND.
IS ELI IN SOME KIND OF TROUBLE?
NOT EXACTLY.
IT SEEMS ELI HAS INHERITED HIS GRANDFATHER'S--
HE'S A SUPER-SOLDIER, FAITH.
LIKE ISAIAH. LIKE ME.

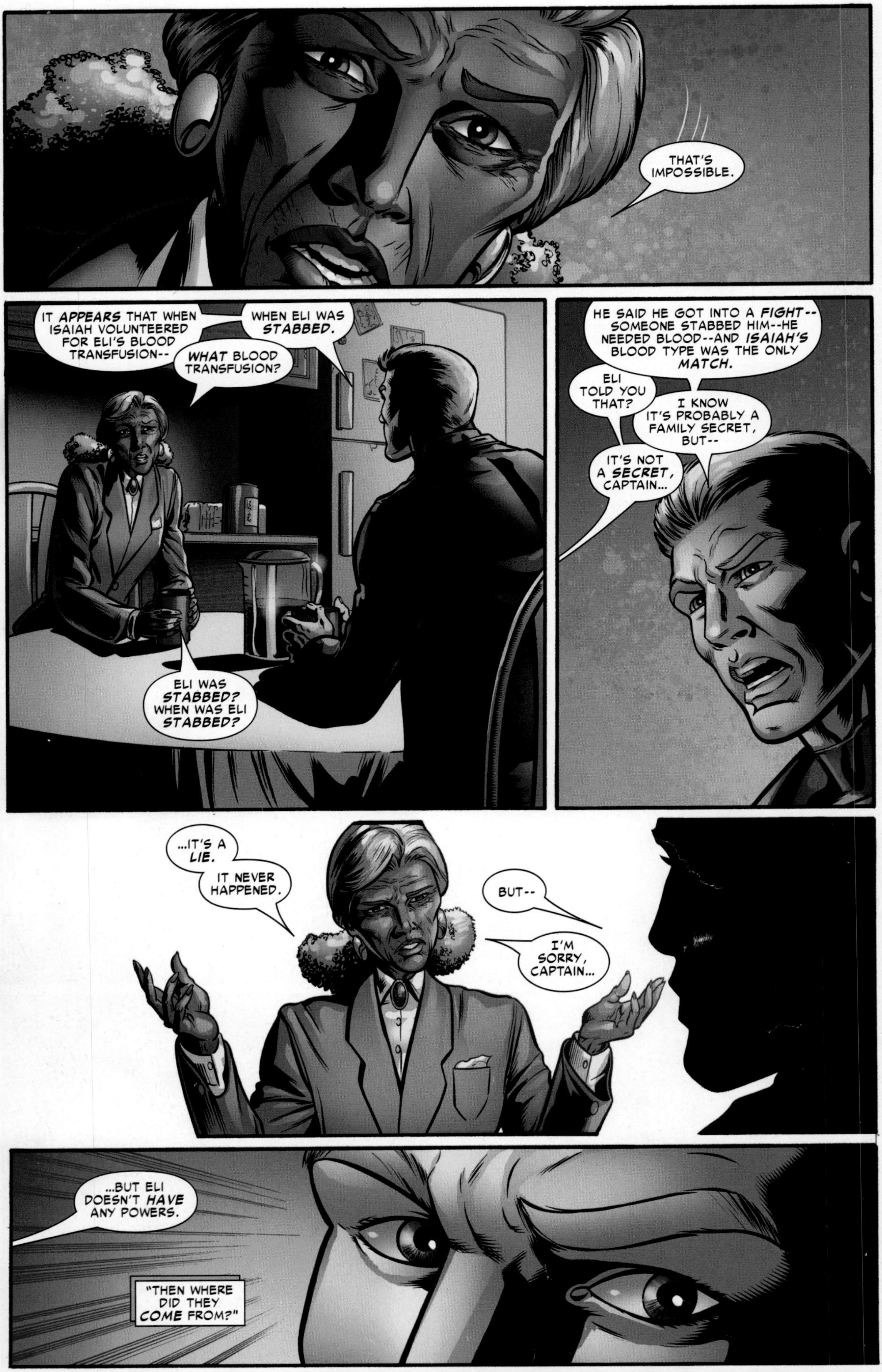
THAT'S IMPOSSIBLE.
IT APPEARS THAT WHEN ISAIAH VOLUNTEERED FOR ELI'S BLOOD TRANSFUSION--
WHAT BLOOD TRANSFUSION?
WHEN ELI WAS STABBED.
ELI WAS STABBED? WHEN WAS ELI STABBED?
HE SAID HE GOT INTO A FIGHT--SOMEONE STABBED HIM--HE NEEDED BLOOD--AND ISAIAH'S BLOOD TYPE WAS THE ONLY MATCH.
ELI TOLD YOU THAT?
I KNOW IT'S PROBABLY A FAMILY SECRET, BUT--
IT'S NOT A SECRET, CAPTAIN...
...IT'S A LIE.
IT NEVER HAPPENED.
BUT--
I'M SORRY, CAPTAIN...
...BUT ELI DOESN'T HAVE ANY POWERS.
"THEN WHERE DID THEY COME FROM?"

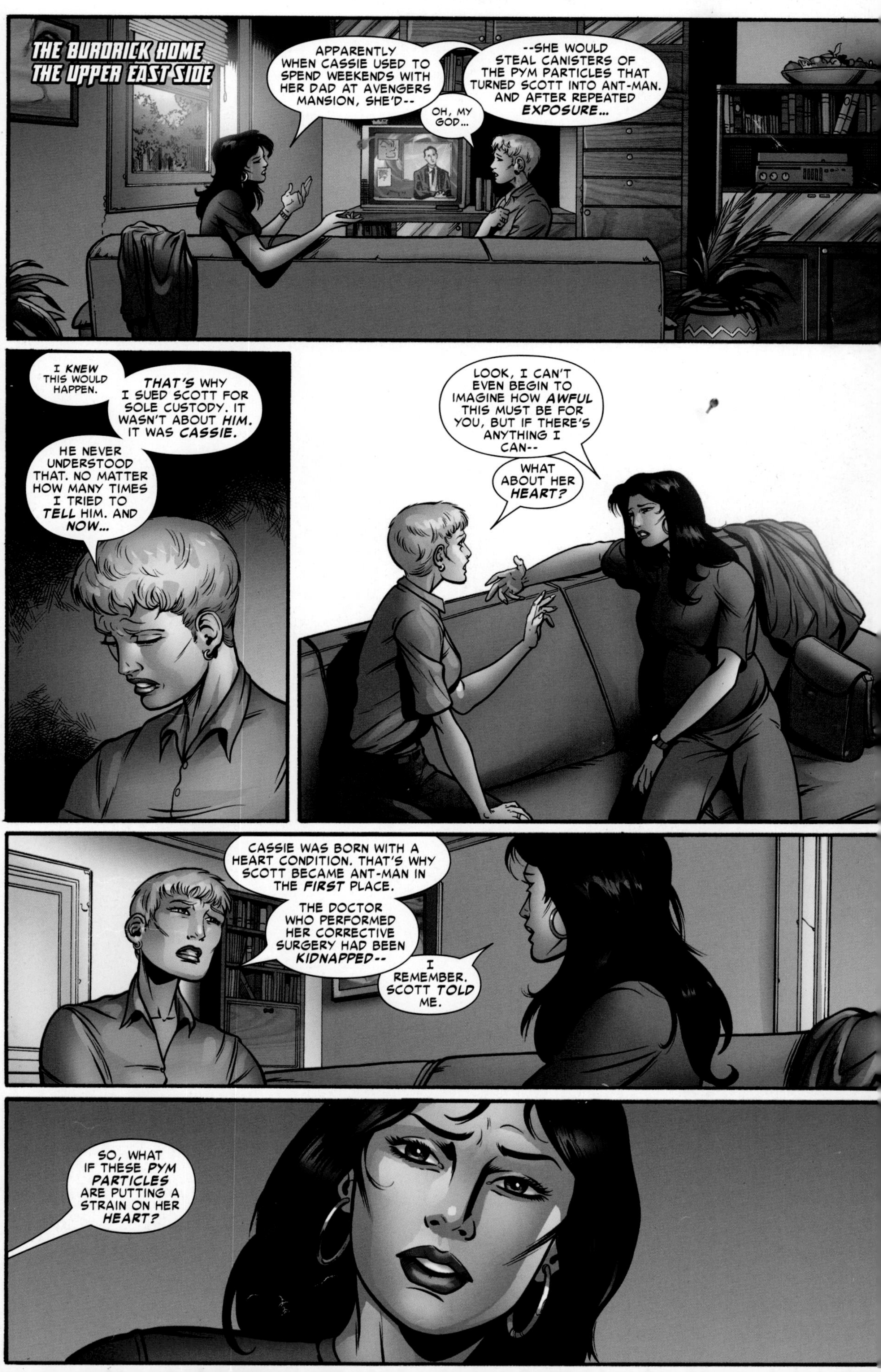
THE BURDRICK HOME
THE UPPER EAST SIDE
APPARENTLY WHEN CASSIE USED TO SPEND WEEKENDS WITH HER DAD AT AVENGERS MANSION, SHE'D--
OH, MY GOD...
--SHE WOULD STEAL CANISTERS OF THE PYM PARTICLES THAT TURNED SCOTT INTO ANT-MAN. AND AFTER REPEATED EXPOSURE...
I KNEW THIS WOULD HAPPEN.
THAT'S WHY I SUED SCOTT FOR SOLE CUSTODY. IT WASN'T ABOUT HIM. IT WAS CASSIE.
HE NEVER UNDERSTOOD THAT. NO MATTER HOW MANY TIMES I TRIED TO TELL HIM. AND NOW...
LOOK, I CAN'T EVEN BEGIN TO IMAGINE HOW AWFUL THIS MUST BE FOR YOU, BUT IF THERE'S ANYTHING I CAN--
WHAT ABOUT HER HEART?
CASSIE WAS BORN WITH A HEART CONDITION. THAT'S WHY SCOTT BECAME ANT-MAN IN THE FIRST PLACE.
THE DOCTOR WHO PERFORMED HER CORRECTIVE SURGERY HAD BEEN KIDNAPPED--
I REMEMBER. SCOTT TOLD ME.
SO, WHAT IF THESE PYM PARTICLES ARE PUTTING A STRAIN ON HER HEART?

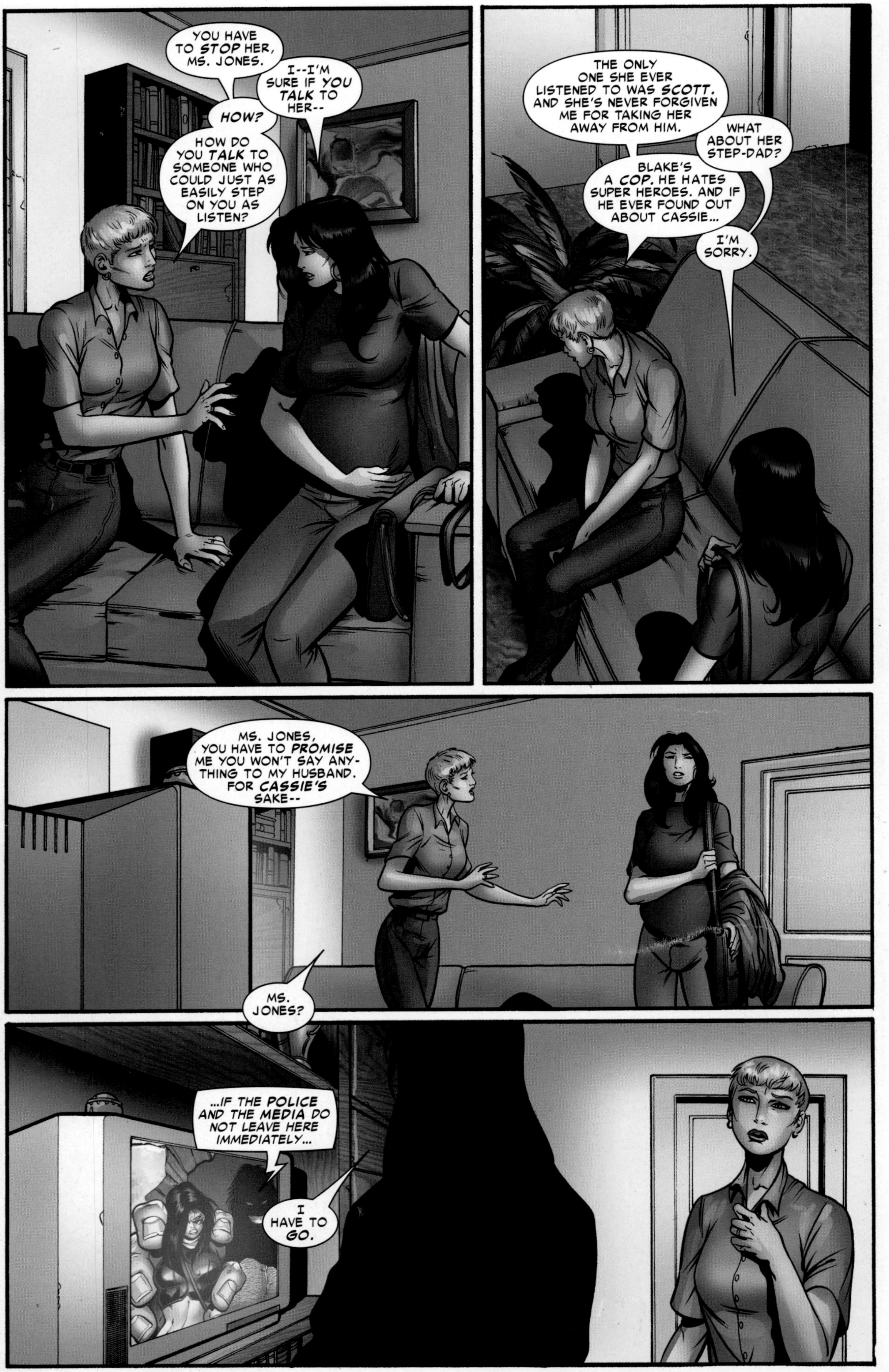
YOU HAVE TO STOP HER, MS. JONES.
I--I'M SURE IF YOU TALK TO HER--
HOW?
HOW DO YOU TALK TO SOMEONE WHO COULD JUST AS EASILY STEP ON YOU AS LISTEN?
THE ONLY ONE SHE EVER LISTENED TO WAS SCOTT. AND SHE'S NEVER FORGIVEN ME FOR TAKING HER AWAY FROM HIM.
WHAT ABOUT HER STEP-DAD?
BLAKE'S A COP. HE HATES SUPER HEROES. AND IF HE EVER FOUND OUT ABOUT CASSIE...
I'M SORRY.
MS. JONES, YOU HAVE TO PROMISE ME YOU WON'T SAY ANY-THING TO MY HUSBAND. FOR CASSIE'S SAKE--
MS. JONES?
...IF THE POLICE AND THE MEDIA DO NOT LEAVE HERE IMMEDIATELY...
I HAVE TO GO.

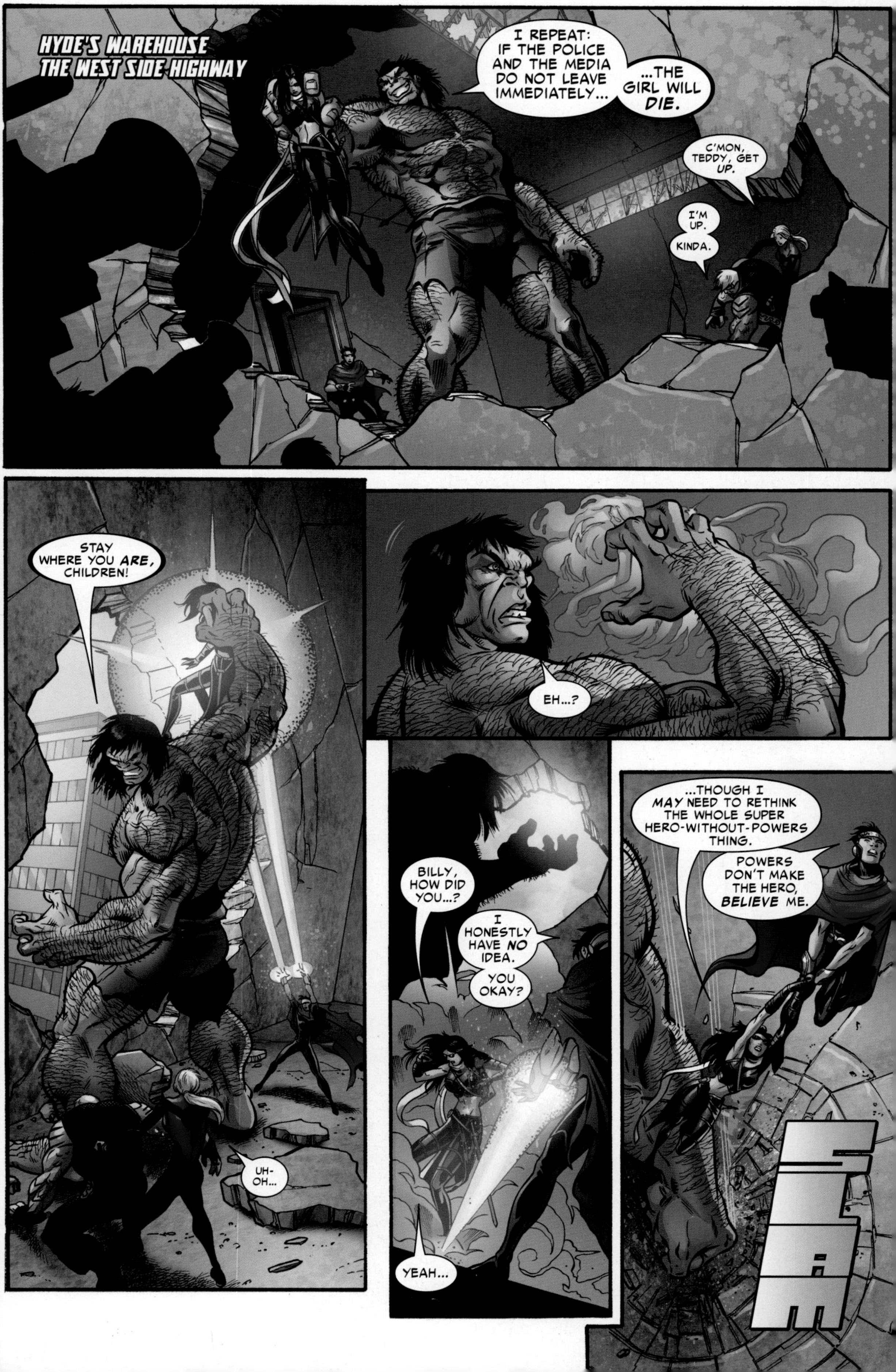
HYDE'S WAREHOUSE
THE WEST SIDE HIGHWAY
I REPEAT: IF THE POLICE AND THE MEDIA DO NOT LEAVE IMMEDIATELY...
...THE GIRL WILL DIE.
C'MON, TEDDY, GET UP.
I'M UP.
KINDA.
STAY WHERE YOU ARE, CHILDREN!
UH-OH...
EH...?
BILLY, HOW DID YOU...?
I HONESTLY HAVE NO IDEA.
YOU OKAY?
YEAH...
...THOUGH I MAY NEED TO RETHINK THE WHOLE SUPER HERO-WITHOUT-POWERS THING.
POWERS DON'T MAKE THE HERO, BELIEVE ME.
SLAM

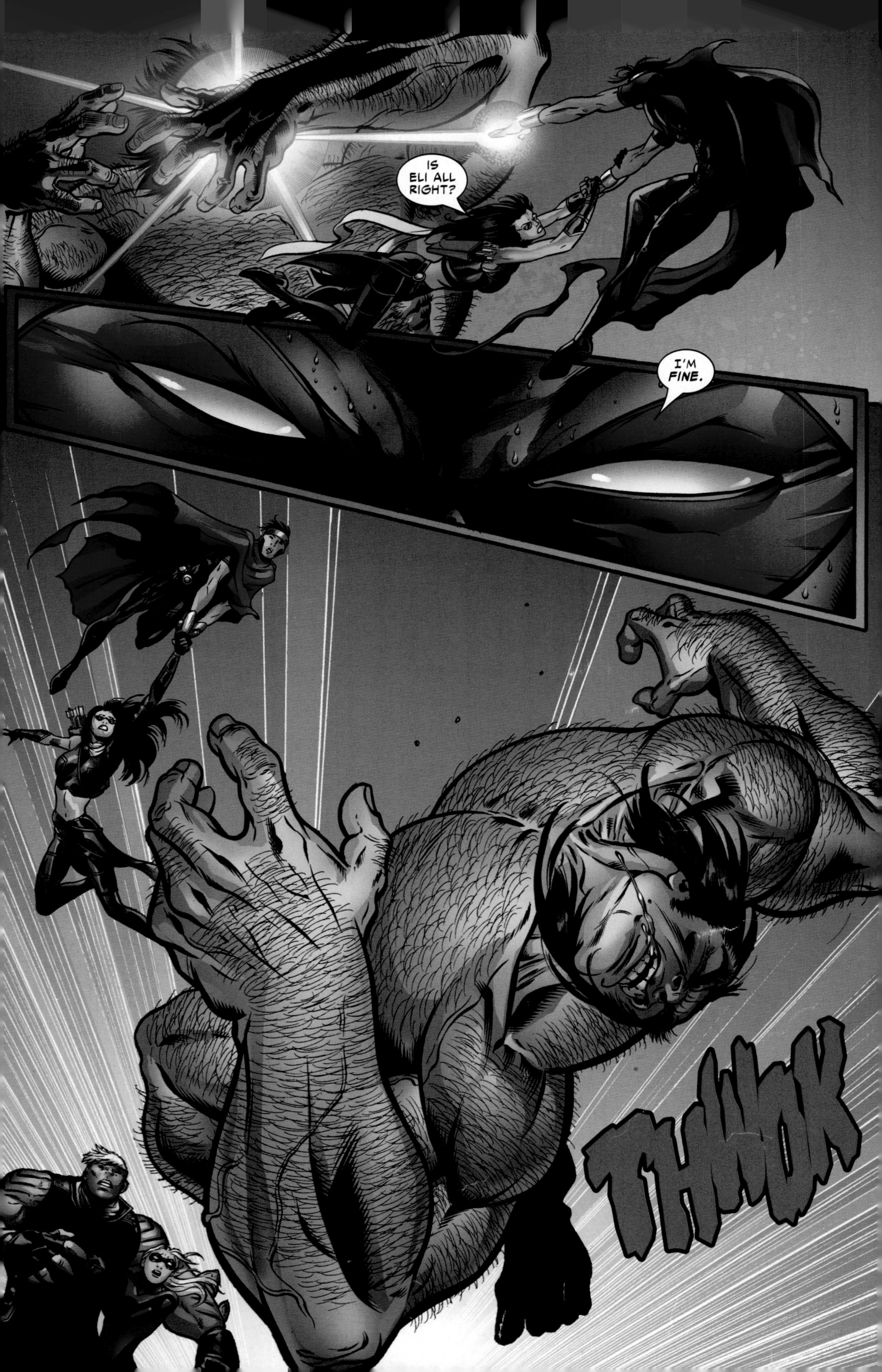
IS ELI ALL RIGHT?
I'M FINE.
THWOK

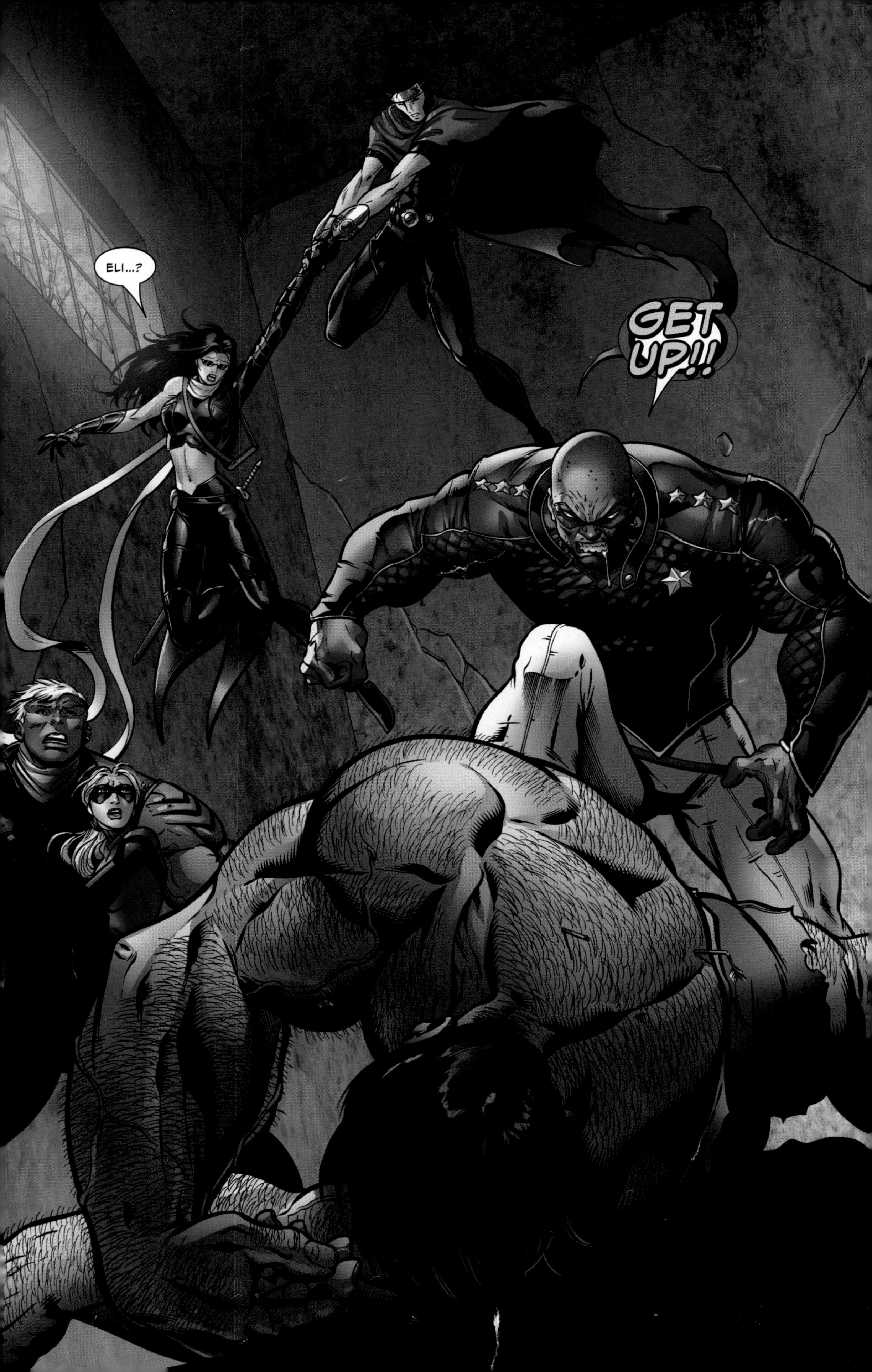
ELI...?
GET UP!!

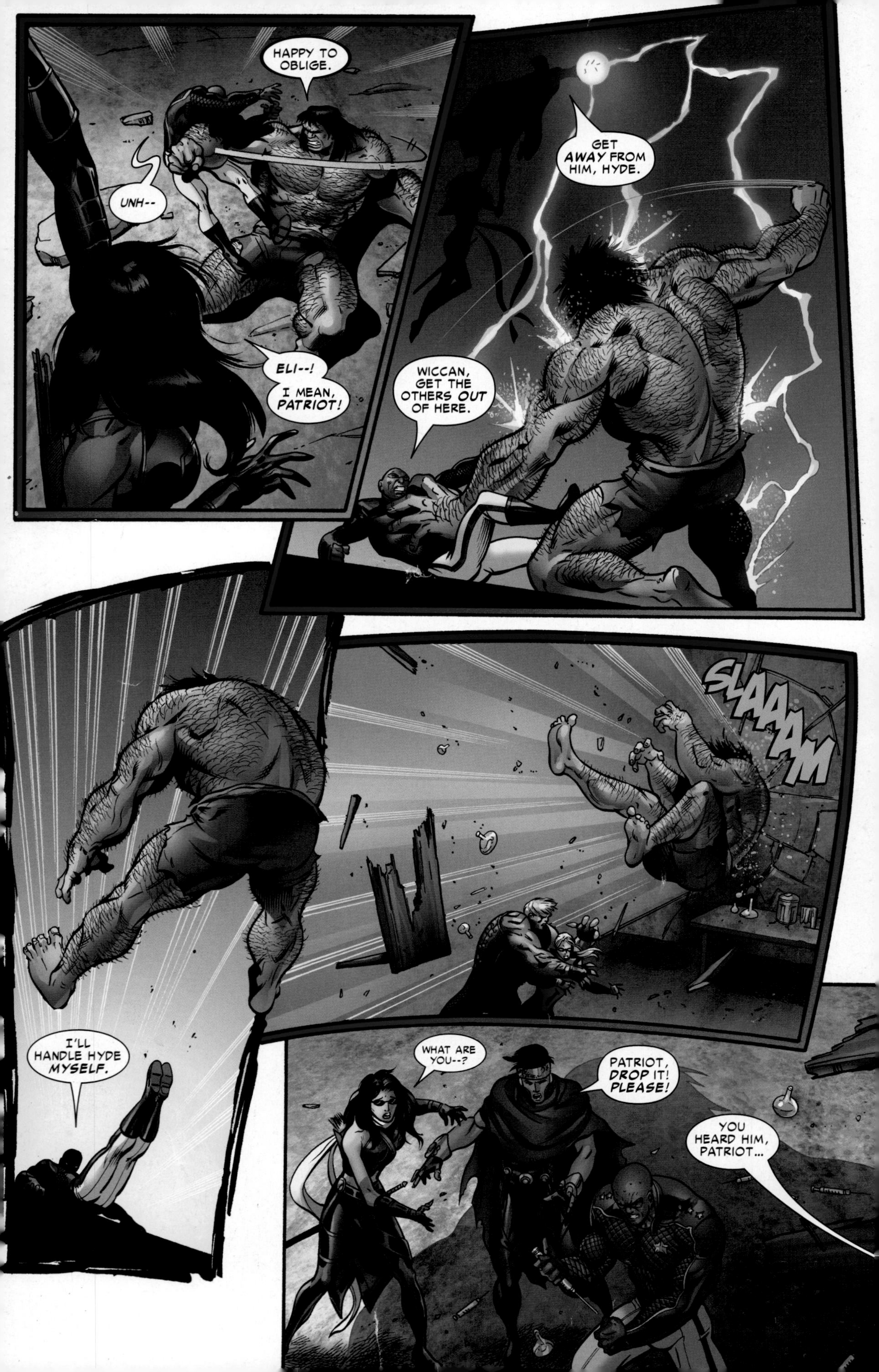

HAPPY TO OBLIGE.
UNH--
ELI--! I MEAN, PATRIOT!
GET AWAY FROM HIM, HYDE.
WICCAN, GET THE OTHERS OUT OF HERE.
SLAAAAM
I'LL HANDLE HYDE MYSELF.
WHAT ARE YOU--?
PATRIOT, DROP IT! PLEASE!
YOU HEARD HIM, PATRIOT...

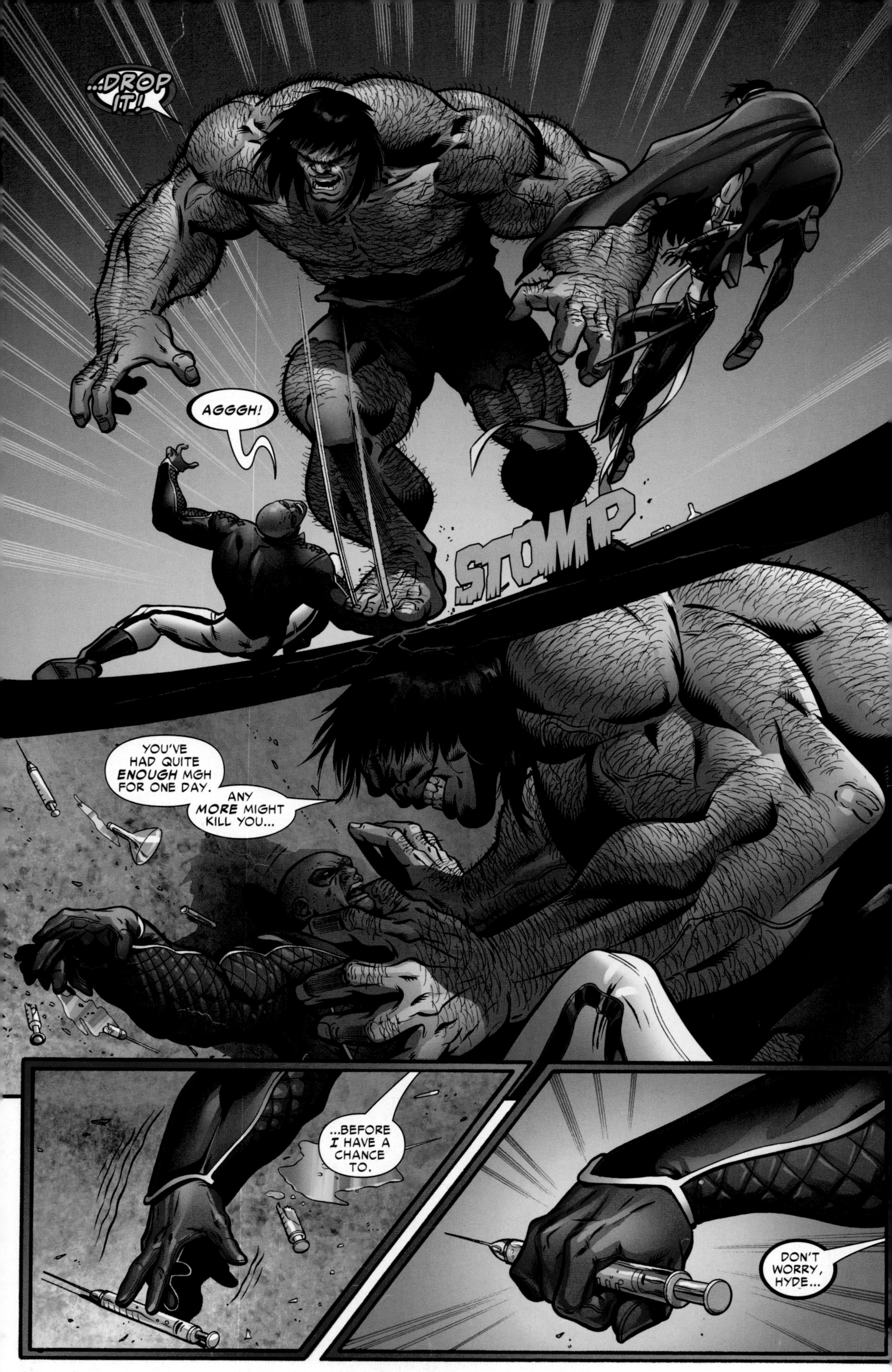
..DROP IT!
AGGGH!
STOMP
YOU'VE HAD QUITE ENOUGH MGH FOR ONE DAY.
ANY MORE MIGHT KILL YOU...
...BEFORE I HAVE A CHANCE TO.
DON'T WORRY, HYDE...

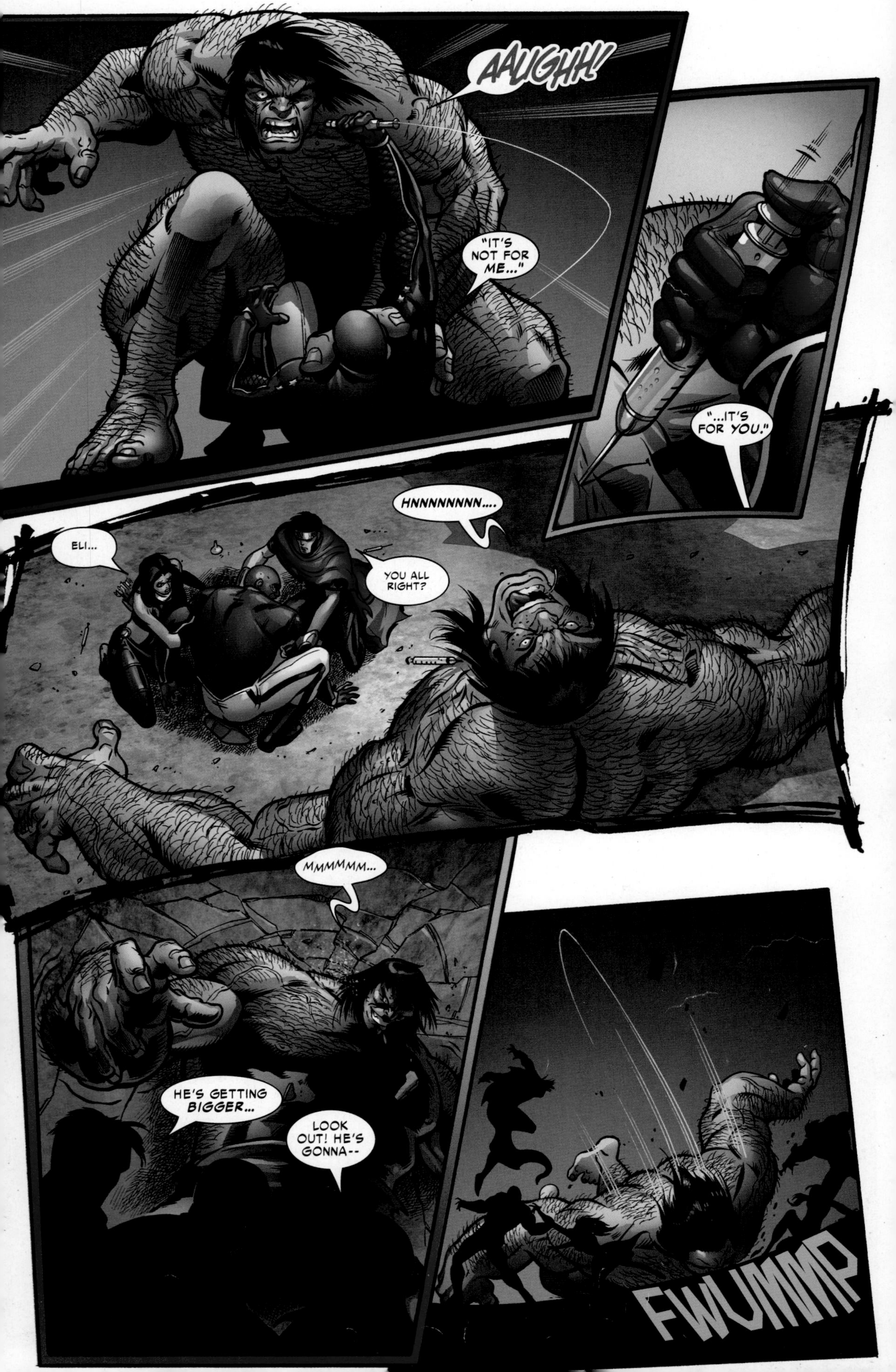

AAUGHH!
"IT'S NOT FOR ME..."
"...IT'S FOR YOU."
HNNNNNNNN....
ELI...
YOU ALL RIGHT?
MMMMMM...
HE'S GETTING BIGGER...
LOOK OUT! HE'S GONNA--
FWUMMP

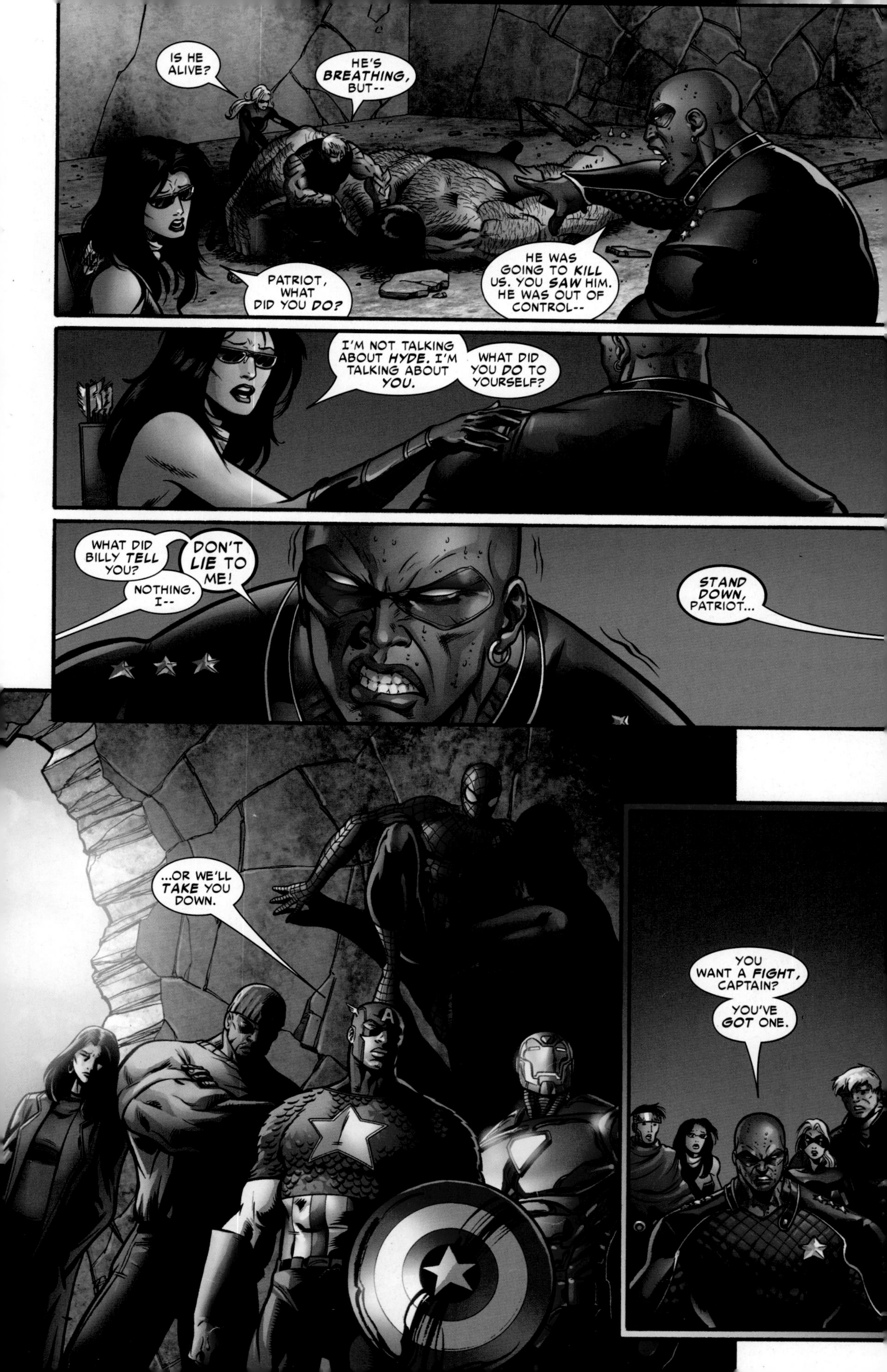
IS HE ALIVE?
HE'S BREATHING, BUT--
PATRIOT, WHAT DID YOU DO?
HE WAS GOING TO KILL US. YOU SAW HIM. HE WAS OUT OF CONTROL--
I'M NOT TALKING ABOUT HYDE. I'M TALKING ABOUT YOU.
WHAT DID YOU DO TO YOURSELF?
WHAT DID BILLY TELL YOU?
NOTHING. I--
DON'T LIE TO ME!
STAND DOWN, PATRIOT...
...OR WE'LL TAKE YOU DOWN.
YOU WANT A FIGHT, CAPTAIN?
YOU'VE GOT ONE.

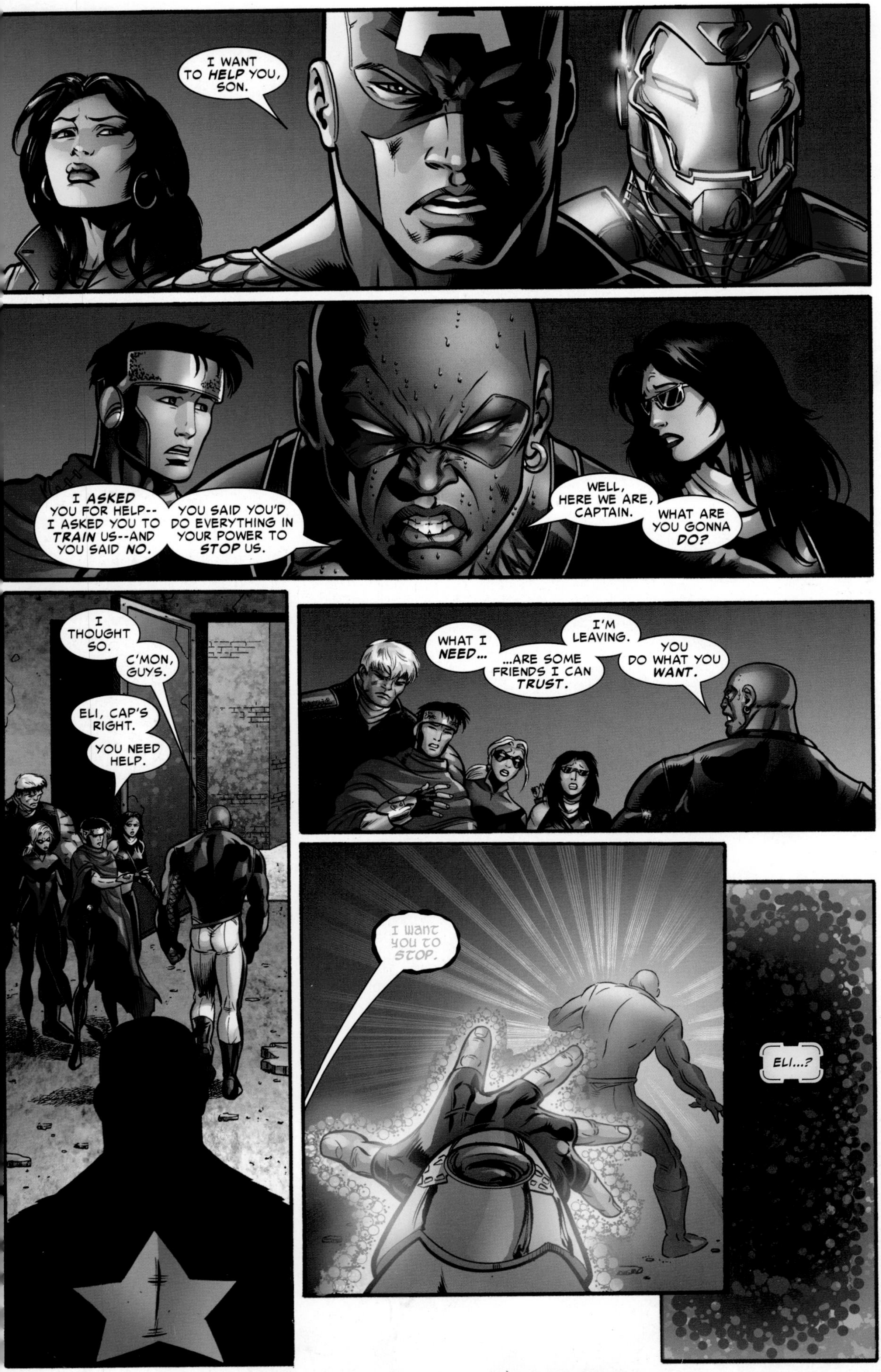
I WANT TO HELP YOU, SON.
I ASKED YOU FOR HELP-- I ASKED YOU TO TRAIN US--AND YOU SAID NO.
YOU SAID YOU'D DO EVERYTHING IN YOUR POWER TO STOP US.
WELL, HERE WE ARE, CAPTAIN.
WHAT ARE YOU GONNA DO?
I THOUGHT SO.
C'MON, GUYS.
ELI, CAP'S RIGHT.
YOU NEED HELP.
WHAT I NEED...
...ARE SOME FRIENDS I CAN TRUST.
I'M LEAVING.
YOU DO WHAT YOU WANT.
I WANT YOU TO STOP.
ELI...?

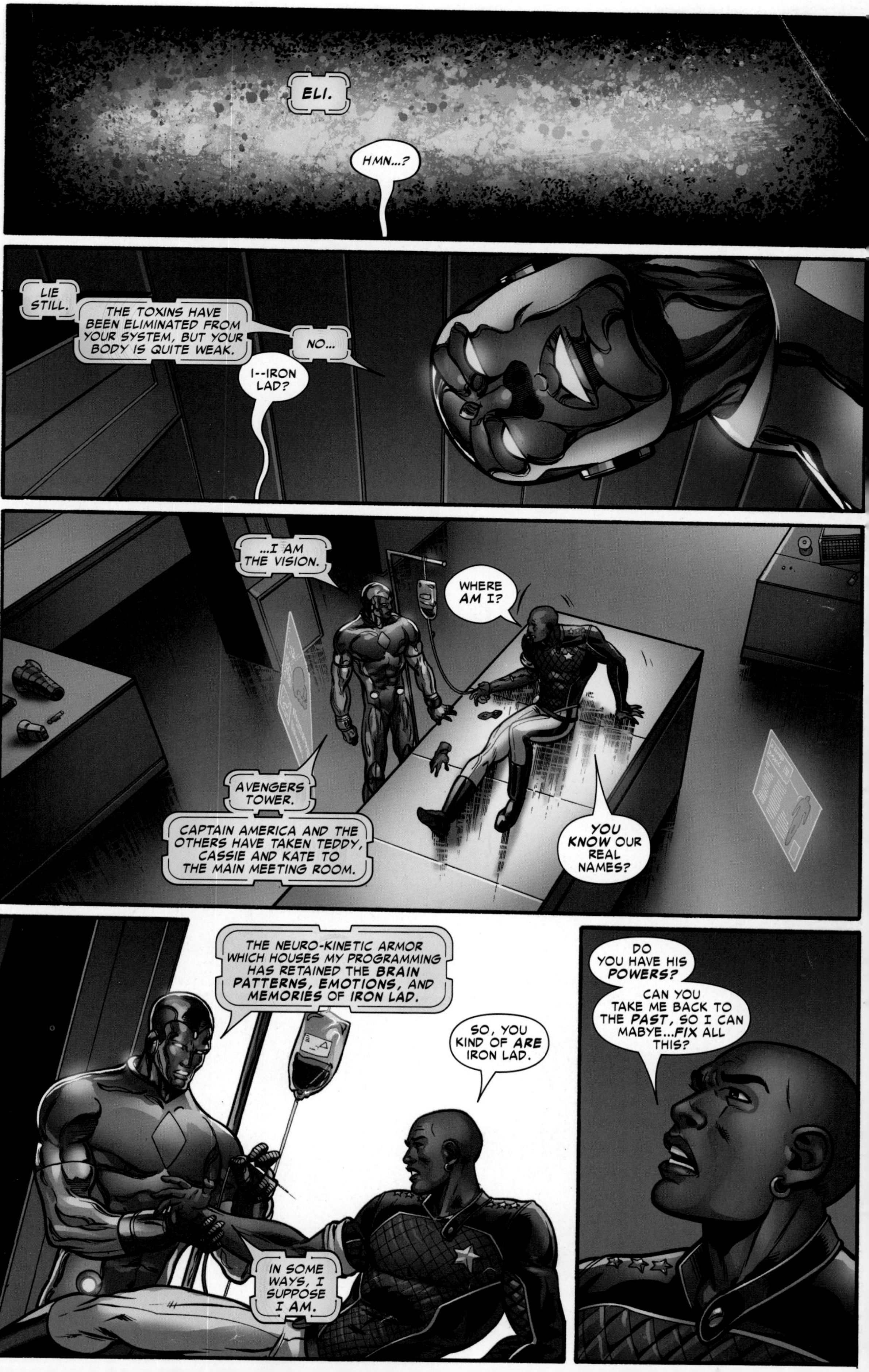
ELI.
HMN...?
LIE STILL.
THE TOXINS HAVE BEEN ELIMINATED FROM YOUR SYSTEM, BUT YOUR BODY IS QUITE WEAK.
NO...
I--IRON LAD?
...I AM THE VISION.
WHERE AM I?
AVENGERS TOWER.
CAPTAIN AMERICA AND THE OTHERS HAVE TAKEN TEDDY, CASSIE AND KATE TO THE MAIN MEETING ROOM.
YOU KNOW OUR REAL NAMES?
THE NEURO-KINETIC ARMOR WHICH HOUSES MY PROGRAMMING HAS RETAINED THE BRAIN PATTERNS, EMOTIONS, AND MEMORIES OF IRON LAD.
SO, YOU KIND OF ARE IRON LAD.
IN SOME WAYS, I SUPPOSE I AM.
DO YOU HAVE HIS POWERS?
CAN YOU TAKE ME BACK TO THE PAST, SO I CAN MABYE...FIX ALL THIS?

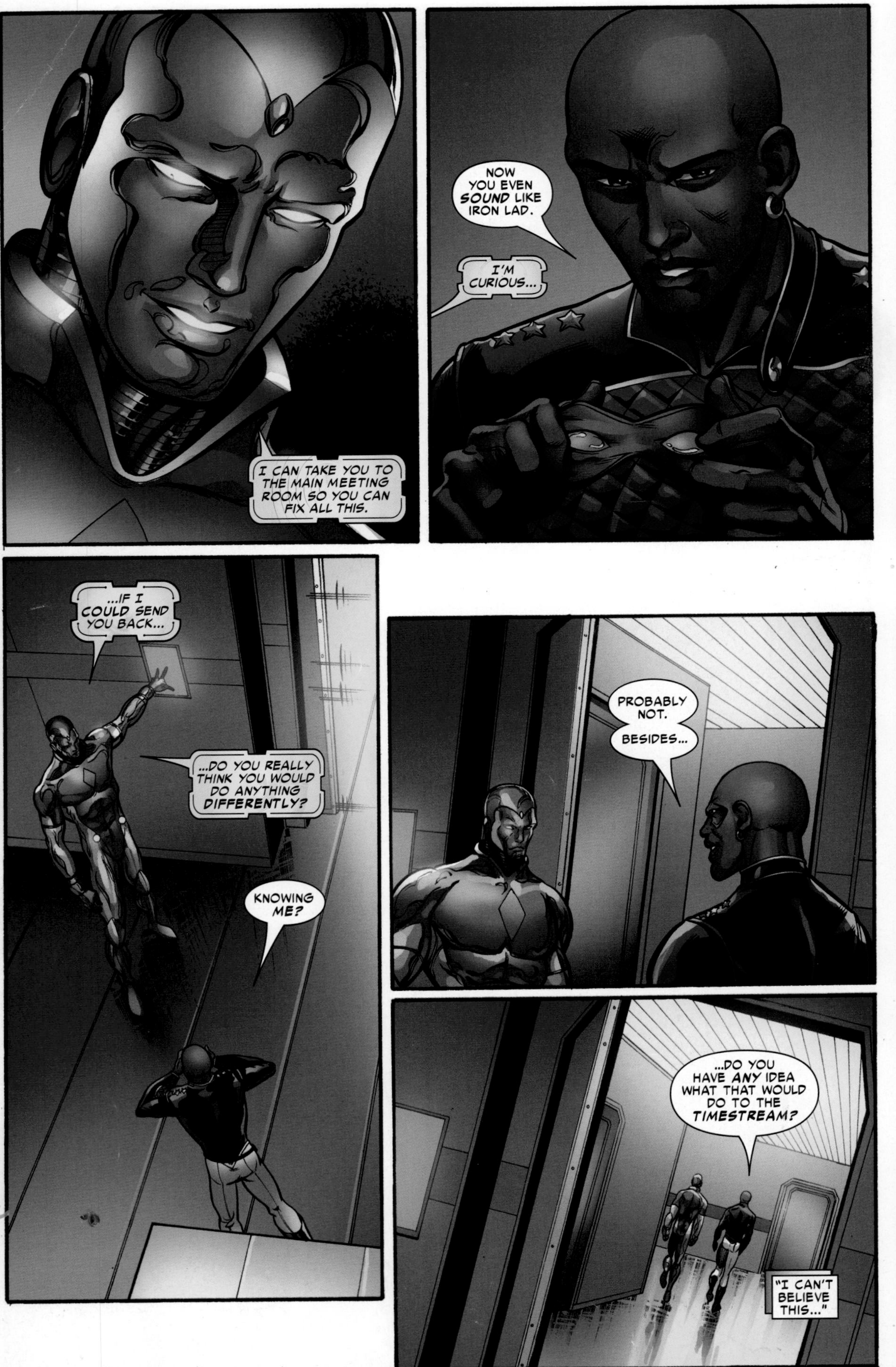
I CAN TAKE YOU TO THE MAIN MEETING ROOM SO YOU CAN FIX ALL THIS.
NOW YOU EVEN SOUND LIKE IRON LAD.
I'M CURIOUS...
...IF I COULD SEND YOU BACK...
...DO YOU REALLY THINK YOU WOULD DO ANYTHING DIFFERENTLY?
KNOWING ME?
PROBABLY NOT.
BESIDES...
...DO YOU HAVE ANY IDEA WHAT THAT WOULD DO TO THE TIMESTREAM?
"I CAN'T BELIEVE THIS..."

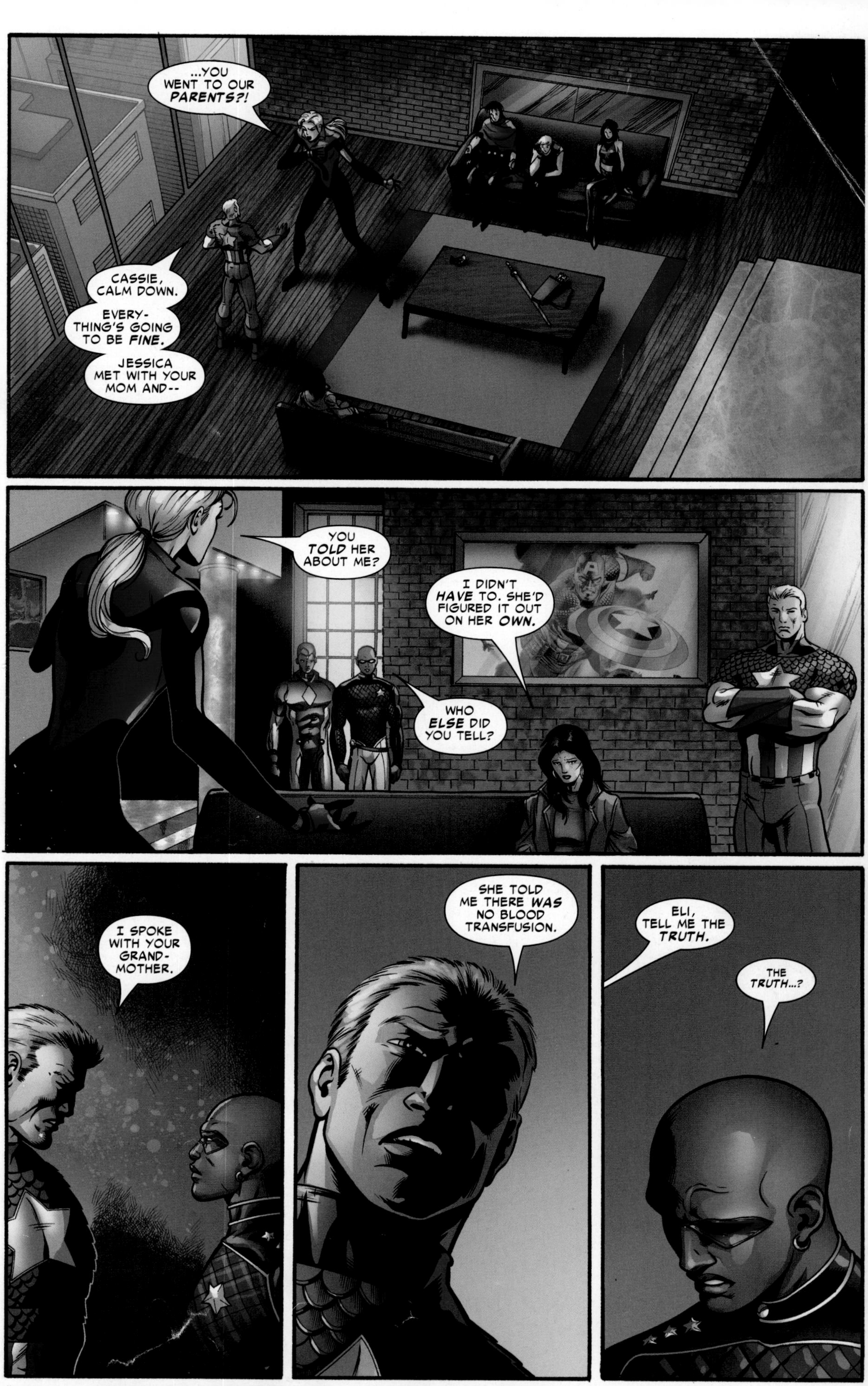
...YOU WENT TO OUR *PARENTS?!*
CASSIE, CALM DOWN.
EVERY-THING'S GOING TO BE *FINE.*
JESSICA MET WITH YOUR MOM AND--
YOU *TOLD* HER ABOUT ME?
I DIDN'T *HAVE* TO. SHE'D FIGURED IT OUT ON HER *OWN.*
WHO *ELSE* DID YOU TELL?
I SPOKE WITH YOUR GRAND-MOTHER.
SHE TOLD ME THERE *WAS* NO BLOOD TRANSFUSION.
ELI, TELL ME THE *TRUTH.*
THE *TRUTH...?*

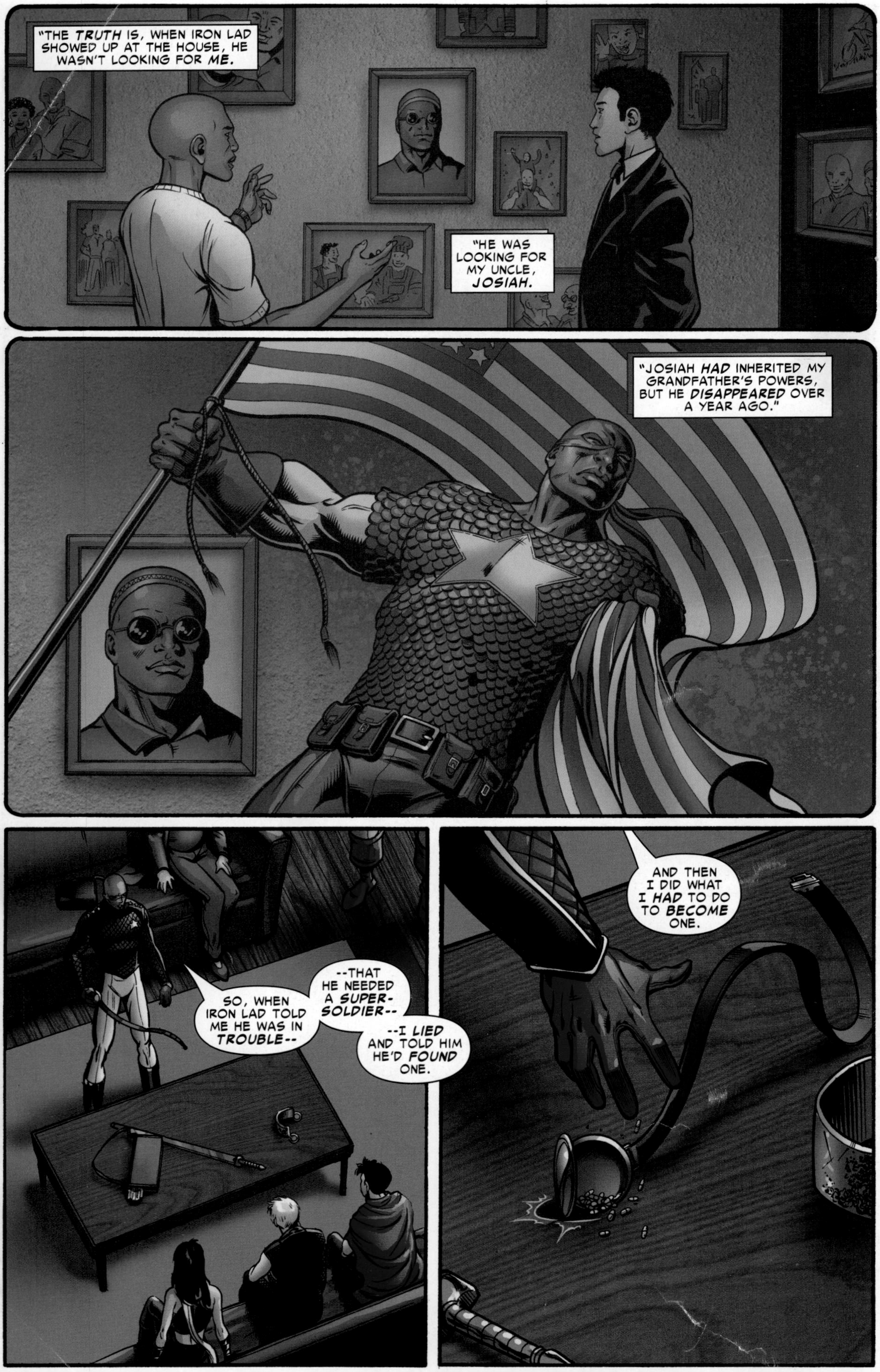
"THE *TRUTH* IS, WHEN IRON LAD SHOWED UP AT THE HOUSE, HE WASN'T LOOKING FOR *ME*.
"HE WAS LOOKING FOR MY UNCLE, **JOSIAH**.
"JOSIAH *HAD* INHERITED MY GRANDFATHER'S POWERS, BUT HE *DISAPPEARED* OVER A YEAR AGO."
SO, WHEN IRON LAD TOLD ME HE WAS IN *TROUBLE*--
--THAT HE NEEDED A *SUPER-SOLDIER*--
--I *LIED* AND TOLD HIM HE'D *FOUND* ONE.
AND THEN I DID WHAT I *HAD* TO DO TO *BECOME* ONE.

I'M SORRY.

SO, ALL THOSE MGH DEALERS YOU BUSTED...?

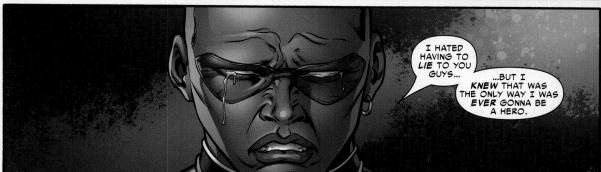

I HATED HAVING TO *LIE* TO YOU GUYS...

...BUT I *KNEW* THAT WAS THE ONLY WAY I WAS *EVER* GONNA BE A HERO.

SO I'LL SAVE YOU THE SPEECH, CAPTAIN.

YOU WON'T HAVE TO WORRY ABOUT MY PLAYING SUPER-SOLDIER ANYMORE...

...BECAUSE I QUIT.

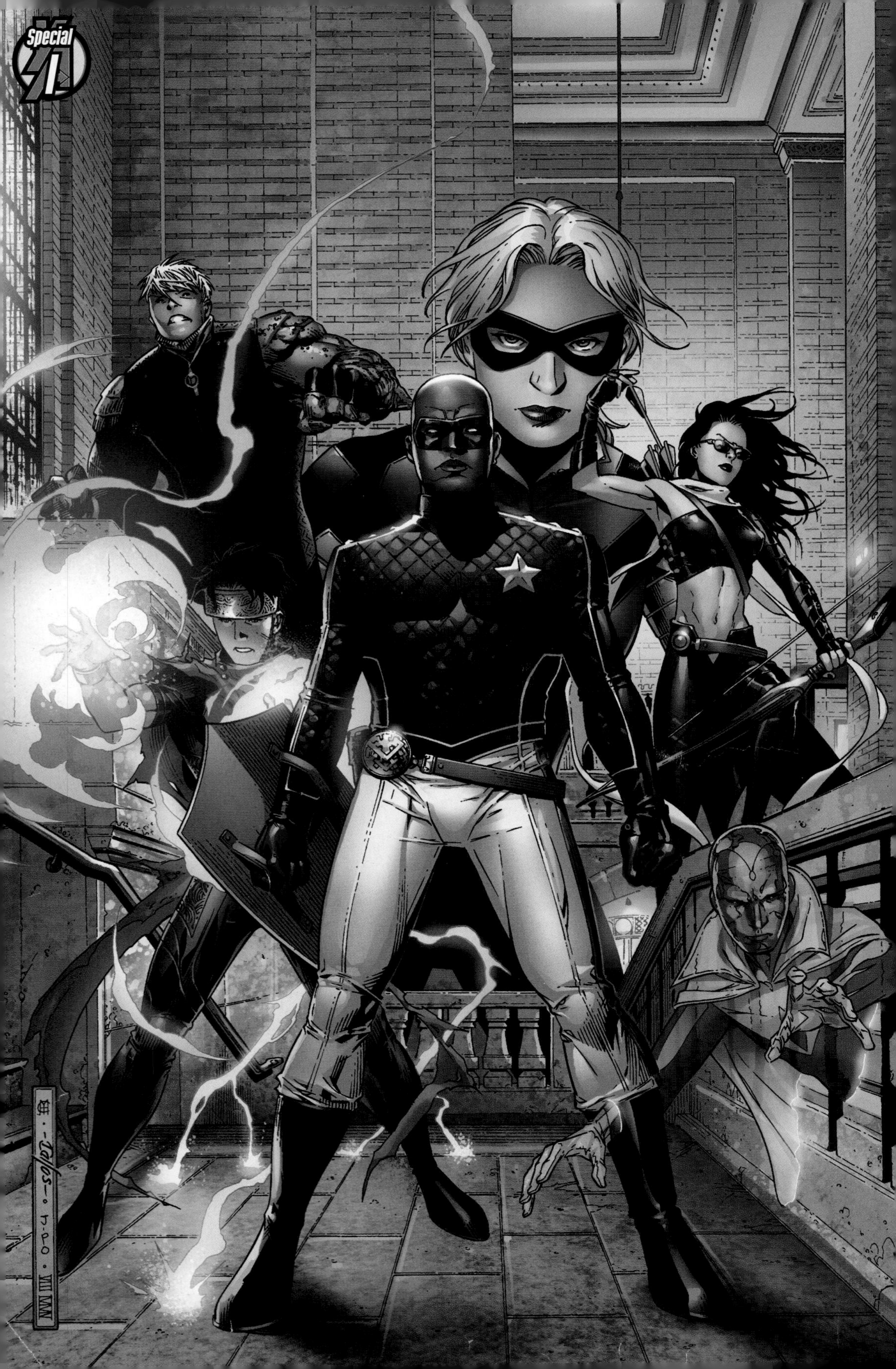
Special

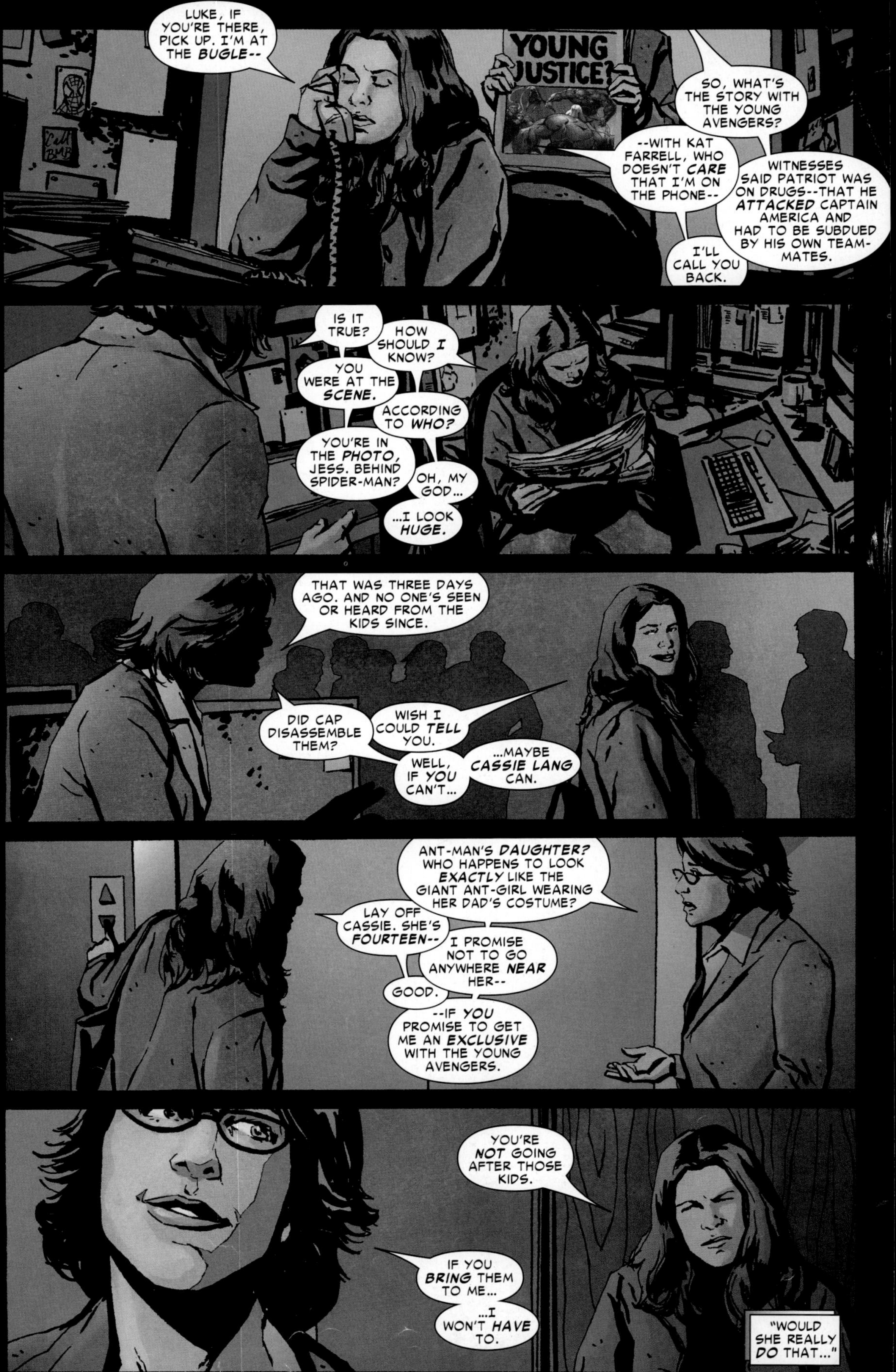

LUKE, IF YOU'RE THERE, PICK UP. I'M AT THE *BUGLE*--
YOUNG JUSTICE?
SO, WHAT'S THE STORY WITH THE YOUNG AVENGERS?
--WITH KAT FARRELL, WHO DOESN'T *CARE* THAT I'M ON THE PHONE--
WITNESSES SAID PATRIOT WAS ON DRUGS--THAT HE *ATTACKED* CAPTAIN AMERICA AND HAD TO BE SUBDUED BY HIS OWN TEAM-MATES.
I'LL CALL YOU BACK.
IS IT TRUE?
HOW SHOULD *I* KNOW?
YOU WERE AT THE *SCENE.*
ACCORDING TO *WHO?*
YOU'RE IN THE *PHOTO*, JESS. BEHIND SPIDER-MAN?
OH, MY GOD...
...I LOOK *HUGE.*
THAT WAS THREE DAYS AGO. AND NO ONE'S SEEN OR HEARD FROM THE KIDS SINCE.
DID CAP DISASSEMBLE THEM?
WISH I COULD *TELL* YOU.
WELL, IF *YOU* CAN'T...
...MAYBE *CASSIE LANG* CAN.
ANT-MAN'S *DAUGHTER?* WHO HAPPENS TO LOOK *EXACTLY* LIKE THE GIANT ANT-GIRL WEARING HER DAD'S COSTUME?
LAY OFF CASSIE. SHE'S *FOURTEEN*--
I PROMISE NOT TO GO ANYWHERE *NEAR* HER--
GOOD.
--IF *YOU* PROMISE TO GET ME AN *EXCLUSIVE* WITH THE YOUNG AVENGERS.
YOU'RE *NOT* GOING AFTER THOSE KIDS.
IF YOU *BRING* THEM TO ME...
...I WON'T *HAVE* TO.
"WOULD SHE REALLY *DO* THAT..."

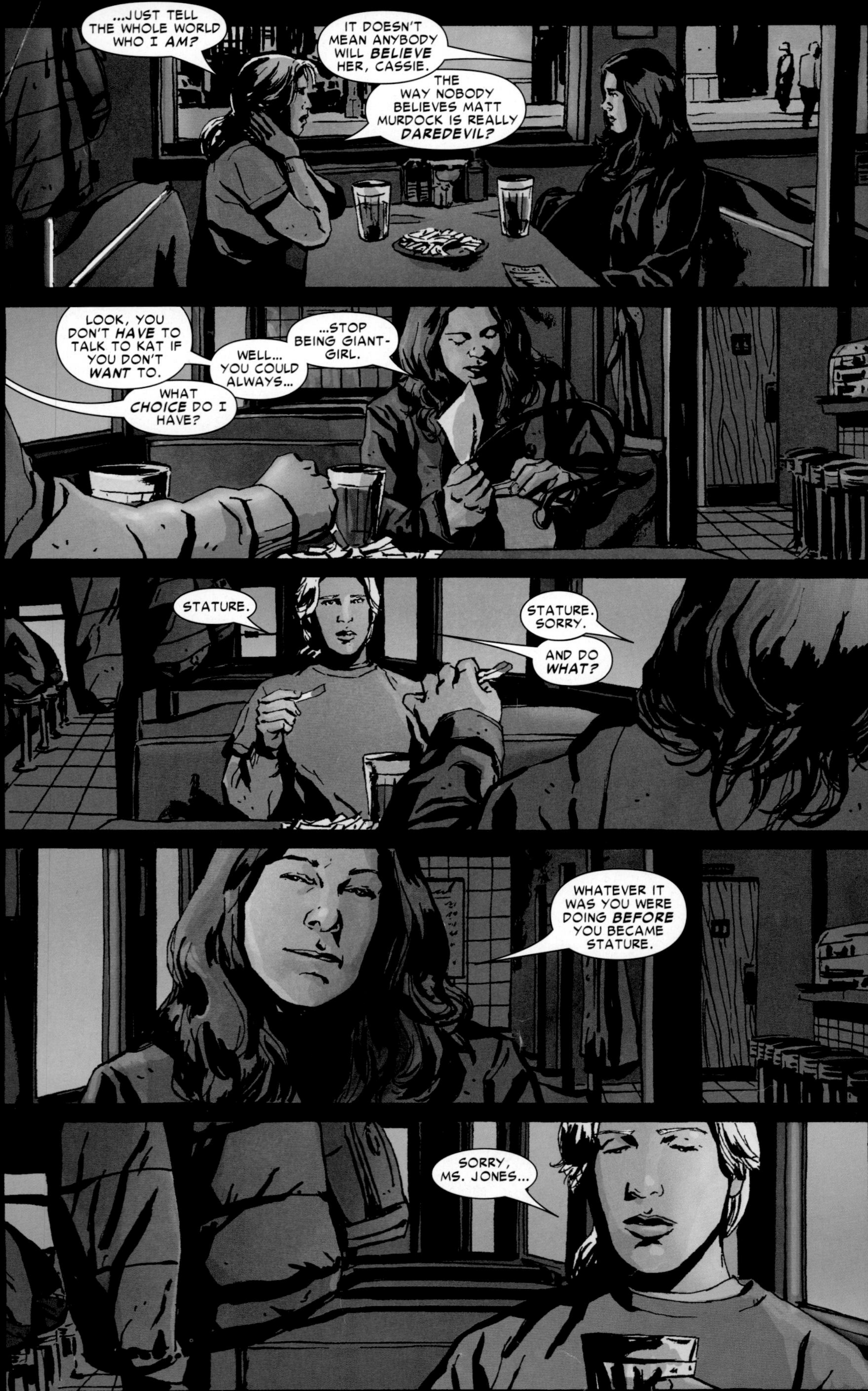
...JUST TELL THE WHOLE WORLD WHO I AM?
IT DOESN'T MEAN ANYBODY WILL BELIEVE HER, CASSIE.
THE WAY NOBODY BELIEVES MATT MURDOCK IS REALLY DAREDEVIL?
LOOK, YOU DON'T HAVE TO TALK TO KAT IF YOU DON'T WANT TO.
WHAT CHOICE DO I HAVE?
WELL... YOU COULD ALWAYS...
...STOP BEING GIANT-GIRL.
STATURE.
STATURE. SORRY.
AND DO WHAT?
WHATEVER IT WAS YOU WERE DOING BEFORE YOU BECAME STATURE.
SORRY, MS. JONES...

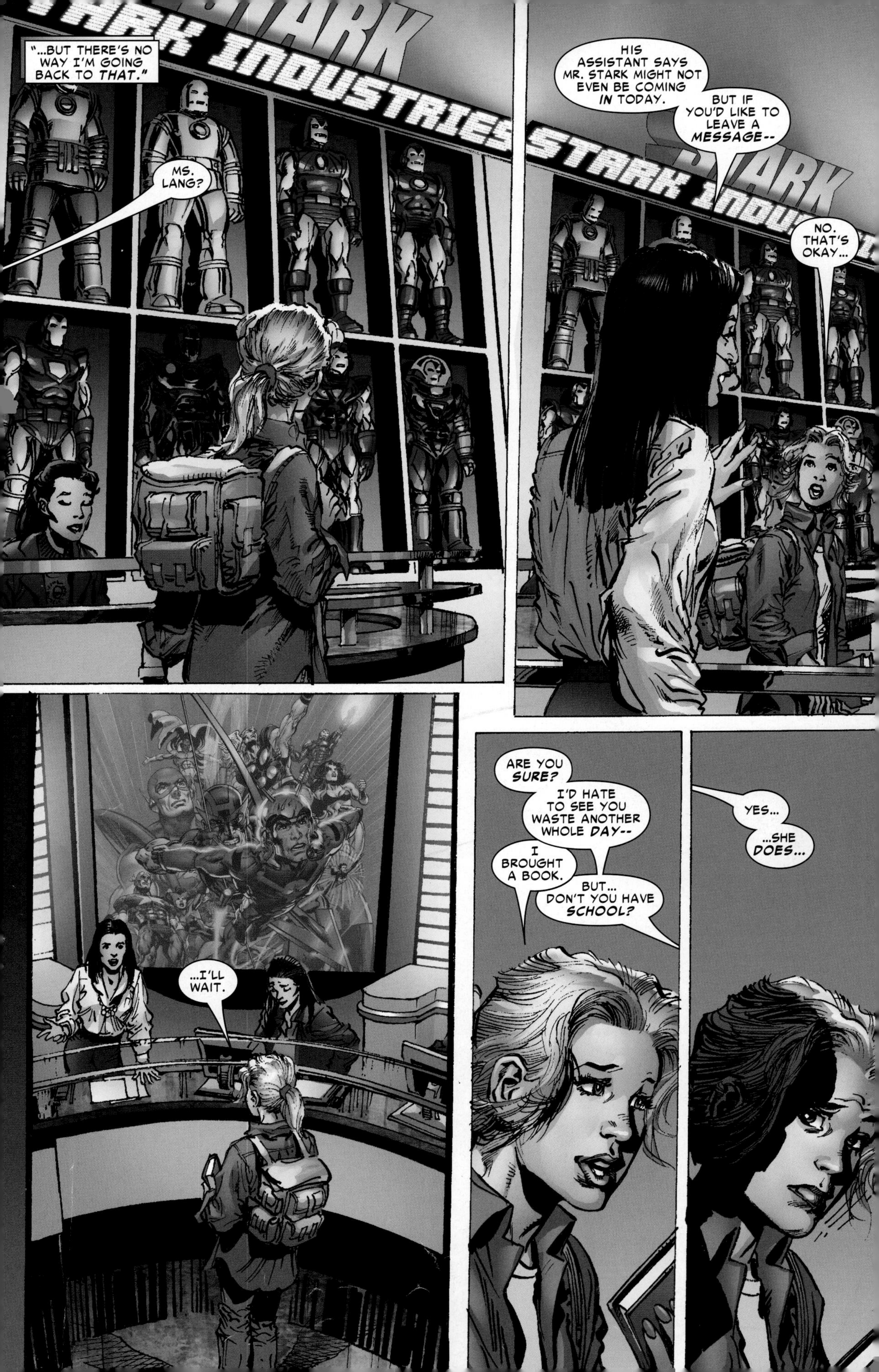
"...BUT THERE'S NO WAY I'M GOING BACK TO *THAT*."
STARK INDUSTRIES
MS. LANG?
HIS ASSISTANT SAYS MR. STARK MIGHT NOT EVEN BE COMING *IN* TODAY.
BUT IF YOU'D LIKE TO LEAVE A *MESSAGE*--
STARK INDUSTRIES
NO. THAT'S OKAY...
...I'LL WAIT.
ARE YOU *SURE?*
I'D HATE TO SEE YOU WASTE ANOTHER WHOLE *DAY*--
I BROUGHT A BOOK.
BUT... DON'T YOU HAVE *SCHOOL?*
YES...
...SHE *DOES*...

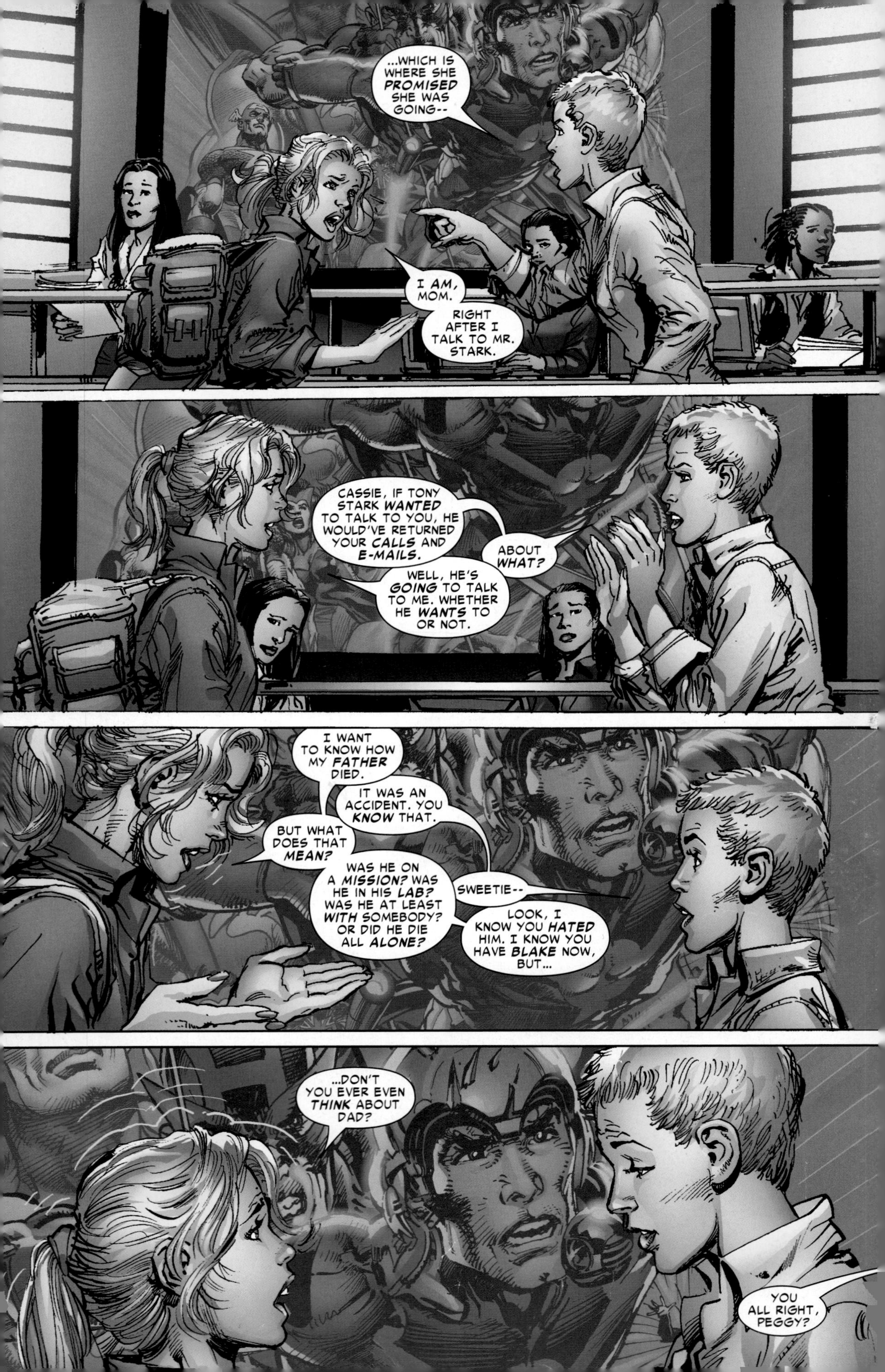
...WHICH IS WHERE SHE PROMISED SHE WAS GOING--
I AM, MOM.
RIGHT AFTER I TALK TO MR. STARK.
CASSIE, IF TONY STARK WANTED TO TALK TO YOU, HE WOULD'VE RETURNED YOUR CALLS AND E-MAILS.
ABOUT WHAT?
WELL, HE'S GOING TO TALK TO ME. WHETHER HE WANTS TO OR NOT.
I WANT TO KNOW HOW MY FATHER DIED.
IT WAS AN ACCIDENT. YOU KNOW THAT.
BUT WHAT DOES THAT MEAN?
WAS HE ON A MISSION? WAS HE IN HIS LAB? WAS HE AT LEAST WITH SOMEBODY? OR DID HE DIE ALL ALONE?
SWEETIE--
LOOK, I KNOW YOU HATED HIM. I KNOW YOU HAVE BLAKE NOW, BUT...
...DON'T YOU EVER EVEN THINK ABOUT DAD?
YOU ALL RIGHT, PEGGY?

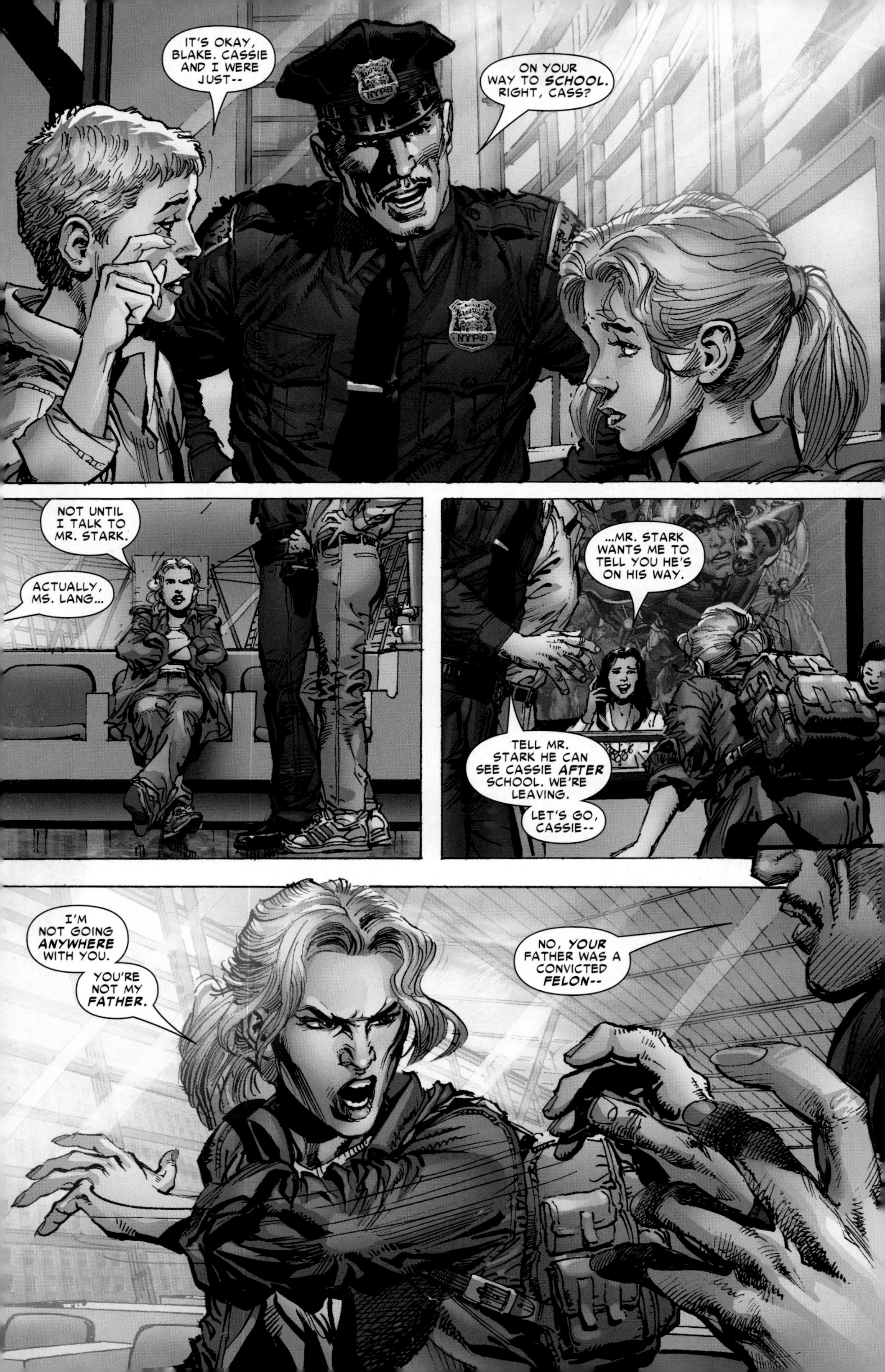
IT'S OKAY, BLAKE. CASSIE AND I WERE JUST--
ON YOUR WAY TO *SCHOOL.* RIGHT, CASS?
NOT UNTIL I TALK TO MR. STARK.
ACTUALLY, MS. LANG...
...MR. STARK WANTS ME TO TELL YOU HE'S ON HIS WAY.
TELL MR. STARK HE CAN SEE CASSIE *AFTER* SCHOOL. WE'RE LEAVING.
LET'S GO, CASSIE--
I'M NOT GOING *ANYWHERE* WITH YOU.
YOU'RE NOT MY *FATHER.*
NO, *YOUR* FATHER WAS A CONVICTED *FELON--*

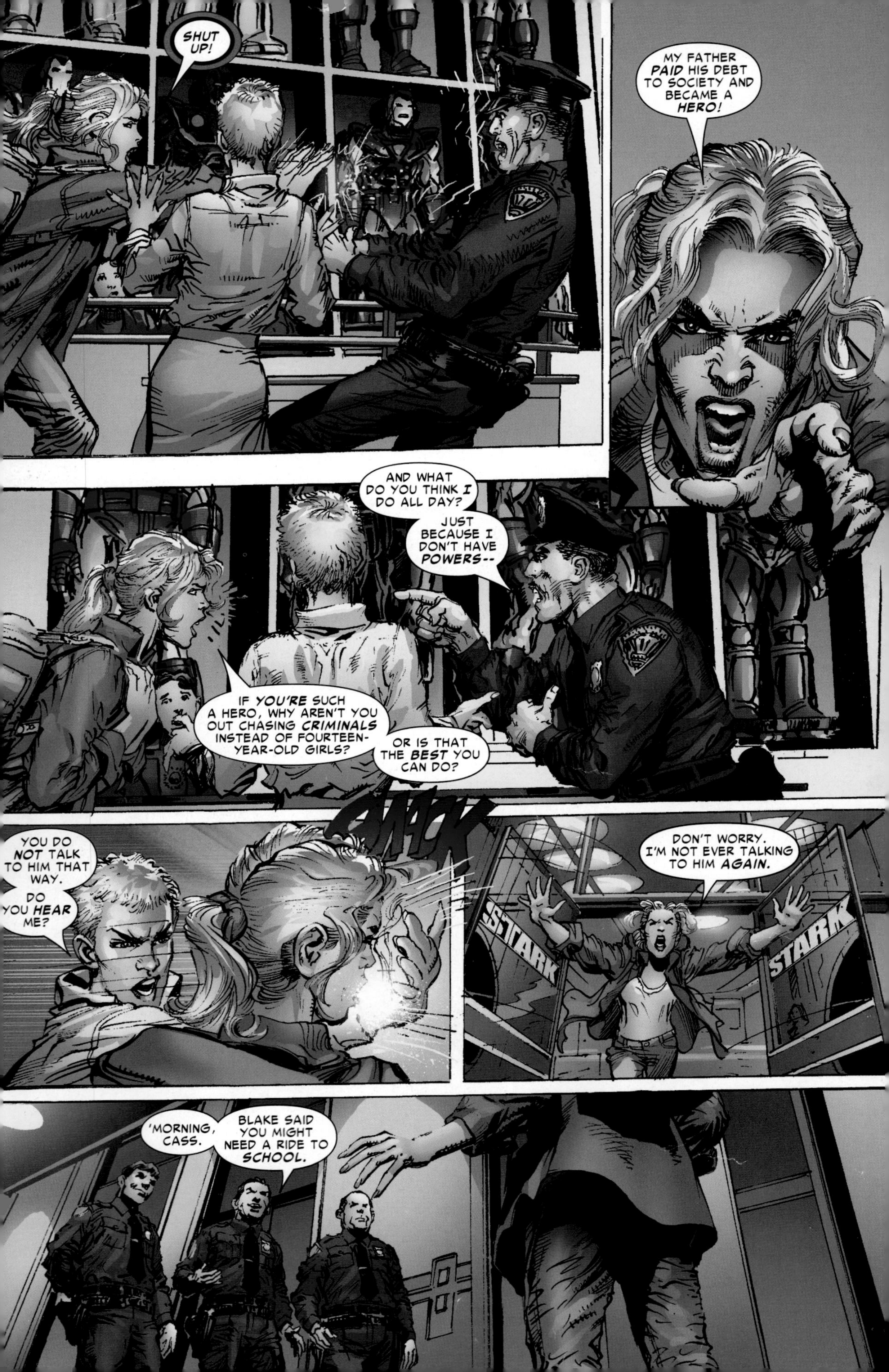
SHUT UP!
MY FATHER PAID HIS DEBT TO SOCIETY AND BECAME A HERO!
AND WHAT DO YOU THINK I DO ALL DAY?
JUST BECAUSE I DON'T HAVE POWERS--
IF YOU'RE SUCH A HERO, WHY AREN'T YOU OUT CHASING CRIMINALS INSTEAD OF FOURTEEN-YEAR-OLD GIRLS?
OR IS THAT THE BEST YOU CAN DO?
CRACK
YOU DO NOT TALK TO HIM THAT WAY.
DO YOU HEAR ME?
DON'T WORRY. I'M NOT EVER TALKING TO HIM AGAIN.
STARK
STARK
'MORNING, CASS.
BLAKE SAID YOU MIGHT NEED A RIDE TO SCHOOL.

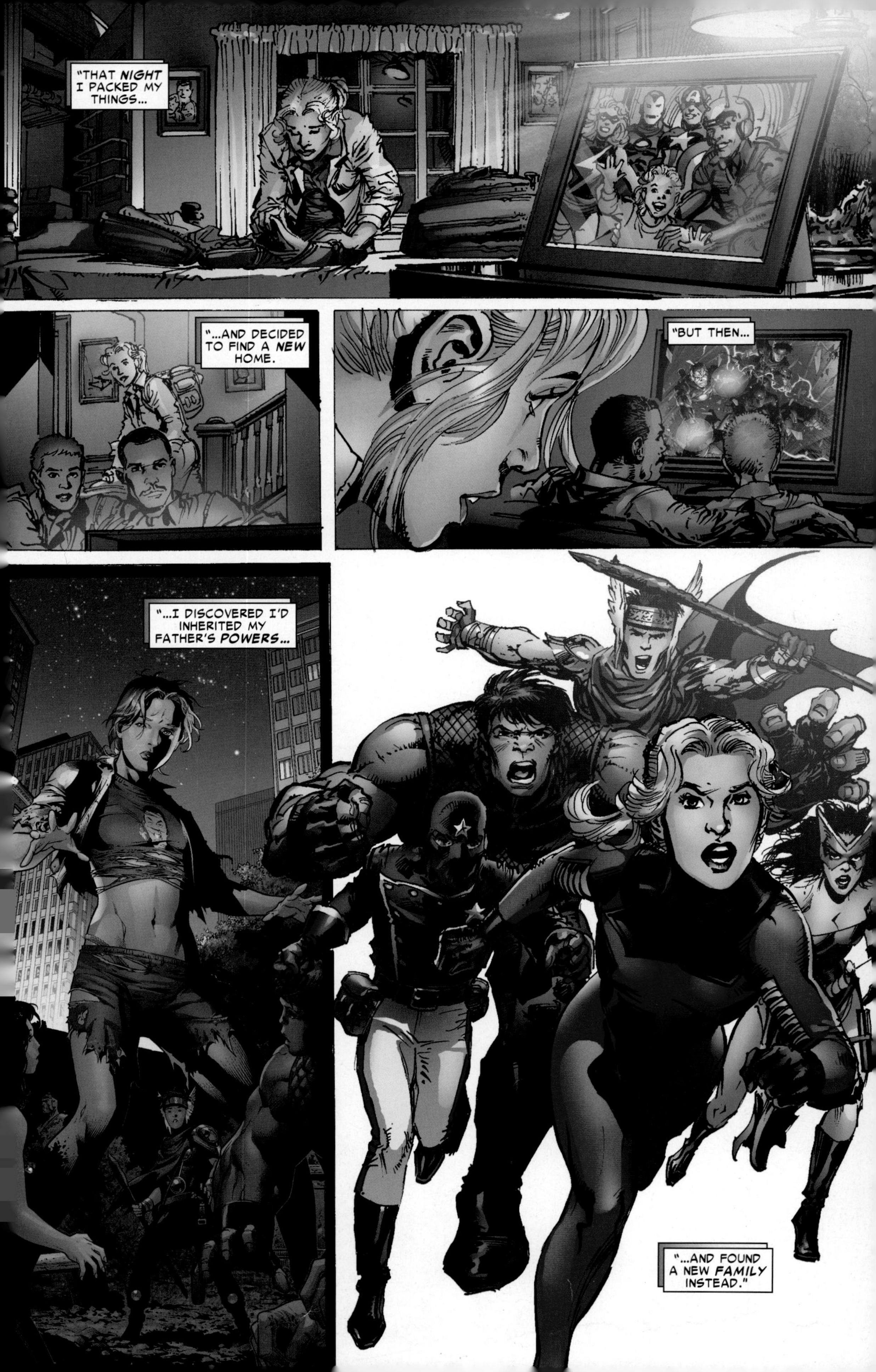
"THAT NIGHT I PACKED MY THINGS...
"...AND DECIDED TO FIND A NEW HOME.
"BUT THEN...
"...I DISCOVERED I'D INHERITED MY FATHER'S POWERS...
"...AND FOUND A NEW FAMILY INSTEAD."

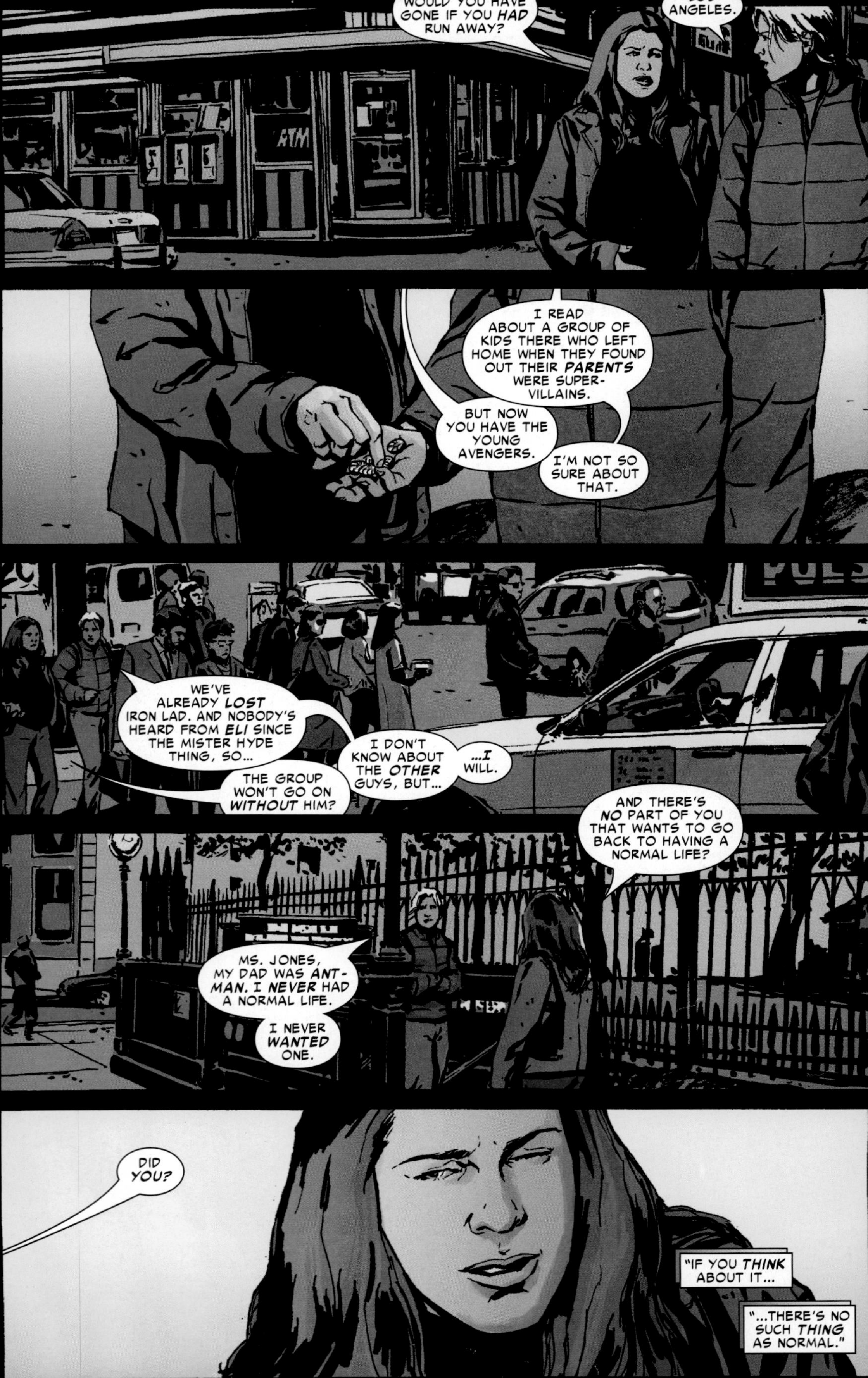
WHERE WOULD YOU HAVE GONE IF YOU HAD RUN AWAY?
LOS ANGELES.
I READ ABOUT A GROUP OF KIDS THERE WHO LEFT HOME WHEN THEY FOUND OUT THEIR PARENTS WERE SUPER-VILLAINS.
BUT NOW YOU HAVE THE YOUNG AVENGERS.
I'M NOT SO SURE ABOUT THAT.
WE'VE ALREADY LOST IRON LAD. AND NOBODY'S HEARD FROM ELI SINCE THE MISTER HYDE THING, SO...
THE GROUP WON'T GO ON WITHOUT HIM?
I DON'T KNOW ABOUT THE OTHER GUYS, BUT...
...I WILL.
AND THERE'S NO PART OF YOU THAT WANTS TO GO BACK TO HAVING A NORMAL LIFE?
MS. JONES, MY DAD WAS ANT-MAN. I NEVER HAD A NORMAL LIFE.
I NEVER WANTED ONE.
DID YOU?
"IF YOU THINK ABOUT IT...
"...THERE'S NO SUCH THING AS NORMAL."

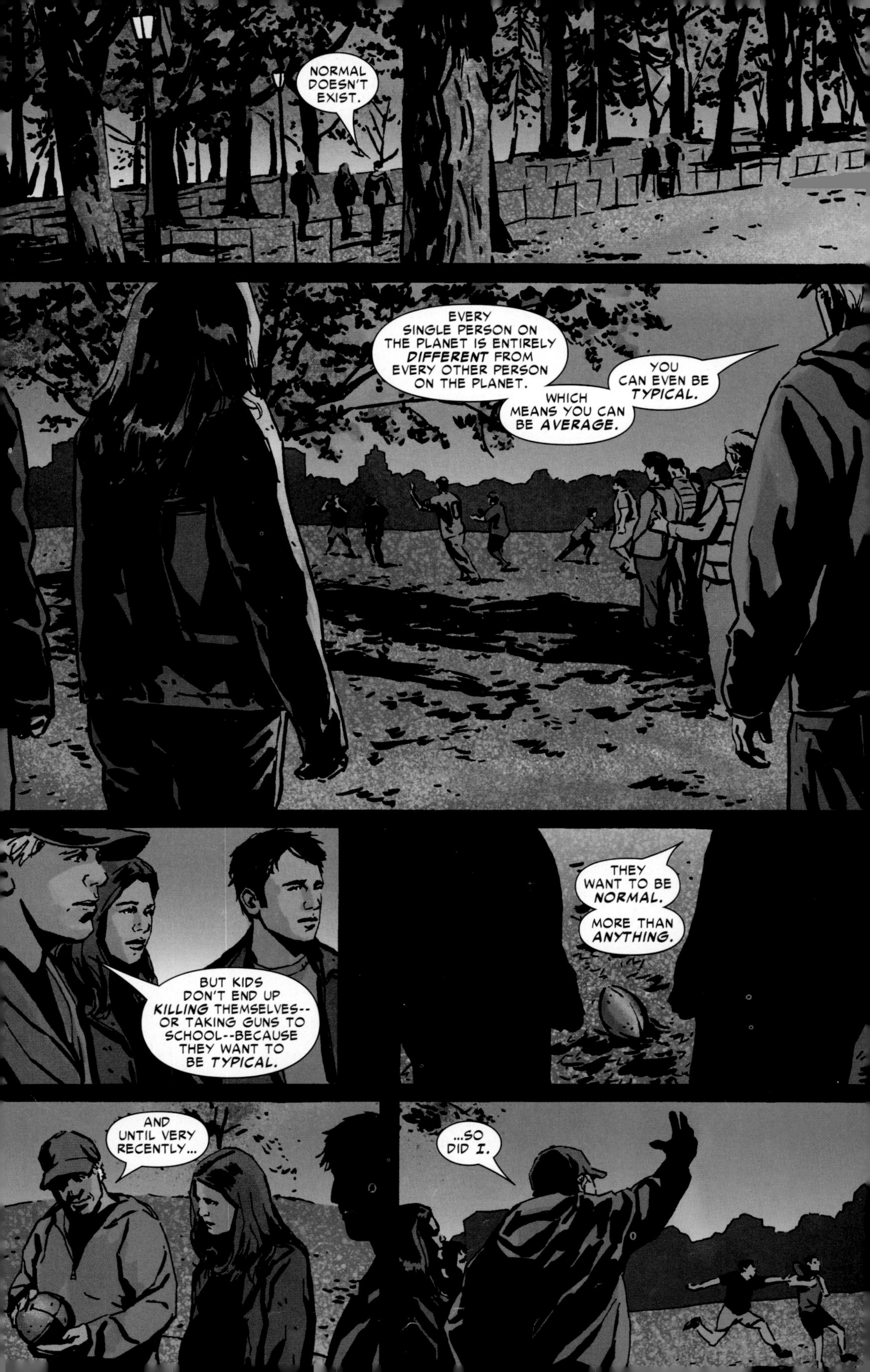
NORMAL DOESN'T EXIST.
EVERY SINGLE PERSON ON THE PLANET IS ENTIRELY *DIFFERENT* FROM EVERY OTHER PERSON ON THE PLANET.
WHICH MEANS YOU CAN BE *AVERAGE*.
YOU CAN EVEN BE *TYPICAL*.
BUT KIDS DON'T END UP *KILLING* THEMSELVES-- OR TAKING GUNS TO SCHOOL--BECAUSE THEY WANT TO BE *TYPICAL*.
THEY WANT TO BE *NORMAL*.
MORE THAN *ANYTHING*.
AND UNTIL VERY RECENTLY...
...SO DID *I*.

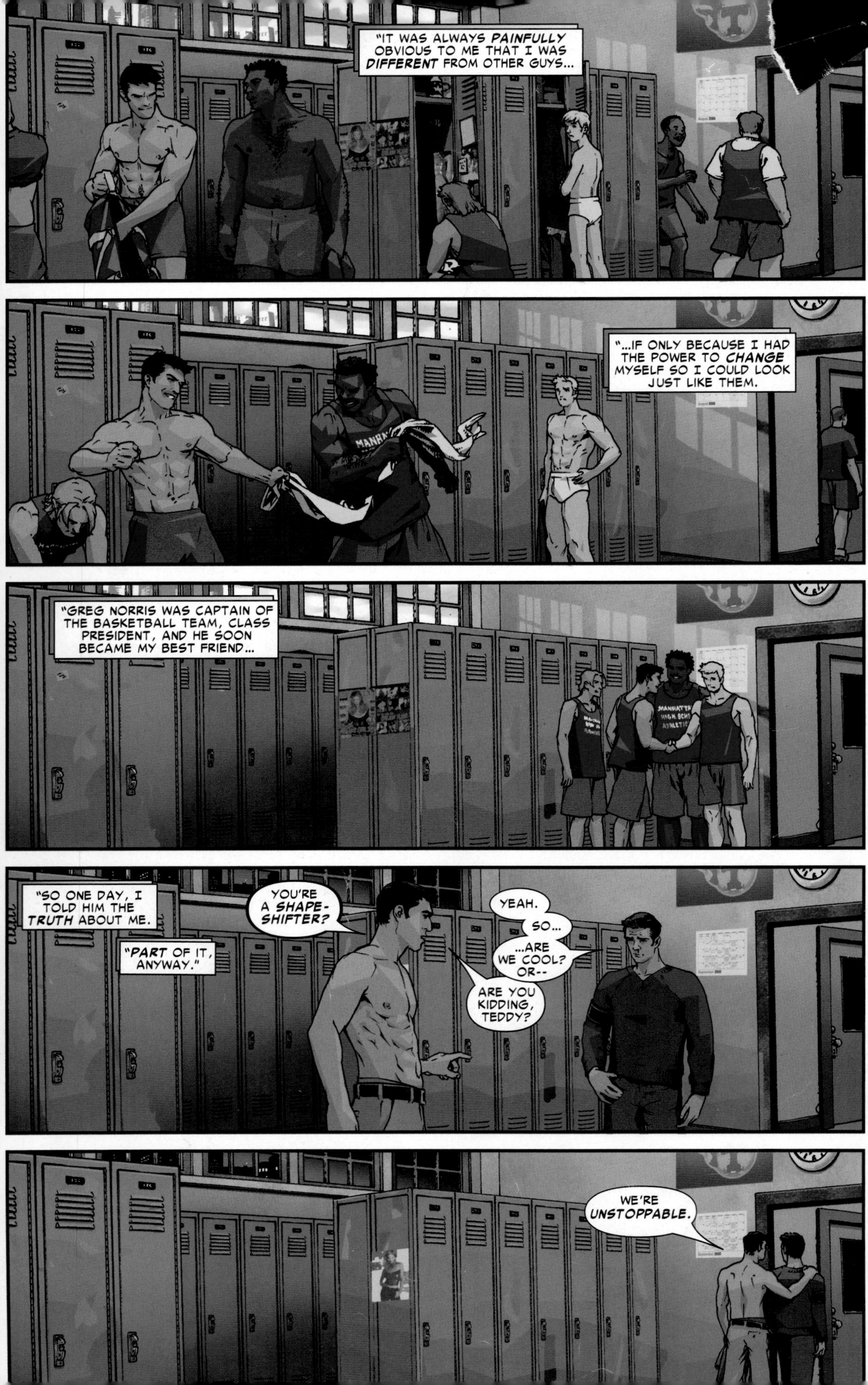
"IT WAS ALWAYS PAINFULLY OBVIOUS TO ME THAT I WAS DIFFERENT FROM OTHER GUYS...
"...IF ONLY BECAUSE I HAD THE POWER TO CHANGE MYSELF SO I COULD LOOK JUST LIKE THEM.
"GREG NORRIS WAS CAPTAIN OF THE BASKETBALL TEAM, CLASS PRESIDENT, AND HE SOON BECAME MY BEST FRIEND...
"SO ONE DAY, I TOLD HIM THE TRUTH ABOUT ME.
"PART OF IT, ANYWAY."
YOU'RE A SHAPE-SHIFTER?
YEAH.
SO...
...ARE WE COOL? OR--
ARE YOU KIDDING, TEDDY?
WE'RE UNSTOPPABLE.

"AND WE WERE.

"TOGETHER, THERE WAS *NOTHING* WE COULDN'T DO.

"AS LONG AS I PRETENDED TO BE *JOHNNY STORM*...

"...OR THE INCREDIBLE HULK...

"...OR TONY STARK."

TONY!

MR. STARK!

GREG, WAIT...

...STARK FOUNDATION IS WORKING WITH THE CITY TO DECLARE AVENGERS MANSION A PUBLIC LANDMARK AND MEMORIAL...

LIVE

GERS DISASSEMBLE!

IRON MAN ANNOUNCES BREAK-UP O PREMIERE SUPER-TEAM

...BECAUSE THE AVENGERS HAVE OFFICIALLY DISBANDED.

OH, MY GOD.

I THINK IT'S TIME WE PAID A VISIT TO AVENGERS MANSION...

...DON'T YOU, "MR. STARK"?

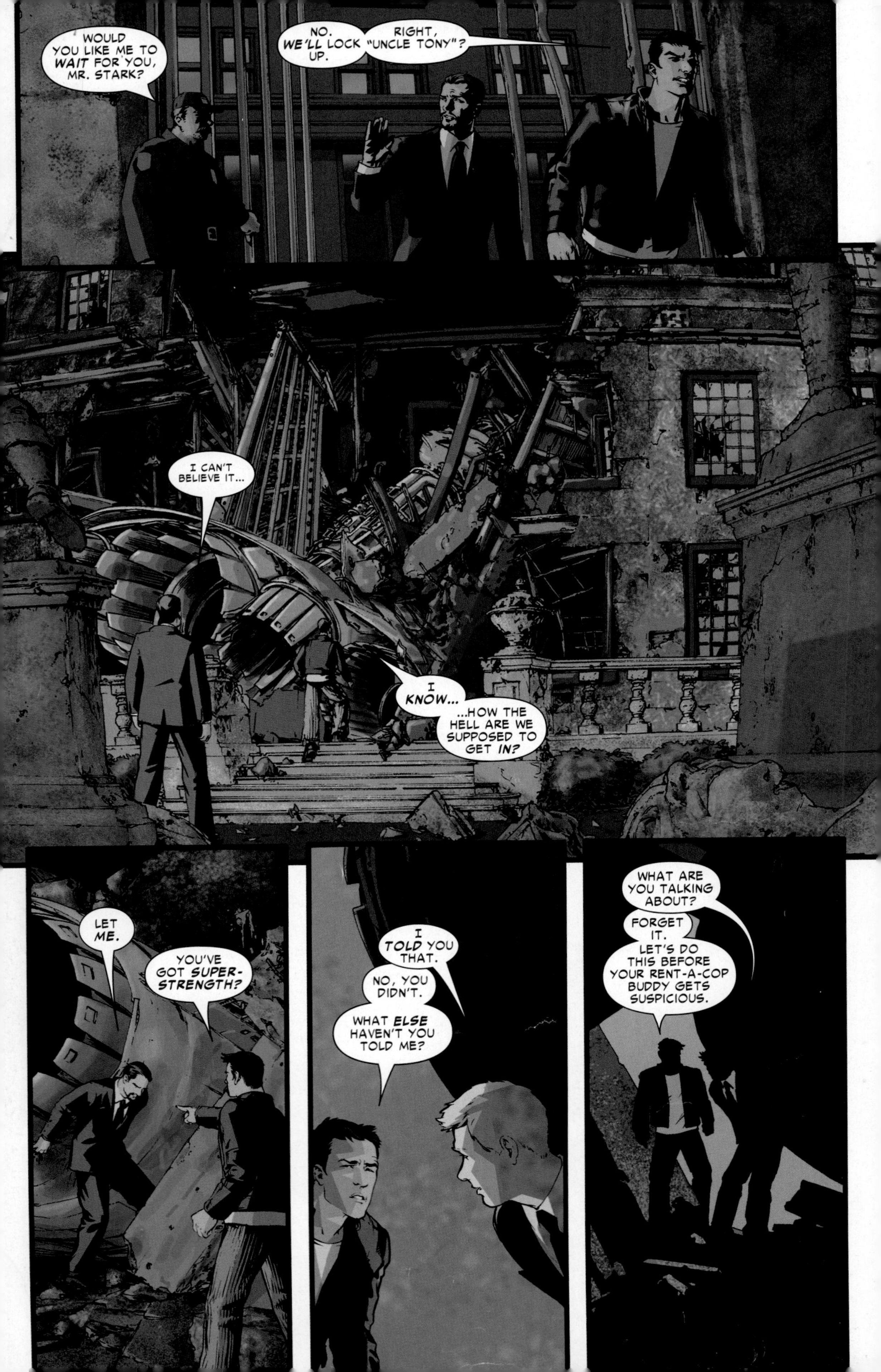
WOULD YOU LIKE ME TO *WAIT* FOR YOU, MR. STARK?
NO. *WE'LL* LOCK UP.
RIGHT, "UNCLE TONY"?
I CAN'T BELIEVE IT...
I *KNOW*...
...HOW THE HELL ARE WE SUPPOSED TO GET *IN?*
LET *ME.*
YOU'VE GOT *SUPER-STRENGTH?*
I *TOLD* YOU THAT.
NO, YOU DIDN'T.
WHAT *ELSE* HAVEN'T YOU TOLD ME?
WHAT ARE YOU TALKING ABOUT?
FORGET IT.
LET'S DO THIS BEFORE YOUR RENT-A-COP BUDDY GETS SUSPICIOUS.

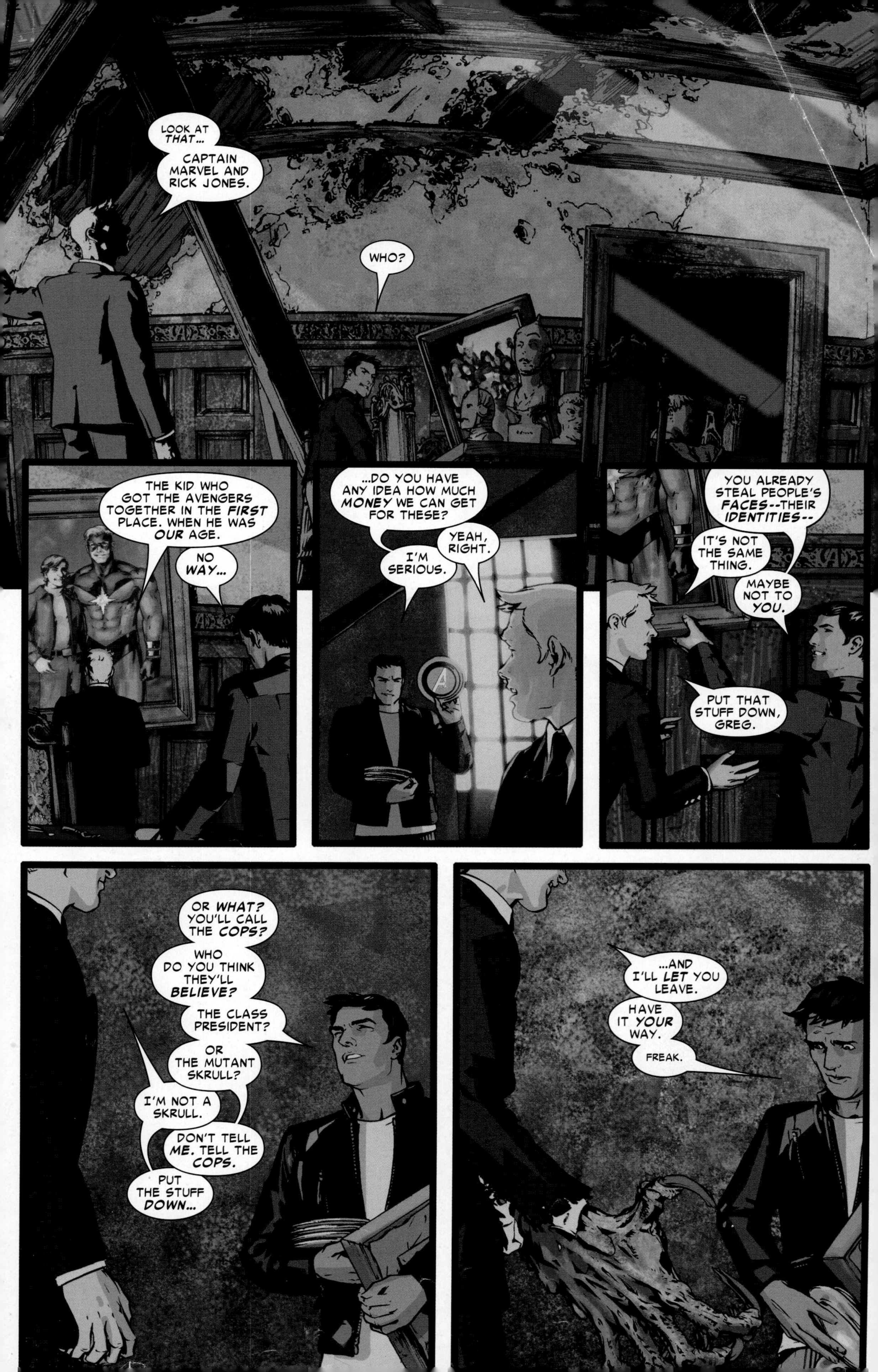
LOOK AT THAT...
CAPTAIN MARVEL AND RICK JONES.
WHO?
THE KID WHO GOT THE AVENGERS TOGETHER IN THE FIRST PLACE. WHEN HE WAS OUR AGE.
NO WAY...
...DO YOU HAVE ANY IDEA HOW MUCH MONEY WE CAN GET FOR THESE?
YEAH, RIGHT.
I'M SERIOUS.
YOU ALREADY STEAL PEOPLE'S FACES--THEIR IDENTITIES--
IT'S NOT THE SAME THING.
MAYBE NOT TO YOU.
PUT THAT STUFF DOWN, GREG.
OR WHAT? YOU'LL CALL THE COPS?
WHO DO YOU THINK THEY'LL BELIEVE?
THE CLASS PRESIDENT?
OR THE MUTANT SKRULL?
I'M NOT A SKRULL.
DON'T TELL ME. TELL THE COPS.
PUT THE STUFF DOWN...
...AND I'LL LET YOU LEAVE.
HAVE IT YOUR WAY.
FREAK.

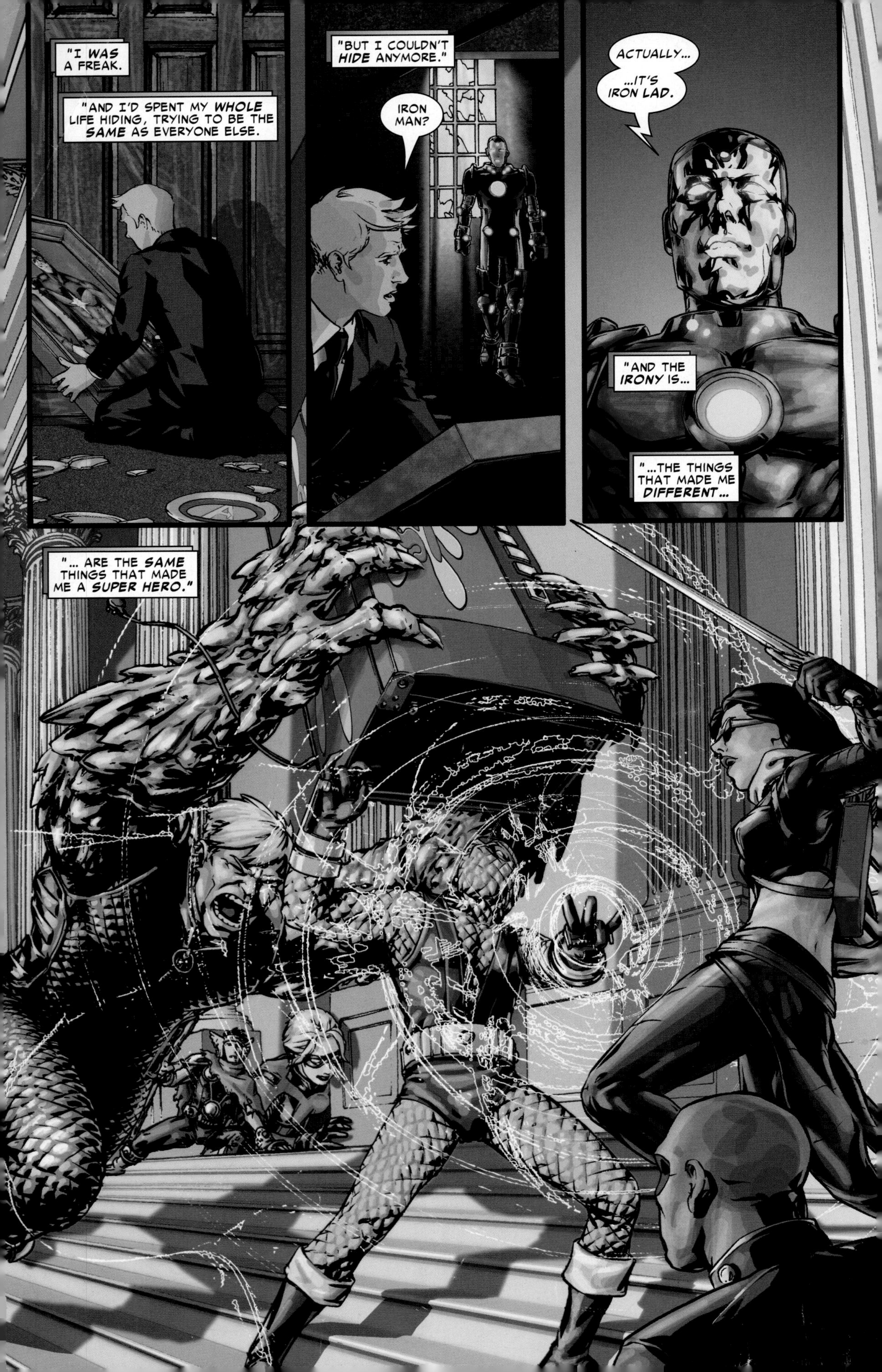
"I WAS A FREAK.
"AND I'D SPENT MY WHOLE LIFE HIDING, TRYING TO BE THE SAME AS EVERYONE ELSE.
"BUT I COULDN'T HIDE ANYMORE."
IRON MAN?
ACTUALLY...
...IT'S IRON LAD.
"AND THE IRONY IS...
"...THE THINGS THAT MADE ME DIFFERENT...
"... ARE THE SAME THINGS THAT MADE ME A SUPER HERO."

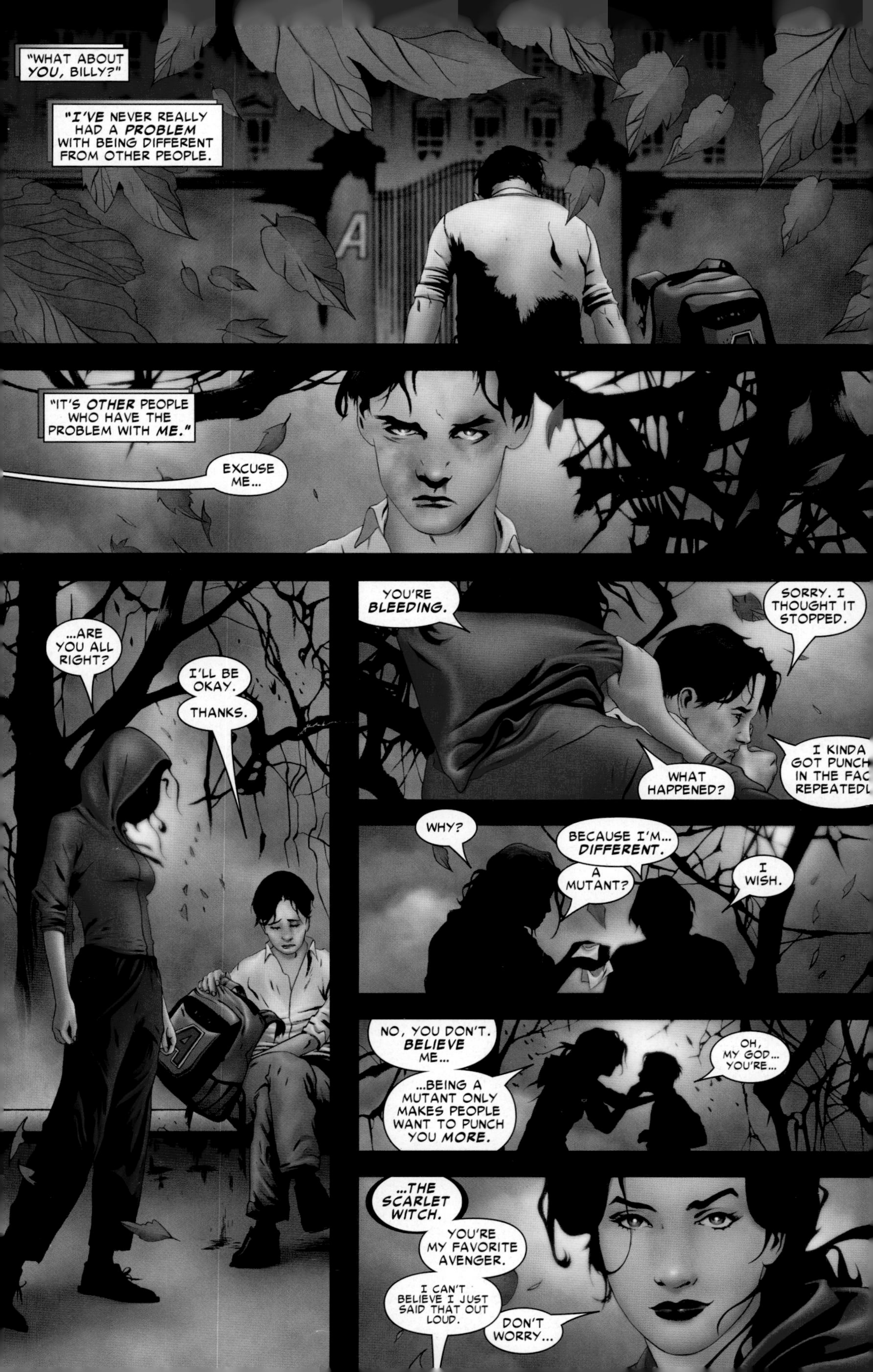
"WHAT ABOUT YOU, BILLY?"
"I'VE NEVER REALLY HAD A PROBLEM WITH BEING DIFFERENT FROM OTHER PEOPLE.
"IT'S OTHER PEOPLE WHO HAVE THE PROBLEM WITH ME."
EXCUSE ME...
...ARE YOU ALL RIGHT?
I'LL BE OKAY.
THANKS.
YOU'RE BLEEDING.
SORRY. I THOUGHT IT STOPPED.
WHAT HAPPENED?
I KINDA GOT PUNCH IN THE FAC REPEATEDL
WHY?
BECAUSE I'M... DIFFERENT.
A MUTANT?
I WISH.
NO, YOU DON'T. BELIEVE ME...
...BEING A MUTANT ONLY MAKES PEOPLE WANT TO PUNCH YOU MORE.
OH, MY GOD... YOU'RE...
...THE SCARLET WITCH.
YOU'RE MY FAVORITE AVENGER.
I CAN'T BELIEVE I JUST SAID THAT OUT LOUD.
DON'T WORRY...

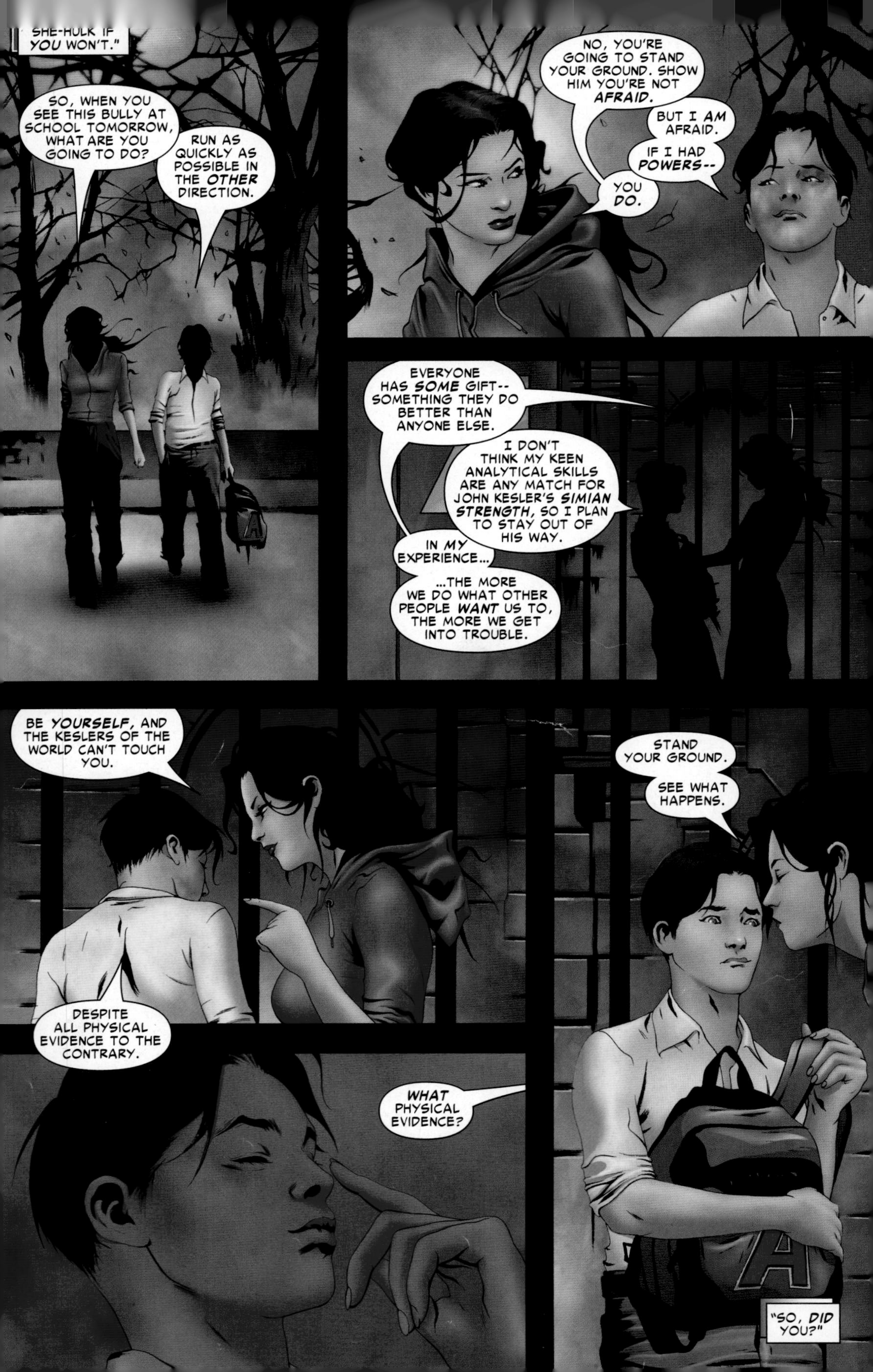
SHE-HULK IF YOU WON'T."
SO, WHEN YOU SEE THIS BULLY AT SCHOOL TOMORROW, WHAT ARE YOU GOING TO DO?
RUN AS QUICKLY AS POSSIBLE IN THE OTHER DIRECTION.
NO, YOU'RE GOING TO STAND YOUR GROUND. SHOW HIM YOU'RE NOT AFRAID.
BUT I AM AFRAID.
IF I HAD POWERS--
YOU DO.
EVERYONE HAS SOME GIFT-- SOMETHING THEY DO BETTER THAN ANYONE ELSE.
I DON'T THINK MY KEEN ANALYTICAL SKILLS ARE ANY MATCH FOR JOHN KESLER'S SIMIAN STRENGTH, SO I PLAN TO STAY OUT OF HIS WAY.
IN MY EXPERIENCE...
...THE MORE WE DO WHAT OTHER PEOPLE WANT US TO, THE MORE WE GET INTO TROUBLE.
BE YOURSELF, AND THE KESLERS OF THE WORLD CAN'T TOUCH YOU.
DESPITE ALL PHYSICAL EVIDENCE TO THE CONTRARY.
WHAT PHYSICAL EVIDENCE?
STAND YOUR GROUND.
SEE WHAT HAPPENS.
"SO, DID YOU?"

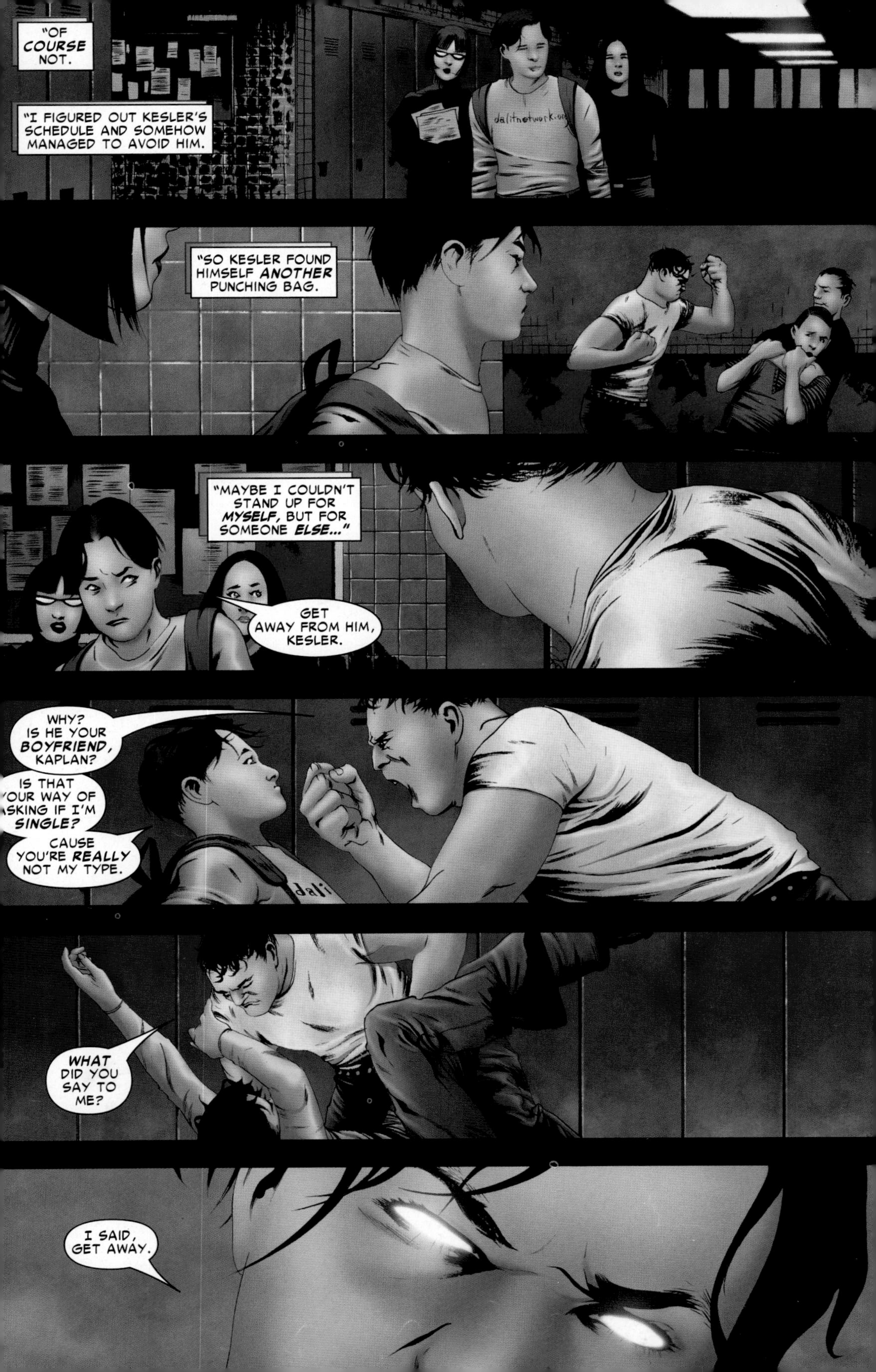
"OF COURSE NOT.
"I FIGURED OUT KESLER'S SCHEDULE AND SOMEHOW MANAGED TO AVOID HIM.
dalitnetwork.org
"SO KESLER FOUND HIMSELF ANOTHER PUNCHING BAG.
"MAYBE I COULDN'T STAND UP FOR MYSELF, BUT FOR SOMEONE ELSE..."
GET AWAY FROM HIM, KESLER.
WHY? IS HE YOUR BOYFRIEND, KAPLAN?
IS THAT YOUR WAY OF ASKING IF I'M SINGLE?
CAUSE YOU'RE REALLY NOT MY TYPE.
dali
WHAT DID YOU SAY TO ME?
I SAID, GET AWAY.

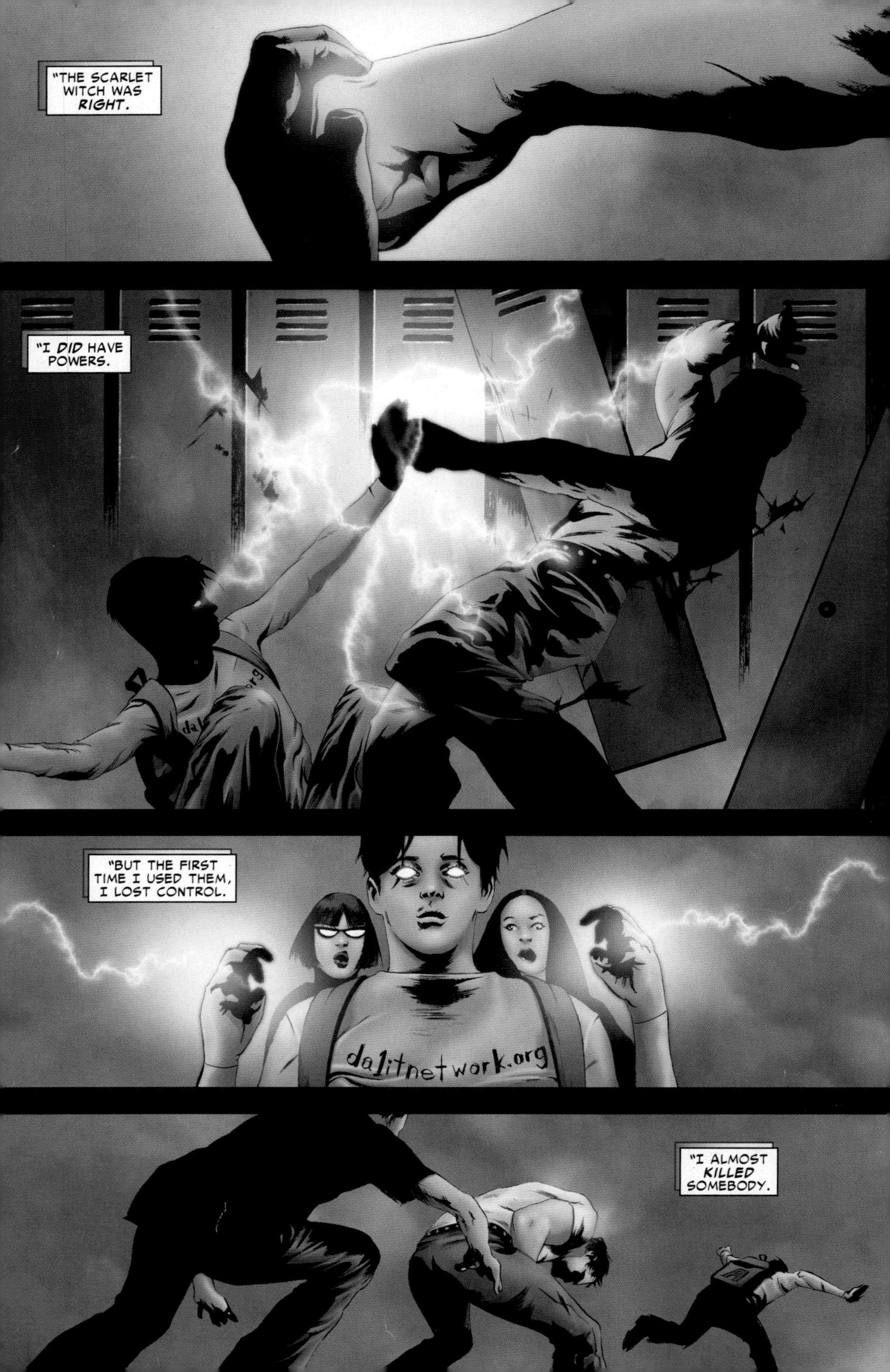
"THE SCARLET WITCH WAS *RIGHT*.
"I *DID* HAVE POWERS.
"BUT THE FIRST TIME I USED THEM, I LOST CONTROL.
da1itnetwork.org
"I ALMOST *KILLED* SOMEBODY.

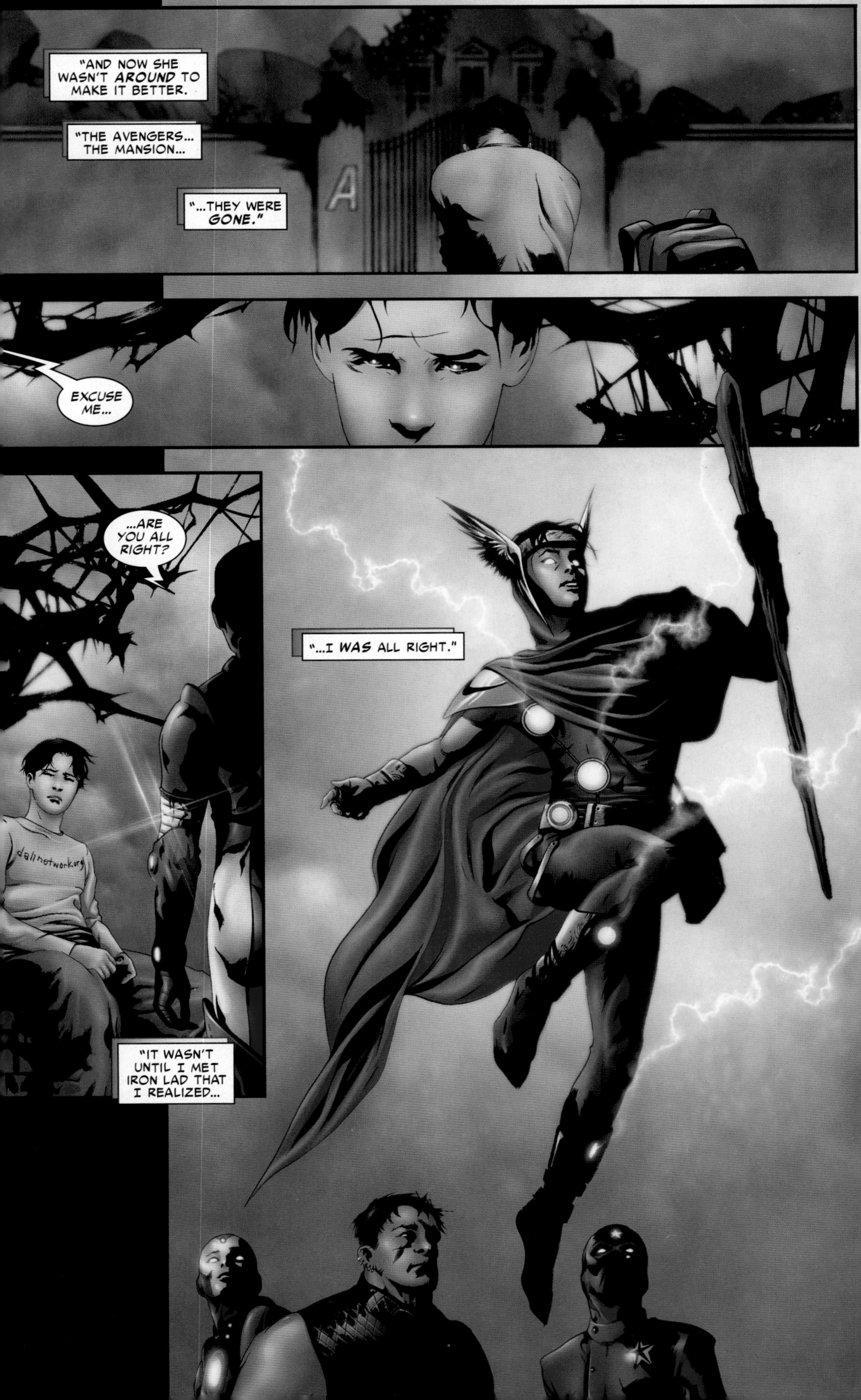
"AND NOW SHE WASN'T AROUND TO MAKE IT BETTER.
"THE AVENGERS... THE MANSION...
"...THEY WERE GONE."
EXCUSE ME...
...ARE YOU ALL RIGHT?
"IT WASN'T UNTIL I MET IRON LAD THAT I REALIZED...
"...I WAS ALL RIGHT."
dalinetwork.org

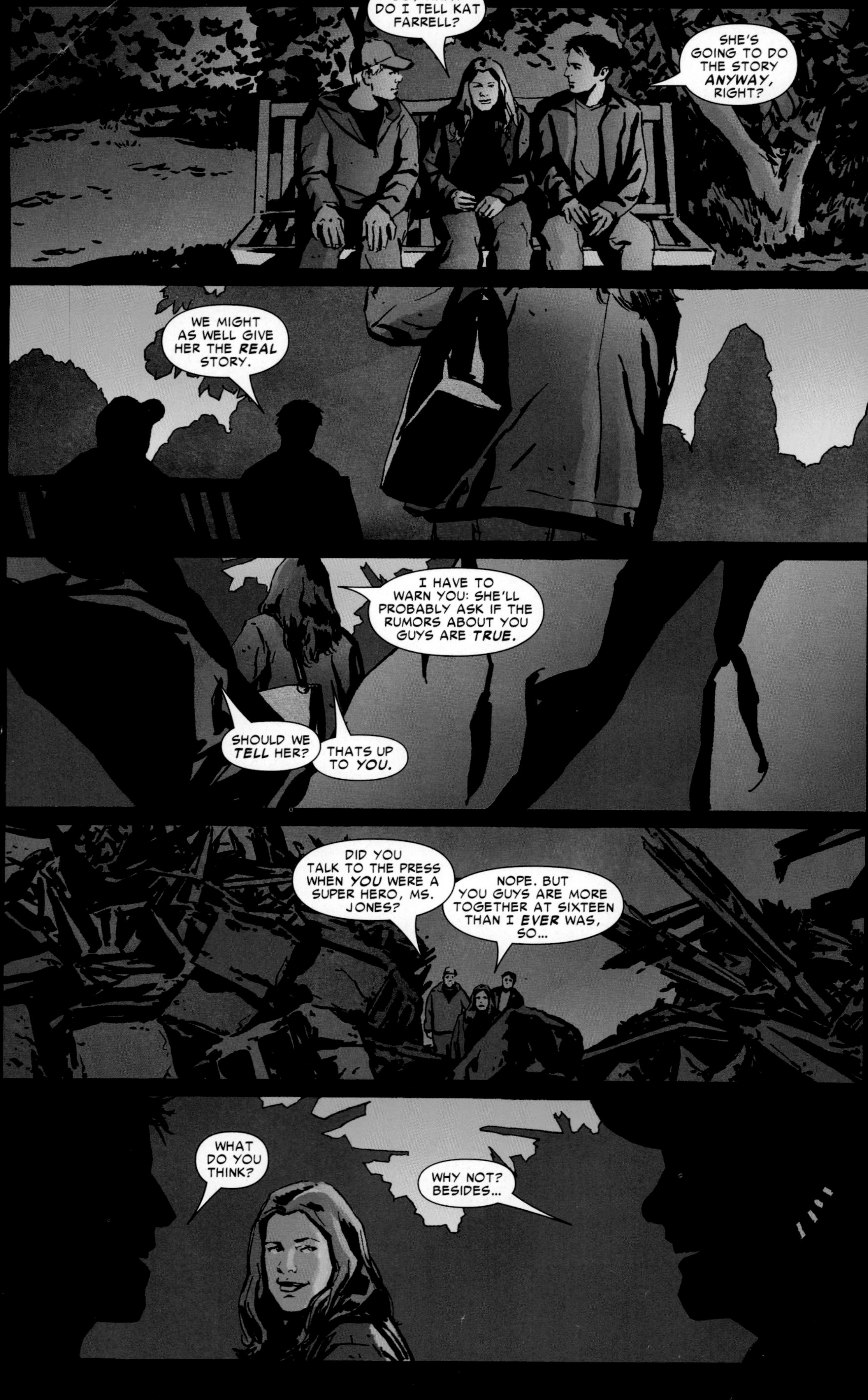
SO, WHAT DO I TELL KAT FARRELL?
SHE'S GOING TO DO THE STORY ANYWAY, RIGHT?
WE MIGHT AS WELL GIVE HER THE REAL STORY.
I HAVE TO WARN YOU: SHE'LL PROBABLY ASK IF THE RUMORS ABOUT YOU GUYS ARE TRUE.
SHOULD WE TELL HER?
THATS UP TO YOU.
DID YOU TALK TO THE PRESS WHEN YOU WERE A SUPER HERO, MS. JONES?
NOPE. BUT YOU GUYS ARE MORE TOGETHER AT SIXTEEN THAN I EVER WAS, SO...
WHAT DO YOU THINK?
WHY NOT? BESIDES...

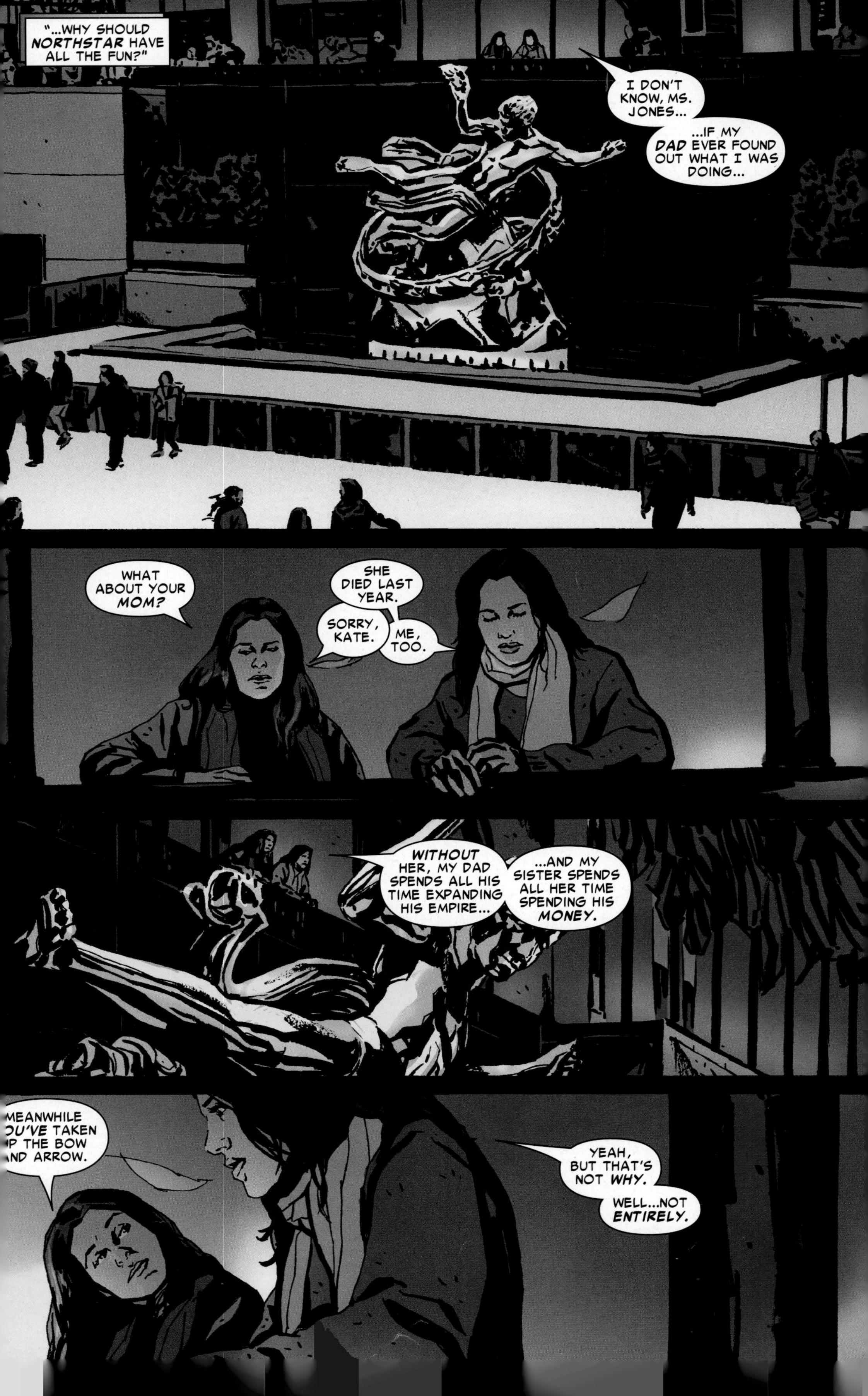
"...WHY SHOULD NORTHSTAR HAVE ALL THE FUN?"
I DON'T KNOW, MS. JONES...
...IF MY DAD EVER FOUND OUT WHAT I WAS DOING...
WHAT ABOUT YOUR MOM?
SHE DIED LAST YEAR.
SORRY, KATE.
ME, TOO.
WITHOUT HER, MY DAD SPENDS ALL HIS TIME EXPANDING HIS EMPIRE...
...AND MY SISTER SPENDS ALL HER TIME SPENDING HIS MONEY.
MEANWHILE OU'VE TAKEN P THE BOW ND ARROW.
YEAH, BUT THAT'S NOT WHY.
WELL...NOT ENTIRELY.

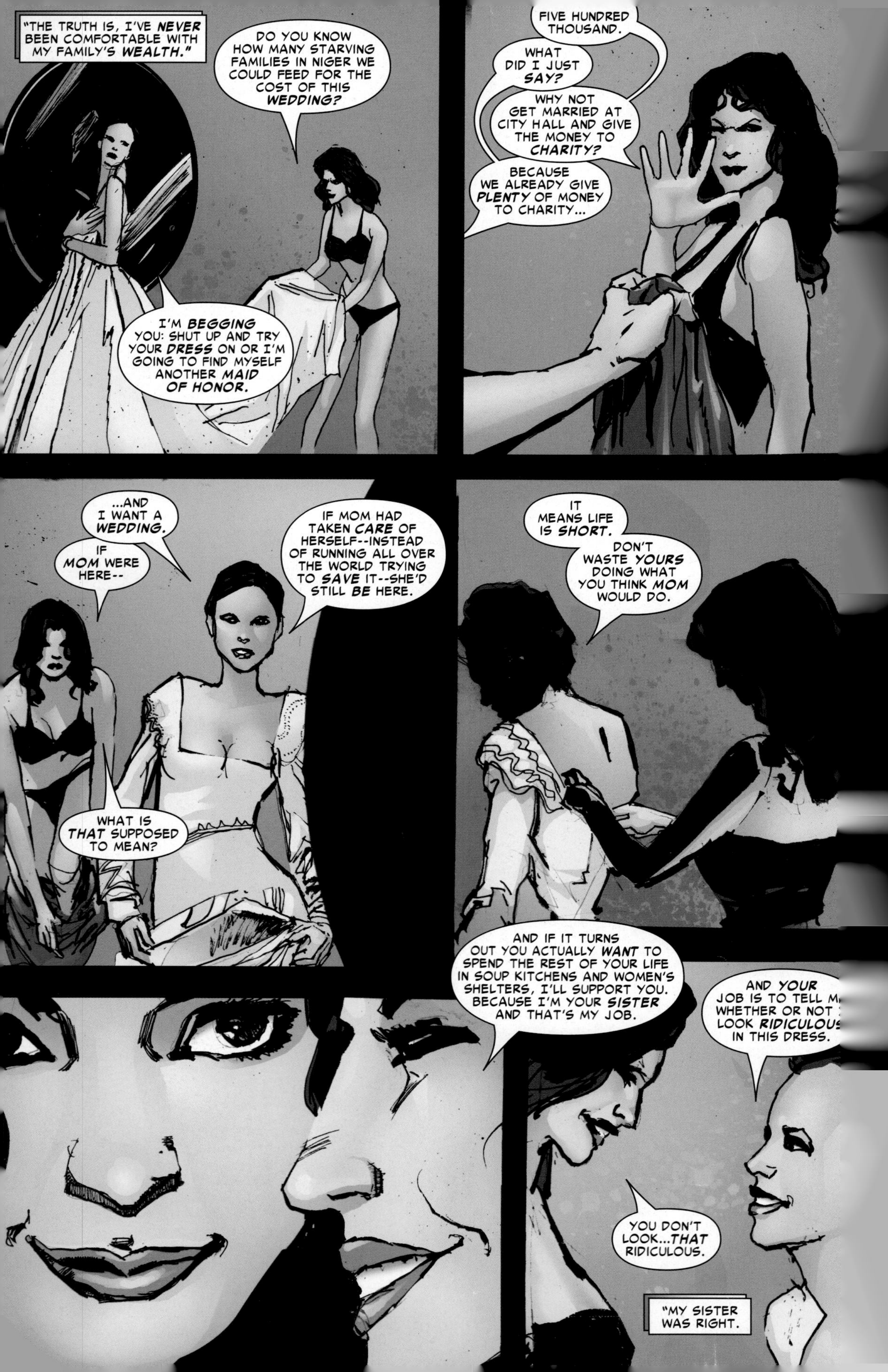

"THE TRUTH IS, I'VE NEVER BEEN COMFORTABLE WITH MY FAMILY'S WEALTH."
DO YOU KNOW HOW MANY STARVING FAMILIES IN NIGER WE COULD FEED FOR THE COST OF THIS WEDDING?
I'M BEGGING YOU: SHUT UP AND TRY YOUR DRESS ON OR I'M GOING TO FIND MYSELF ANOTHER MAID OF HONOR.
FIVE HUNDRED THOUSAND.
WHAT DID I JUST SAY?
WHY NOT GET MARRIED AT CITY HALL AND GIVE THE MONEY TO CHARITY?
BECAUSE WE ALREADY GIVE PLENTY OF MONEY TO CHARITY...
...AND I WANT A WEDDING.
IF MOM WERE HERE--
IF MOM HAD TAKEN CARE OF HERSELF--INSTEAD OF RUNNING ALL OVER THE WORLD TRYING TO SAVE IT--SHE'D STILL BE HERE.
WHAT IS THAT SUPPOSED TO MEAN?
IT MEANS LIFE IS SHORT.
DON'T WASTE YOURS DOING WHAT YOU THINK MOM WOULD DO.
AND IF IT TURNS OUT YOU ACTUALLY WANT TO SPEND THE REST OF YOUR LIFE IN SOUP KITCHENS AND WOMEN'S SHELTERS, I'LL SUPPORT YOU. BECAUSE I'M YOUR SISTER AND THAT'S MY JOB.
AND YOUR JOB IS TO TELL M WHETHER OR NOT LOOK RIDICULOU IN THIS DRESS.
YOU DON'T LOOK...THAT RIDICULOUS.
"MY SISTER WAS RIGHT.

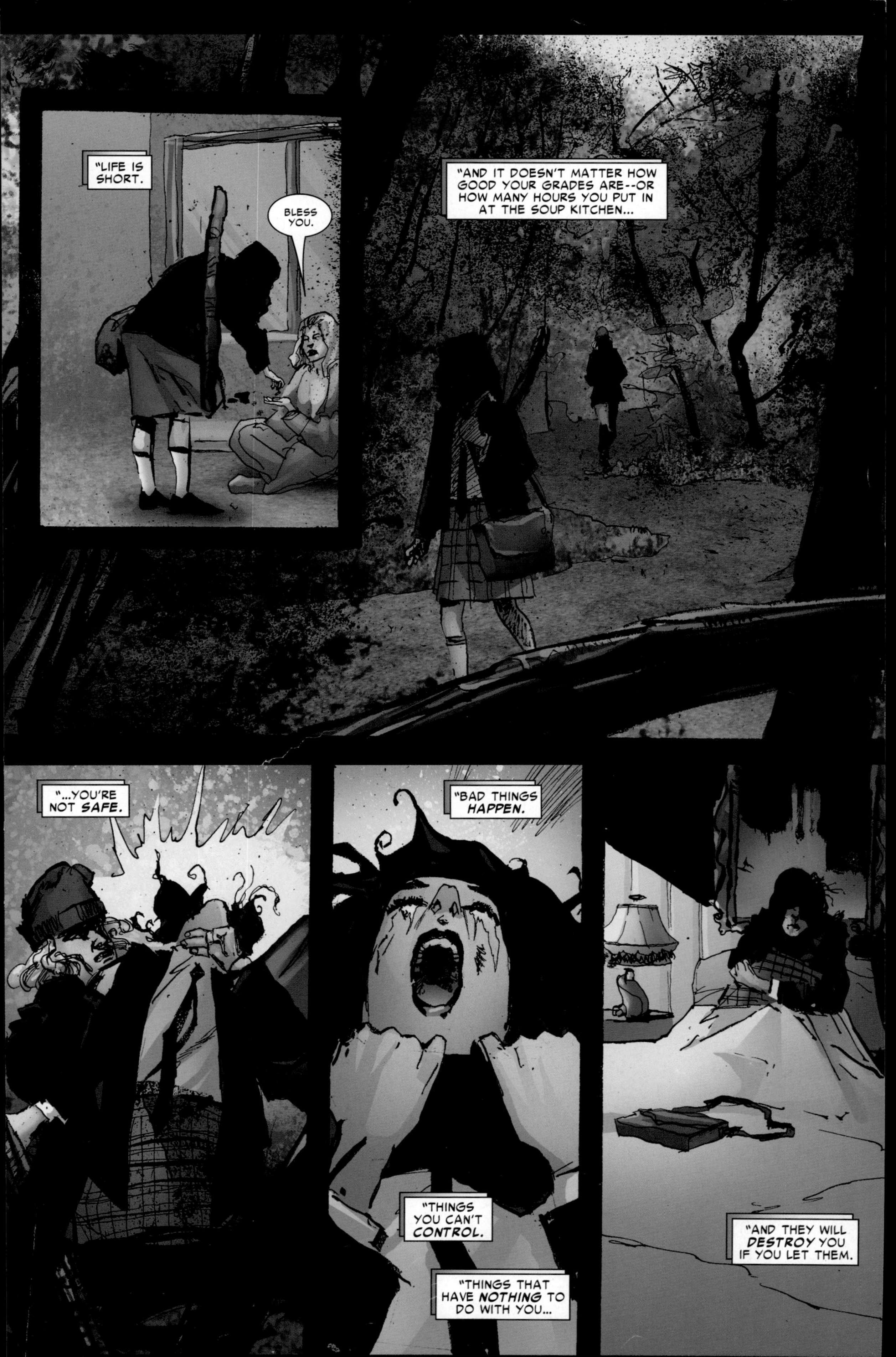
"LIFE IS SHORT.
BLESS YOU.
"AND IT DOESN'T MATTER HOW GOOD YOUR GRADES ARE--OR HOW MANY HOURS YOU PUT IN AT THE SOUP KITCHEN...
"...YOU'RE NOT SAFE.
"BAD THINGS HAPPEN.
"THINGS YOU CAN'T CONTROL.
"THINGS THAT HAVE NOTHING TO DO WITH YOU...
"AND THEY WILL DESTROY YOU IF YOU LET THEM.

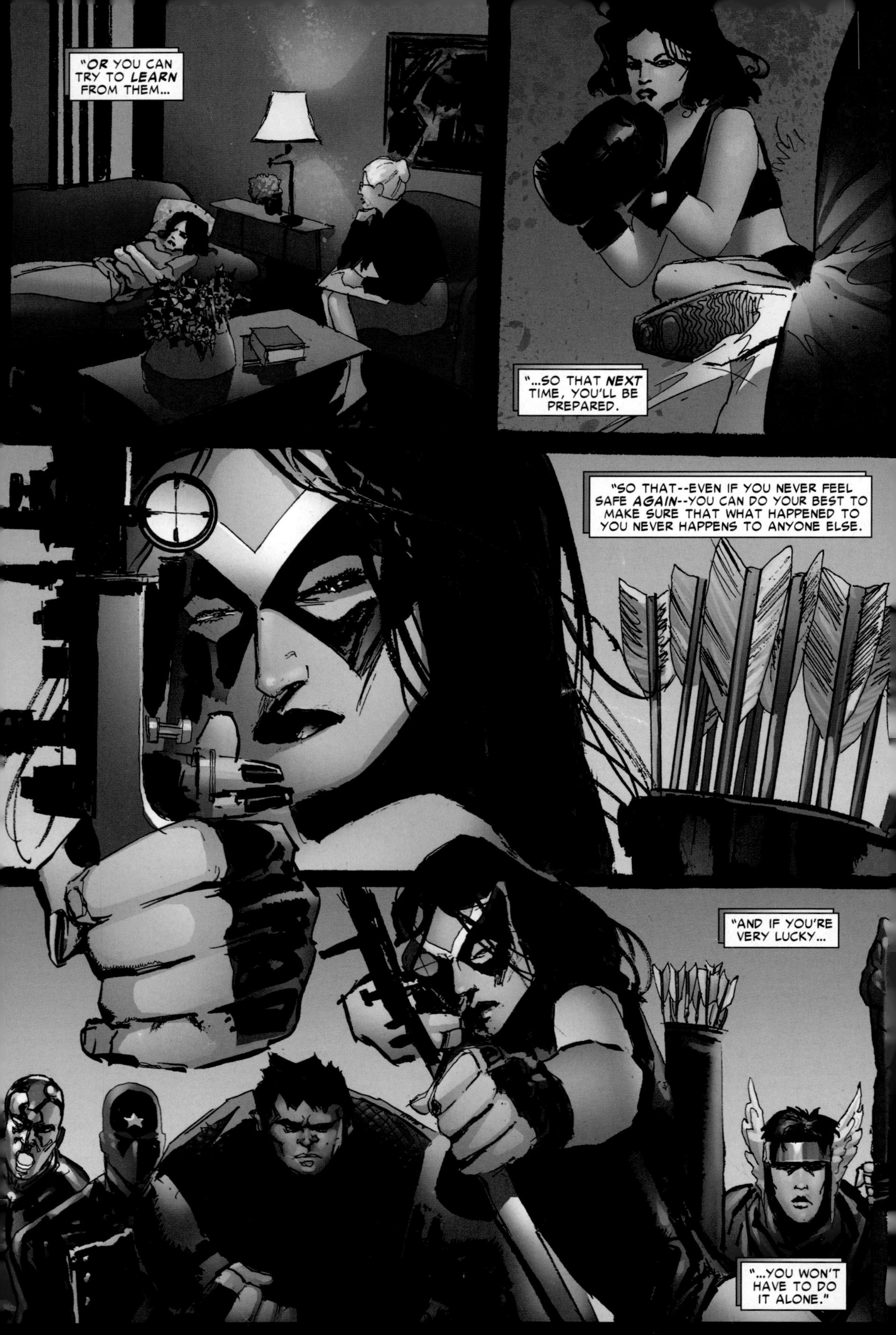
"OR YOU CAN TRY TO LEARN FROM THEM...
"...SO THAT NEXT TIME, YOU'LL BE PREPARED.
"SO THAT--EVEN IF YOU NEVER FEEL SAFE AGAIN--YOU CAN DO YOUR BEST TO MAKE SURE THAT WHAT HAPPENED TO YOU NEVER HAPPENS TO ANYONE ELSE.
"AND IF YOU'RE VERY LUCKY...
"...YOU WON'T HAVE TO DO IT ALONE."

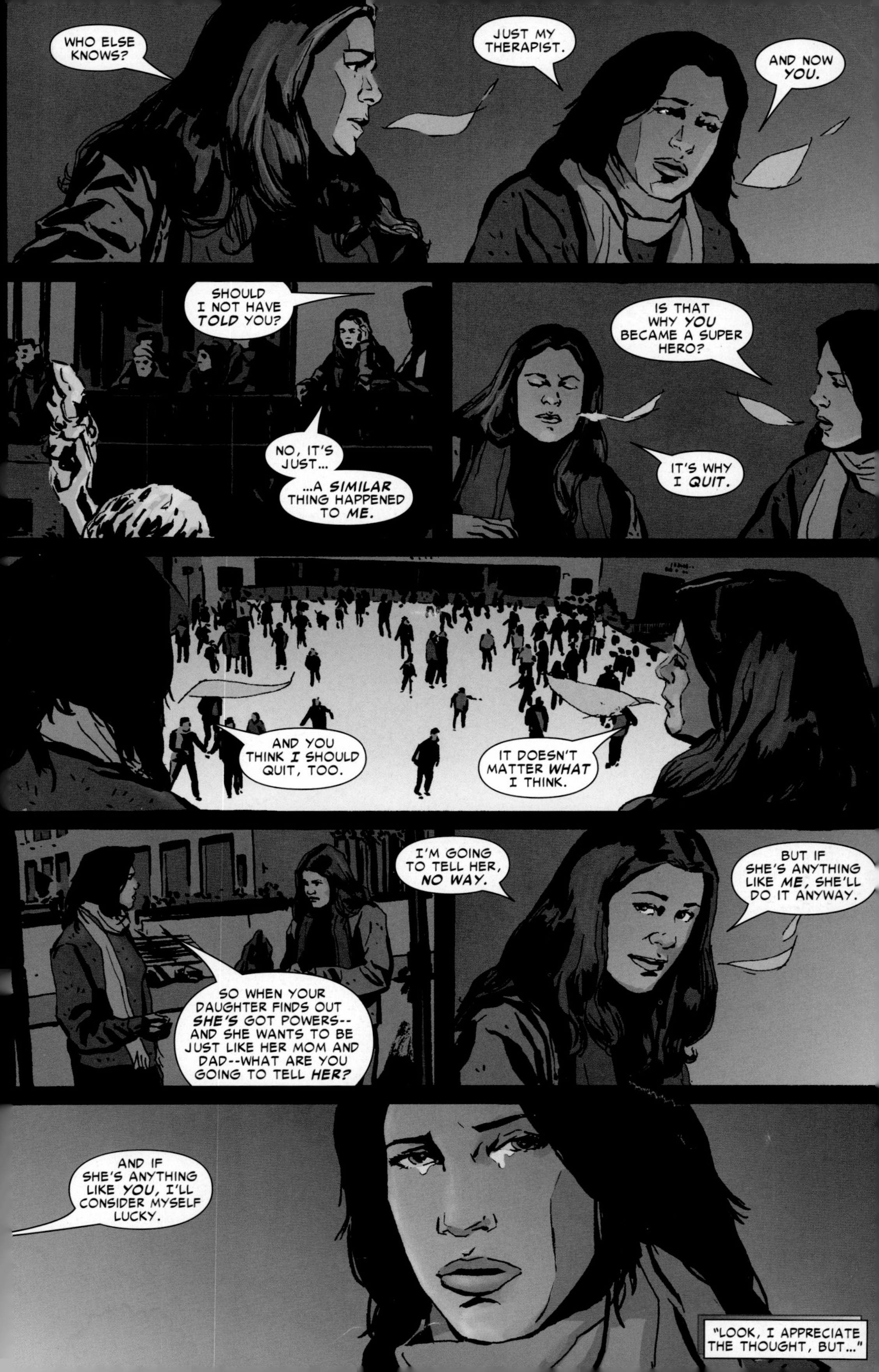
WHO ELSE KNOWS?
JUST MY THERAPIST.
AND NOW YOU.
SHOULD I NOT HAVE TOLD YOU?
NO, IT'S JUST...
...A SIMILAR THING HAPPENED TO ME.
IS THAT WHY YOU BECAME A SUPER HERO?
IT'S WHY I QUIT.
AND YOU THINK I SHOULD QUIT, TOO.
IT DOESN'T MATTER WHAT I THINK.
SO WHEN YOUR DAUGHTER FINDS OUT SHE'S GOT POWERS-- AND SHE WANTS TO BE JUST LIKE HER MOM AND DAD--WHAT ARE YOU GOING TO TELL HER?
I'M GOING TO TELL HER, NO WAY.
BUT IF SHE'S ANYTHING LIKE ME, SHE'LL DO IT ANYWAY.
AND IF SHE'S ANYTHING LIKE YOU, I'LL CONSIDER MYSELF LUCKY.
"LOOK, I APPRECIATE THE THOUGHT, BUT..."

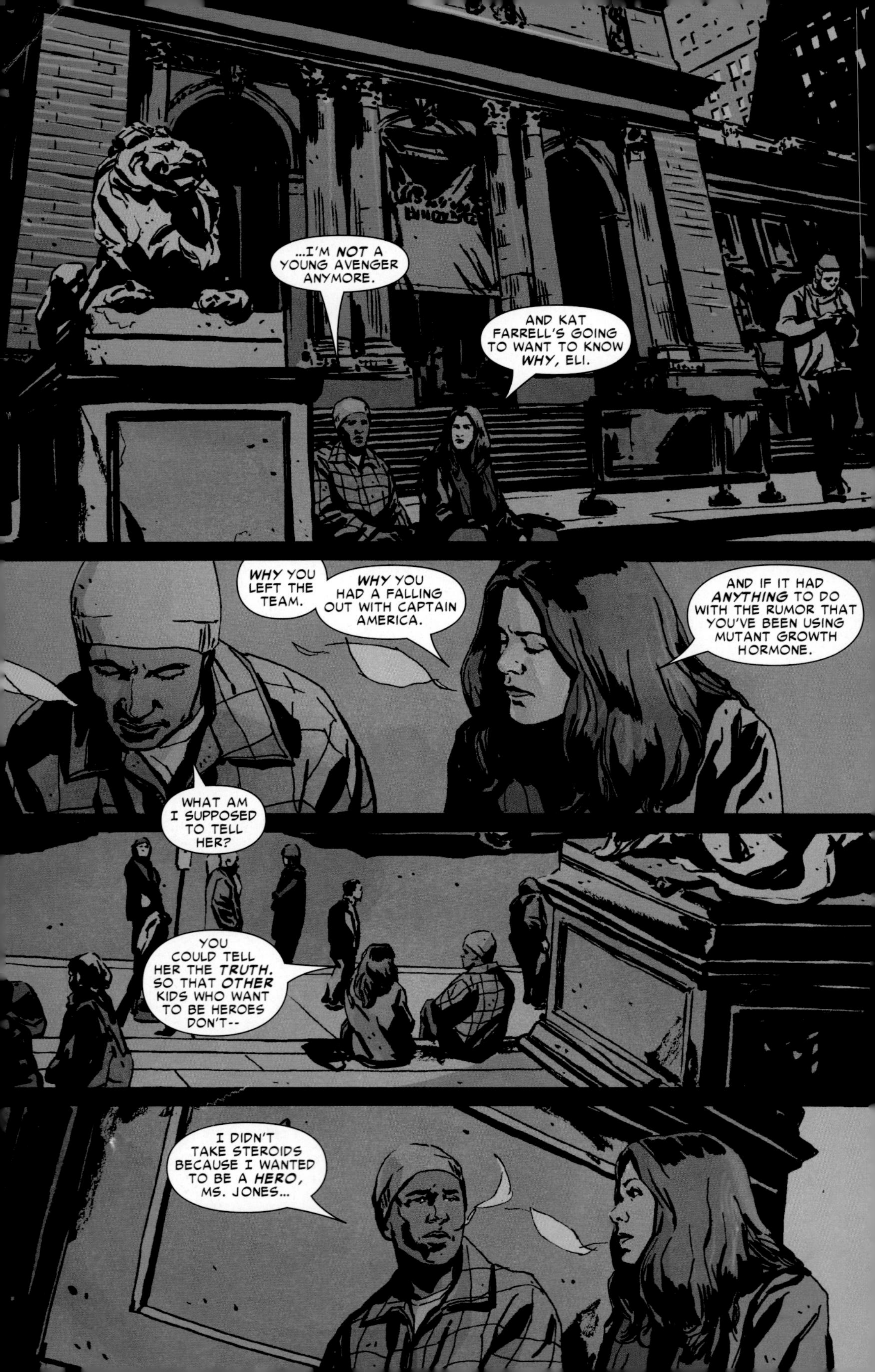
...I'M NOT A YOUNG AVENGER ANYMORE.
AND KAT FARRELL'S GOING TO WANT TO KNOW WHY, ELI.
WHY YOU LEFT THE TEAM.
WHY YOU HAD A FALLING OUT WITH CAPTAIN AMERICA.
AND IF IT HAD ANYTHING TO DO WITH THE RUMOR THAT YOU'VE BEEN USING MUTANT GROWTH HORMONE.
WHAT AM I SUPPOSED TO TELL HER?
YOU COULD TELL HER THE TRUTH. SO THAT OTHER KIDS WHO WANT TO BE HEROES DON'T--
I DIDN'T TAKE STEROIDS BECAUSE I WANTED TO BE A HERO, MS. JONES...

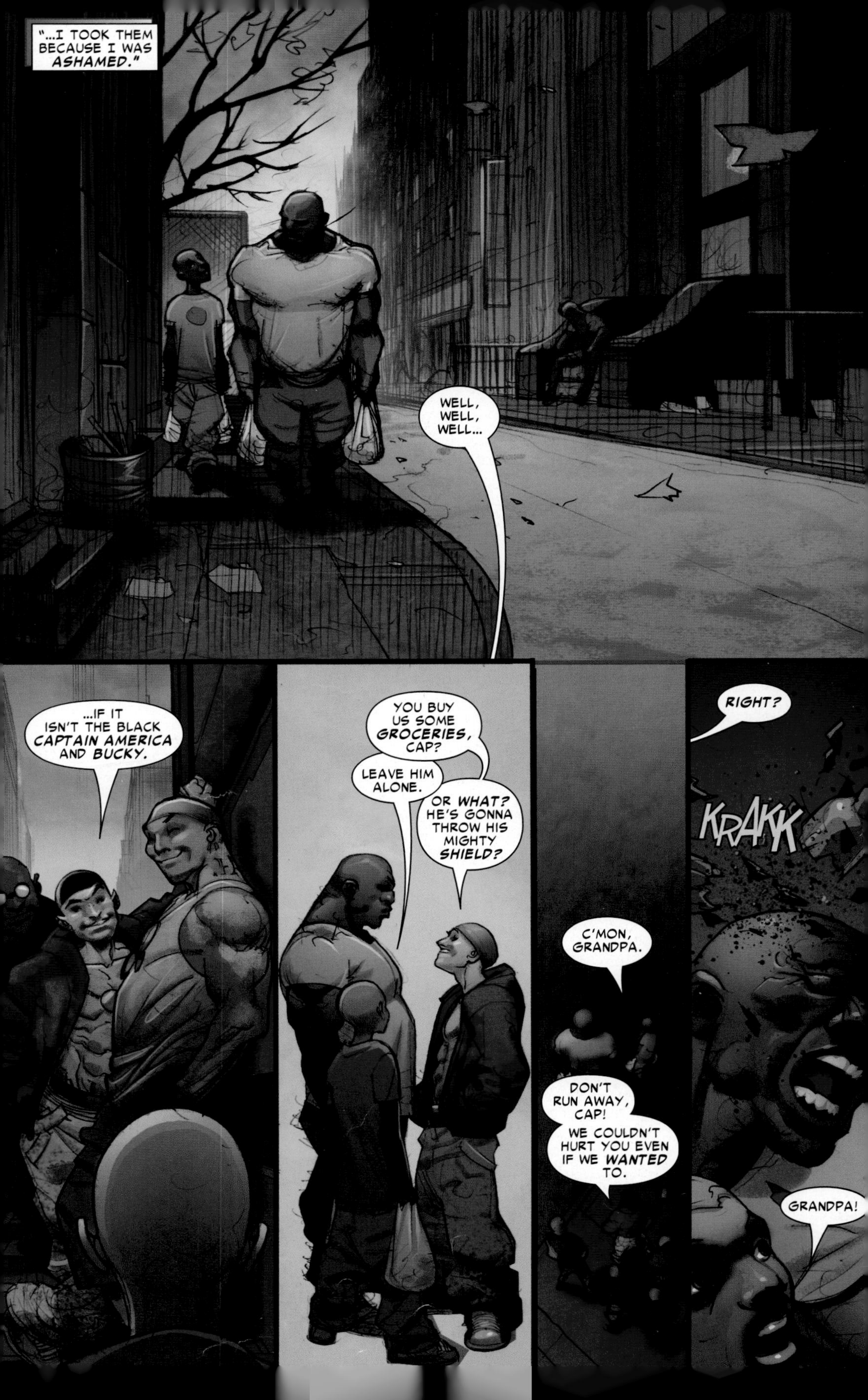
"...I TOOK THEM BECAUSE I WAS ASHAMED."
WELL, WELL, WELL...
...IF IT ISN'T THE BLACK CAPTAIN AMERICA AND BUCKY.
YOU BUY US SOME GROCERIES, CAP?
LEAVE HIM ALONE.
OR WHAT? HE'S GONNA THROW HIS MIGHTY SHIELD?
C'MON, GRANDPA.
DON'T RUN AWAY, CAP!
WE COULDN'T HURT YOU EVEN IF WE WANTED TO.
RIGHT?
KRAKK
GRANDPA!

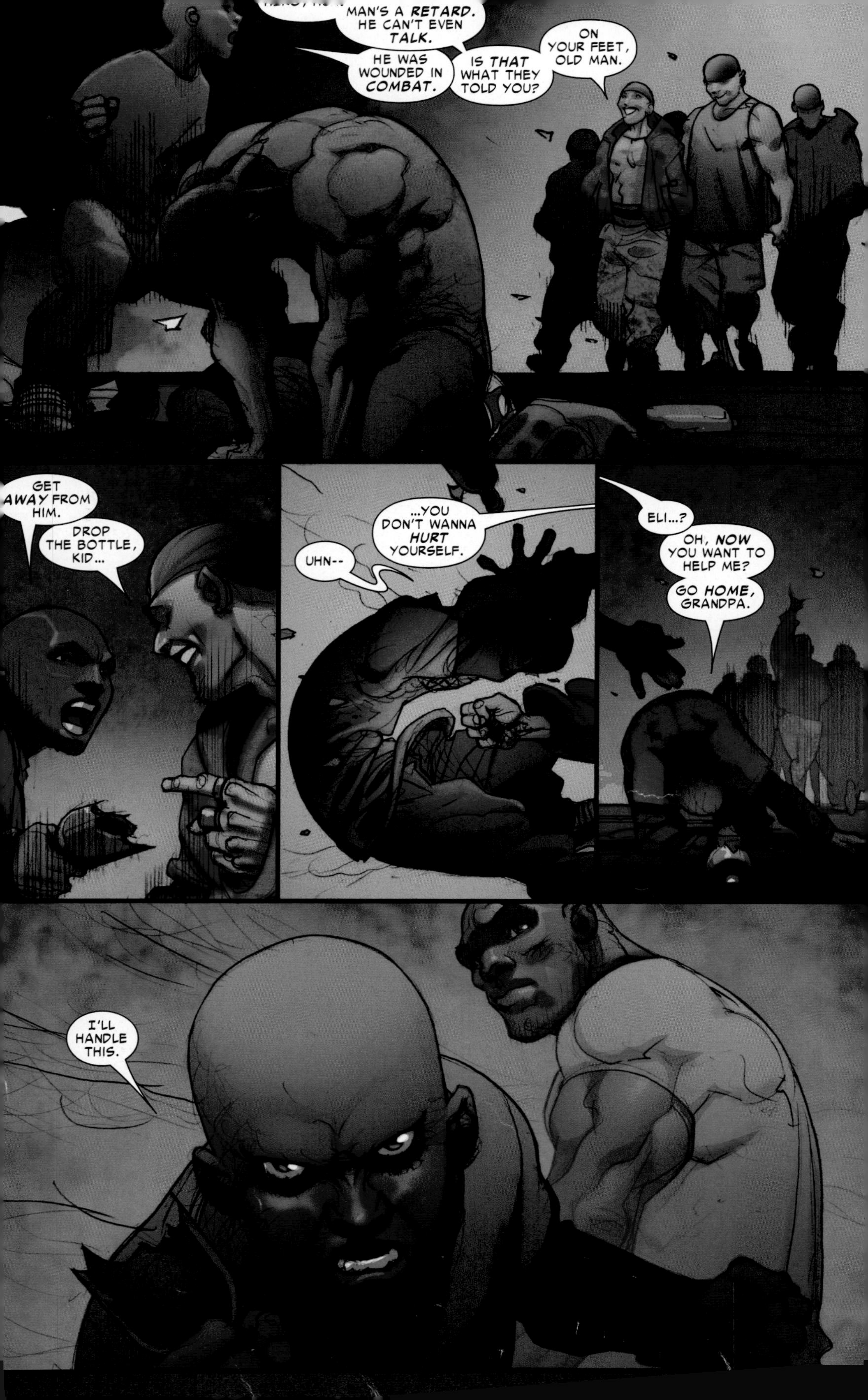
MAN'S A RETARD. HE CAN'T EVEN TALK.
HE WAS WOUNDED IN COMBAT.
IS THAT WHAT THEY TOLD YOU?
ON YOUR FEET, OLD MAN.
GET AWAY FROM HIM.
DROP THE BOTTLE, KID...
...YOU DON'T WANNA HURT YOURSELF.
UHN--
ELI...?
OH, NOW YOU WANT TO HELP ME?
GO HOME, GRANDPA.
I'LL HANDLE THIS.

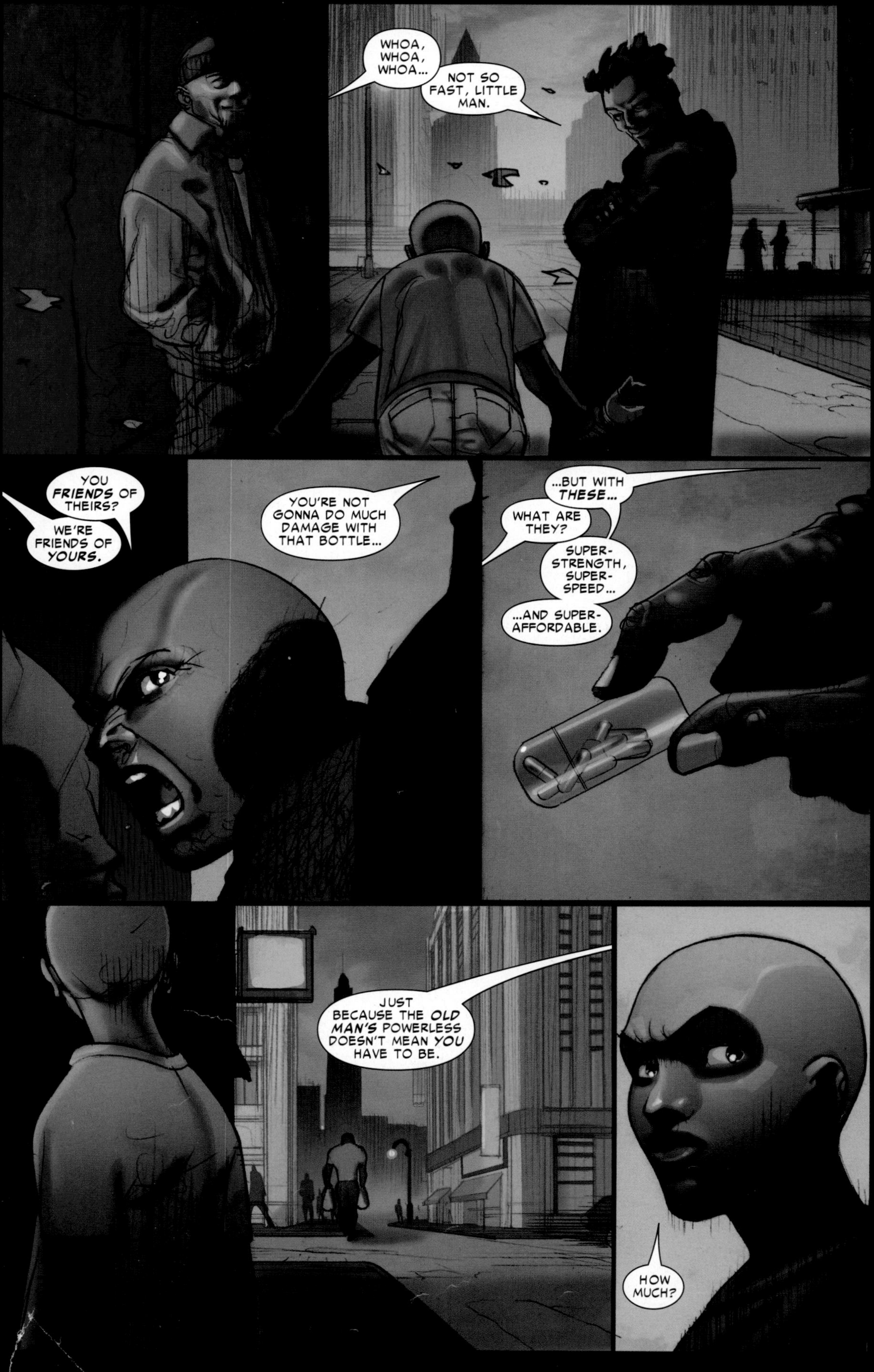
WHOA, WHOA, WHOA...
NOT SO FAST, LITTLE MAN.
YOU FRIENDS OF THEIRS?
WE'RE FRIENDS OF YOURS.
YOU'RE NOT GONNA DO MUCH DAMAGE WITH THAT BOTTLE...
...BUT WITH THESE...
WHAT ARE THEY?
SUPER-STRENGTH, SUPER-SPEED...
...AND SUPER-AFFORDABLE.
JUST BECAUSE THE OLD MAN'S POWERLESS DOESN'T MEAN YOU HAVE TO BE.
HOW MUCH?

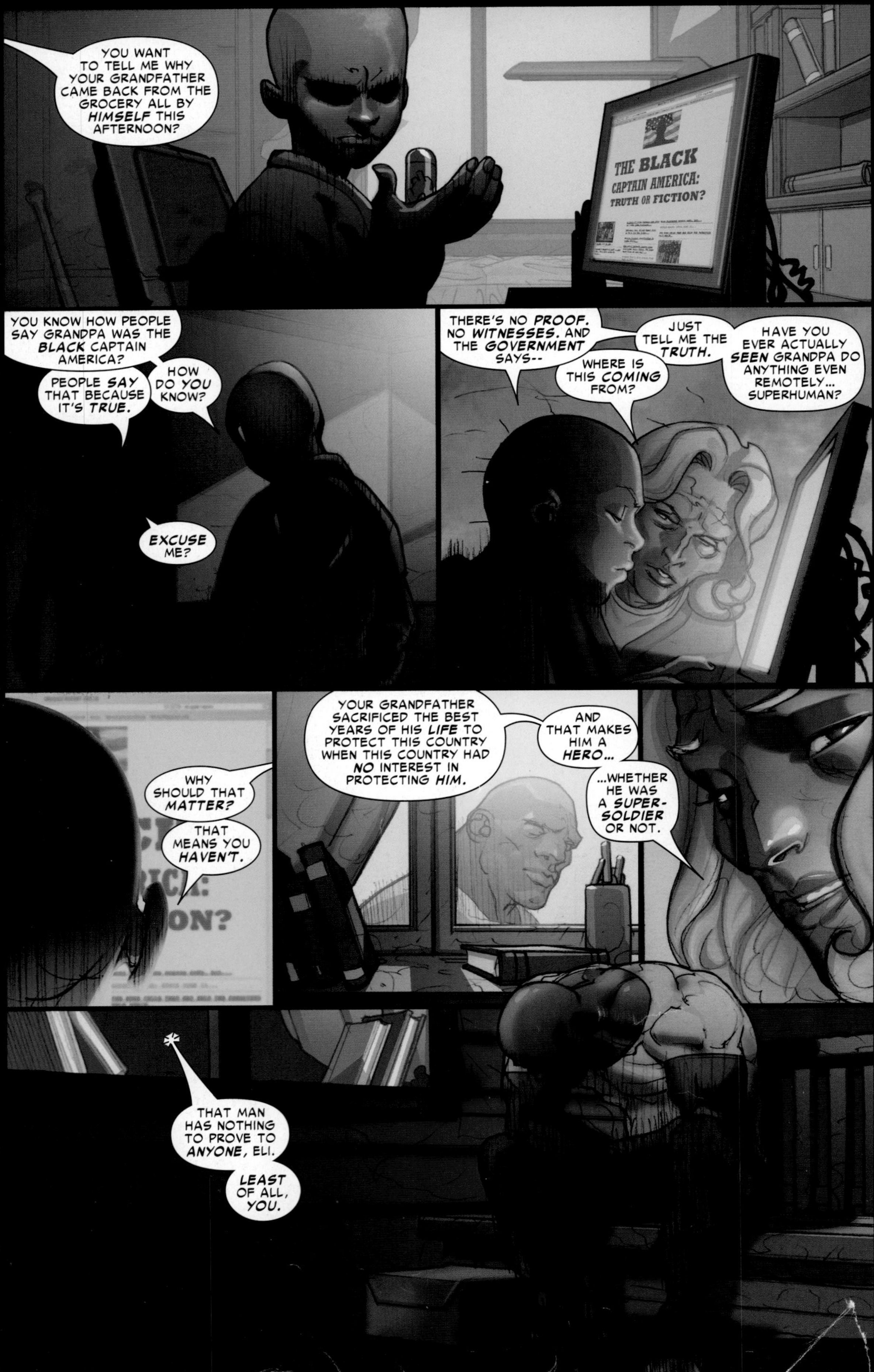

YOU WANT TO TELL ME WHY YOUR GRANDFATHER CAME BACK FROM THE GROCERY ALL BY HIMSELF THIS AFTERNOON?
THE BLACK CAPTAIN AMERICA: TRUTH OR FICTION?
YOU KNOW HOW PEOPLE SAY GRANDPA WAS THE BLACK CAPTAIN AMERICA?
PEOPLE SAY THAT BECAUSE IT'S TRUE.
HOW DO YOU KNOW?
EXCUSE ME?
THERE'S NO PROOF. NO WITNESSES. AND THE GOVERNMENT SAYS--
JUST TELL ME THE TRUTH.
WHERE IS THIS COMING FROM?
HAVE YOU EVER ACTUALLY SEEN GRANDPA DO ANYTHING EVEN REMOTELY... SUPERHUMAN?
WHY SHOULD THAT MATTER?
THAT MEANS YOU HAVEN'T.
YOUR GRANDFATHER SACRIFICED THE BEST YEARS OF HIS LIFE TO PROTECT THIS COUNTRY WHEN THIS COUNTRY HAD NO INTEREST IN PROTECTING HIM.
AND THAT MAKES HIM A HERO...
...WHETHER HE WAS A SUPER-SOLDIER OR NOT.
THAT MAN HAS NOTHING TO PROVE TO ANYONE, ELI.
LEAST OF ALL, YOU.

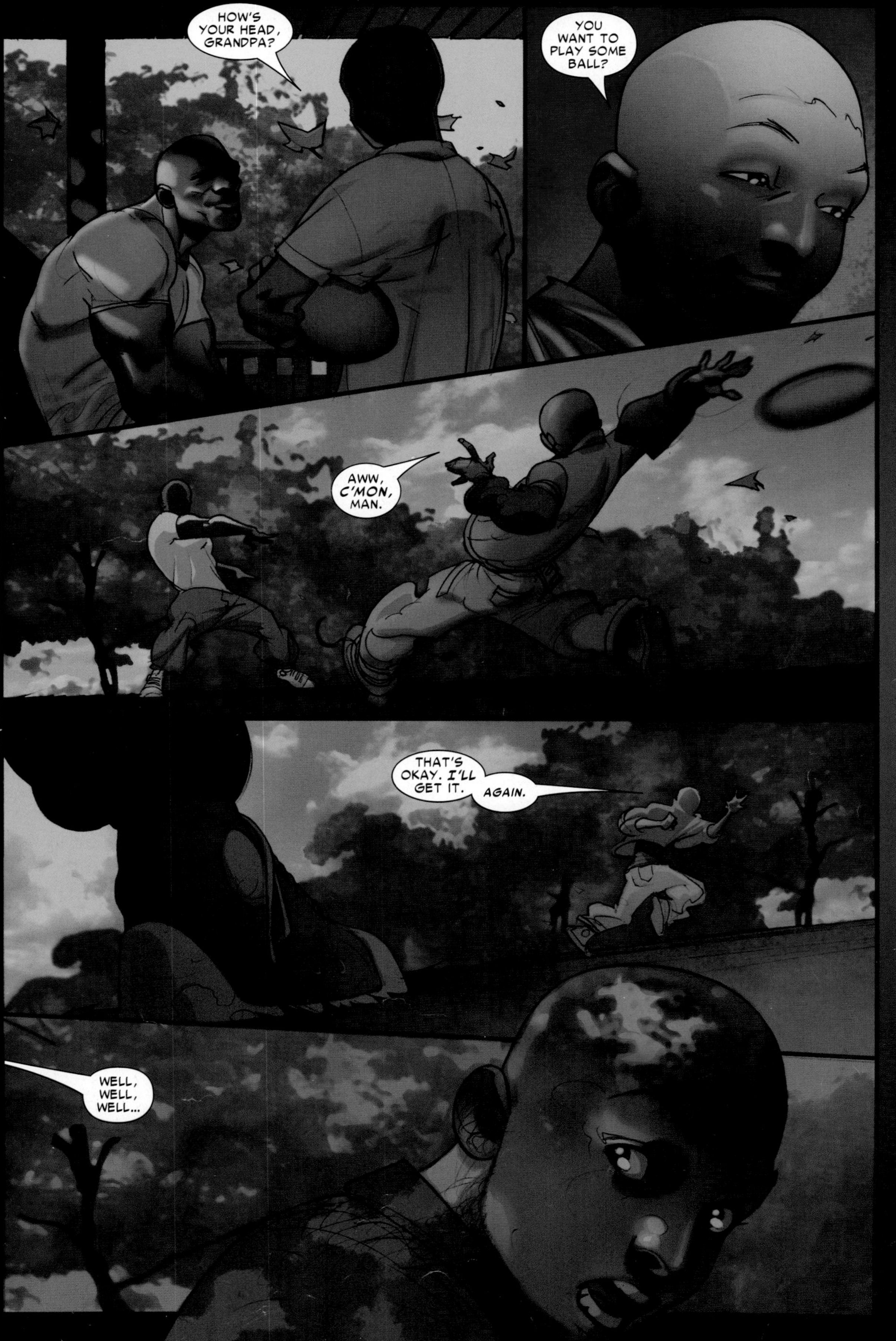
HOW'S YOUR HEAD, GRANDPA?
YOU WANT TO PLAY SOME BALL?
AWW, C'MON, MAN.
THAT'S OKAY. I'LL GET IT.
AGAIN.
WELL, WELL, WELL...

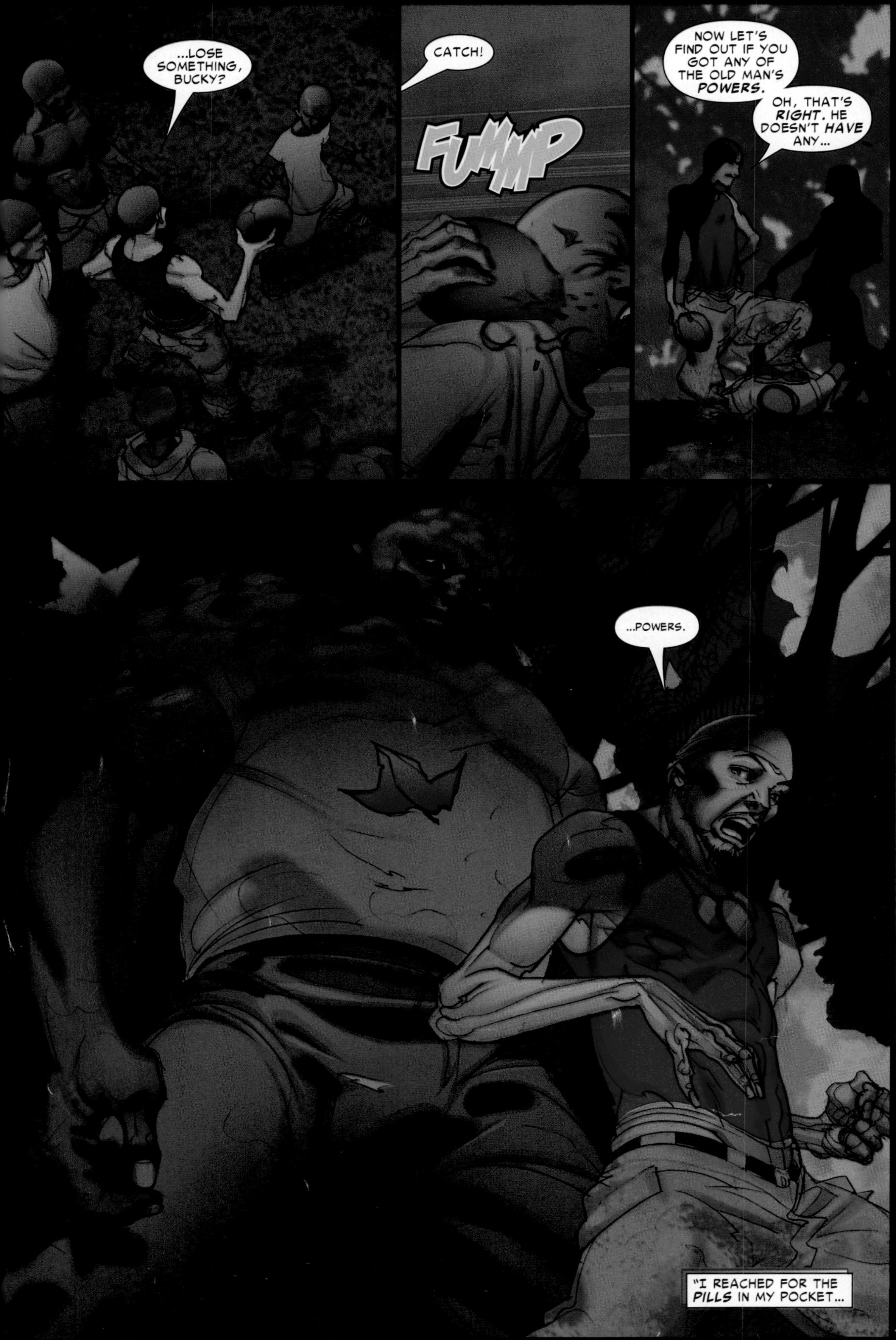
...LOSE SOMETHING, BUCKY?
CATCH!
FUMMP
NOW LET'S FIND OUT IF YOU GOT ANY OF THE OLD MAN'S POWERS.
OH, THAT'S RIGHT. HE DOESN'T HAVE ANY...
...POWERS.
"I REACHED FOR THE PILLS IN MY POCKET...

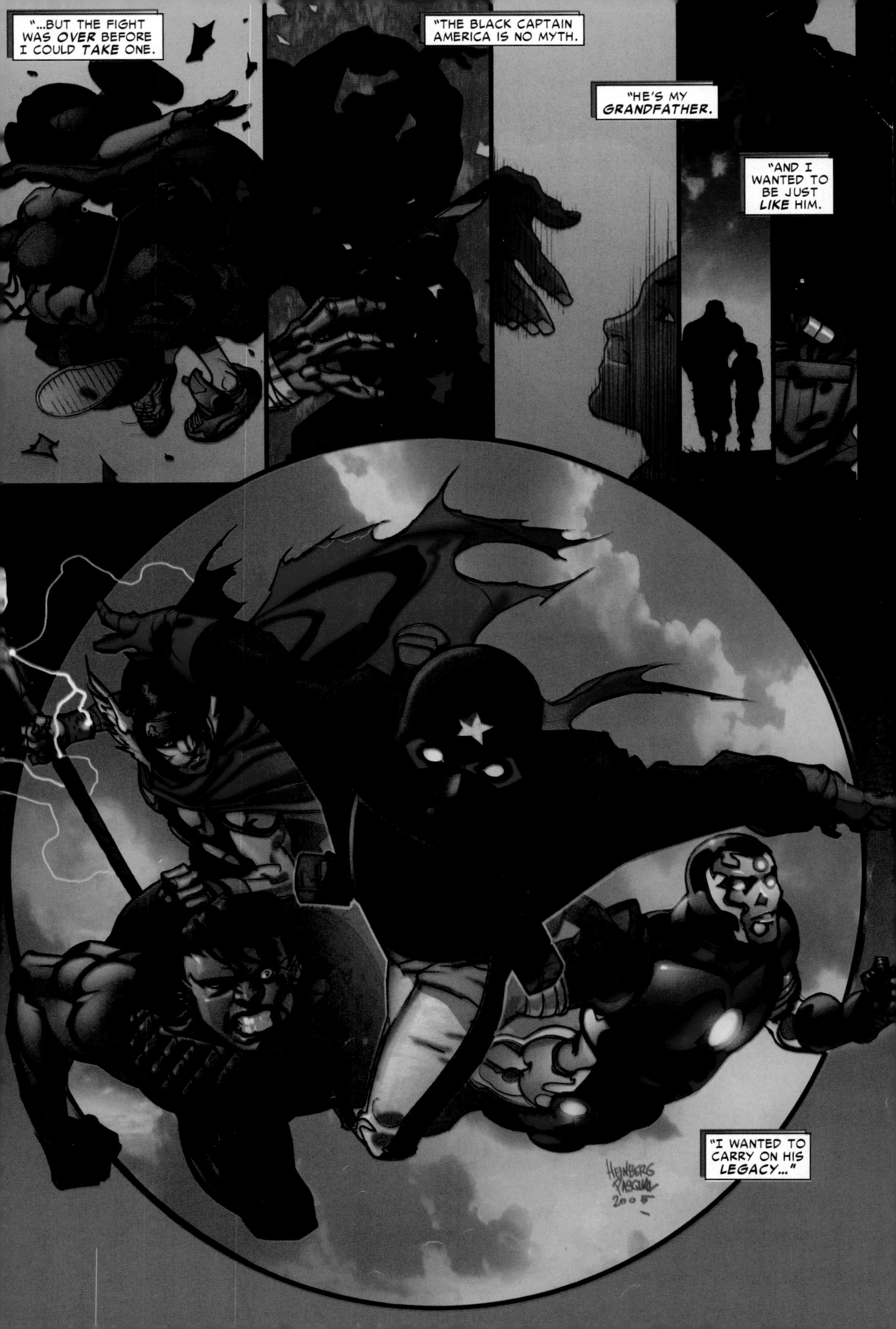
"...BUT THE FIGHT WAS OVER BEFORE I COULD TAKE ONE.
"THE BLACK CAPTAIN AMERICA IS NO MYTH.
"HE'S MY GRANDFATHER.
"AND I WANTED TO BE JUST LIKE HIM.
"I WANTED TO CARRY ON HIS LEGACY..."
HEINBERG PASQUAL 2005

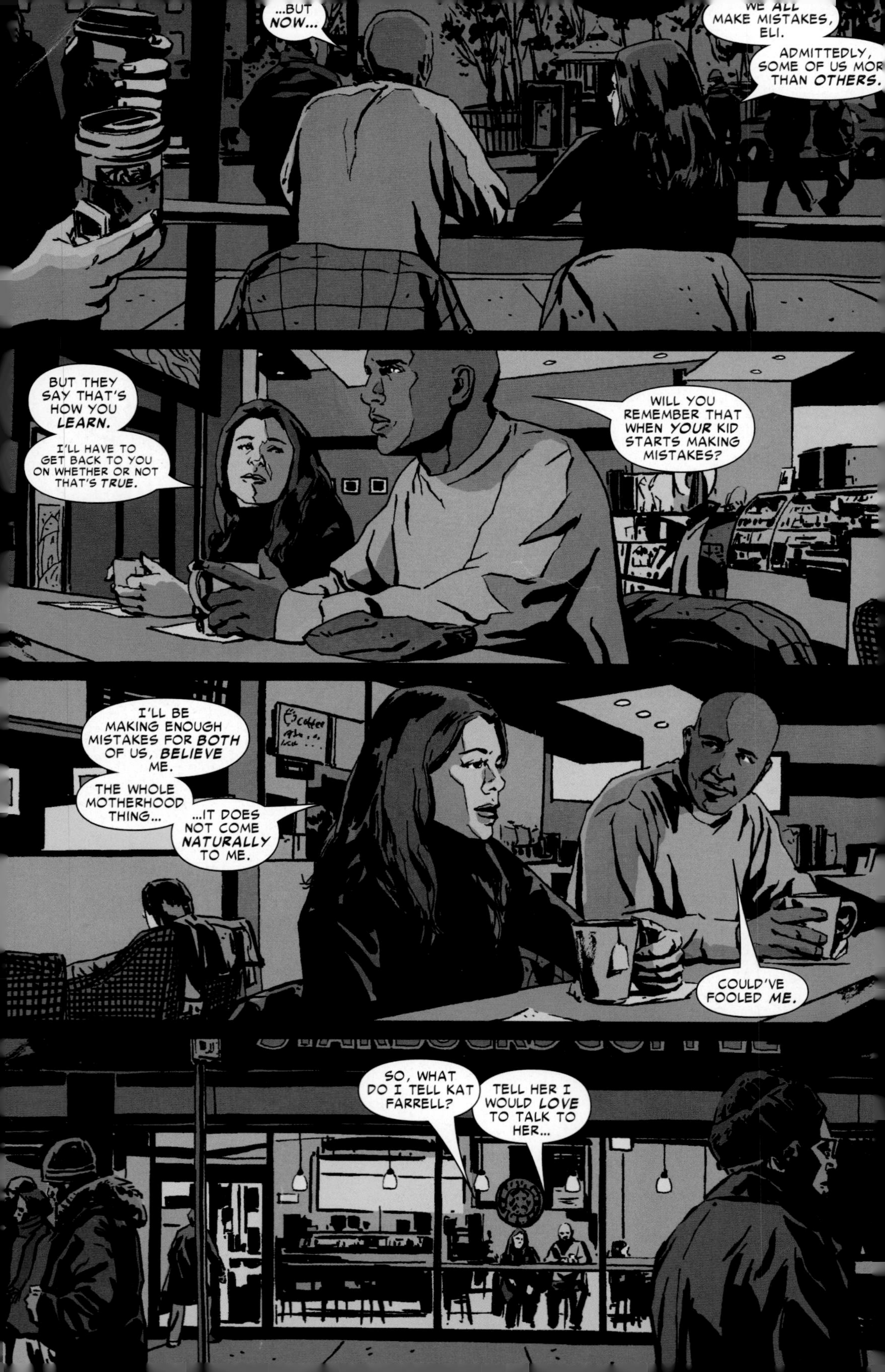

...BUT NOW...
WE ALL MAKE MISTAKES, ELI.
ADMITTEDLY, SOME OF US MOR THAN OTHERS.
BUT THEY SAY THAT'S HOW YOU LEARN.
I'LL HAVE TO GET BACK TO YOU ON WHETHER OR NOT THAT'S TRUE.
WILL YOU REMEMBER THAT WHEN YOUR KID STARTS MAKING MISTAKES?
I'LL BE MAKING ENOUGH MISTAKES FOR BOTH OF US, BELIEVE ME.
THE WHOLE MOTHERHOOD THING...
...IT DOES NOT COME NATURALLY TO ME.
COULD'VE FOOLED ME.
SO, WHAT DO I TELL KAT FARRELL?
TELL HER I WOULD LOVE TO TALK TO HER...

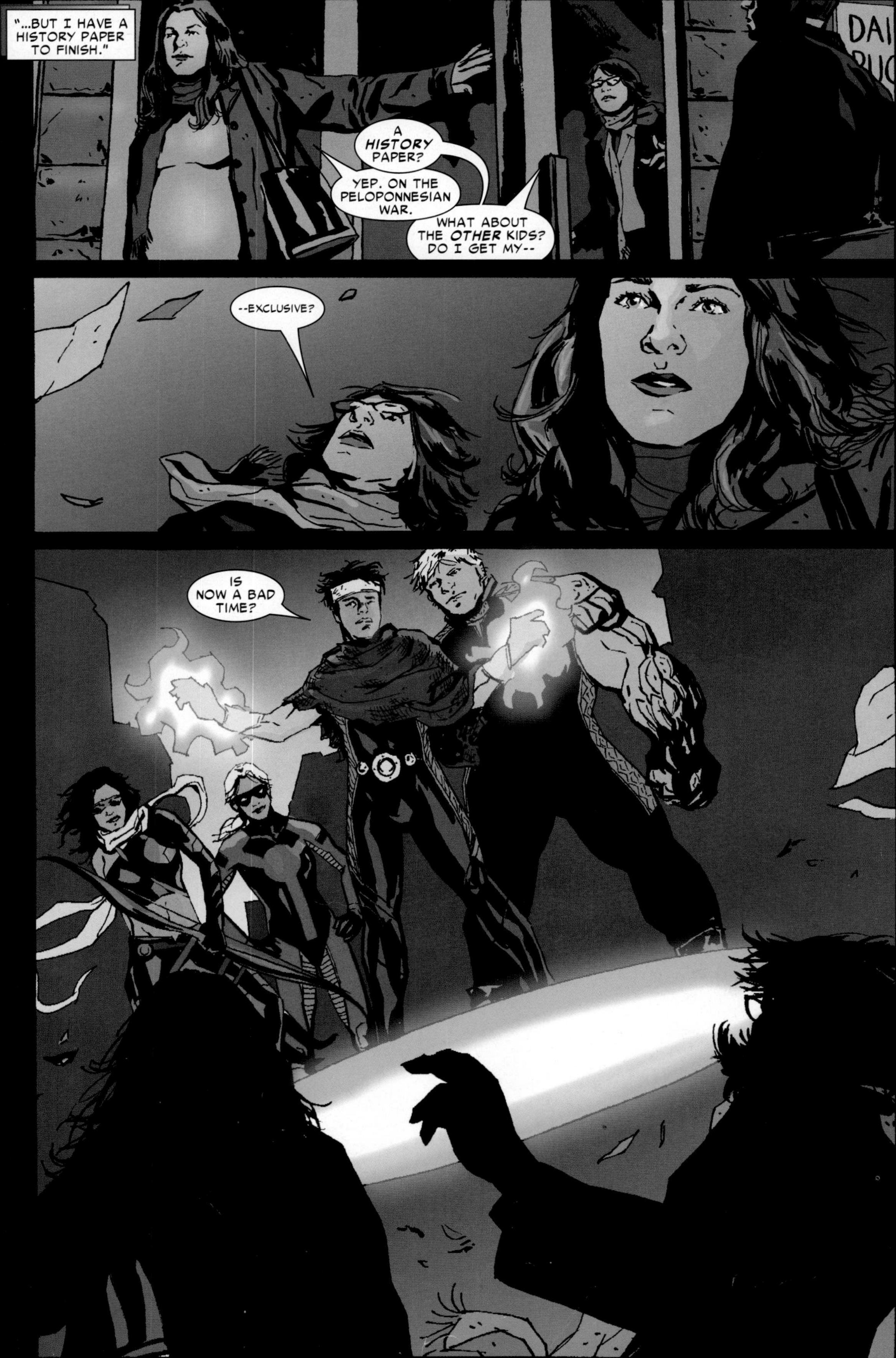
"...BUT I HAVE A HISTORY PAPER TO FINISH."
A HISTORY PAPER?
YEP. ON THE PELOPONNESIAN WAR.
WHAT ABOUT THE OTHER KIDS? DO I GET MY--
--EXCLUSIVE?
IS NOW A BAD TIME?

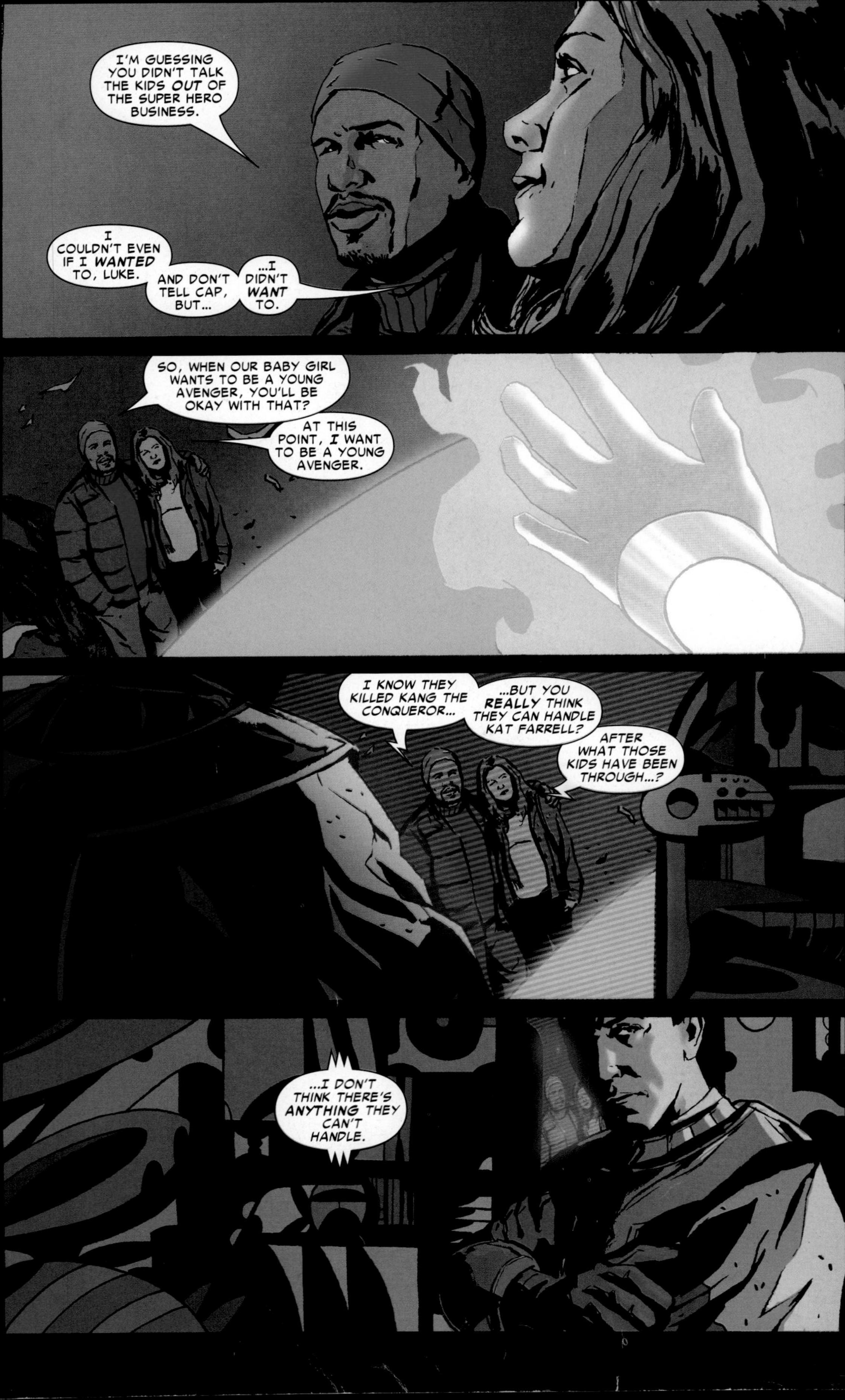
I'M GUESSING YOU DIDN'T TALK THE KIDS OUT OF THE SUPER HERO BUSINESS.
I COULDN'T EVEN IF I WANTED TO, LUKE.
AND DON'T TELL CAP, BUT...
...I DIDN'T WANT TO.
SO, WHEN OUR BABY GIRL WANTS TO BE A YOUNG AVENGER, YOU'LL BE OKAY WITH THAT?
AT THIS POINT, I WANT TO BE A YOUNG AVENGER.
I KNOW THEY KILLED KANG THE CONQUEROR...
...BUT YOU REALLY THINK THEY CAN HANDLE KAT FARRELL?
AFTER WHAT THOSE KIDS HAVE BEEN THROUGH...?
...I DON'T THINK THERE'S ANYTHING THEY CAN'T HANDLE.

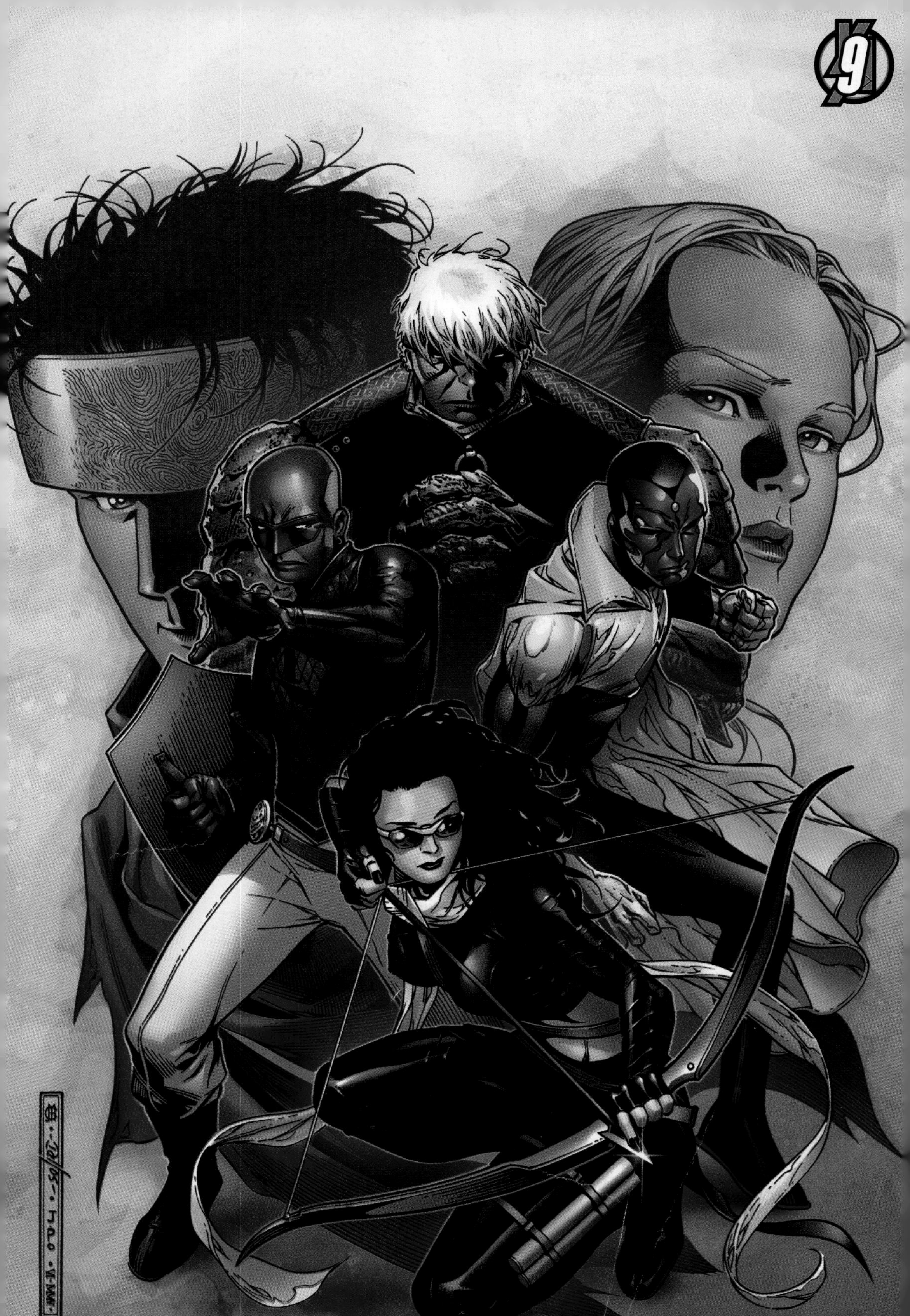

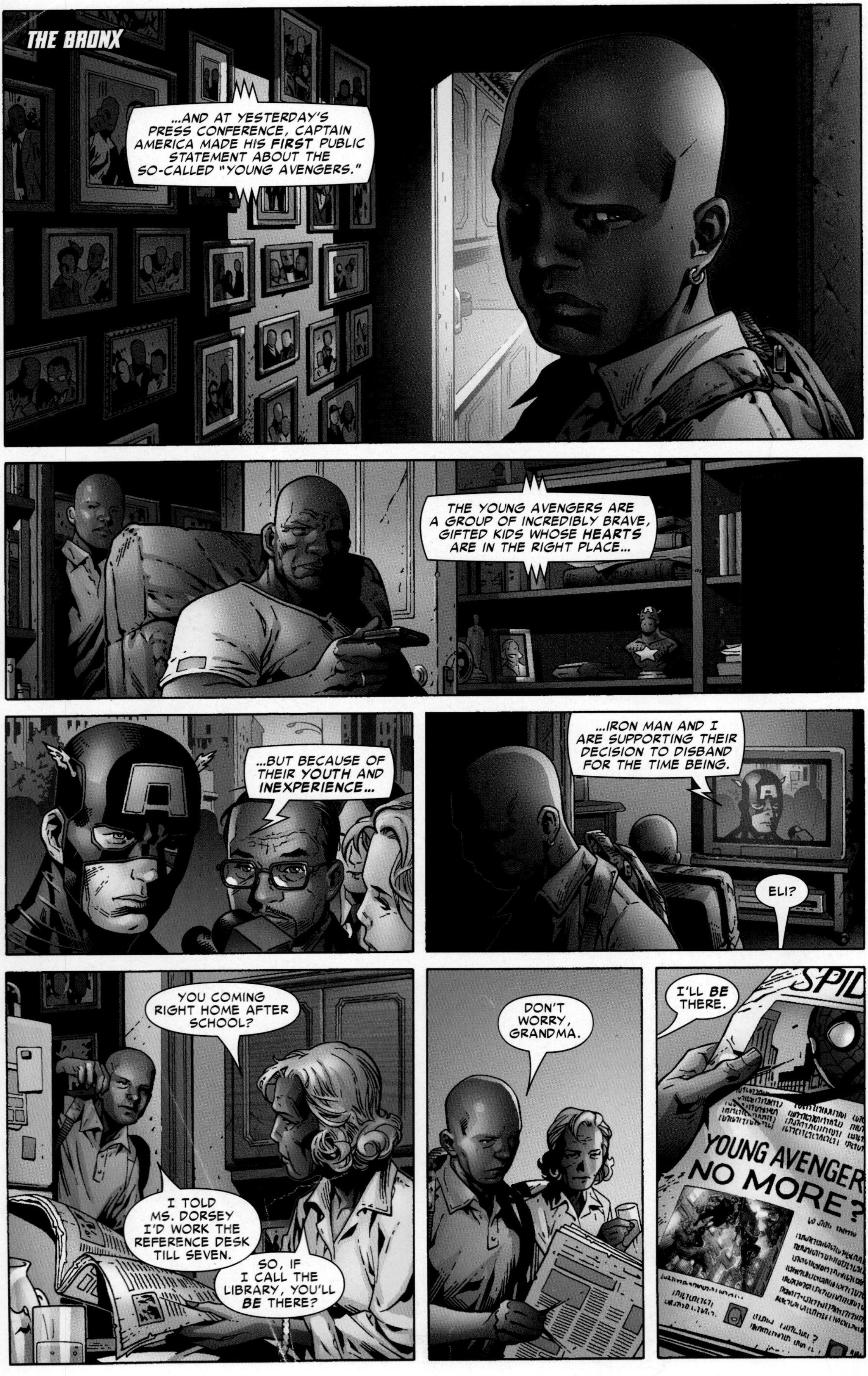
THE BRONX
...AND AT YESTERDAY'S PRESS CONFERENCE, CAPTAIN AMERICA MADE HIS FIRST PUBLIC STATEMENT ABOUT THE SO-CALLED "YOUNG AVENGERS."
THE YOUNG AVENGERS ARE A GROUP OF INCREDIBLY BRAVE, GIFTED KIDS WHOSE HEARTS ARE IN THE RIGHT PLACE...
...BUT BECAUSE OF THEIR YOUTH AND INEXPERIENCE...
...IRON MAN AND I ARE SUPPORTING THEIR DECISION TO DISBAND FOR THE TIME BEING.
ELI?
YOU COMING RIGHT HOME AFTER SCHOOL?
I TOLD MS. DORSEY I'D WORK THE REFERENCE DESK TILL SEVEN.
SO, IF I CALL THE LIBRARY, YOU'LL BE THERE?
DON'T WORRY, GRANDMA.
I'LL BE THERE.
YOUNG AVENGER NO MORE?

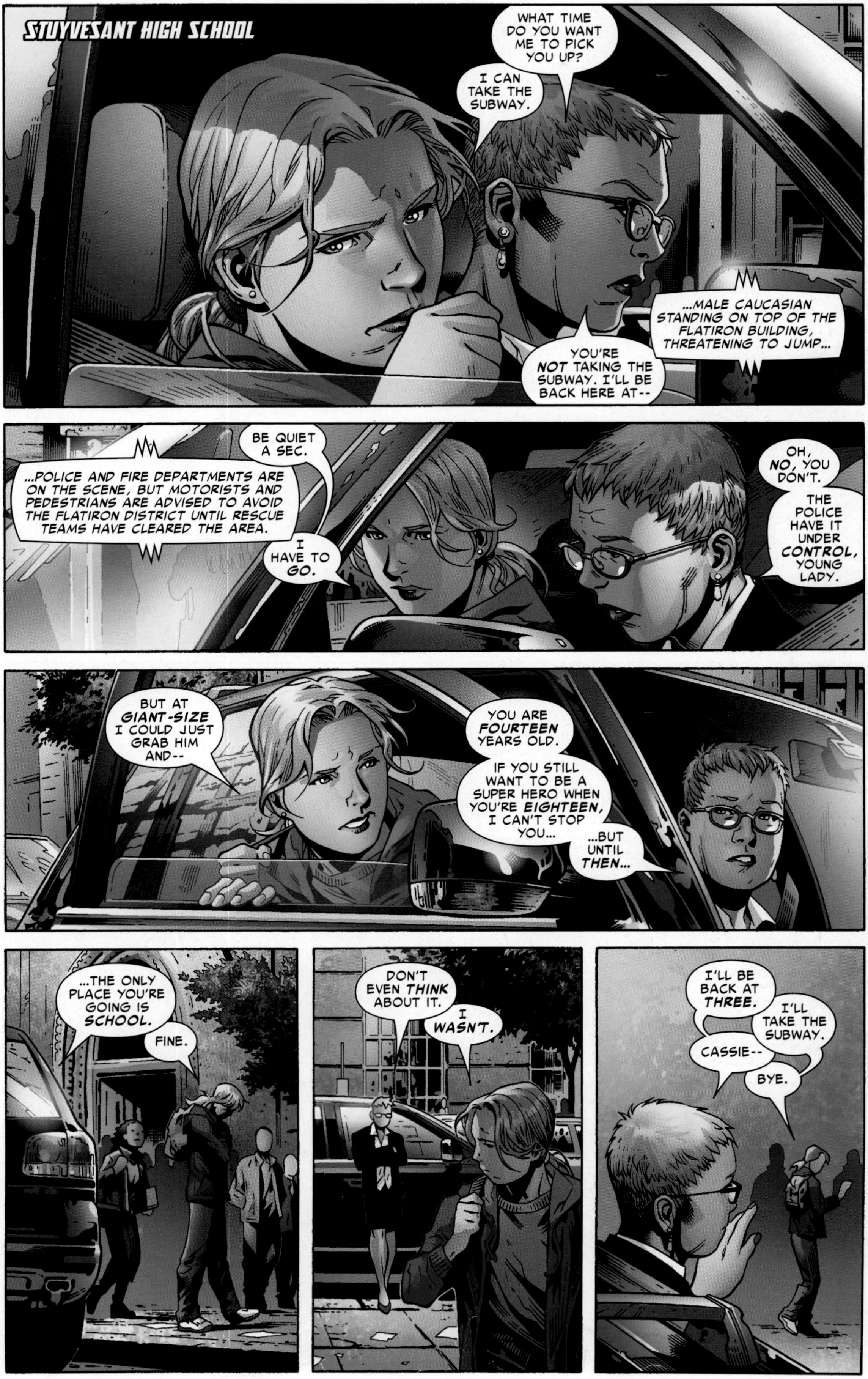
STUYVESANT HIGH SCHOOL
WHAT TIME DO YOU WANT ME TO PICK YOU UP?
I CAN TAKE THE SUBWAY.
YOU'RE NOT TAKING THE SUBWAY. I'LL BE BACK HERE AT--
...MALE CAUCASIAN STANDING ON TOP OF THE FLATIRON BUILDING, THREATENING TO JUMP...
BE QUIET A SEC.
...POLICE AND FIRE DEPARTMENTS ARE ON THE SCENE, BUT MOTORISTS AND PEDESTRIANS ARE ADVISED TO AVOID THE FLATIRON DISTRICT UNTIL RESCUE TEAMS HAVE CLEARED THE AREA.
I HAVE TO GO.
OH, NO, YOU DON'T.
THE POLICE HAVE IT UNDER CONTROL, YOUNG LADY.
BUT AT GIANT-SIZE I COULD JUST GRAB HIM AND--
YOU ARE FOURTEEN YEARS OLD.
IF YOU STILL WANT TO BE A SUPER HERO WHEN YOU'RE EIGHTEEN, I CAN'T STOP YOU...
...BUT UNTIL THEN...
...THE ONLY PLACE YOU'RE GOING IS SCHOOL.
FINE.
DON'T EVEN THINK ABOUT IT.
I WASN'T.
I'LL BE BACK AT THREE.
I'LL TAKE THE SUBWAY.
CASSIE--
BYE.

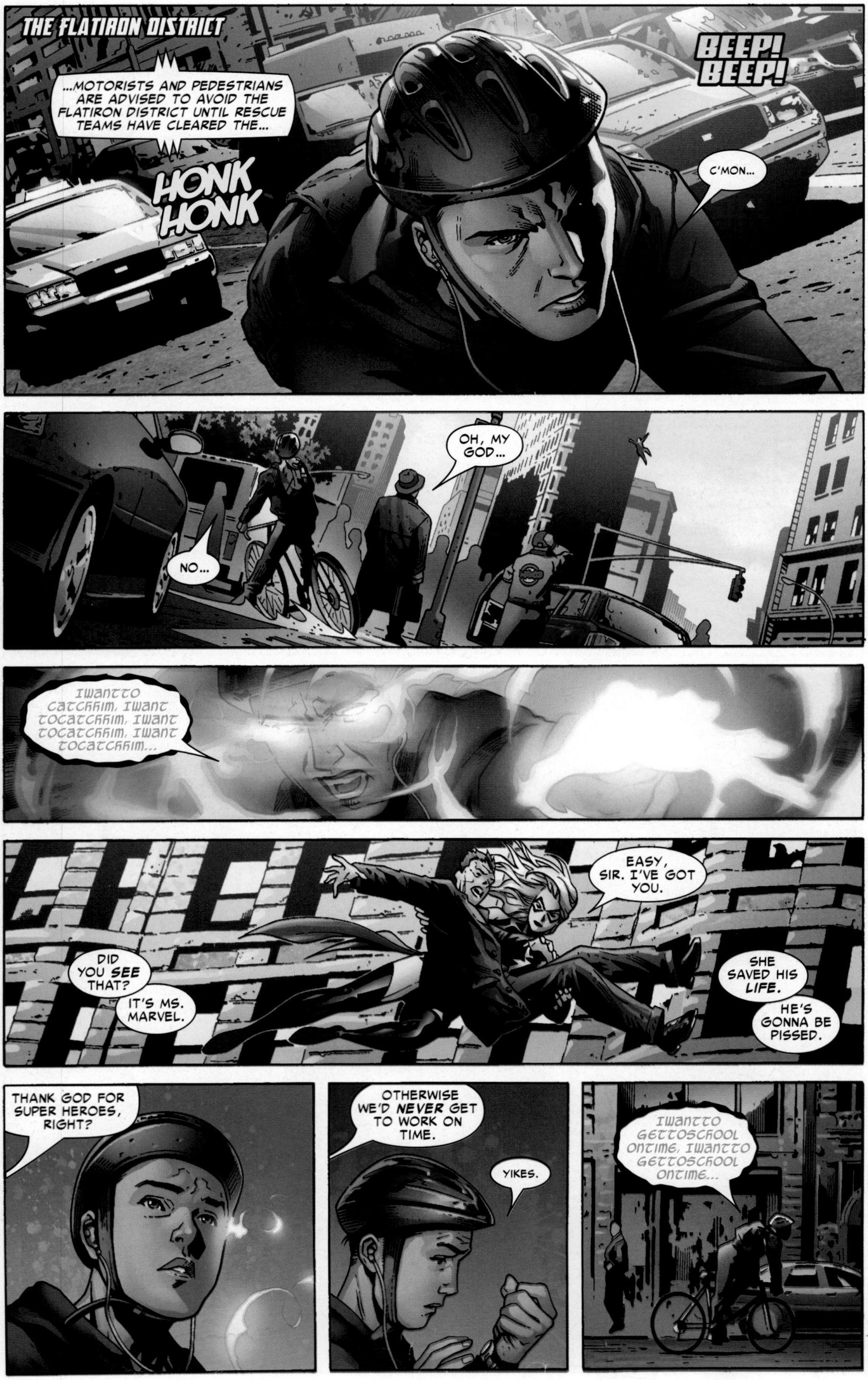
THE FLATIRON DISTRICT
...MOTORISTS AND PEDESTRIANS ARE ADVISED TO AVOID THE FLATIRON DISTRICT UNTIL RESCUE TEAMS HAVE CLEARED THE...
HONK HONK
BEEP! BEEP!
C'MON...
OH, MY GOD...
NO...
IWANTTO CATCHHIM, IWANT TOCATCHHIM, IWANT TOCATCHHIM, IWANT TOCATCHHIM...
EASY, SIR. I'VE GOT YOU.
DID YOU SEE THAT?
IT'S MS. MARVEL.
SHE SAVED HIS LIFE.
HE'S GONNA BE PISSED.
THANK GOD FOR SUPER HEROES, RIGHT?
OTHERWISE WE'D NEVER GET TO WORK ON TIME.
YIKES.
IWANTTO GETTOSCHOOL ONTIME, IWANTTO GETTOSCHOOL ONTIME...

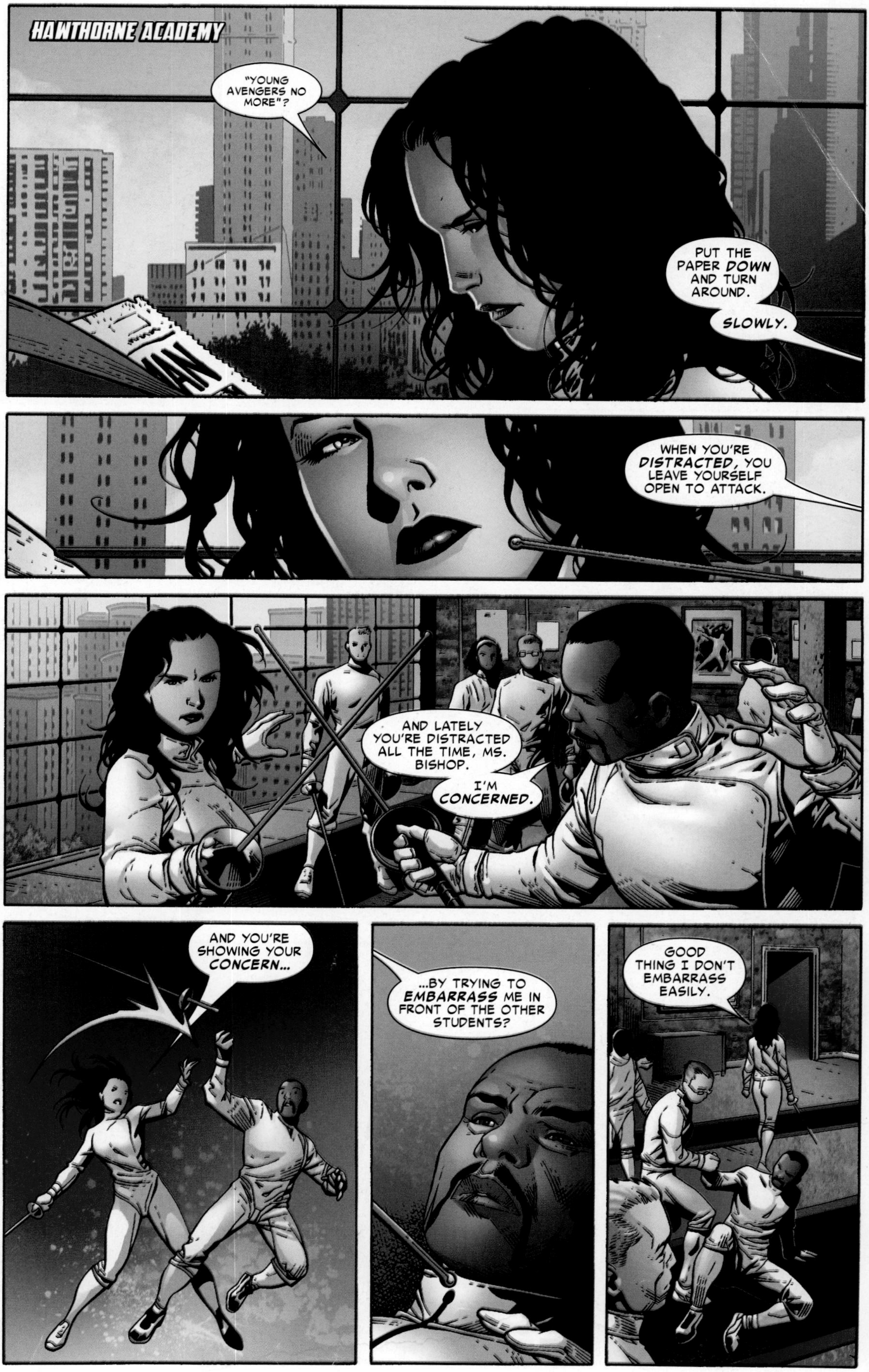
HAWTHORNE ACADEMY
"YOUNG AVENGERS NO MORE"?
PUT THE PAPER DOWN AND TURN AROUND.
SLOWLY.
WHEN YOU'RE DISTRACTED, YOU LEAVE YOURSELF OPEN TO ATTACK.
AND LATELY YOU'RE DISTRACTED ALL THE TIME, MS. BISHOP.
I'M CONCERNED.
AND YOU'RE SHOWING YOUR CONCERN...
...BY TRYING TO EMBARRASS ME IN FRONT OF THE OTHER STUDENTS?
GOOD THING I DON'T EMBARRASS EASILY.

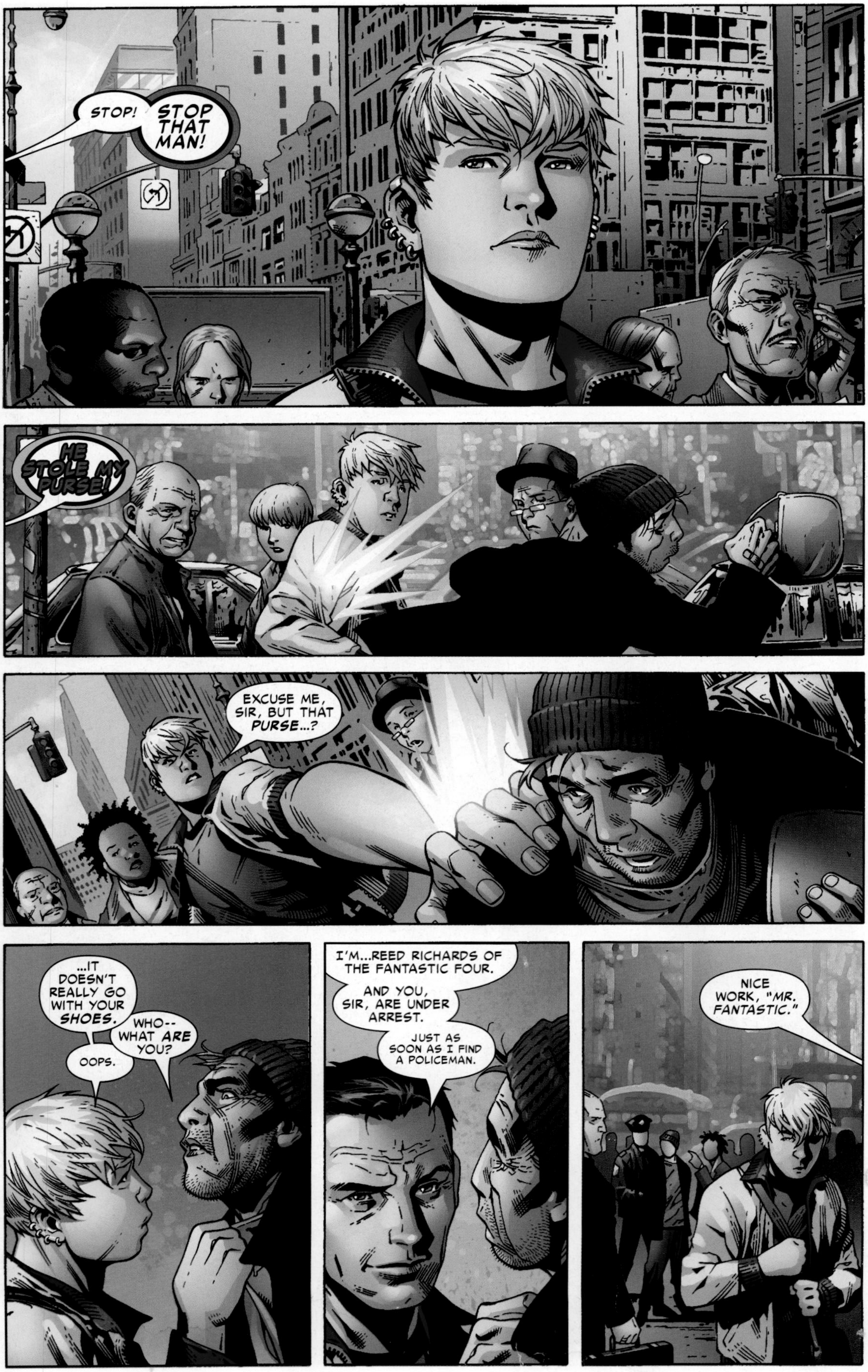
STOP!
STOP THAT MAN!
HE STOLE MY PURSE!
EXCUSE ME, SIR, BUT THAT PURSE...?
...IT DOESN'T REALLY GO WITH YOUR SHOES.
OOPS.
WHO-- WHAT ARE YOU?
I'M...REED RICHARDS OF THE FANTASTIC FOUR.
AND YOU, SIR, ARE UNDER ARREST.
JUST AS SOON AS I FIND A POLICEMAN.
NICE WORK, "MR. FANTASTIC."

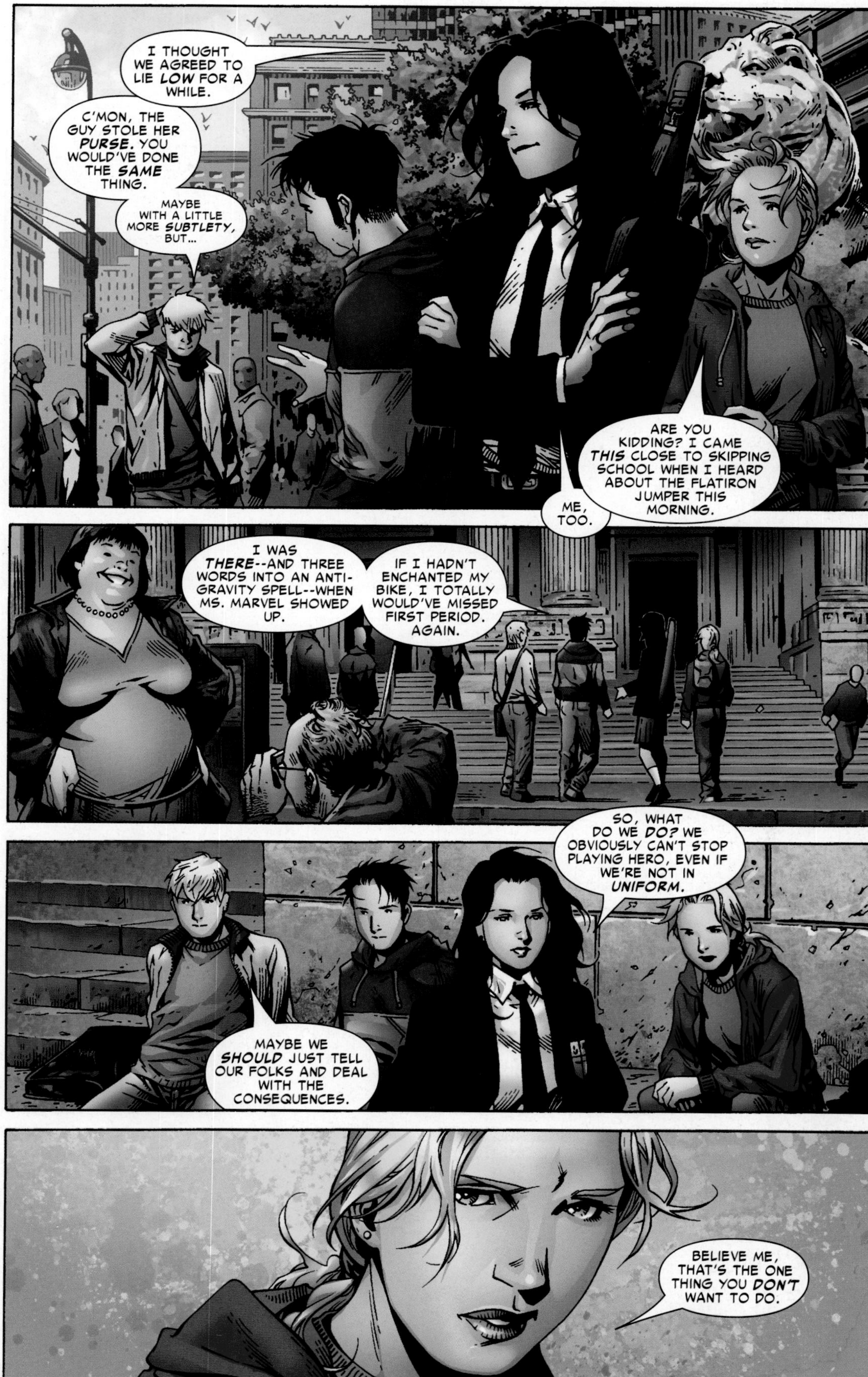
I THOUGHT WE AGREED TO LIE LOW FOR A WHILE.
C'MON, THE GUY STOLE HER PURSE. YOU WOULD'VE DONE THE SAME THING.
MAYBE WITH A LITTLE MORE SUBTLETY, BUT...
ARE YOU KIDDING? I CAME THIS CLOSE TO SKIPPING SCHOOL WHEN I HEARD ABOUT THE FLATIRON JUMPER THIS MORNING.
ME, TOO.
I WAS THERE--AND THREE WORDS INTO AN ANTI-GRAVITY SPELL--WHEN MS. MARVEL SHOWED UP.
IF I HADN'T ENCHANTED MY BIKE, I TOTALLY WOULD'VE MISSED FIRST PERIOD. AGAIN.
SO, WHAT DO WE DO? WE OBVIOUSLY CAN'T STOP PLAYING HERO, EVEN IF WE'RE NOT IN UNIFORM.
MAYBE WE SHOULD JUST TELL OUR FOLKS AND DEAL WITH THE CONSEQUENCES.
BELIEVE ME, THAT'S THE ONE THING YOU DON'T WANT TO DO.

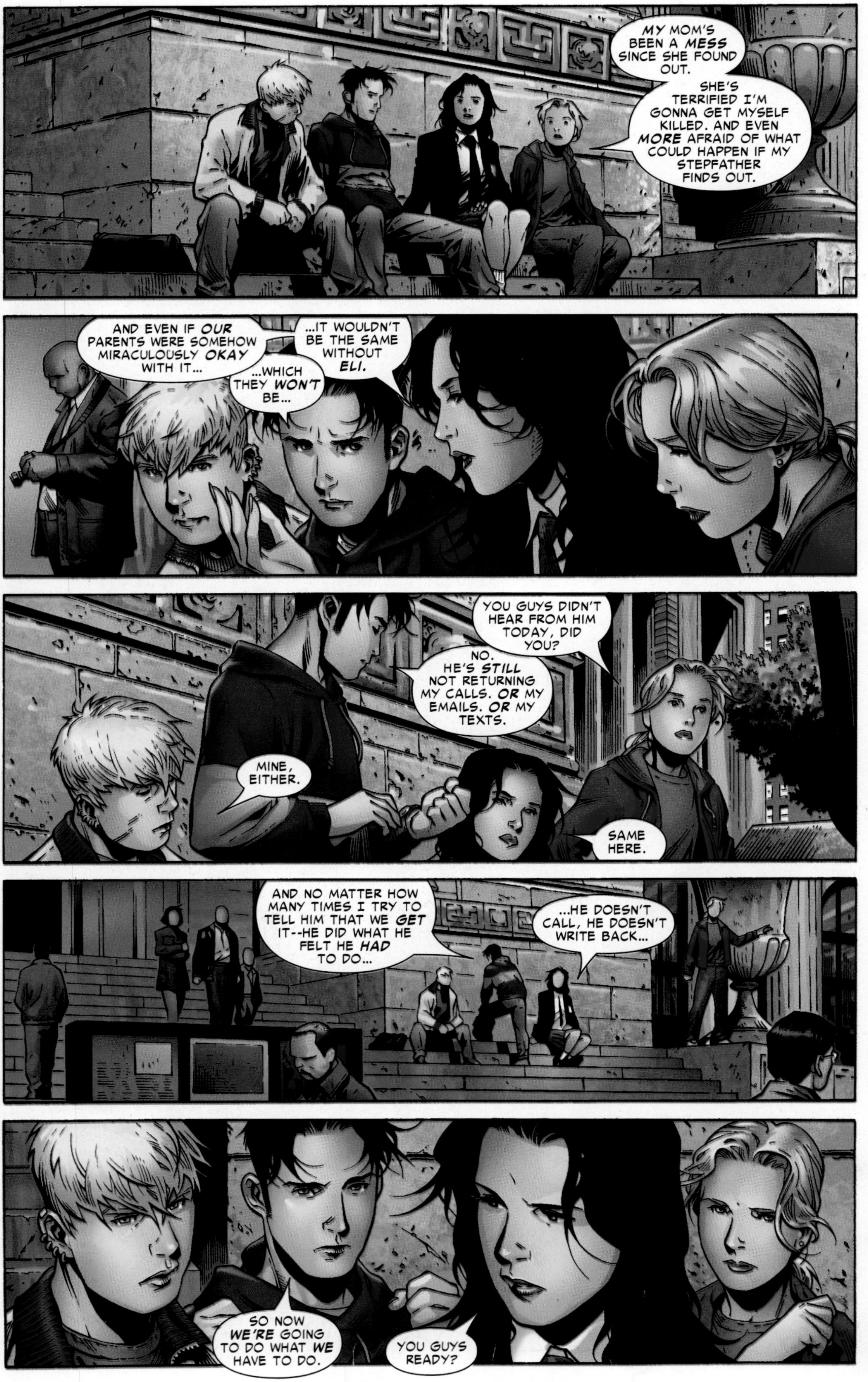
MY MOM'S BEEN A MESS SINCE SHE FOUND OUT.
SHE'S TERRIFIED I'M GONNA GET MYSELF KILLED. AND EVEN MORE AFRAID OF WHAT COULD HAPPEN IF MY STEPFATHER FINDS OUT.
AND EVEN IF OUR PARENTS WERE SOMEHOW MIRACULOUSLY OKAY WITH IT...
...WHICH THEY WON'T BE...
...IT WOULDN'T BE THE SAME WITHOUT ELI.
YOU GUYS DIDN'T HEAR FROM HIM TODAY, DID YOU?
NO. HE'S STILL NOT RETURNING MY CALLS. OR MY EMAILS. OR MY TEXTS.
MINE, EITHER.
SAME HERE.
AND NO MATTER HOW MANY TIMES I TRY TO TELL HIM THAT WE GET IT--HE DID WHAT HE FELT HE HAD TO DO...
...HE DOESN'T CALL, HE DOESN'T WRITE BACK...
SO NOW WE'RE GOING TO DO WHAT WE HAVE TO DO.
YOU GUYS READY?

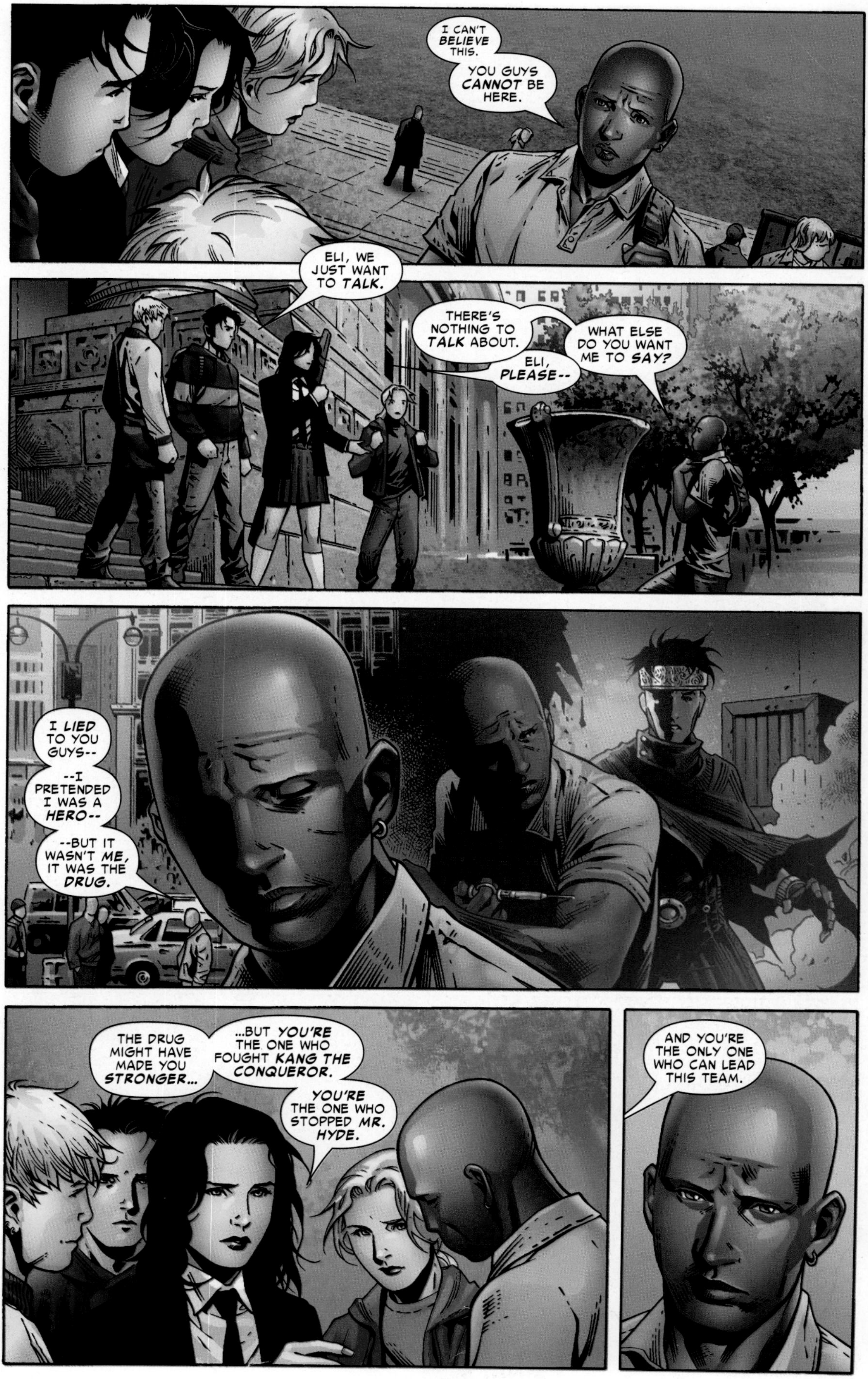
I CAN'T BELIEVE THIS.
YOU GUYS CANNOT BE HERE.
ELI, WE JUST WANT TO TALK.
THERE'S NOTHING TO TALK ABOUT.
ELI, PLEASE--
WHAT ELSE DO YOU WANT ME TO SAY?
I LIED TO YOU GUYS--
--I PRETENDED I WAS A HERO--
--BUT IT WASN'T ME, IT WAS THE DRUG.
THE DRUG MIGHT HAVE MADE YOU STRONGER...
...BUT YOU'RE THE ONE WHO FOUGHT KANG THE CONQUEROR.
YOU'RE THE ONE WHO STOPPED MR. HYDE.
AND YOU'RE THE ONLY ONE WHO CAN LEAD THIS TEAM.

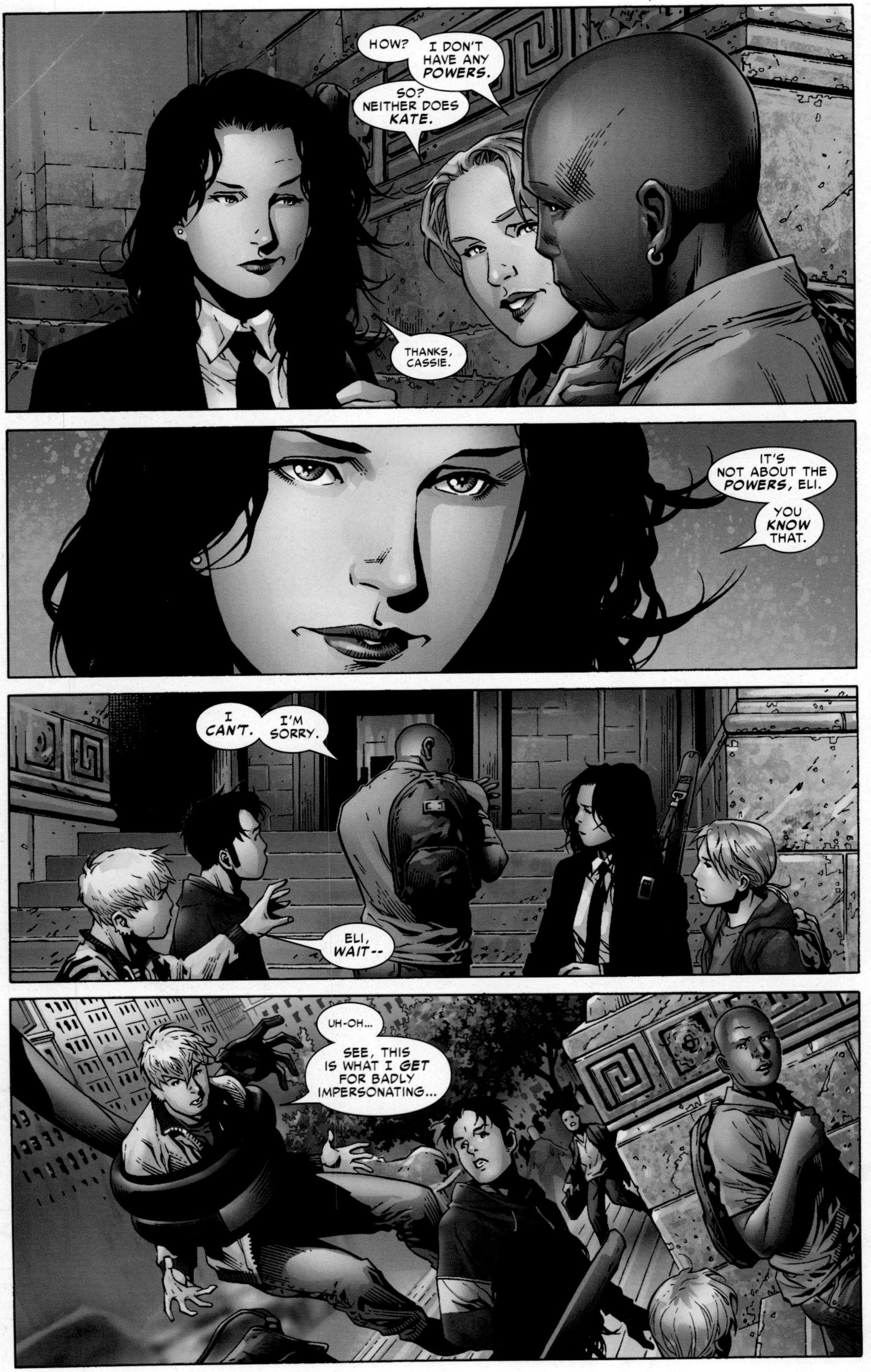
HOW?
I DON'T HAVE ANY POWERS.
SO? NEITHER DOES KATE.
THANKS, CASSIE.
IT'S NOT ABOUT THE POWERS, ELI.
YOU KNOW THAT.
I CAN'T.
I'M SORRY.
ELI, WAIT--
UH-OH...
SEE, THIS IS WHAT I GET FOR BADLY IMPERSONATING...

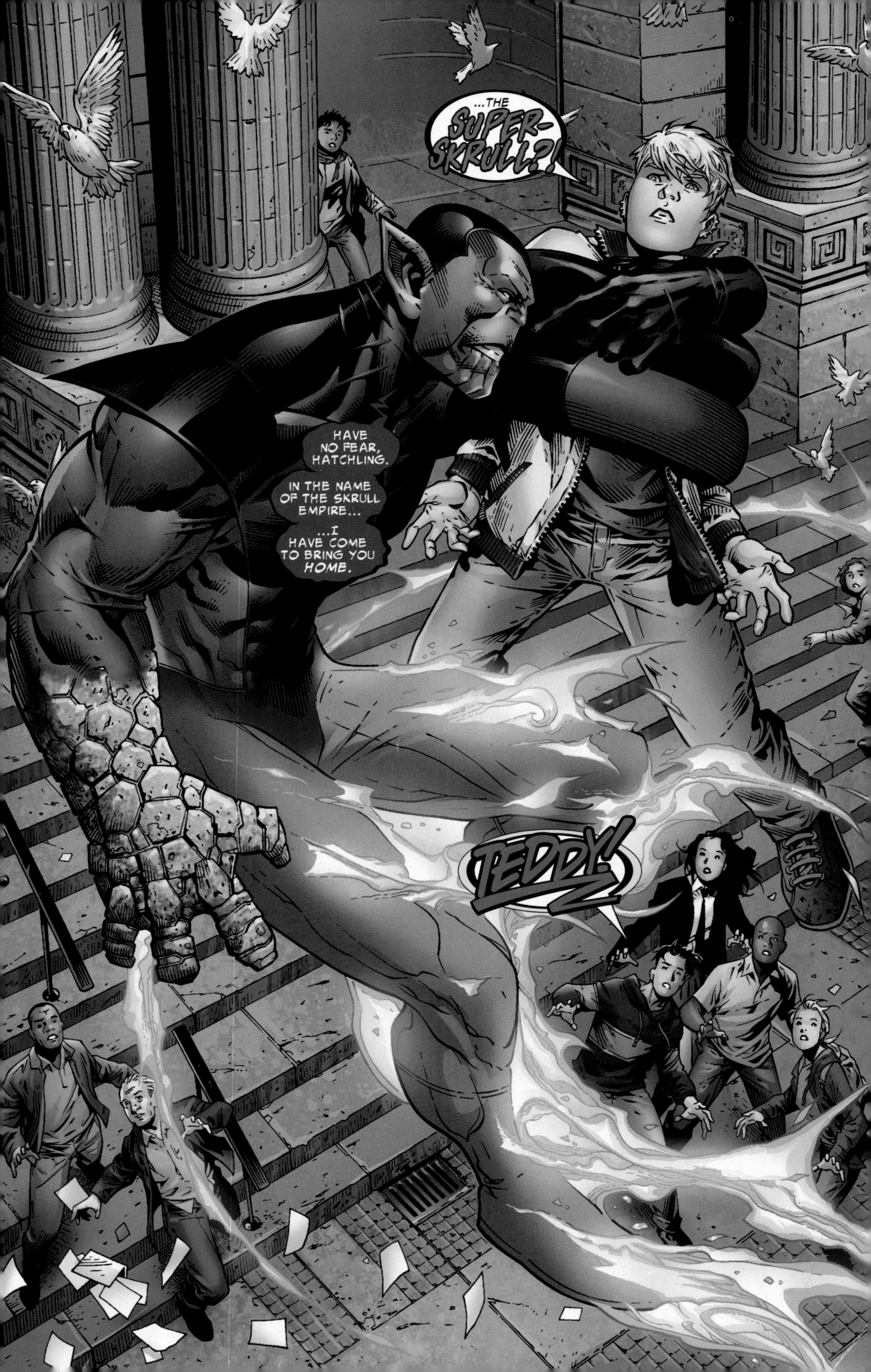
...THE SUPER-SKRULL?!
HAVE NO FEAR, HATCHLING.
IN THE NAME OF THE SKRULL EMPIRE...
...I HAVE COME TO BRING YOU *HOME*.
TEDDY!

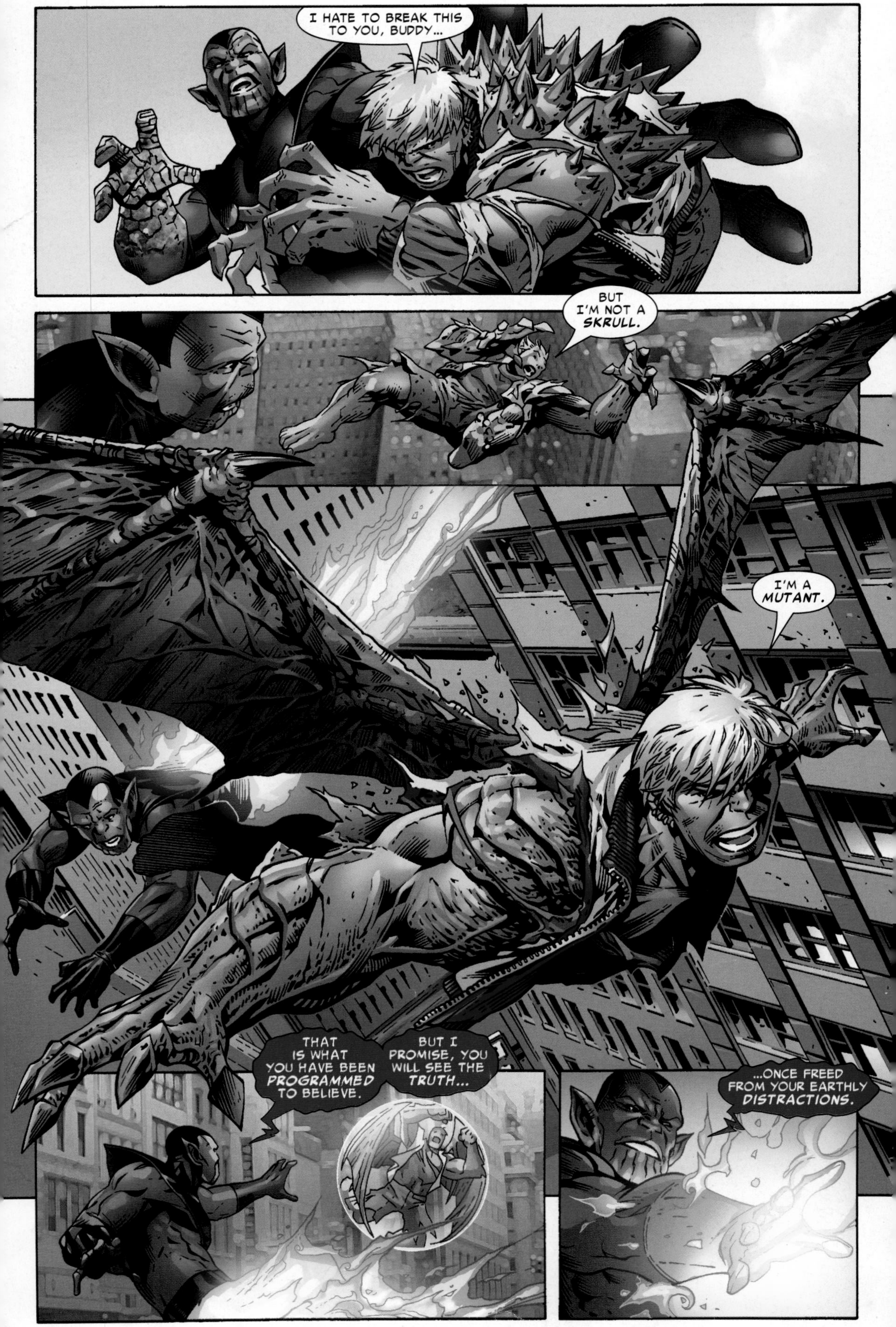
I HATE TO BREAK THIS TO YOU, BUDDY...
BUT I'M NOT A *SKRULL.*
I'M A *MUTANT.*
THAT IS WHAT YOU HAVE BEEN *PROGRAMMED* TO BELIEVE.
BUT I PROMISE, YOU WILL SEE THE *TRUTH*...
...ONCE FREED FROM YOUR EARTHLY *DISTRACTIONS.*

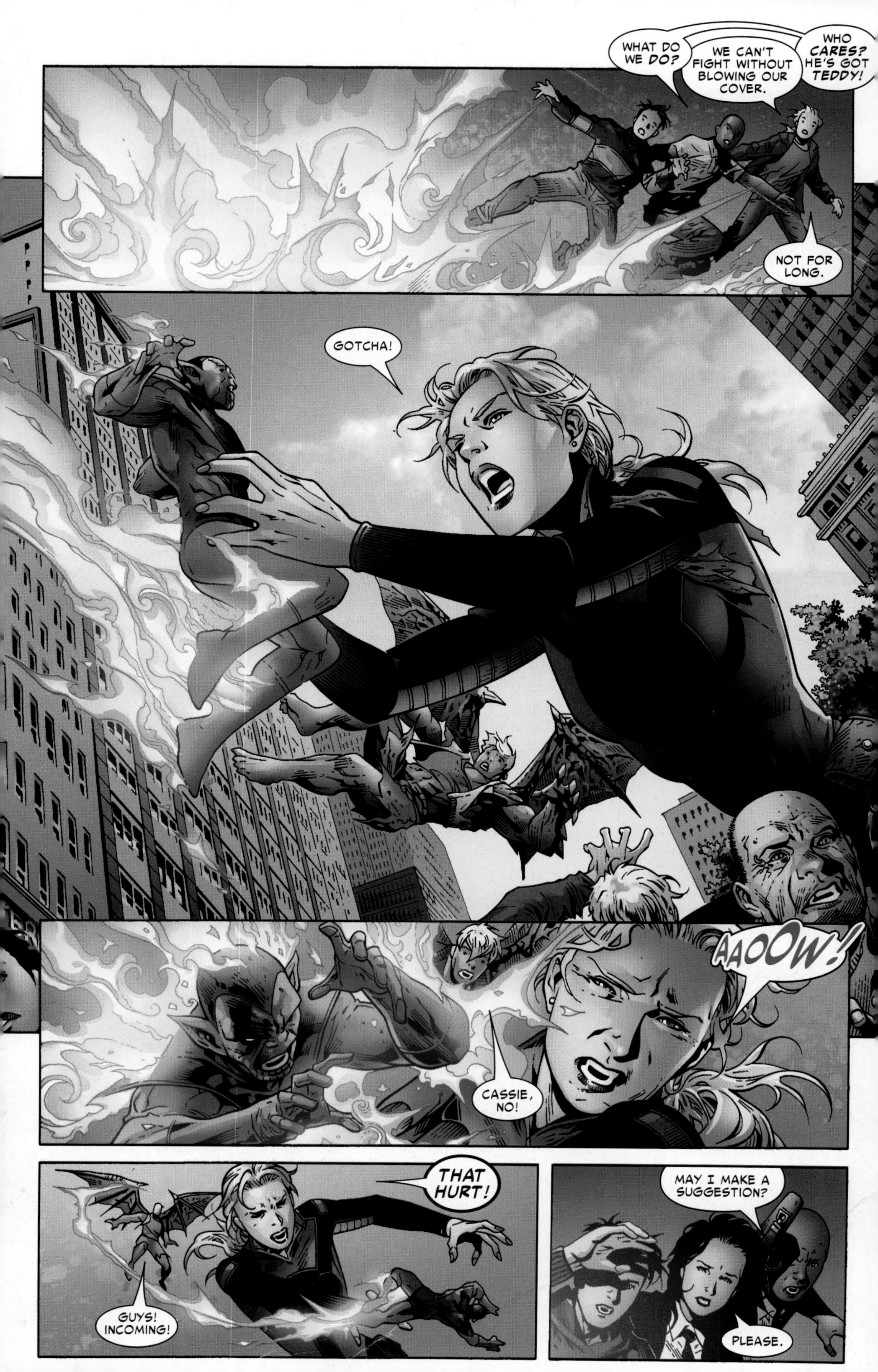
WHAT DO WE DO?
WE CAN'T FIGHT WITHOUT BLOWING OUR COVER.
WHO CARES? HE'S GOT TEDDY!
NOT FOR LONG.
GOTCHA!
AAOOW!
CASSIE, NO!
THAT HURT!
GUYS! INCOMING!
MAY I MAKE A SUGGESTION?
PLEASE.

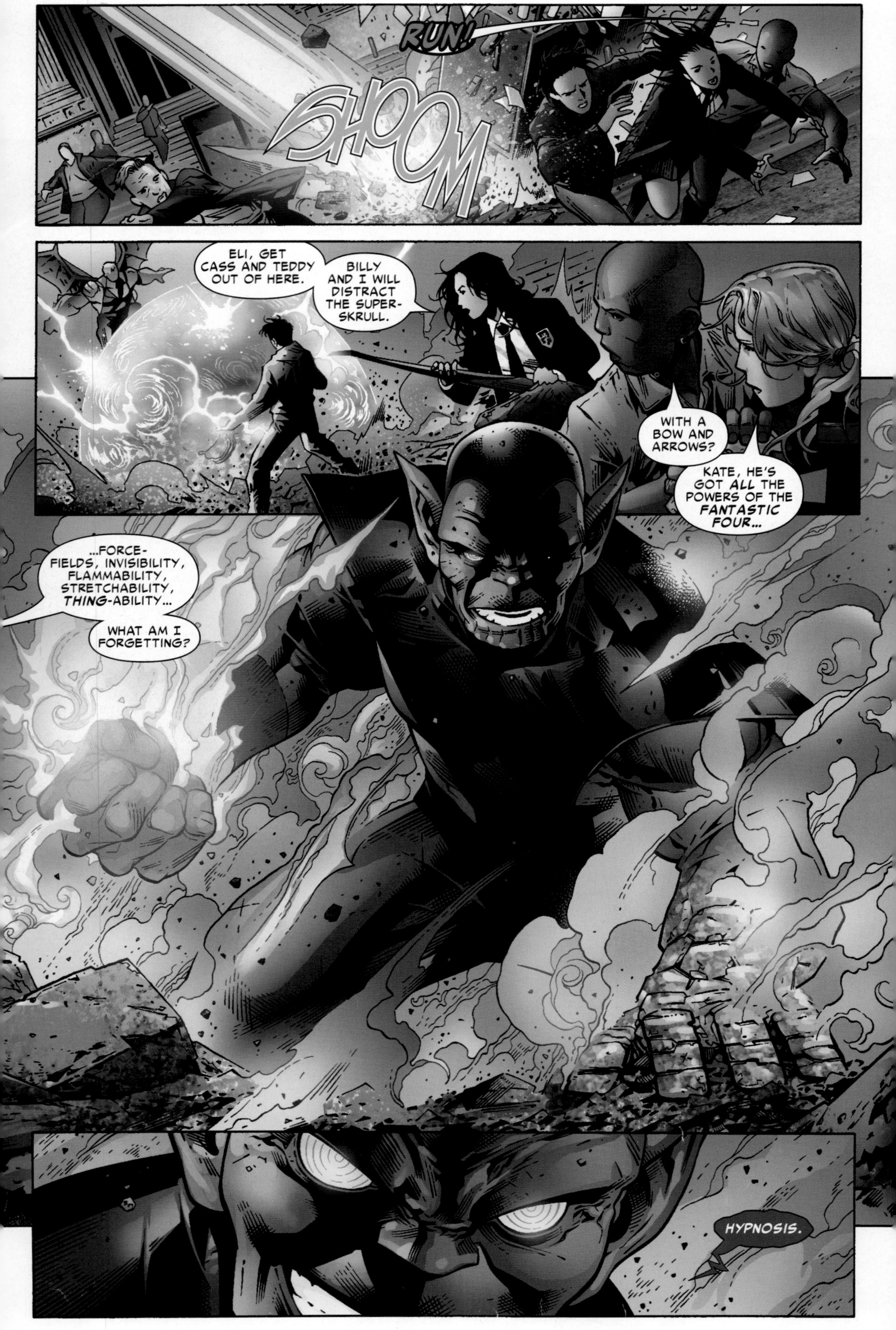
RUN!
SHOOOM
ELI, GET CASS AND TEDDY OUT OF HERE.
BILLY AND I WILL DISTRACT THE SUPER-SKRULL.
WITH A BOW AND ARROWS?
KATE, HE'S GOT ALL THE POWERS OF THE FANTASTIC FOUR...
...FORCE-FIELDS, INVISIBILITY, FLAMMABILITY, STRETCHABILITY, THING-ABILITY...
WHAT AM I FORGETTING?
HYPNOSIS.

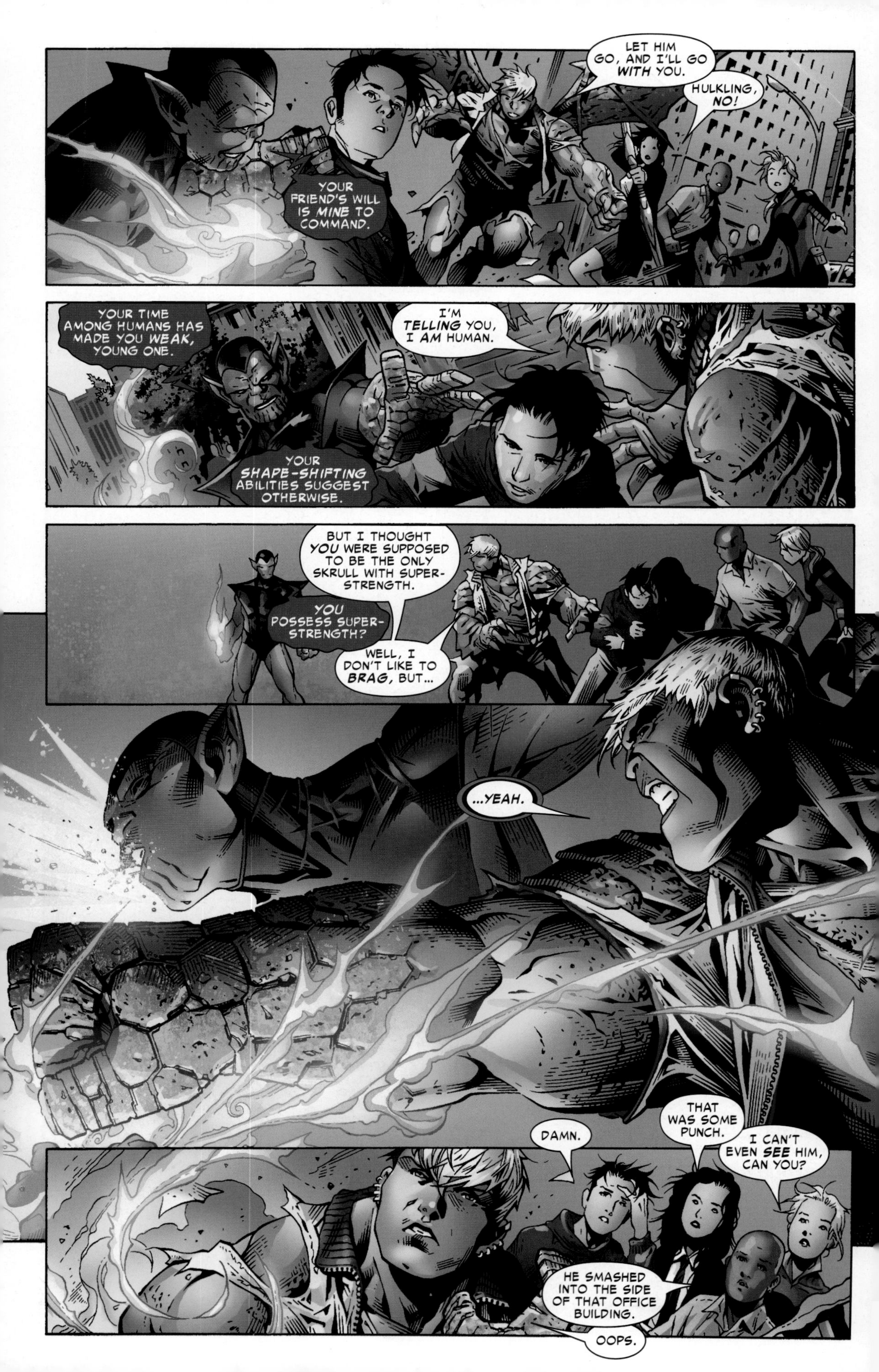
LET HIM GO, AND I'LL GO WITH YOU.
HULKLING, NO!
YOUR FRIEND'S WILL IS MINE TO COMMAND.
YOUR TIME AMONG HUMANS HAS MADE YOU WEAK, YOUNG ONE.
I'M TELLING YOU, I AM HUMAN.
YOUR SHAPE-SHIFTING ABILITIES SUGGEST OTHERWISE.
BUT I THOUGHT YOU WERE SUPPOSED TO BE THE ONLY SKRULL WITH SUPER-STRENGTH.
YOU POSSESS SUPER-STRENGTH?
WELL, I DON'T LIKE TO BRAG, BUT...
...YEAH.
DAMN.
THAT WAS SOME PUNCH.
I CAN'T EVEN SEE HIM, CAN YOU?
HE SMASHED INTO THE SIDE OF THAT OFFICE BUILDING.
OOPS.

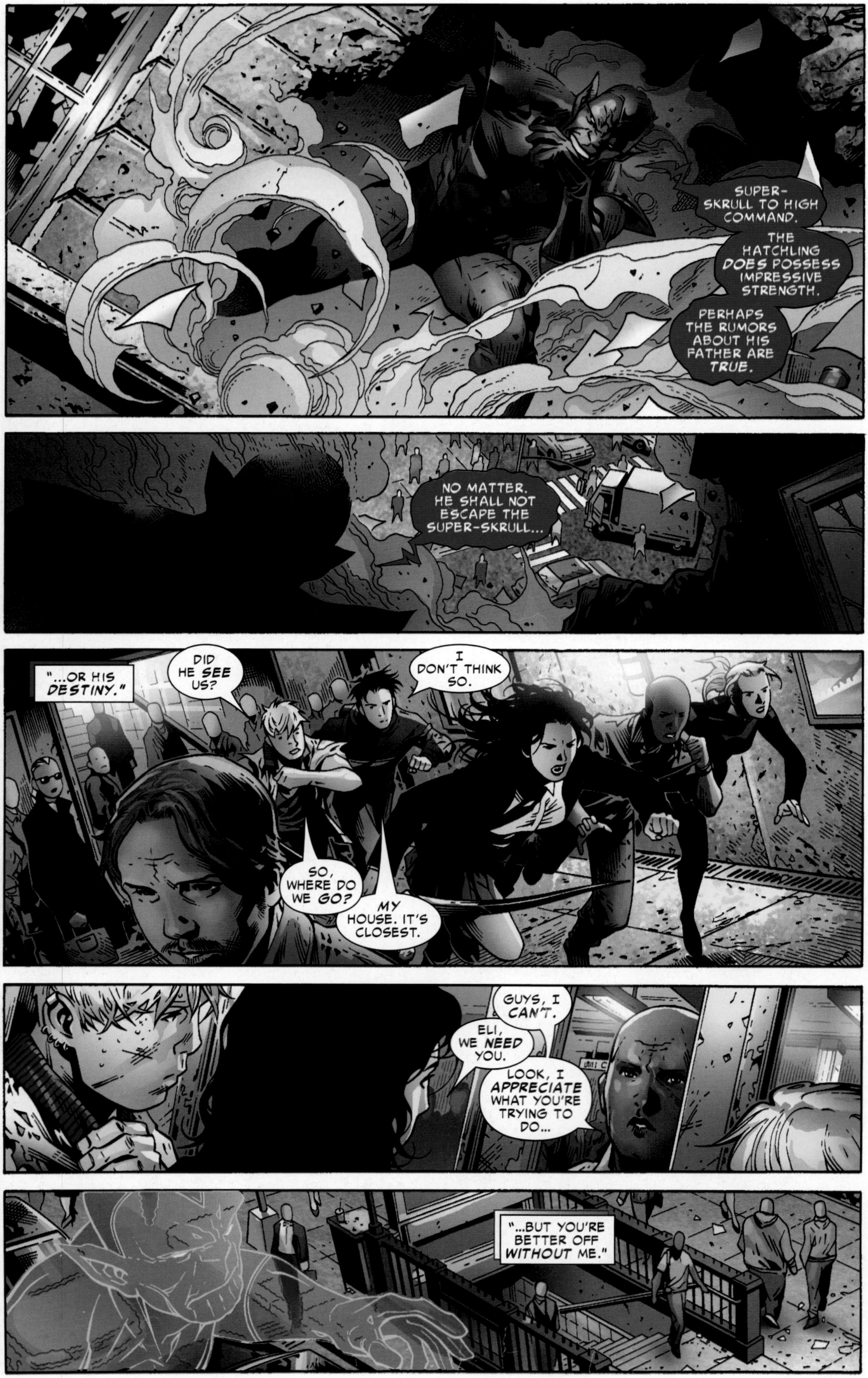
SUPER-SKRULL TO HIGH COMMAND.
THE HATCHLING DOES POSSESS IMPRESSIVE STRENGTH.
PERHAPS THE RUMORS ABOUT HIS FATHER ARE TRUE.
NO MATTER. HE SHALL NOT ESCAPE THE SUPER-SKRULL...
"...OR HIS DESTINY."
DID HE SEE US?
I DON'T THINK SO.
SO, WHERE DO WE GO?
MY HOUSE. IT'S CLOSEST.
GUYS, I CAN'T.
ELI, WE NEED YOU.
LOOK, I APPRECIATE WHAT YOU'RE TRYING TO DO...
"...BUT YOU'RE BETTER OFF WITHOUT ME."

MY MOM'S NOT ANSWERING HER PHONE.

YOU THINK THE SUPER-SKRULL WOULD GO AFTER YOUR MOM?

IF HE THINKS *I'M* A SKRULL--

CAN I ASK A TERRIBLE QUESTION?

THAT'S THE ONE.

"HOW DO I KNOW MY MOM'S *NOT* A SKRULL?"

BECAUSE SHE'S MY MOM.

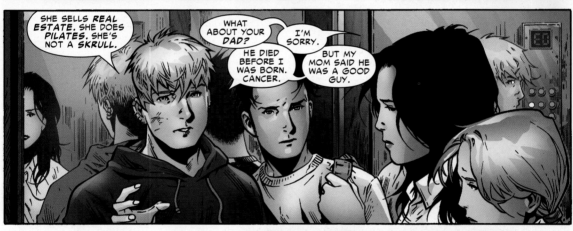

SHE SELLS *REAL* ESTATE. SHE DOES *PILATES*. SHE'S NOT A *SKRULL*.

WHAT ABOUT YOUR *DAD*?

I'M SORRY.

HE DIED BEFORE I WAS BORN. CANCER.

BUT MY MOM SAID HE WAS A GOOD GUY.

I SHOULD GO HOME AND SEE IF SHE'S OKAY.

HOME IS THE *FIRST* PLACE THE SUPER-SKRULL'S GOING TO LOOK FOR YOU.

RIGHT, BUT IF MY *MOM* IS THERE, HE'LL--

TEDDY, WE'RE OUT OF OUR *LEAGUE*.

WE NEED TO CALL THE AVENGERS, COME UP WITH A *PLAN*, AND *THEN* WE'LL FIND YOUR--

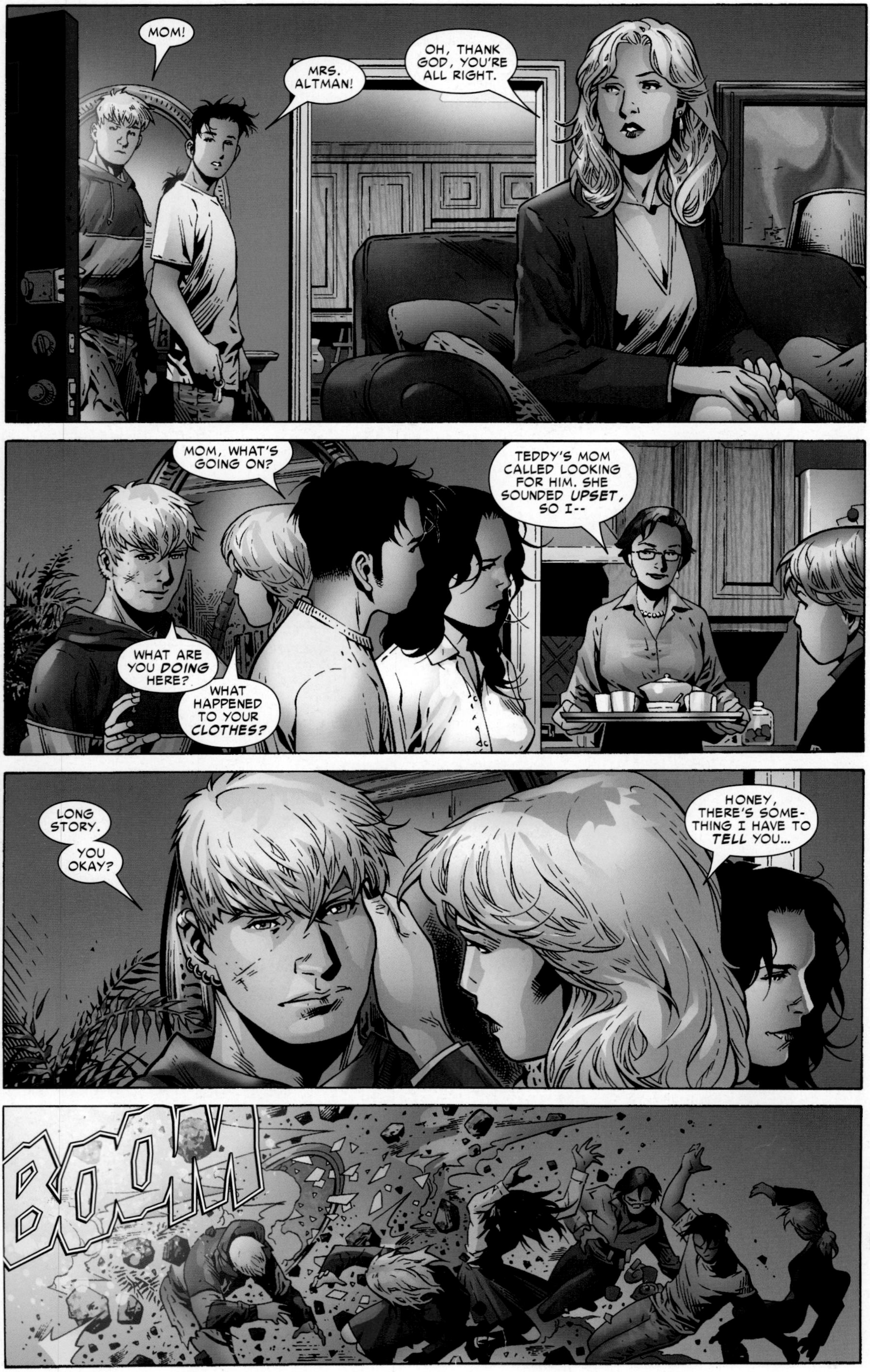
MOM!
MRS. ALTMAN!
OH, THANK GOD, YOU'RE ALL RIGHT.
MOM, WHAT'S GOING ON?
TEDDY'S MOM CALLED LOOKING FOR HIM. SHE SOUNDED UPSET, SO I--
WHAT ARE YOU DOING HERE?
WHAT HAPPENED TO YOUR CLOTHES?
LONG STORY.
YOU OKAY?
HONEY, THERE'S SOME-THING I HAVE TO TELL YOU...
BOOM

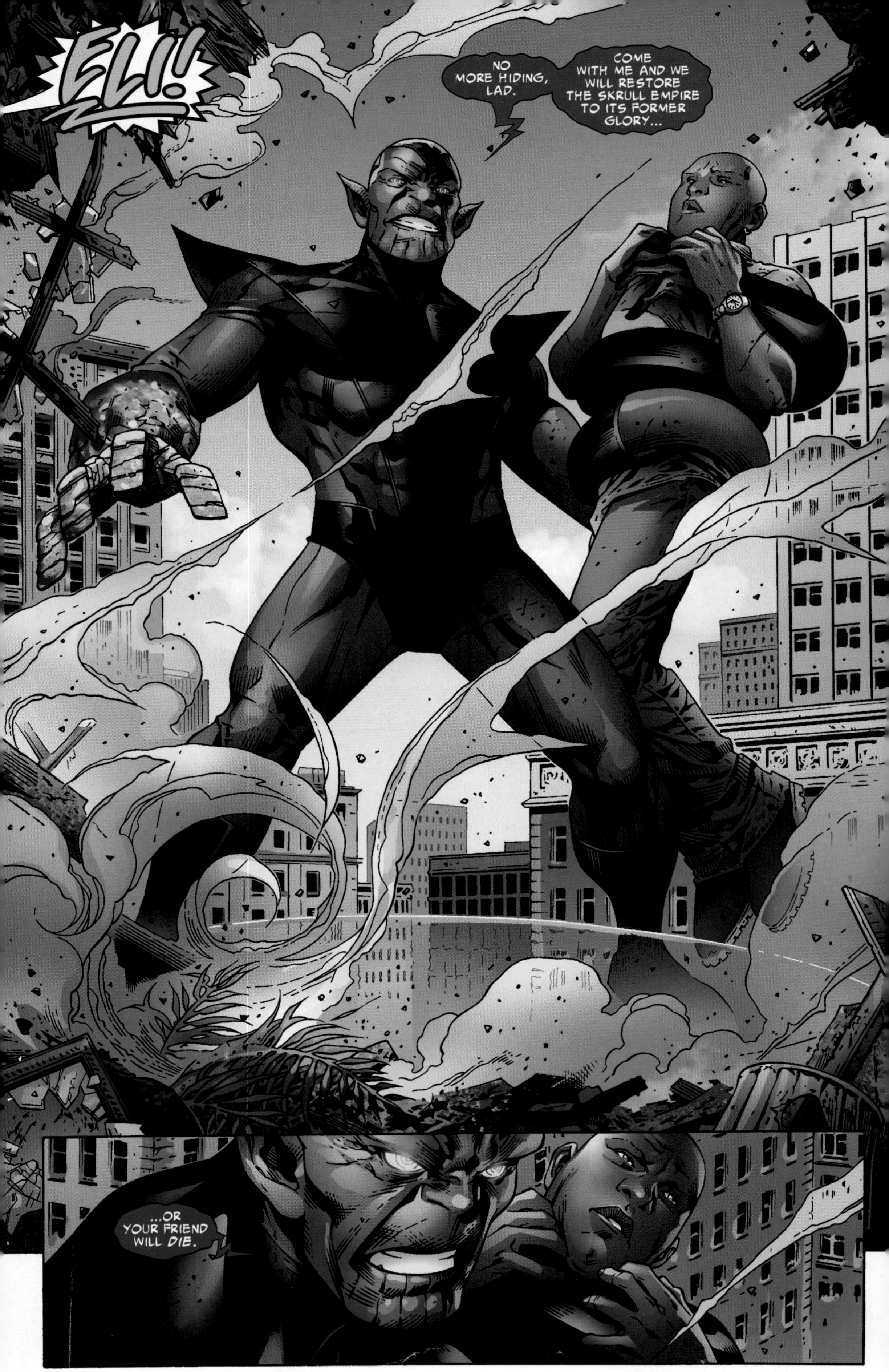
ELI!
NO MORE HIDING, LAD.
COME WITH ME AND WE WILL RESTORE THE SKRULL EMPIRE TO ITS FORMER GLORY...
...OR YOUR FRIEND WILL *DIE*.

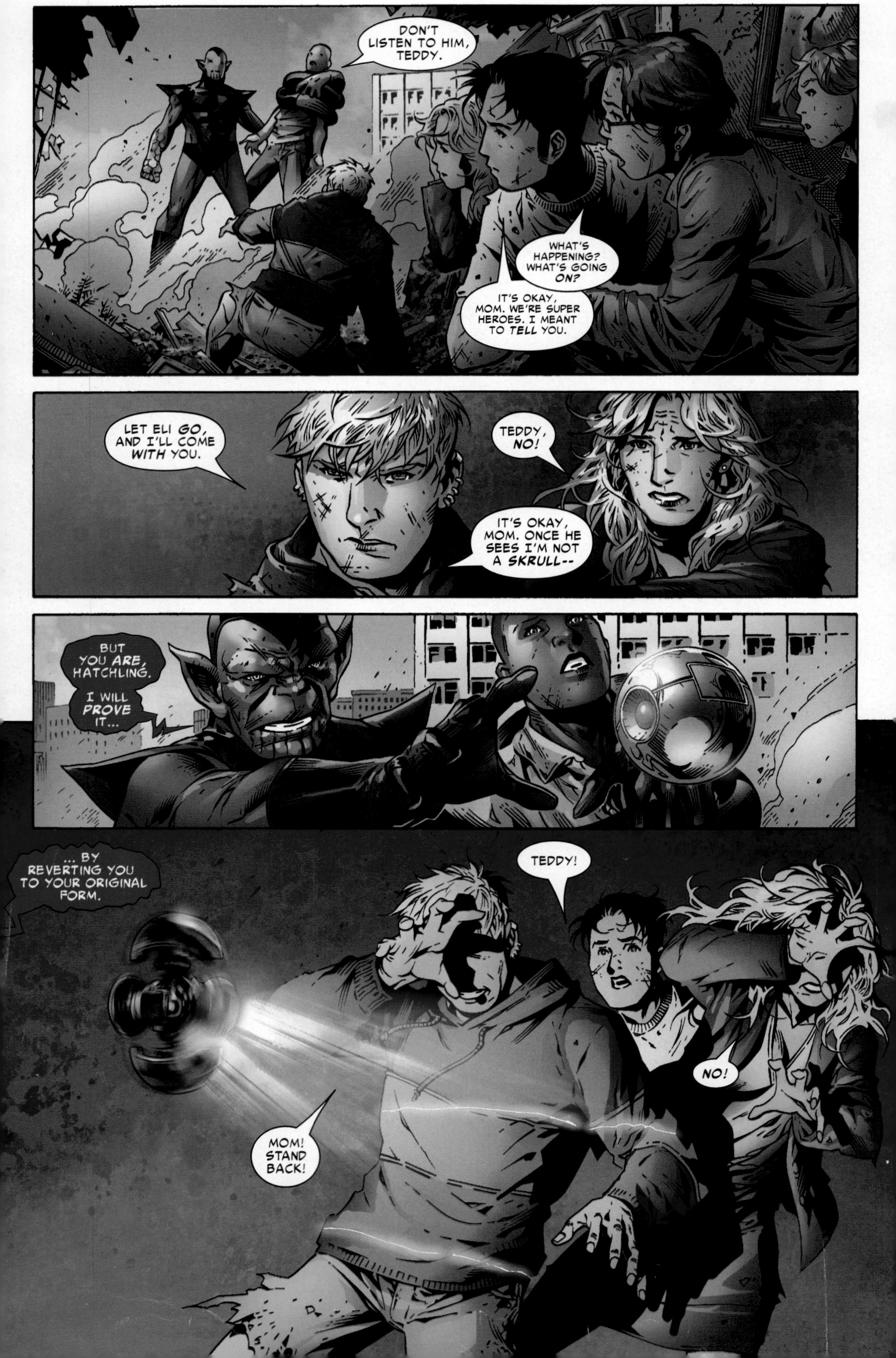
DON'T LISTEN TO HIM, TEDDY.
WHAT'S HAPPENING? WHAT'S GOING ON?
IT'S OKAY, MOM. WE'RE SUPER HEROES. I MEANT TO TELL YOU.
LET ELI GO, AND I'LL COME WITH YOU.
TEDDY, NO!
IT'S OKAY, MOM. ONCE HE SEES I'M NOT A SKRULL--
BUT YOU ARE, HATCHLING.
I WILL PROVE IT...
... BY REVERTING YOU TO YOUR ORIGINAL FORM.
TEDDY!
NO!
MOM! STAND BACK!

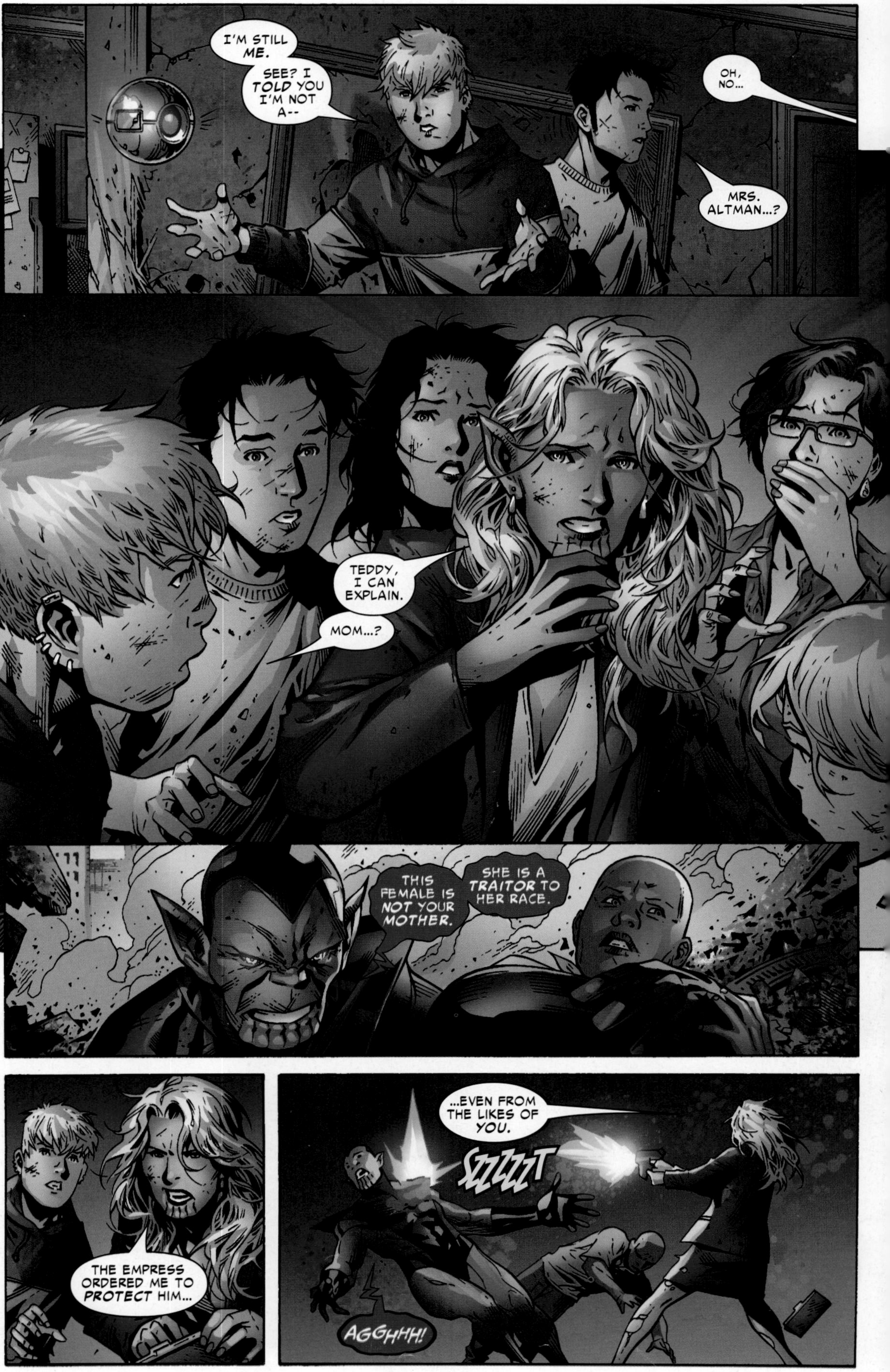
I'M STILL ME.
SEE? I TOLD YOU I'M NOT A--
OH, NO...
MRS. ALTMAN...?
TEDDY, I CAN EXPLAIN.
MOM...?
THIS FEMALE IS NOT YOUR MOTHER.
SHE IS A TRAITOR TO HER RACE.
THE EMPRESS ORDERED ME TO PROTECT HIM...
...EVEN FROM THE LIKES OF YOU.
SZZZZZT
AGGHHH!

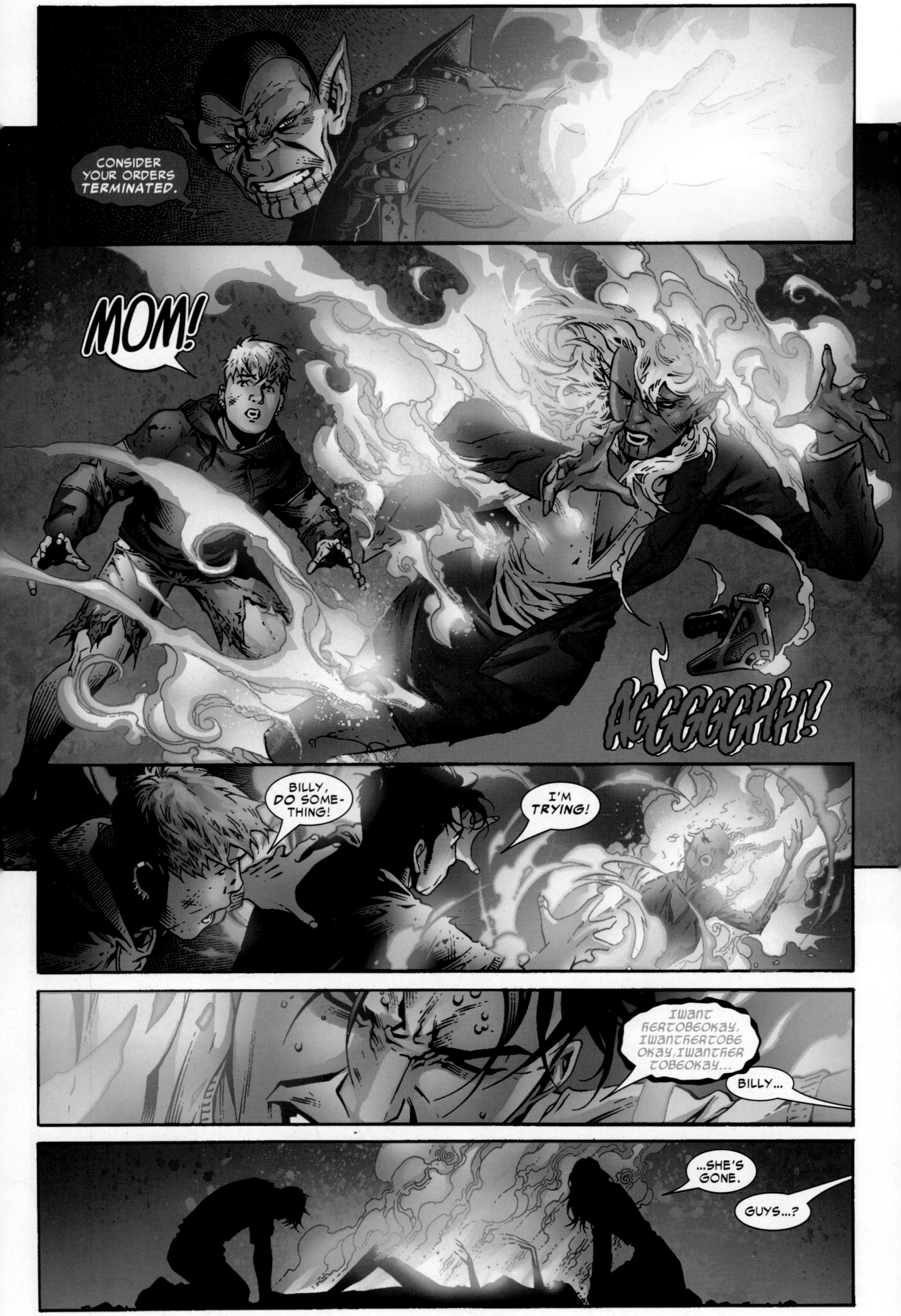

CONSIDER YOUR ORDERS TERMINATED.
MOM!
AGGGGGHH!
BILLY, DO SOME-THING!
I'M TRYING!
IWANT HERTOBEOKAY, IWANTHERTOBE OKAY,IWANTHER TOBEOKAY...
BILLY...
...SHE'S GONE.
GUYS...?

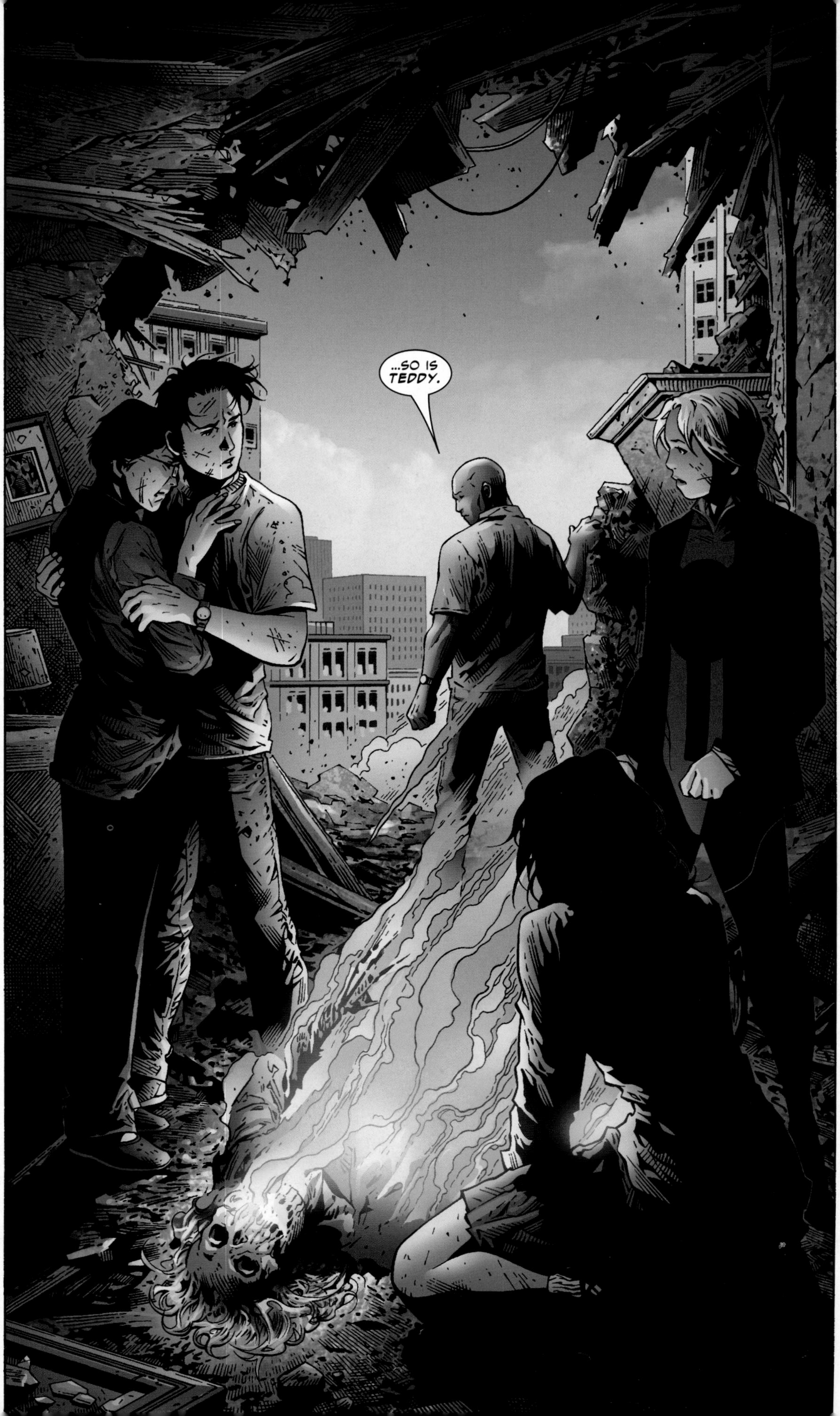
...SO IS TEDDY.

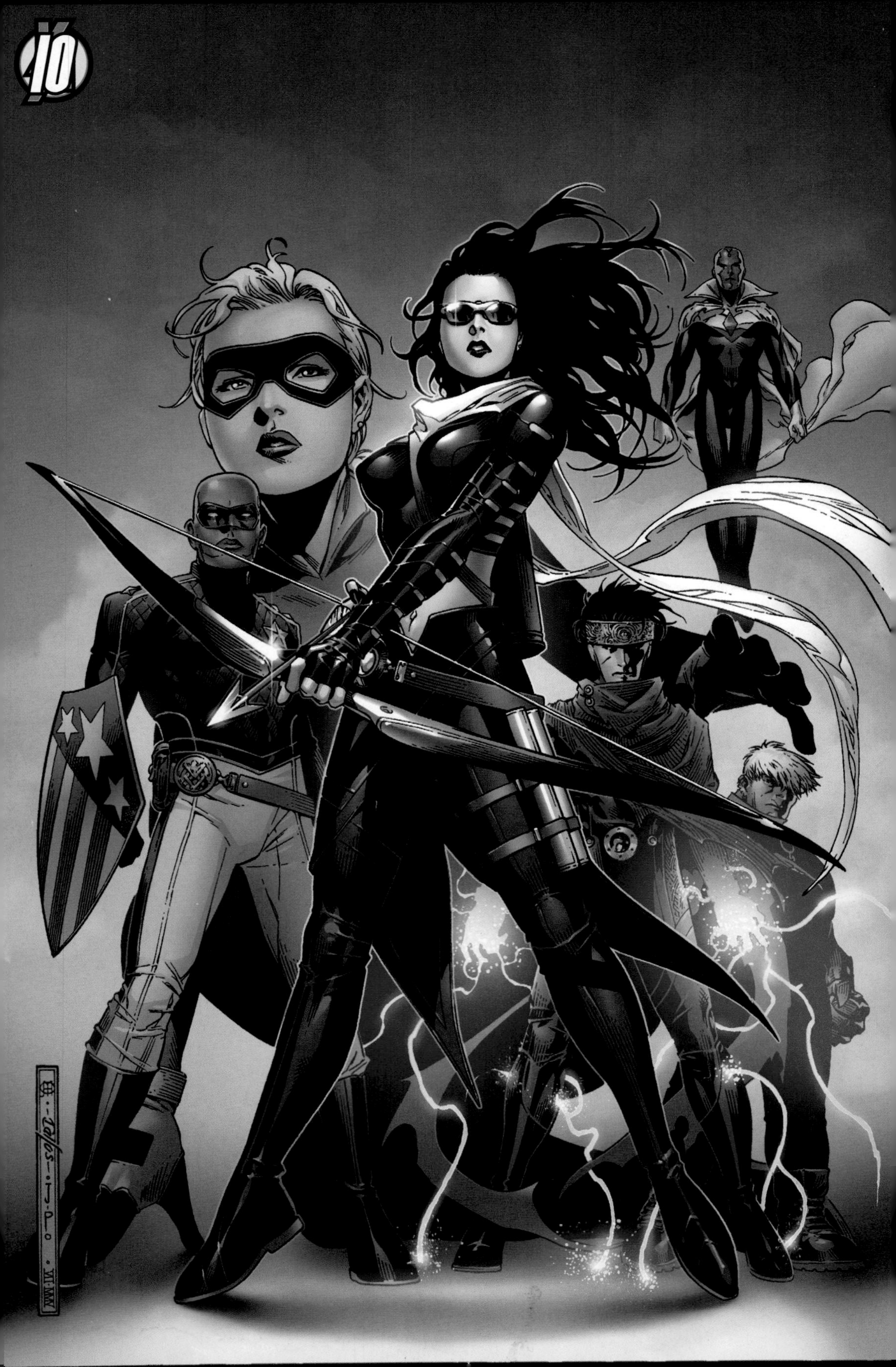

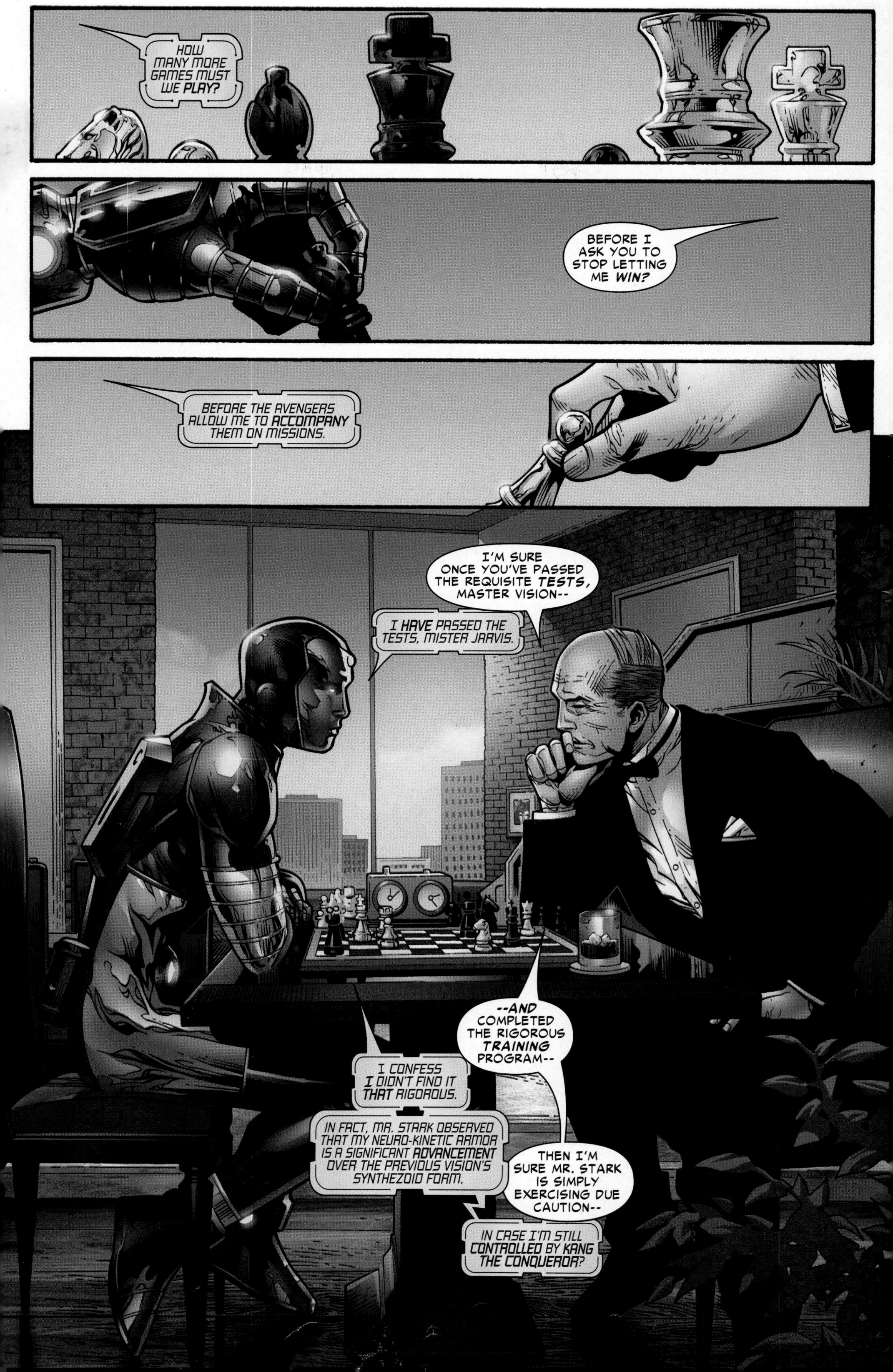
HOW MANY MORE GAMES MUST WE PLAY?
BEFORE I ASK YOU TO STOP LETTING ME WIN?
BEFORE THE AVENGERS ALLOW ME TO ACCOMPANY THEM ON MISSIONS.
I'M SURE ONCE YOU'VE PASSED THE REQUISITE TESTS, MASTER VISION--
I HAVE PASSED THE TESTS, MISTER JARVIS.
--AND COMPLETED THE RIGOROUS TRAINING PROGRAM--
I CONFESS I DIDN'T FIND IT THAT RIGOROUS.
IN FACT, MR. STARK OBSERVED THAT MY NEURO-KINETIC ARMOR IS A SIGNIFICANT ADVANCEMENT OVER THE PREVIOUS VISION'S SYNTHEZOID FORM.
THEN I'M SURE MR. STARK IS SIMPLY EXERCISING DUE CAUTION--
IN CASE I'M STILL CONTROLLED BY KANG THE CONQUEROR?

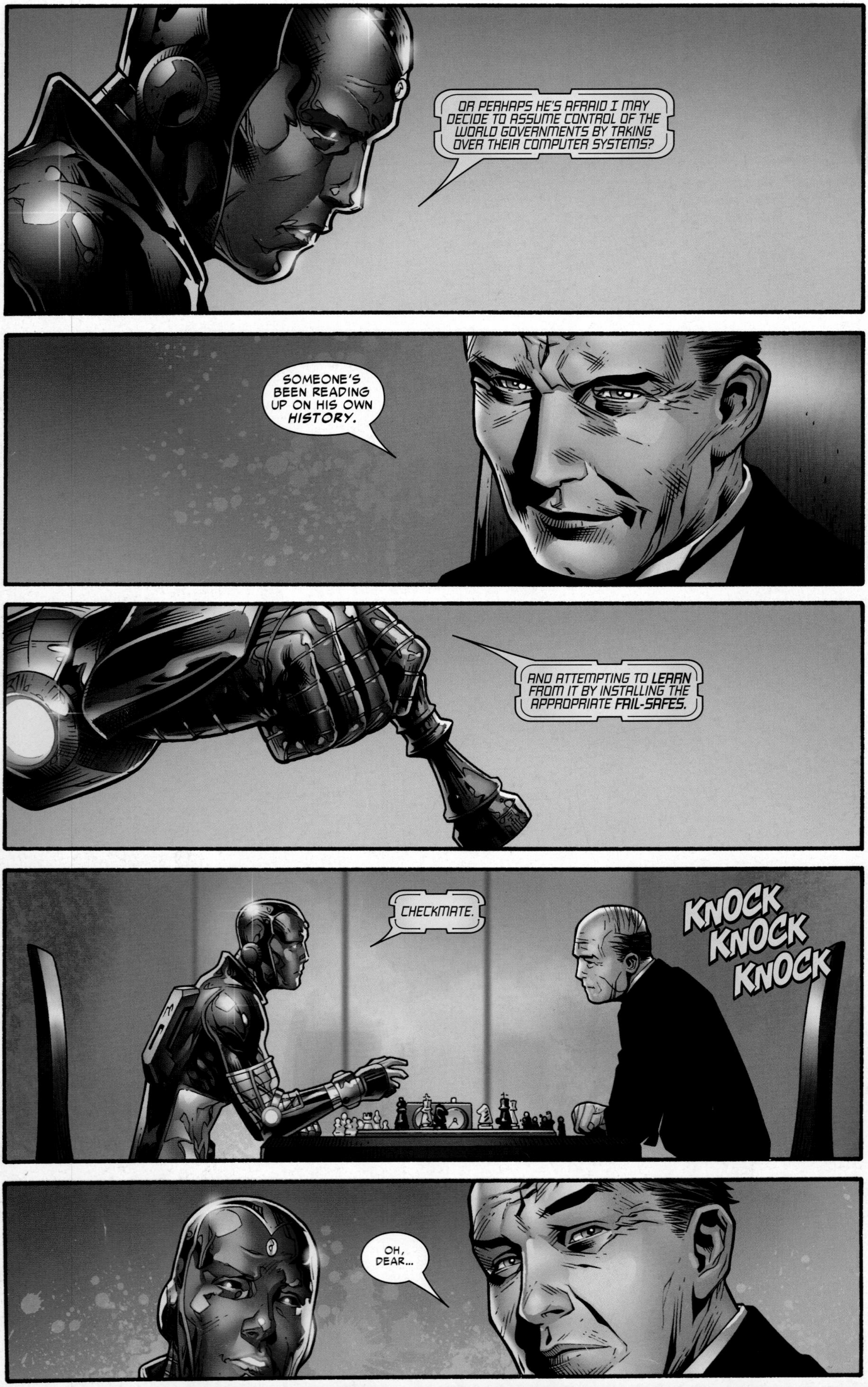
OR PERHAPS HE'S AFRAID I MAY DECIDE TO ASSUME CONTROL OF THE WORLD GOVERNMENTS BY TAKING OVER THEIR COMPUTER SYSTEMS?
SOMEONE'S BEEN READING UP ON HIS OWN HISTORY.
AND ATTEMPTING TO LEARN FROM IT BY INSTALLING THE APPROPRIATE FAIL-SAFES.
CHECKMATE.
KNOCK KNOCK KNOCK
OH, DEAR...

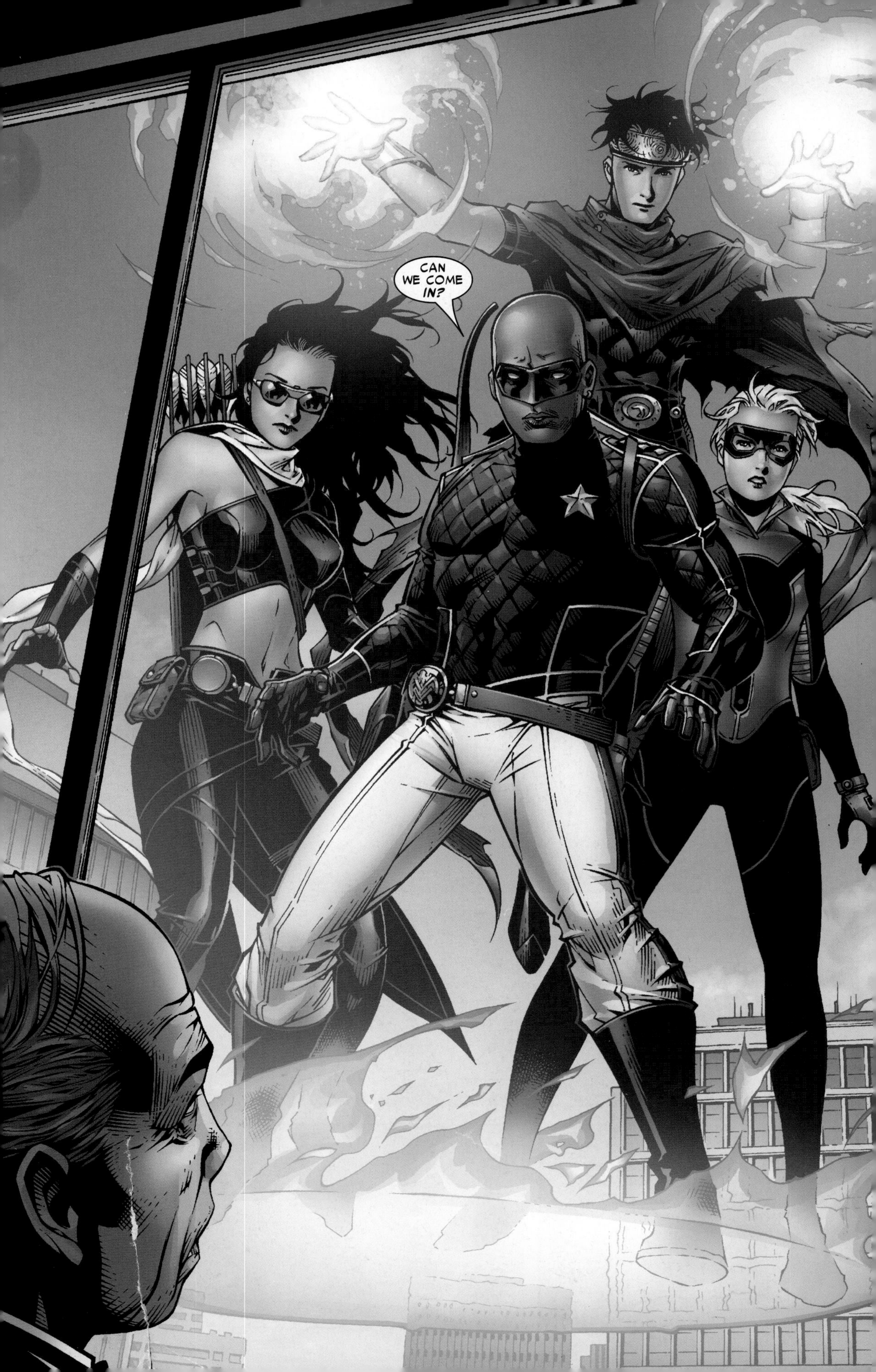
CAN WE COME IN?

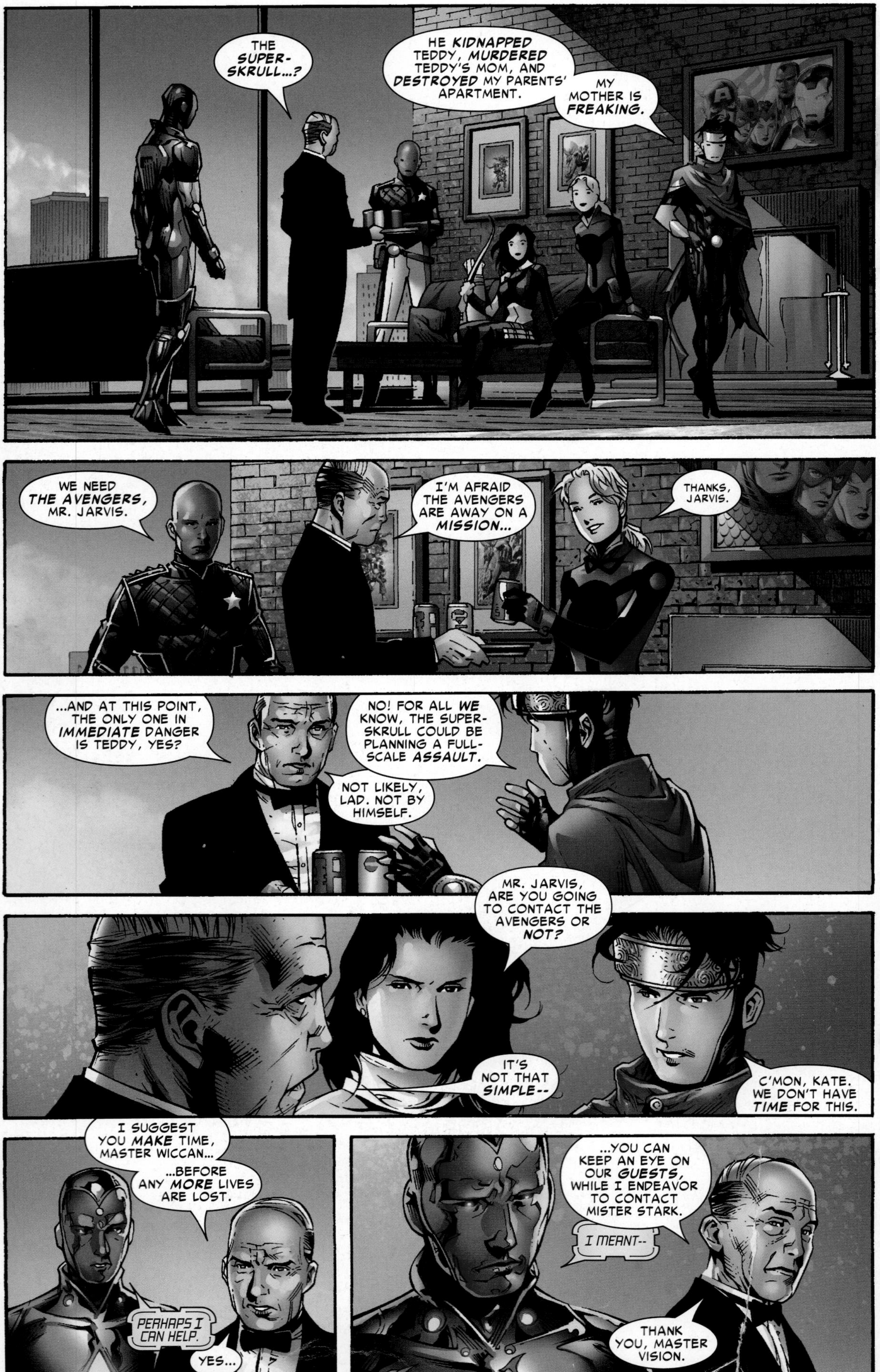
THE SUPER-SKRULL...?
HE KIDNAPPED TEDDY, MURDERED TEDDY'S MOM, AND DESTROYED MY PARENTS' APARTMENT.
MY MOTHER IS FREAKING.
WE NEED THE AVENGERS, MR. JARVIS.
I'M AFRAID THE AVENGERS ARE AWAY ON A MISSION...
THANKS, JARVIS.
...AND AT THIS POINT, THE ONLY ONE IN IMMEDIATE DANGER IS TEDDY, YES?
NO! FOR ALL WE KNOW, THE SUPER-SKRULL COULD BE PLANNING A FULL-SCALE ASSAULT.
NOT LIKELY, LAD. NOT BY HIMSELF.
MR. JARVIS, ARE YOU GOING TO CONTACT THE AVENGERS OR NOT?
IT'S NOT THAT SIMPLE--
C'MON, KATE. WE DON'T HAVE TIME FOR THIS.
I SUGGEST YOU MAKE TIME, MASTER WICCAN...
...BEFORE ANY MORE LIVES ARE LOST.
PERHAPS I CAN HELP.
YES...
...YOU CAN KEEP AN EYE ON OUR GUESTS, WHILE I ENDEAVOR TO CONTACT MISTER STARK.
I MEANT--
THANK YOU, MASTER VISION.

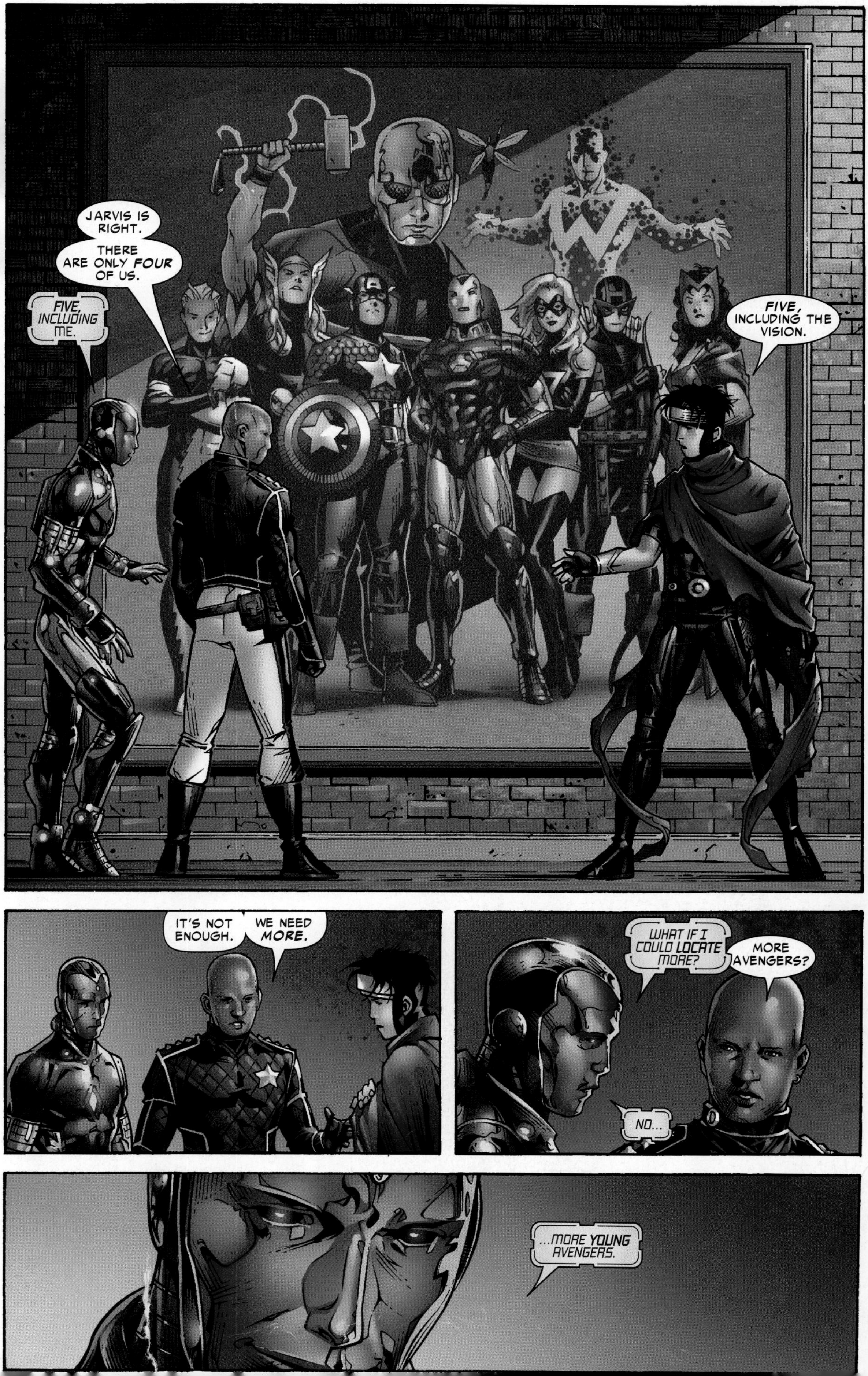
JARVIS IS RIGHT.
THERE ARE ONLY FOUR OF US.
FIVE, INCLUDING ME.
FIVE, INCLUDING THE VISION.
IT'S NOT ENOUGH.
WE NEED MORE.
WHAT IF I COULD LOCATE MORE?
MORE AVENGERS?
NO...
...MORE YOUNG AVENGERS.

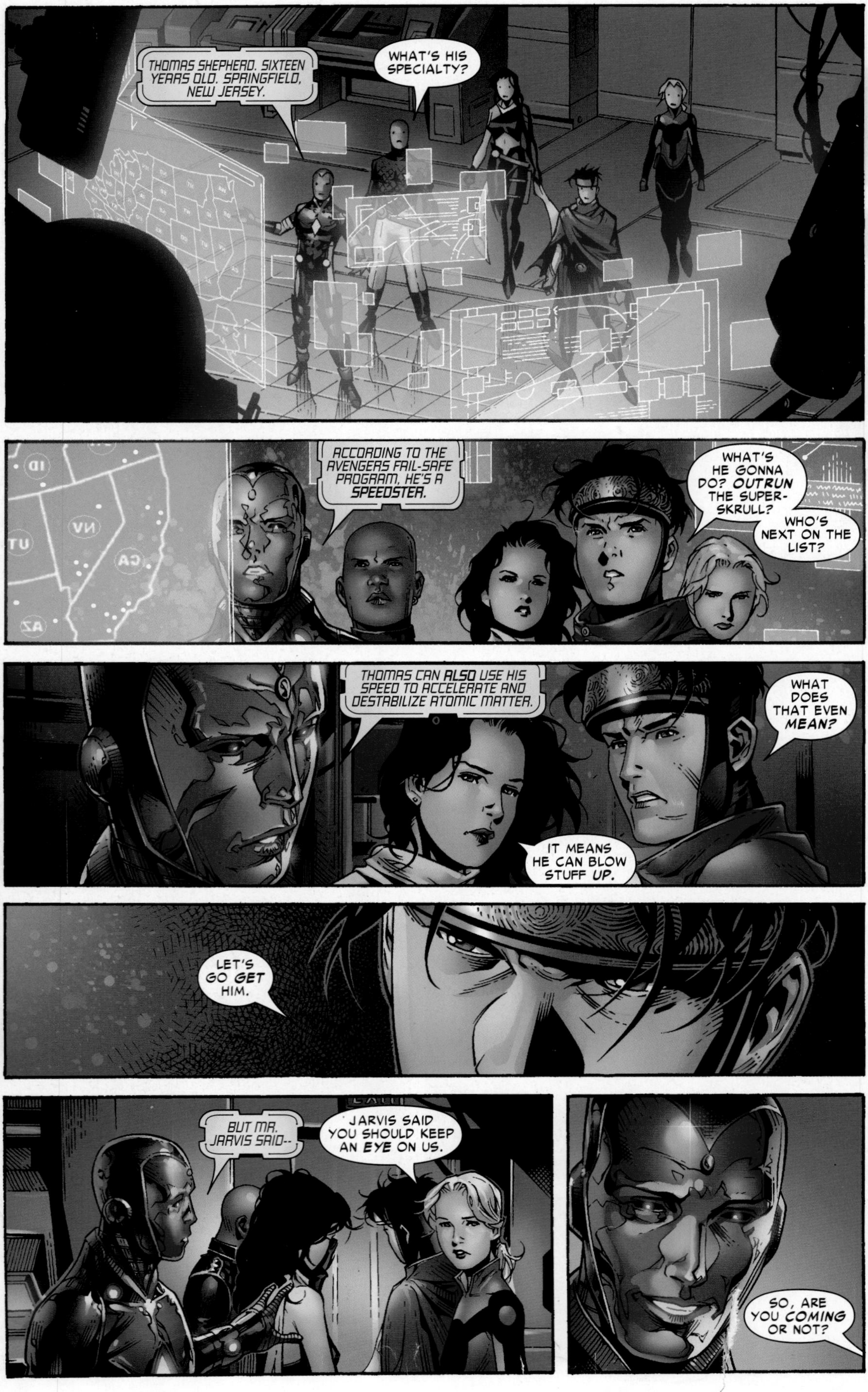
THOMAS SHEPHERD. SIXTEEN YEARS OLD. SPRINGFIELD, NEW JERSEY.
WHAT'S HIS SPECIALTY?
ACCORDING TO THE AVENGERS FAIL-SAFE PROGRAM, HE'S A SPEEDSTER.
WHAT'S HE GONNA DO? OUTRUN THE SUPER-SKRULL?
WHO'S NEXT ON THE LIST?
THOMAS CAN ALSO USE HIS SPEED TO ACCELERATE AND DESTABILIZE ATOMIC MATTER.
WHAT DOES THAT EVEN MEAN?
IT MEANS HE CAN BLOW STUFF UP.
LET'S GO GET HIM.
BUT MR. JARVIS SAID--
JARVIS SAID YOU SHOULD KEEP AN EYE ON US.
SO, ARE YOU COMING OR NOT?

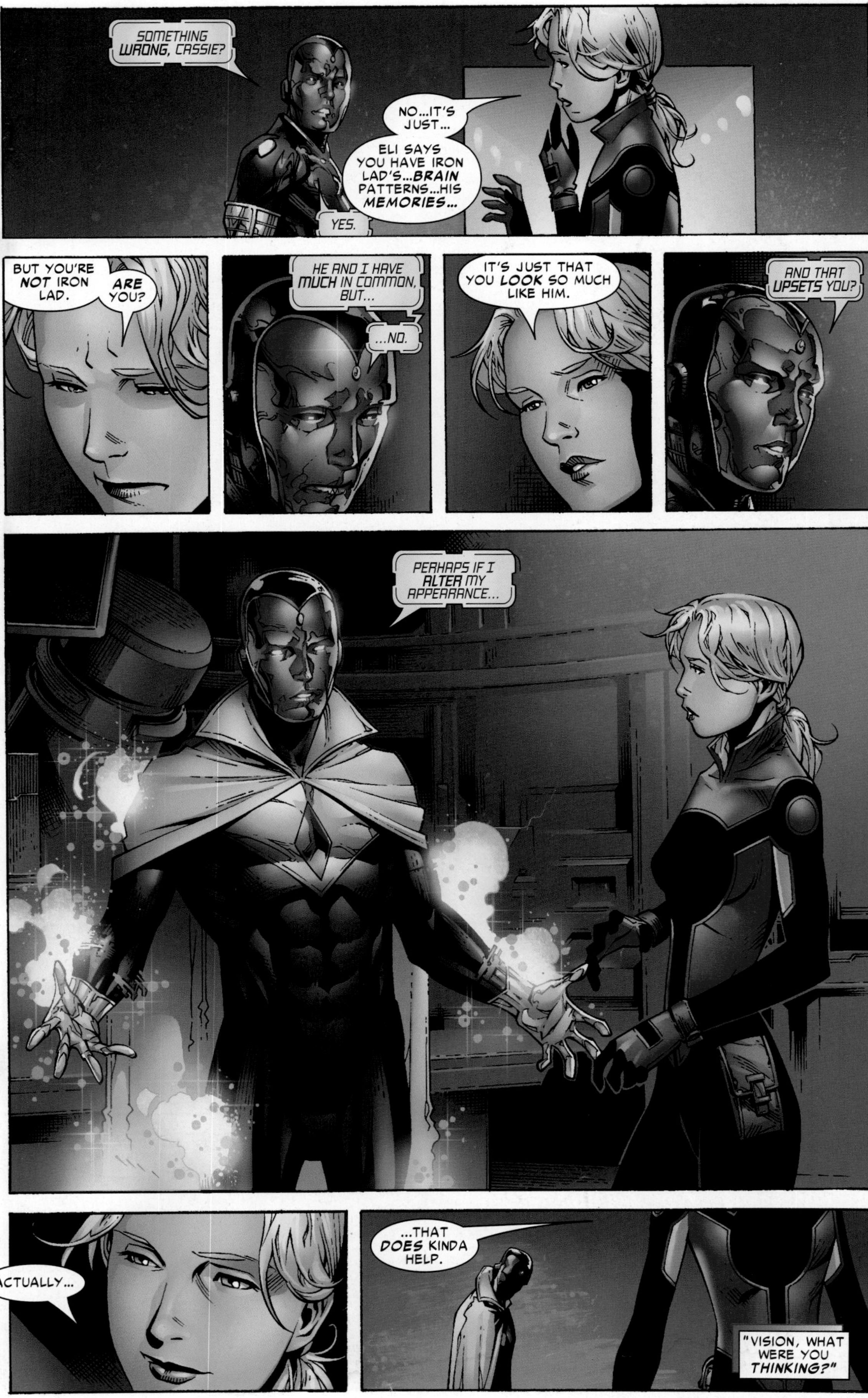
SOMETHING WRONG, CASSIE?
NO...IT'S JUST...
ELI SAYS YOU HAVE IRON LAD'S...BRAIN PATTERNS...HIS MEMORIES...
YES.
BUT YOU'RE NOT IRON LAD.
ARE YOU?
HE AND I HAVE MUCH IN COMMON, BUT...
...NO.
IT'S JUST THAT YOU LOOK SO MUCH LIKE HIM.
AND THAT UPSETS YOU?
PERHAPS IF I ALTER MY APPEARANCE...
ACTUALLY...
...THAT DOES KINDA HELP.
"VISION, WHAT WERE YOU THINKING?"

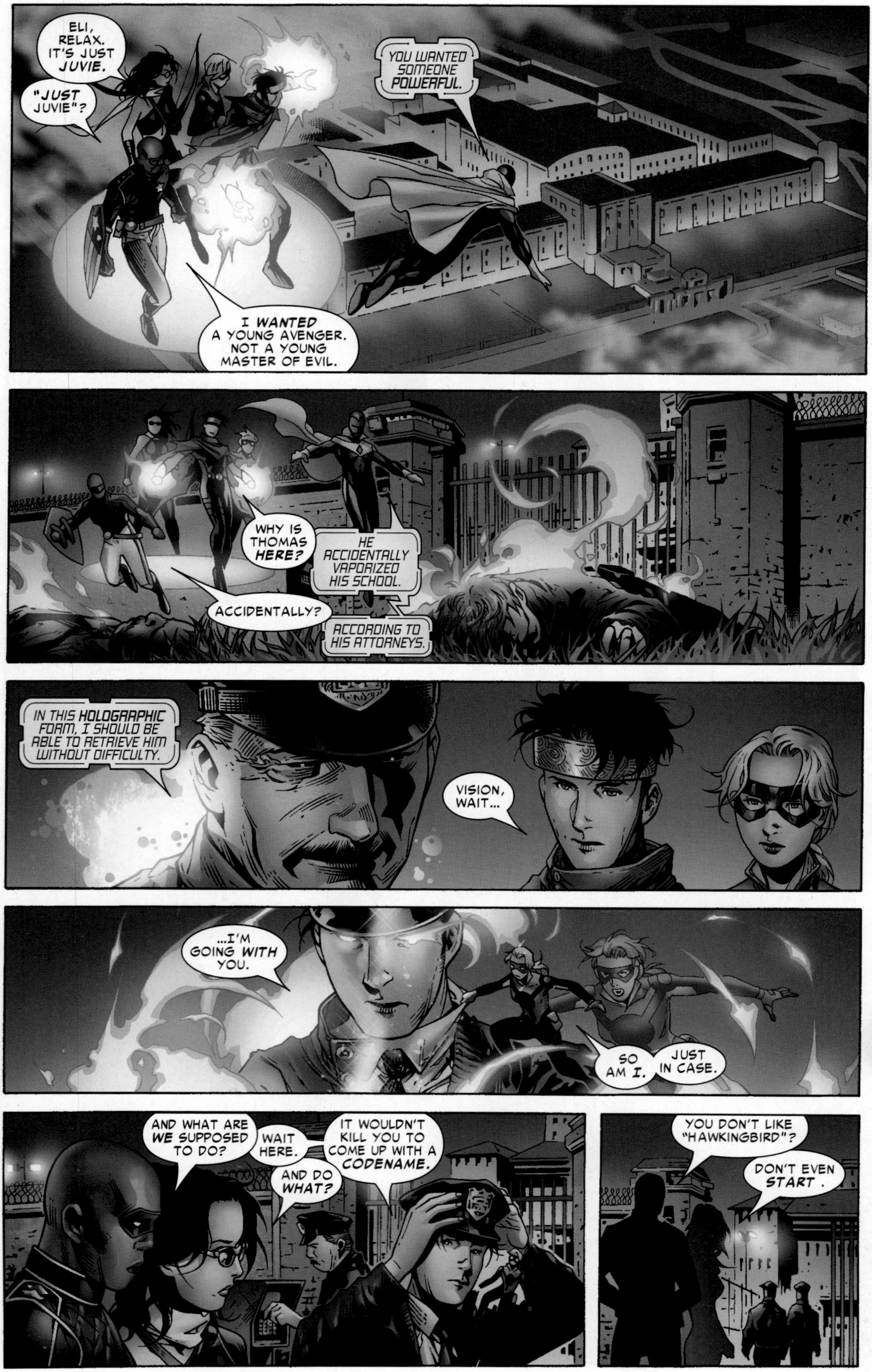
ELI, RELAX. IT'S JUST JUVIE.
"JUST JUVIE"?
YOU WANTED SOMEONE POWERFUL.
I WANTED A YOUNG AVENGER. NOT A YOUNG MASTER OF EVIL.
WHY IS THOMAS HERE?
HE ACCIDENTALLY VAPORIZED HIS SCHOOL.
ACCIDENTALLY?
ACCORDING TO HIS ATTORNEYS.
IN THIS HOLOGRAPHIC FORM, I SHOULD BE ABLE TO RETRIEVE HIM WITHOUT DIFFICULTY.
VISION, WAIT...
...I'M GOING WITH YOU.
SO AM I.
JUST IN CASE.
AND WHAT ARE WE SUPPOSED TO DO?
WAIT HERE.
AND DO WHAT?
IT WOULDN'T KILL YOU TO COME UP WITH A CODENAME.
YOU DON'T LIKE "HAWKINGBIRD"?
DON'T EVEN START .

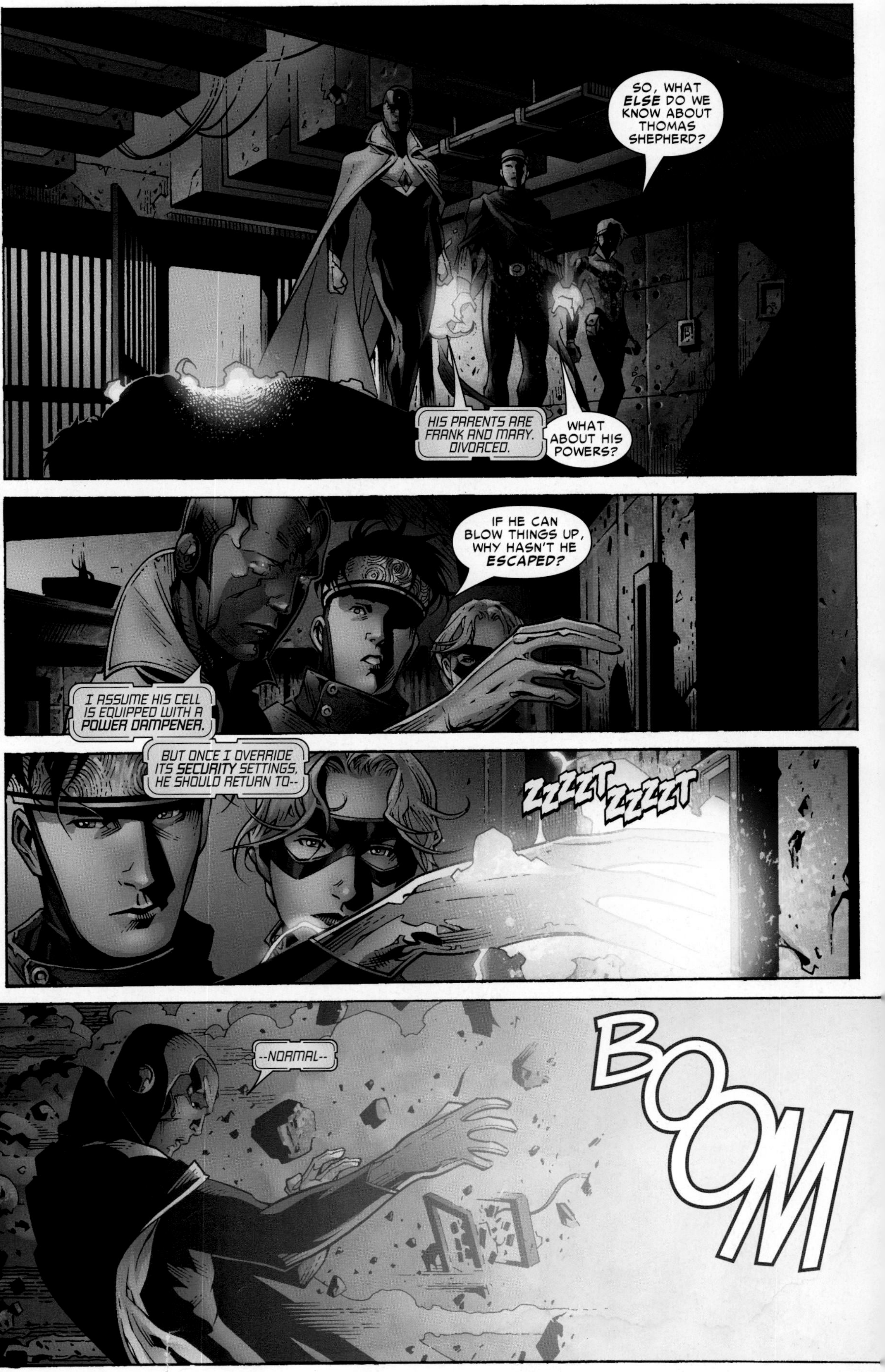
SO, WHAT ELSE DO WE KNOW ABOUT THOMAS SHEPHERD?
HIS PARENTS ARE FRANK AND MARY. DIVORCED.
WHAT ABOUT HIS POWERS?
IF HE CAN BLOW THINGS UP, WHY HASN'T HE ESCAPED?
I ASSUME HIS CELL IS EQUIPPED WITH A POWER DAMPENER.
BUT ONCE I OVERRIDE ITS SECURITY SETTINGS, HE SHOULD RETURN TO--
ZZZZT ZZZZT
--NORMAL--
BOOM

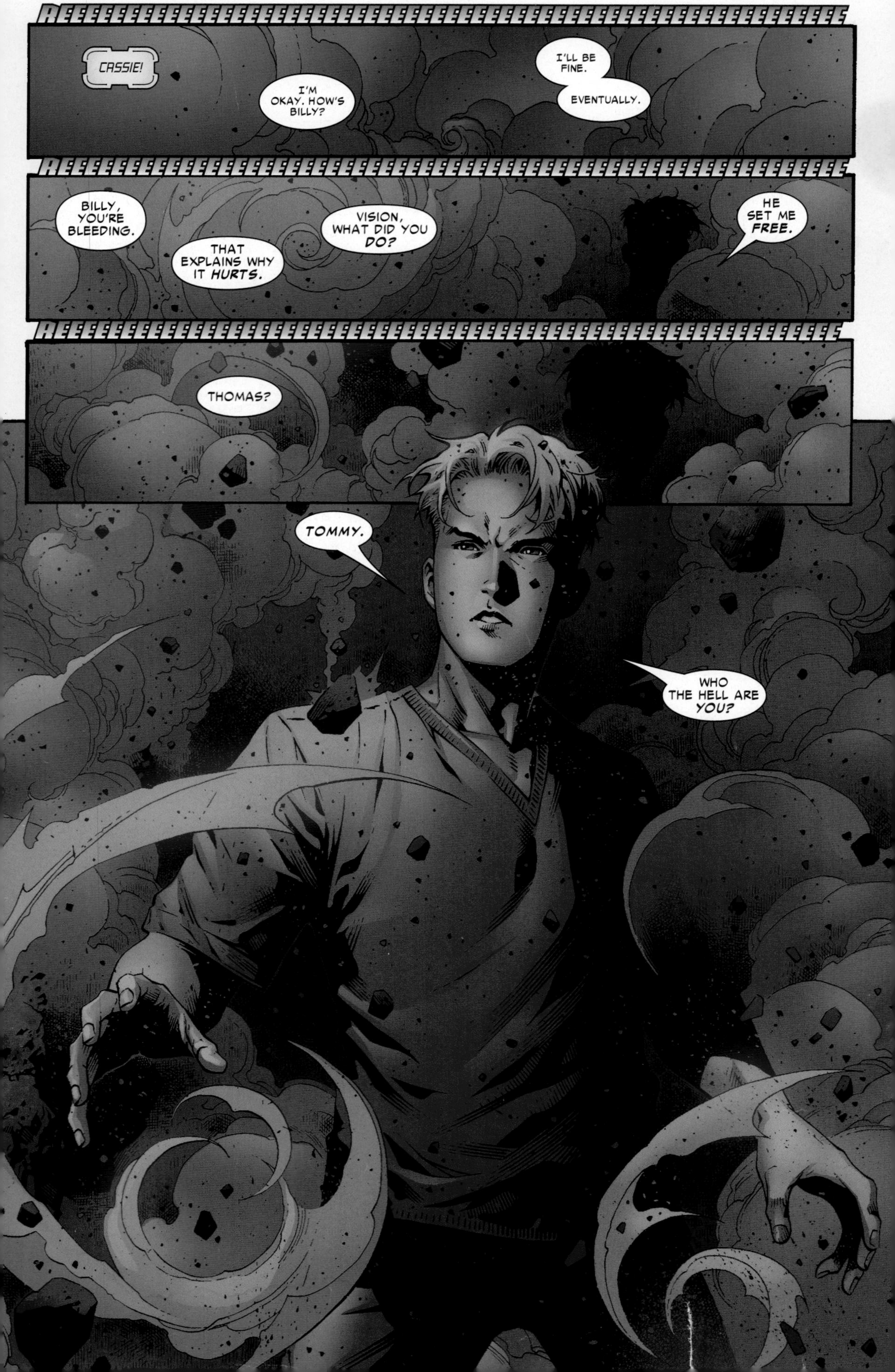
REEEEEEEEEEEEEEEEEEEEEEEEEEEEEEEEEEEEEEEEEEEEEEEEEEEEE
CASSIE!
I'M OKAY. HOW'S BILLY?
I'LL BE FINE.
EVENTUALLY.
REEEEEEEEEEEEEEEEEEEEEEEEEEEEEEEEEEEEEEEEEEEEEEEEEEEEE
BILLY, YOU'RE BLEEDING.
THAT EXPLAINS WHY IT HURTS.
VISION, WHAT DID YOU DO?
HE SET ME FREE.
REEEEEEEEEEEEEEEEEEEEEEEEEEEEEEEEEEEEEEEEEEEEEEEEEEEEE
THOMAS?
TOMMY.
WHO THE HELL ARE YOU?

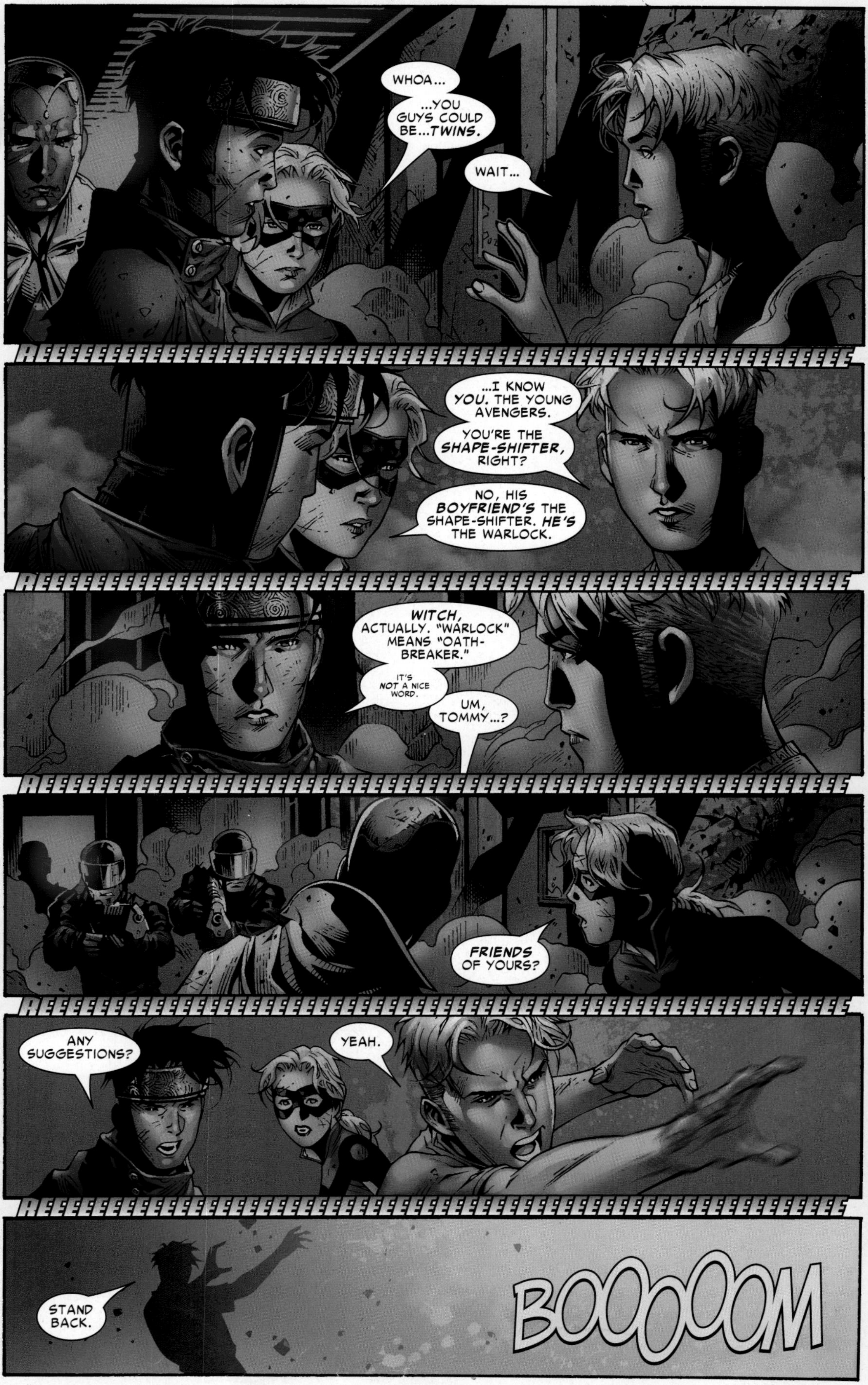
WHOA...
...YOU GUYS COULD BE...TWINS.
WAIT...
REEEEEEEEEEEEEEEEEEEEEEEEEEEEEEEEEEEEEEEEEEEEEEEEEEEEEE
...I KNOW YOU. THE YOUNG AVENGERS.
YOU'RE THE SHAPE-SHIFTER, RIGHT?
NO, HIS BOYFRIEND'S THE SHAPE-SHIFTER. HE'S THE WARLOCK.
WITCH, ACTUALLY. "WARLOCK" MEANS "OATH-BREAKER."
IT'S NOT A NICE WORD.
UM, TOMMY...?
FRIENDS OF YOURS?
ANY SUGGESTIONS?
YEAH.
STAND BACK.
BOOOOOM

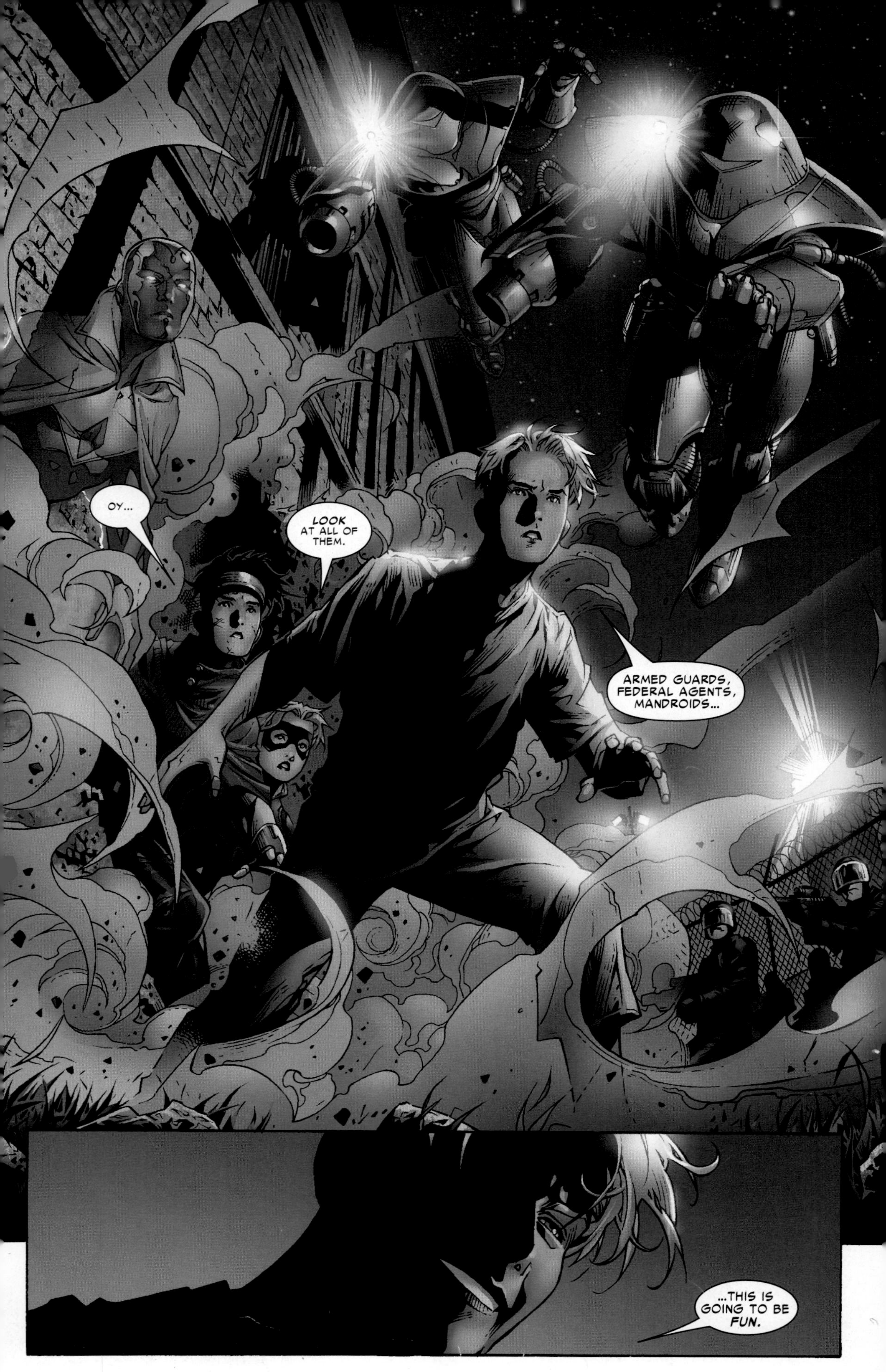
OY...
LOOK AT ALL OF THEM.
ARMED GUARDS, FEDERAL AGENTS, MANDROIDS...
...THIS IS GOING TO BE FUN.

THEY'VE KEPT ME LOCKED UP FOR MONTHS...

...TESTING ME...

...PROBING ME...

...TRYING TO TURN ME INTO A LIVING WEAPON.

WELL, CONGRATULATIONS, OFFICERS...

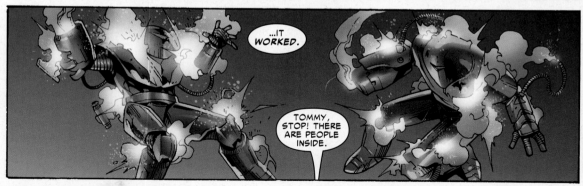

...IT WORKED.

TOMMY, STOP! THERE ARE PEOPLE INSIDE.

I'VE GOT THEM, CASS.

STAY WITH TOMMY...

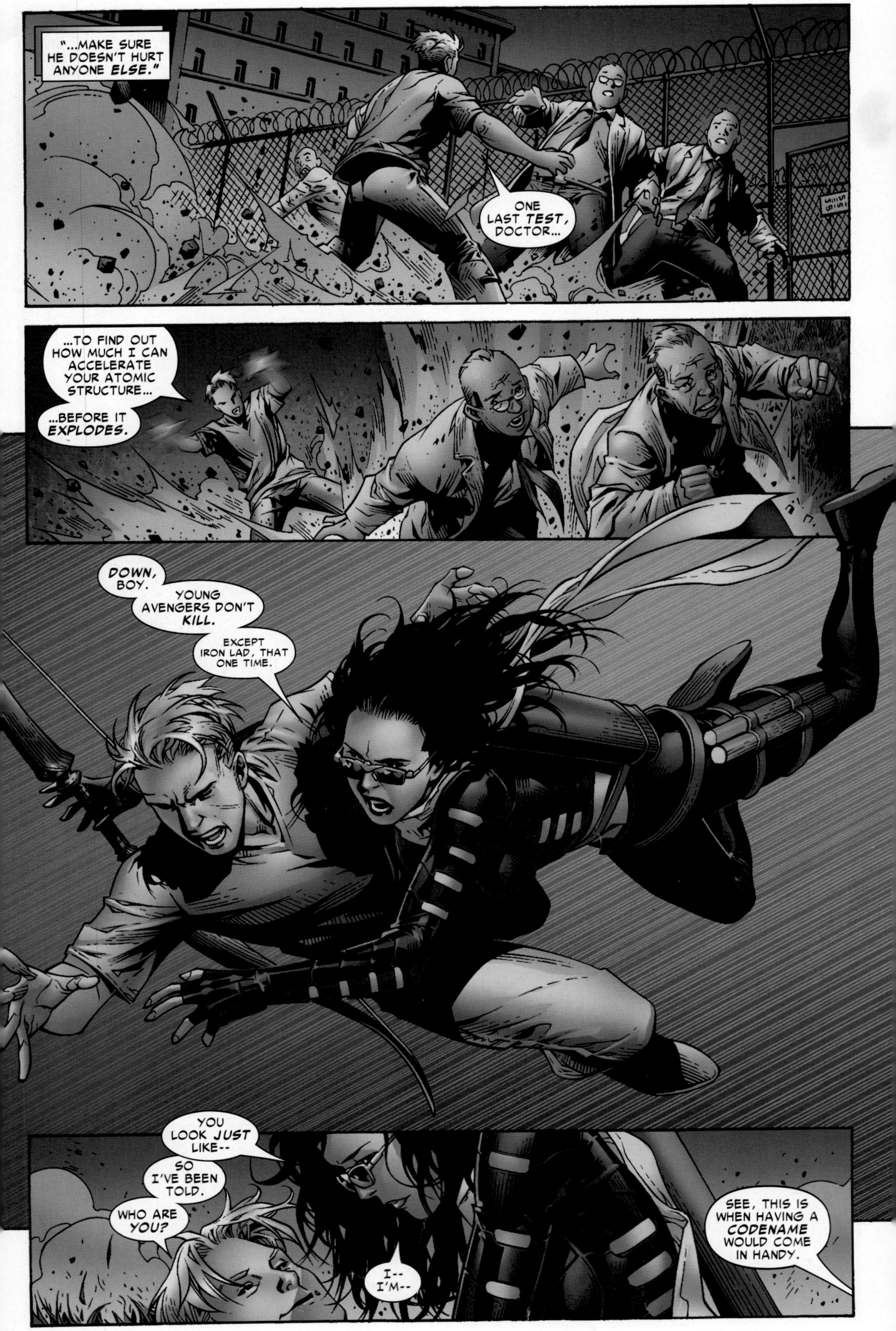
"...MAKE SURE HE DOESN'T HURT ANYONE ELSE."
ONE LAST TEST, DOCTOR...
...TO FIND OUT HOW MUCH I CAN ACCELERATE YOUR ATOMIC STRUCTURE...
...BEFORE IT EXPLODES.
DOWN, BOY.
YOUNG AVENGERS DON'T KILL.
EXCEPT IRON LAD, THAT ONE TIME.
YOU LOOK JUST LIKE--
SO I'VE BEEN TOLD.
WHO ARE YOU?
I-- I'M--
SEE, THIS IS WHEN HAVING A CODENAME WOULD COME IN HANDY.

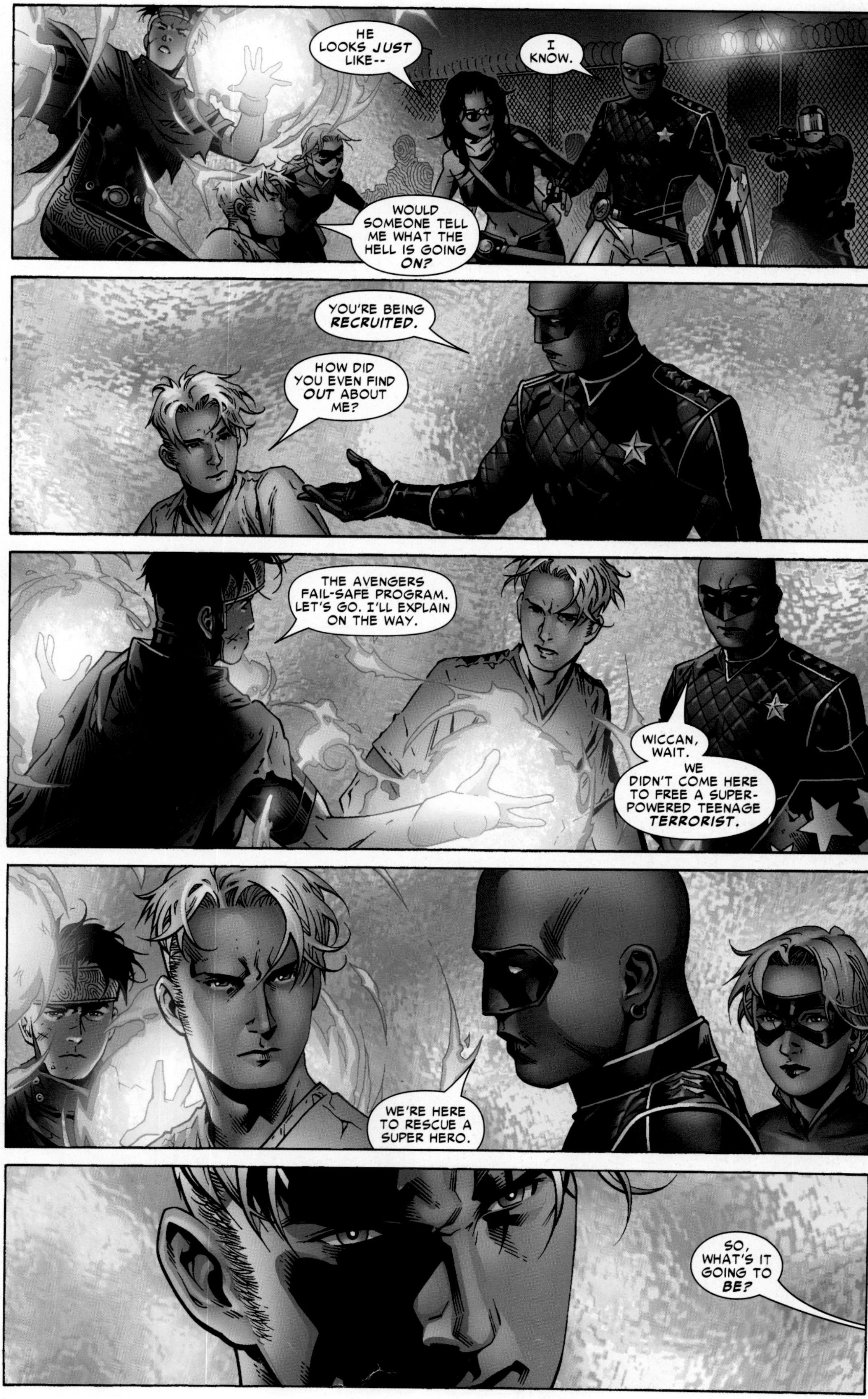
HE LOOKS JUST LIKE--
I KNOW.
WOULD SOMEONE TELL ME WHAT THE HELL IS GOING ON?
YOU'RE BEING RECRUITED.
HOW DID YOU EVEN FIND OUT ABOUT ME?
THE AVENGERS FAIL-SAFE PROGRAM. LET'S GO. I'LL EXPLAIN ON THE WAY.
WICCAN, WAIT.
WE DIDN'T COME HERE TO FREE A SUPER-POWERED TEENAGE TERRORIST.
WE'RE HERE TO RESCUE A SUPER HERO.
SO, WHAT'S IT GOING TO BE?

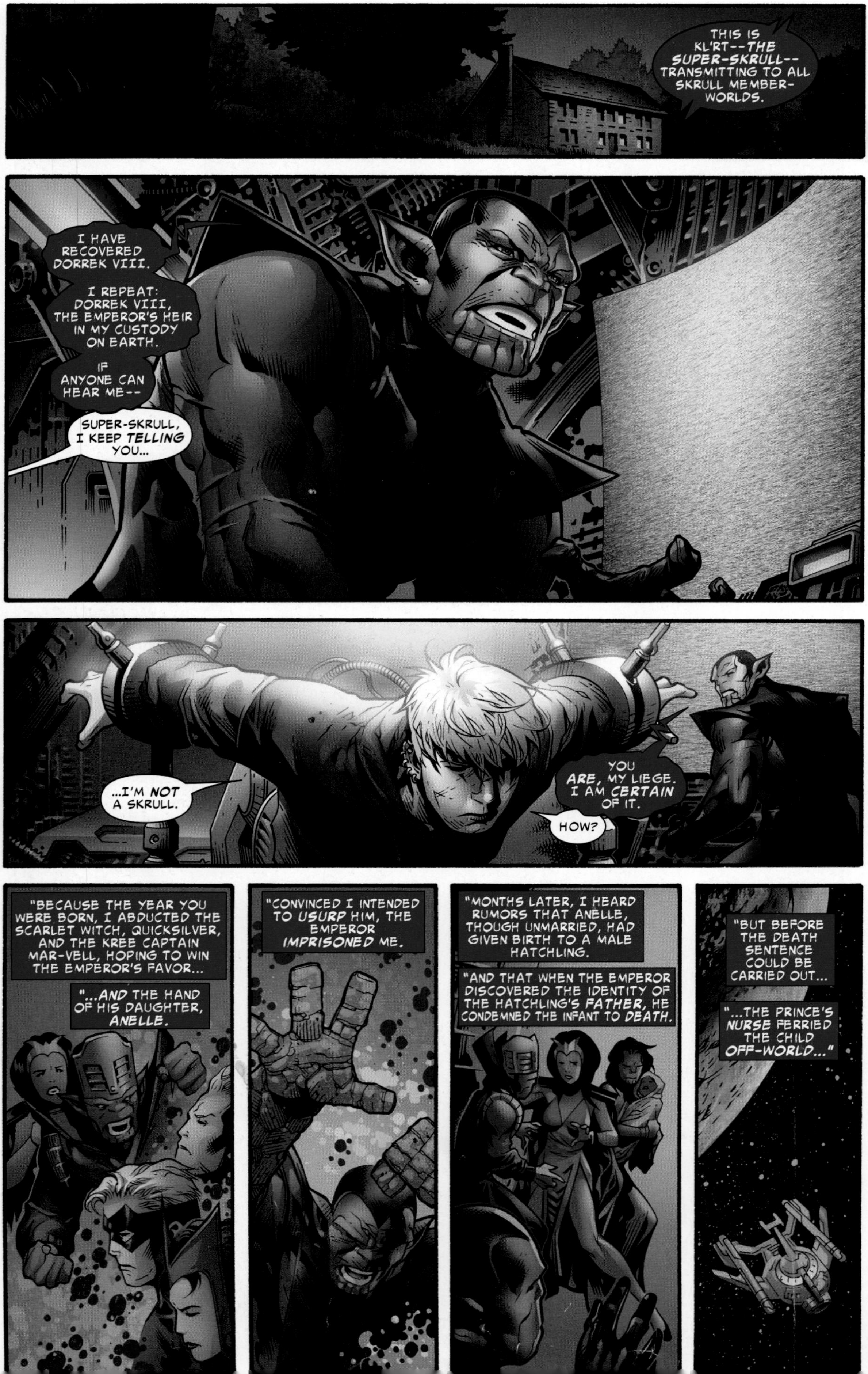
THIS IS KL'RT--*THE SUPER-SKRULL*--TRANSMITTING TO ALL SKRULL MEMBER-WORLDS.
I HAVE RECOVERED DORREK VIII.
I REPEAT: DORREK VIII, THE EMPEROR'S HEIR IN MY CUSTODY ON EARTH.
IF ANYONE CAN HEAR ME--
SUPER-SKRULL, I KEEP *TELLING* YOU...
...I'M *NOT* A SKRULL.
YOU *ARE*, MY LIEGE. I AM *CERTAIN* OF IT.
HOW?
"BECAUSE THE YEAR YOU WERE BORN, I ABDUCTED THE SCARLET WITCH, QUICKSILVER, AND THE KREE CAPTAIN MAR-VELL, HOPING TO WIN THE EMPEROR'S FAVOR...
"...*AND* THE HAND OF HIS DAUGHTER, *ANELLE*.
"CONVINCED I INTENDED TO *USURP* HIM, THE EMPEROR *IMPRISONED* ME.
"MONTHS LATER, I HEARD RUMORS THAT ANELLE, THOUGH UNMARRIED, HAD GIVEN BIRTH TO A MALE HATCHLING.
"AND THAT WHEN THE EMPEROR DISCOVERED THE IDENTITY OF THE HATCHLING'S *FATHER*, HE CONDEMNED THE INFANT TO *DEATH*.
"BUT BEFORE THE DEATH SENTENCE COULD BE CARRIED OUT...
"...THE PRINCE'S *NURSE* FERRIED THE CHILD *OFF-WORLD*..."

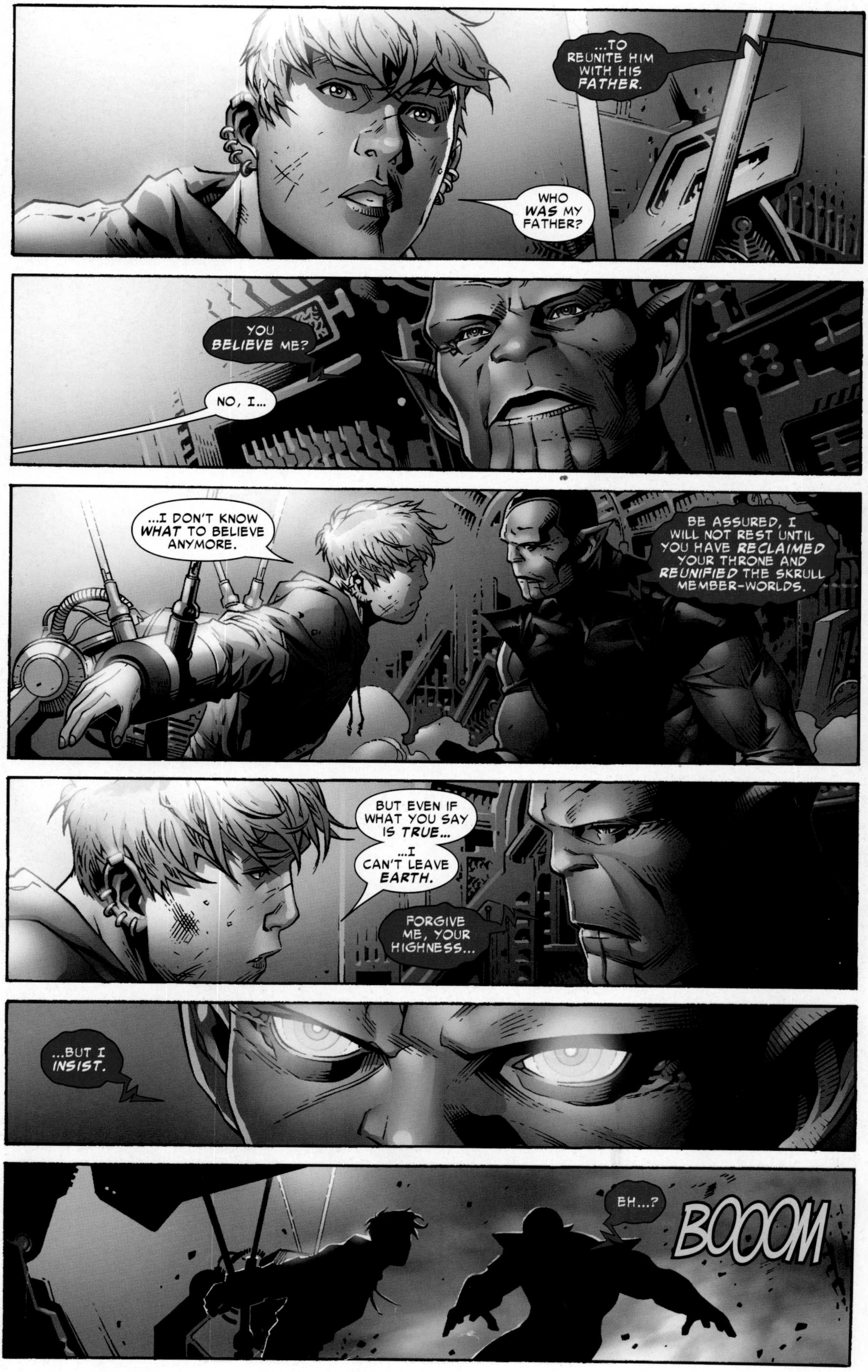
...TO REUNITE HIM WITH HIS FATHER.
WHO WAS MY FATHER?
YOU BELIEVE ME?
NO, I...
...I DON'T KNOW WHAT TO BELIEVE ANYMORE.
BE ASSURED, I WILL NOT REST UNTIL YOU HAVE RECLAIMED YOUR THRONE AND REUNIFIED THE SKRULL MEMBER-WORLDS.
BUT EVEN IF WHAT YOU SAY IS TRUE...
...I CAN'T LEAVE EARTH.
FORGIVE ME, YOUR HIGHNESS...
...BUT I INSIST.
EH...?
BOOOM

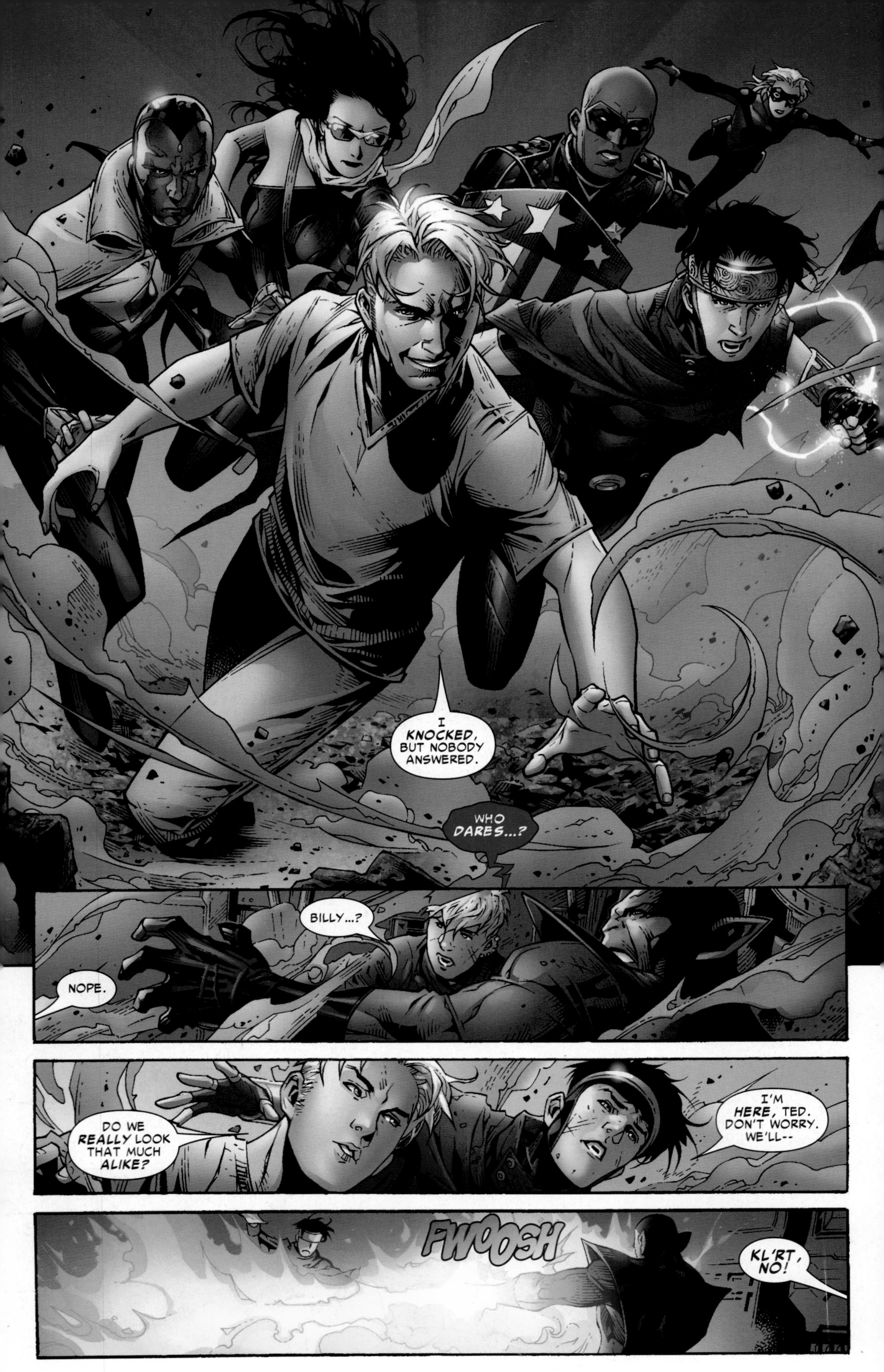

I KNOCKED, BUT NOBODY ANSWERED.
WHO DARES...?
BILLY...?
NOPE.
DO WE REALLY LOOK THAT MUCH ALIKE?
I'M HERE, TED. DON'T WORRY. WE'LL--
FWOOSH
KL'RT, NO!

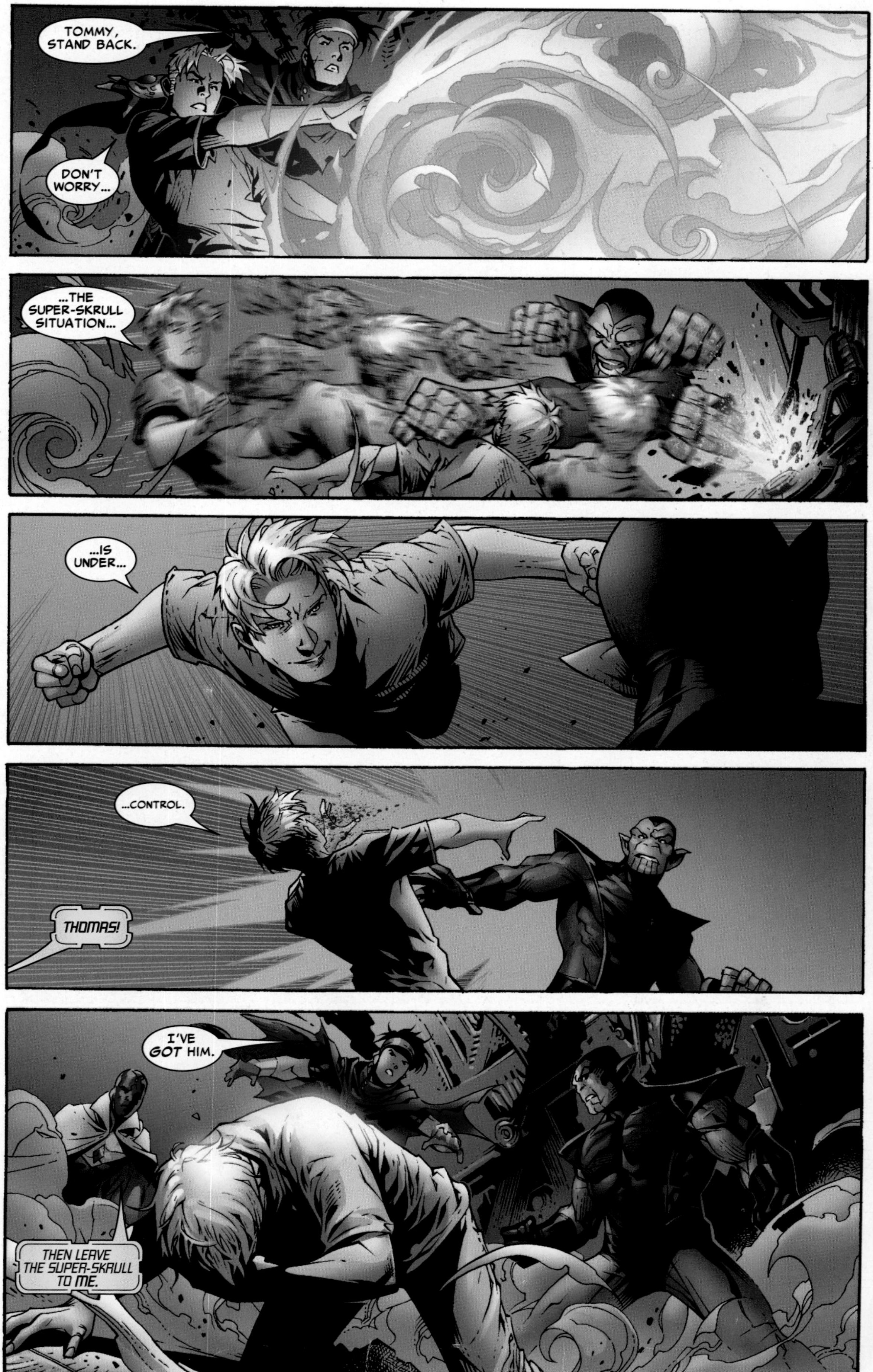
TOMMY, STAND BACK.
DON'T WORRY...
...THE SUPER-SKRULL SITUATION...
...IS UNDER...
...CONTROL.
THOMAS!
I'VE GOT HIM.
THEN LEAVE THE SUPER-SKRULL TO ME.

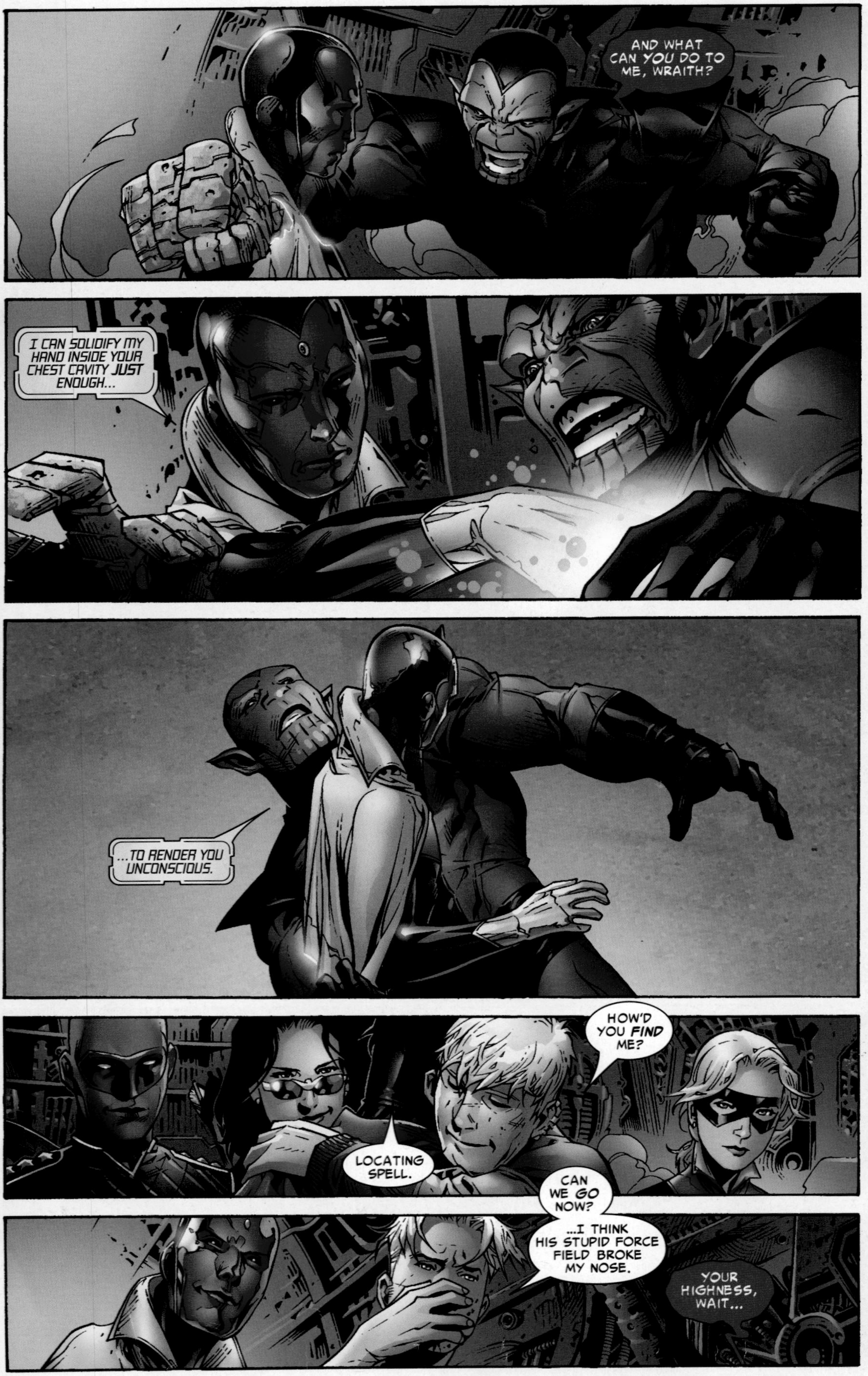
AND WHAT CAN YOU DO TO ME, WRAITH?
I CAN SOLIDIFY MY HAND INSIDE YOUR CHEST CAVITY JUST ENOUGH...
...TO RENDER YOU UNCONSCIOUS.
HOW'D YOU FIND ME?
LOCATING SPELL.
CAN WE GO NOW?
...I THINK HIS STUPID FORCE FIELD BROKE MY NOSE.
YOUR HIGHNESS, WAIT...

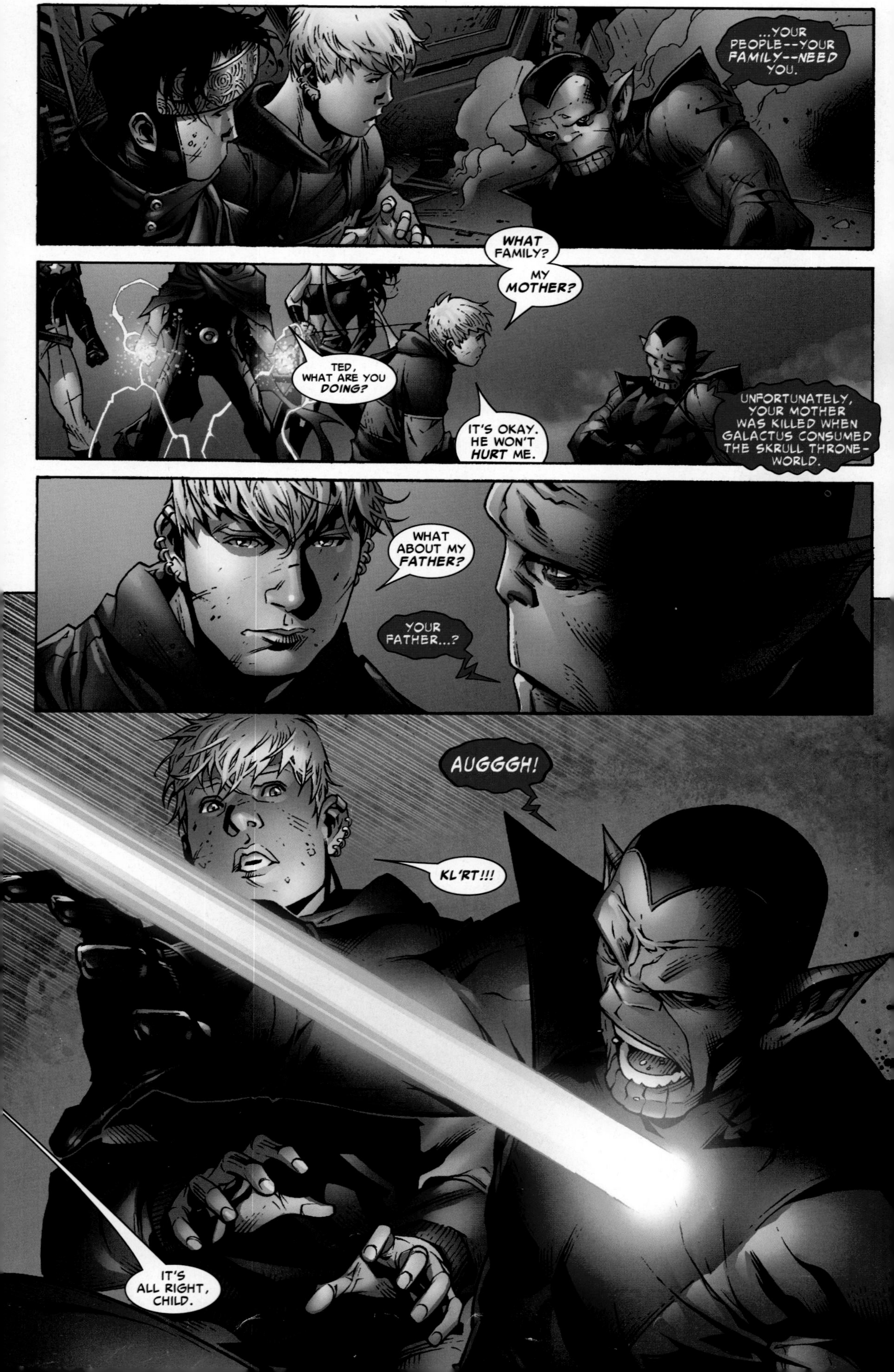
...YOUR PEOPLE--YOUR FAMILY--NEED YOU.
WHAT FAMILY?
MY MOTHER?
TED, WHAT ARE YOU DOING?
IT'S OKAY. HE WON'T HURT ME.
UNFORTUNATELY, YOUR MOTHER WAS KILLED WHEN GALACTUS CONSUMED THE SKRULL THRONE-WORLD.
WHAT ABOUT MY FATHER?
YOUR FATHER...?
AUGGGH!
KL'RT!!!
IT'S ALL RIGHT, CHILD.

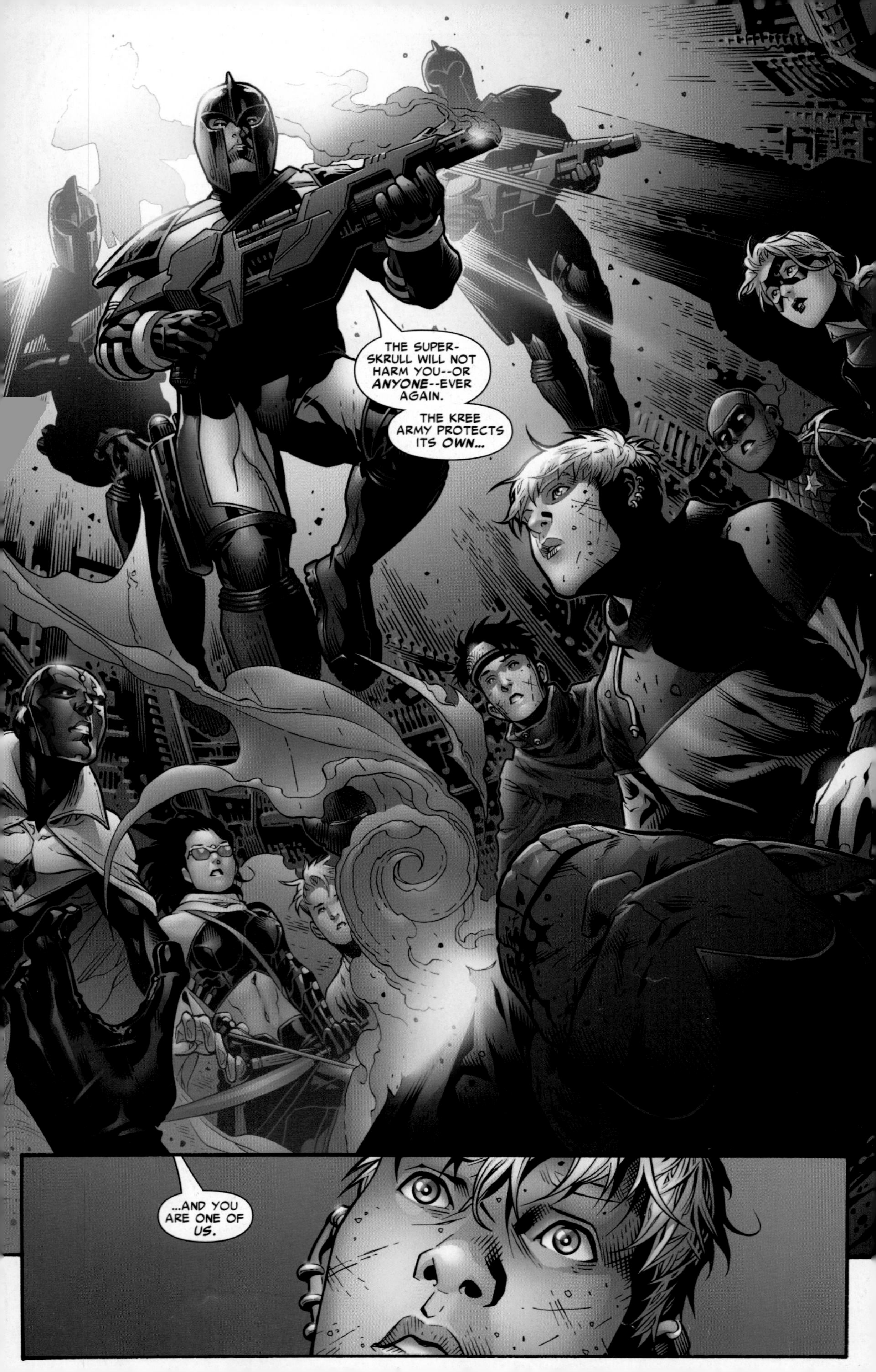
THE SUPER-SKRULL WILL NOT HARM YOU--OR ANYONE--EVER AGAIN.
THE KREE ARMY PROTECTS ITS OWN...
...AND YOU ARE ONE OF US.

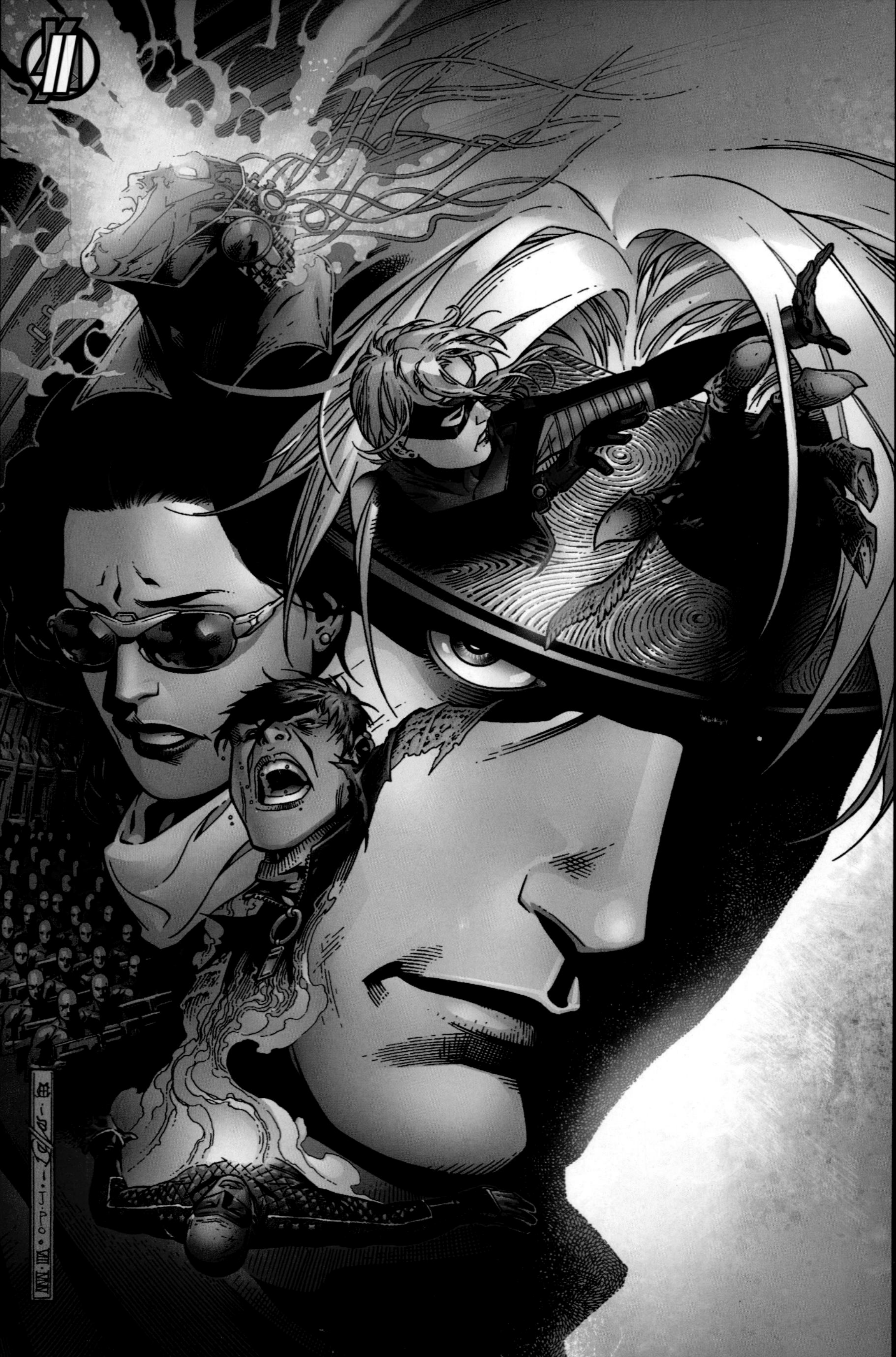

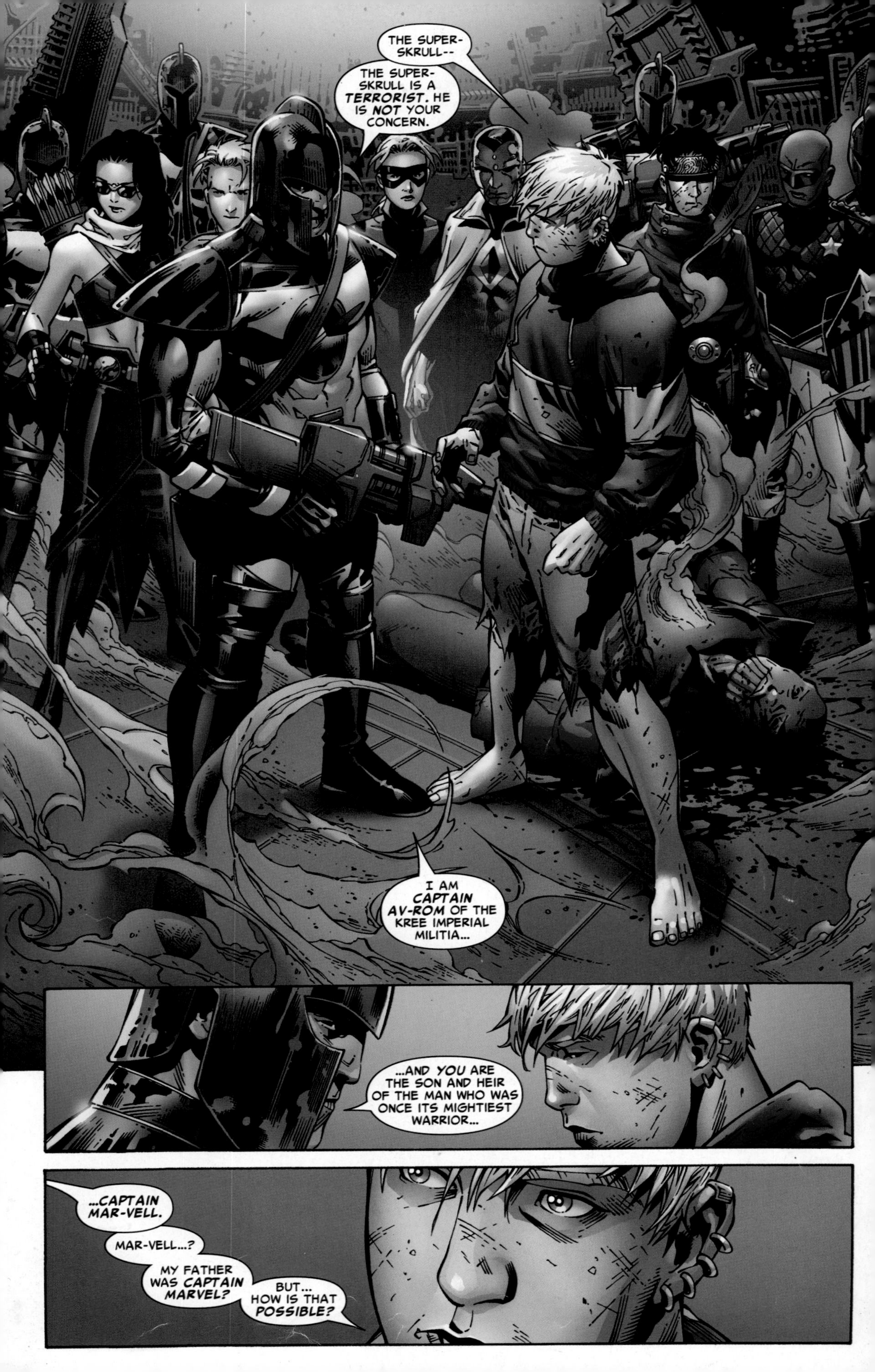
THE SUPER-SKRULL--
THE SUPER-SKRULL IS A TERRORIST. HE IS NOT YOUR CONCERN.
I AM CAPTAIN AV-ROM OF THE KREE IMPERIAL MILITIA...
...AND YOU ARE THE SON AND HEIR OF THE MAN WHO WAS ONCE ITS MIGHTIEST WARRIOR...
...CAPTAIN MAR-VELL.
MAR-VELL...?
MY FATHER WAS CAPTAIN MARVEL?
BUT... HOW IS THAT POSSIBLE?

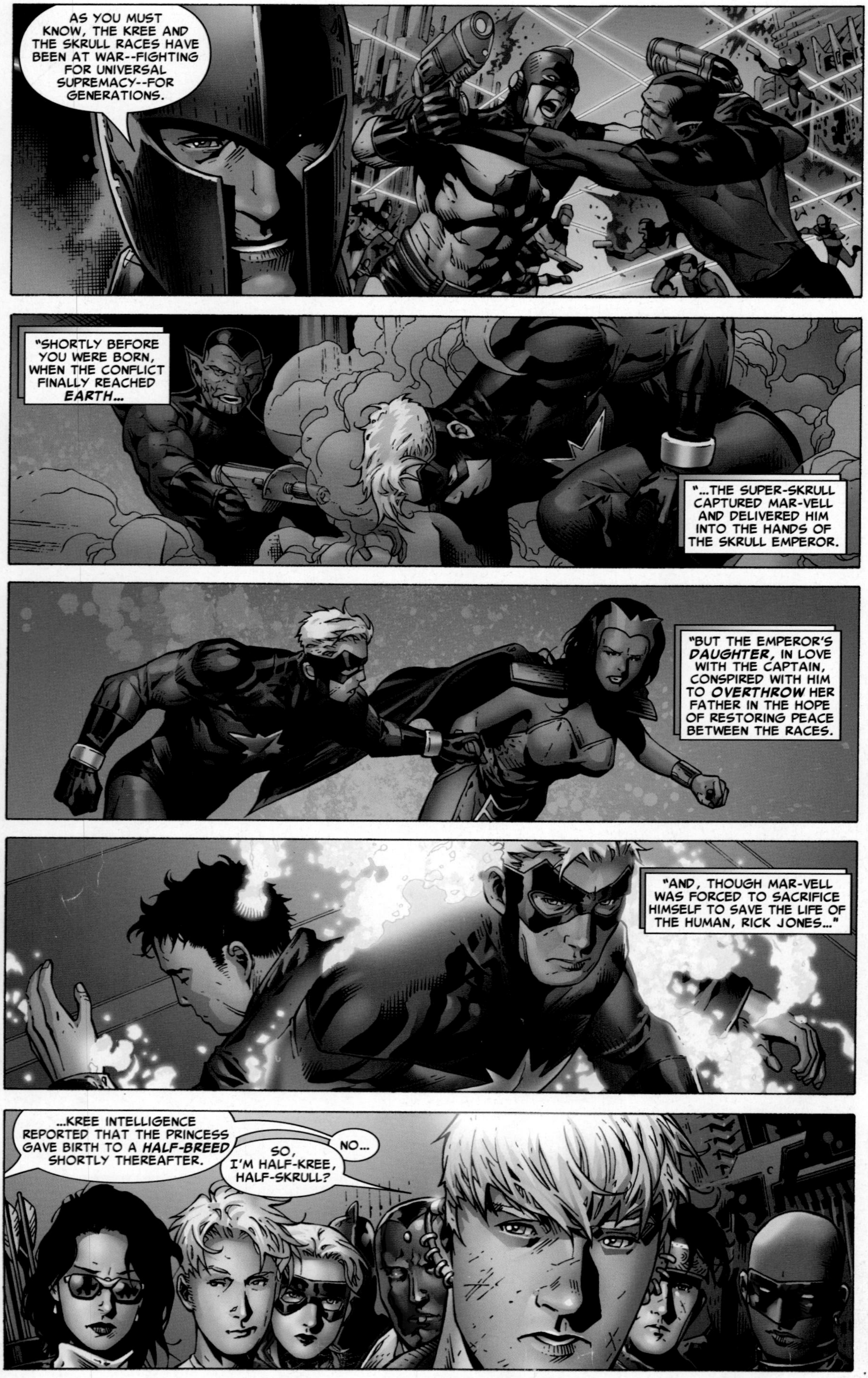
AS YOU MUST KNOW, THE KREE AND THE SKRULL RACES HAVE BEEN AT WAR--FIGHTING FOR UNIVERSAL SUPREMACY--FOR GENERATIONS.
"SHORTLY BEFORE YOU WERE BORN, WHEN THE CONFLICT FINALLY REACHED EARTH...
"...THE SUPER-SKRULL CAPTURED MAR-VELL AND DELIVERED HIM INTO THE HANDS OF THE SKRULL EMPEROR.
"BUT THE EMPEROR'S DAUGHTER, IN LOVE WITH THE CAPTAIN, CONSPIRED WITH HIM TO OVERTHROW HER FATHER IN THE HOPE OF RESTORING PEACE BETWEEN THE RACES.
"AND, THOUGH MAR-VELL WAS FORCED TO SACRIFICE HIMSELF TO SAVE THE LIFE OF THE HUMAN, RICK JONES..."
...KREE INTELLIGENCE REPORTED THAT THE PRINCESS GAVE BIRTH TO A HALF-BREED SHORTLY THEREAFTER.
SO, I'M HALF-KREE, HALF-SKRULL?
NO...

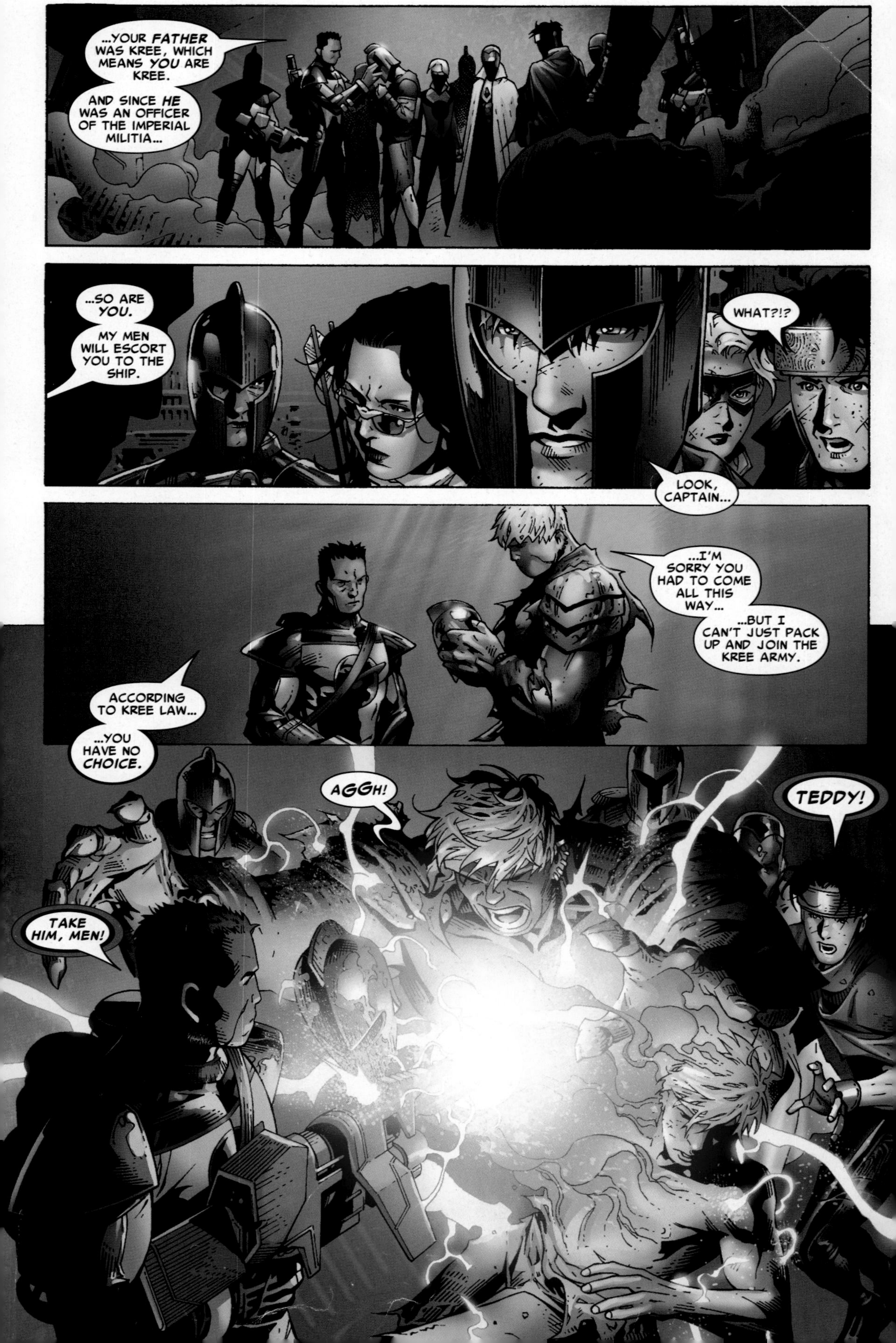
...YOUR FATHER WAS KREE, WHICH MEANS YOU ARE KREE.
AND SINCE HE WAS AN OFFICER OF THE IMPERIAL MILITIA...
...SO ARE YOU.
MY MEN WILL ESCORT YOU TO THE SHIP.
WHAT?!?
LOOK, CAPTAIN...
...I'M SORRY YOU HAD TO COME ALL THIS WAY...
...BUT I CAN'T JUST PACK UP AND JOIN THE KREE ARMY.
ACCORDING TO KREE LAW...
...YOU HAVE NO CHOICE.
AGGH!
TEDDY!
TAKE HIM, MEN!

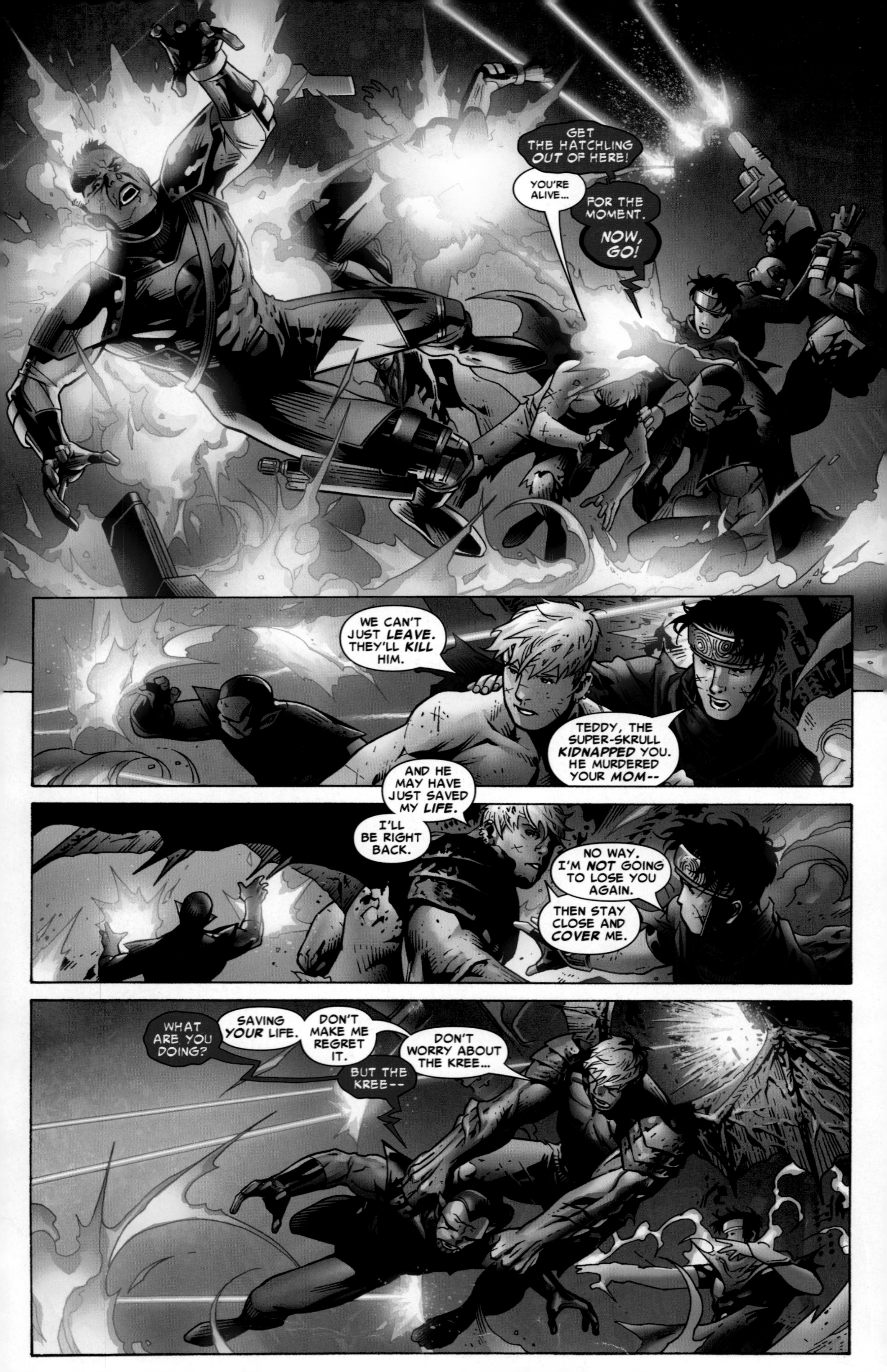
GET THE HATCHLING OUT OF HERE!
YOU'RE ALIVE...
FOR THE MOMENT.
NOW, GO!
WE CAN'T JUST LEAVE. THEY'LL KILL HIM.
TEDDY, THE SUPER-SKRULL KIDNAPPED YOU. HE MURDERED YOUR MOM--
AND HE MAY HAVE JUST SAVED MY LIFE.
I'LL BE RIGHT BACK.
NO WAY. I'M NOT GOING TO LOSE YOU AGAIN.
THEN STAY CLOSE AND COVER ME.
WHAT ARE YOU DOING?
SAVING YOUR LIFE.
DON'T MAKE ME REGRET IT.
BUT THE KREE--
DON'T WORRY ABOUT THE KREE...

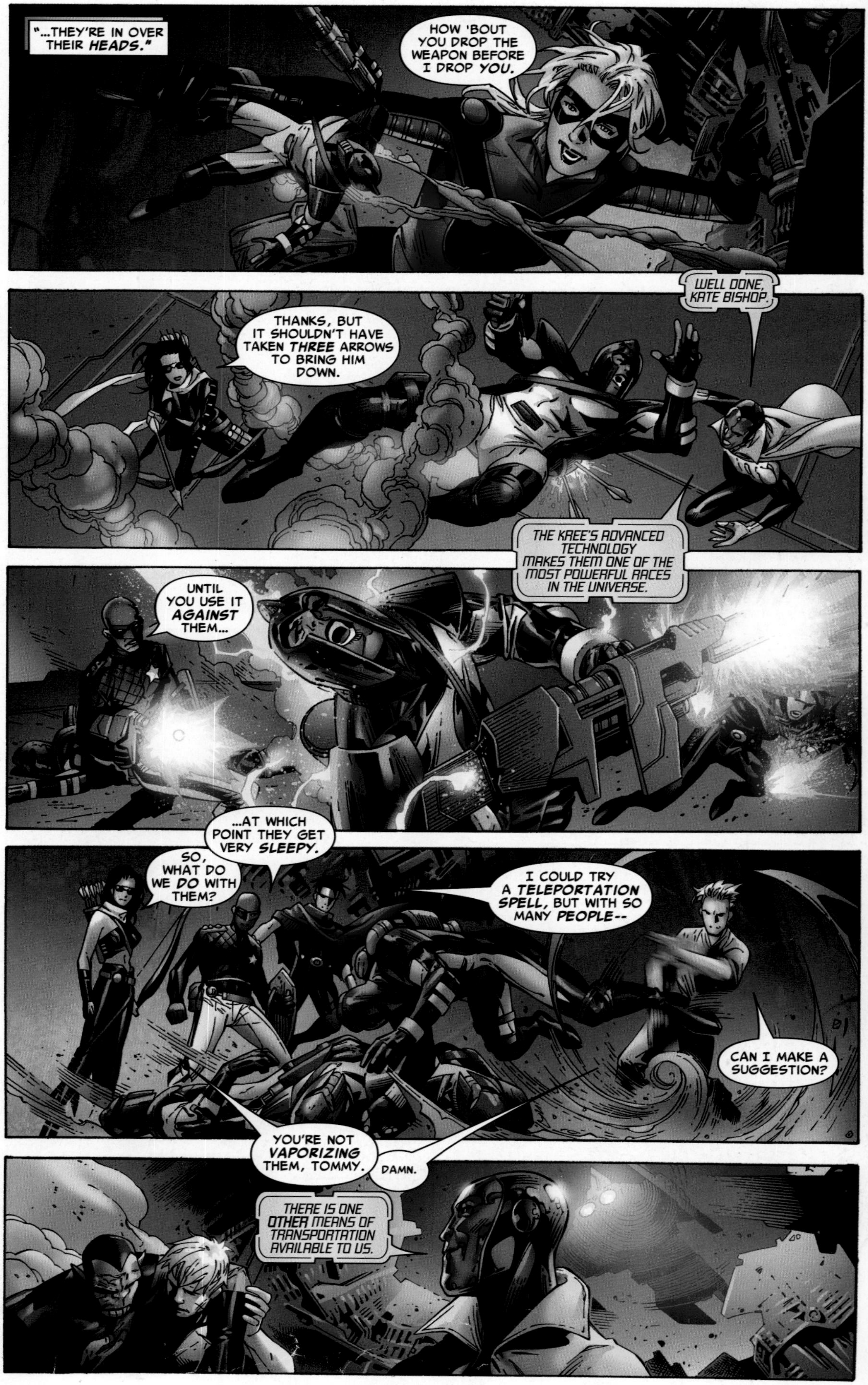
"...THEY'RE IN OVER THEIR HEADS."
HOW 'BOUT YOU DROP THE WEAPON BEFORE I DROP YOU.
THANKS, BUT IT SHOULDN'T HAVE TAKEN THREE ARROWS TO BRING HIM DOWN.
WELL DONE, KATE BISHOP.
THE KREE'S ADVANCED TECHNOLOGY MAKES THEM ONE OF THE MOST POWERFUL RACES IN THE UNIVERSE.
UNTIL YOU USE IT AGAINST THEM...
...AT WHICH POINT THEY GET VERY SLEEPY.
SO, WHAT DO WE DO WITH THEM?
I COULD TRY A TELEPORTATION SPELL, BUT WITH SO MANY PEOPLE--
CAN I MAKE A SUGGESTION?
YOU'RE NOT VAPORIZING THEM, TOMMY.
DAMN.
THERE IS ONE OTHER MEANS OF TRANSPORTATION AVAILABLE TO US.

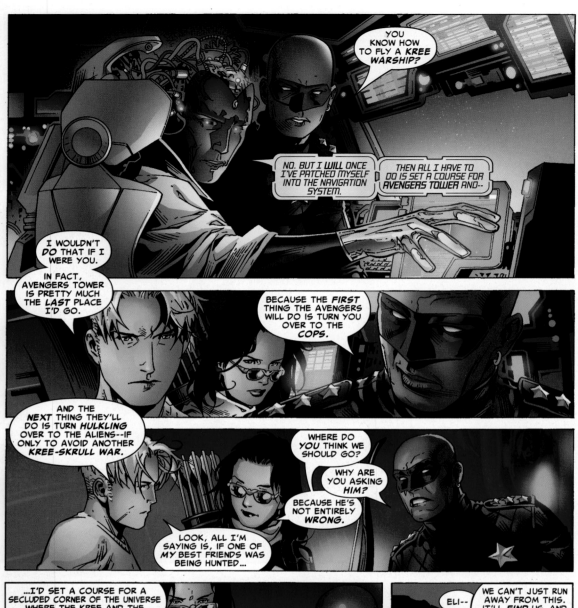

YOU KNOW HOW TO FLY A *KREE WARSHIP?*

NO. BUT I *WILL* ONCE I'VE PATCHED MYSELF INTO THE NAVIGATION SYSTEM.

THEN ALL I HAVE TO DO IS SET A COURSE FOR *AVENGERS TOWER AND--*

I WOULDN'T *DO* THAT IF I WERE YOU.

IN FACT, AVENGERS TOWER IS PRETTY MUCH THE *LAST* PLACE I'D GO.

BECAUSE THE *FIRST* THING THE AVENGERS WILL DO IS TURN YOU OVER TO THE *COPS.*

AND THE *NEXT* THING THEY'LL DO IS TURN *HULKLING* OVER TO THE ALIENS--IF ONLY TO AVOID ANOTHER *KREE-SKRULL WAR.*

WHERE DO *YOU* THINK WE SHOULD GO?

WHY ARE YOU ASKING *HIM?*

BECAUSE HE'S NOT ENTIRELY *WRONG.*

LOOK, ALL I'M SAYING IS, IF ONE OF MY BEST FRIENDS WAS BEING HUNTED...

...I'D SET A COURSE FOR A SECLUDED CORNER OF THE UNIVERSE WHERE THE KREE AND THE SKRULLS AND THE AVENGERS COULD NEVER *FIND* US.

AND WHERE WOULD THAT *BE,* EXACTLY?

NO IDEA, BUT--

SET A COURSE FOR AVENGERS TOWER.

ELI--

WE CAN'T JUST RUN AWAY FROM THIS. IT'LL *FIND* US. AND WHEN IT *DOES,* WE WON'T BE ABLE TO FIGHT IT BY *OURSELVES.*

AND ANYONE WHO FEELS DIFFERENTLY IS WELCOME TO *LEAVE.*

YOUR BOYFRIEND HAS *CONTROL* ISSUES.

HE'S *NOT* MY BOYFRIEND.

GOOD TO KNOW.

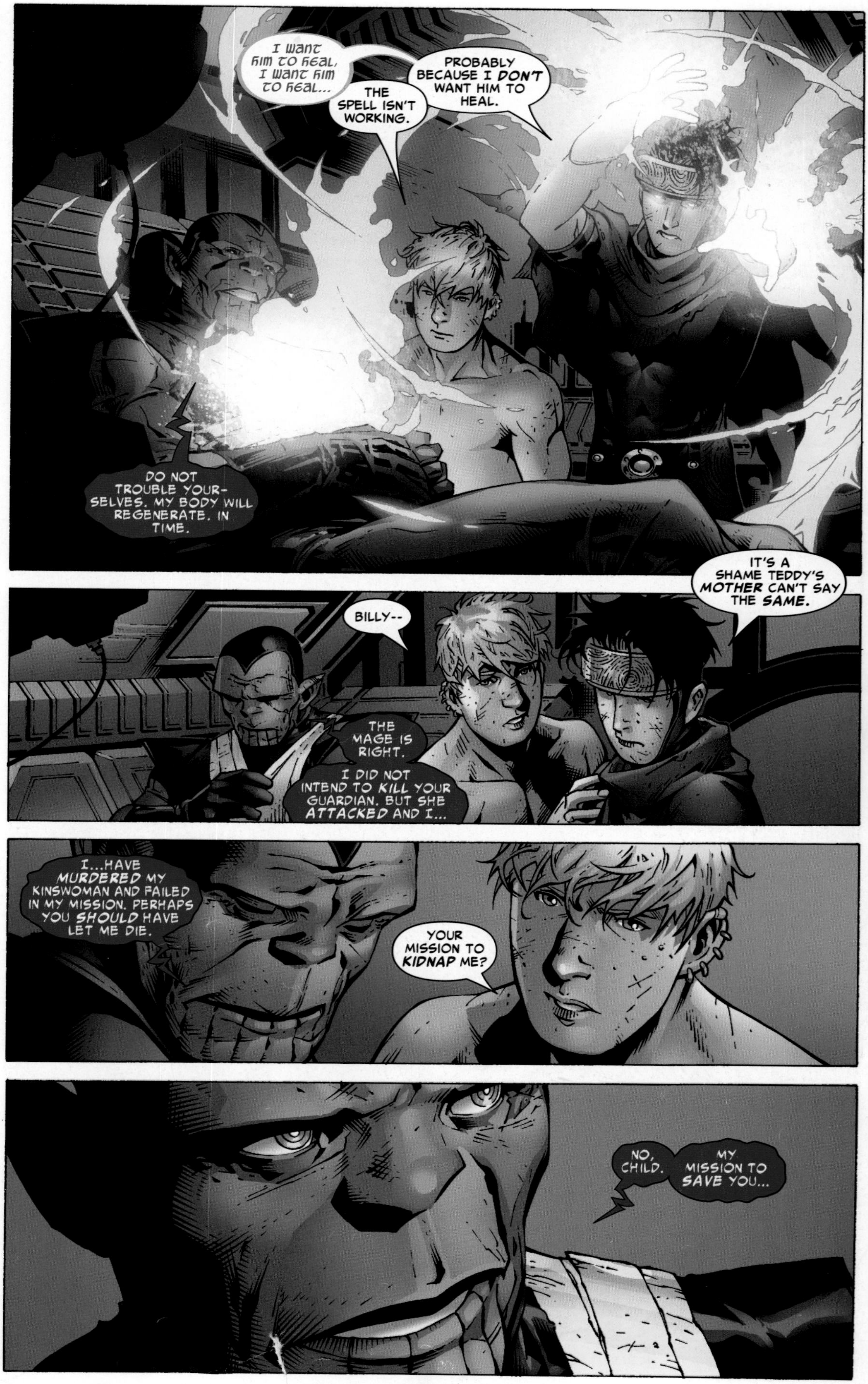
I WANT HIM TO HEAL, I WANT HIM TO HEAL...
THE SPELL ISN'T WORKING.
PROBABLY BECAUSE I DON'T WANT HIM TO HEAL.
DO NOT TROUBLE YOURSELVES. MY BODY WILL REGENERATE. IN TIME.
BILLY--
IT'S A SHAME TEDDY'S MOTHER CAN'T SAY THE SAME.
THE MAGE IS RIGHT.
I DID NOT INTEND TO KILL YOUR GUARDIAN. BUT SHE ATTACKED AND I...
I...HAVE MURDERED MY KINSWOMAN AND FAILED IN MY MISSION. PERHAPS YOU SHOULD HAVE LET ME DIE.
YOUR MISSION TO KIDNAP ME?
NO, CHILD.
MY MISSION TO SAVE YOU...

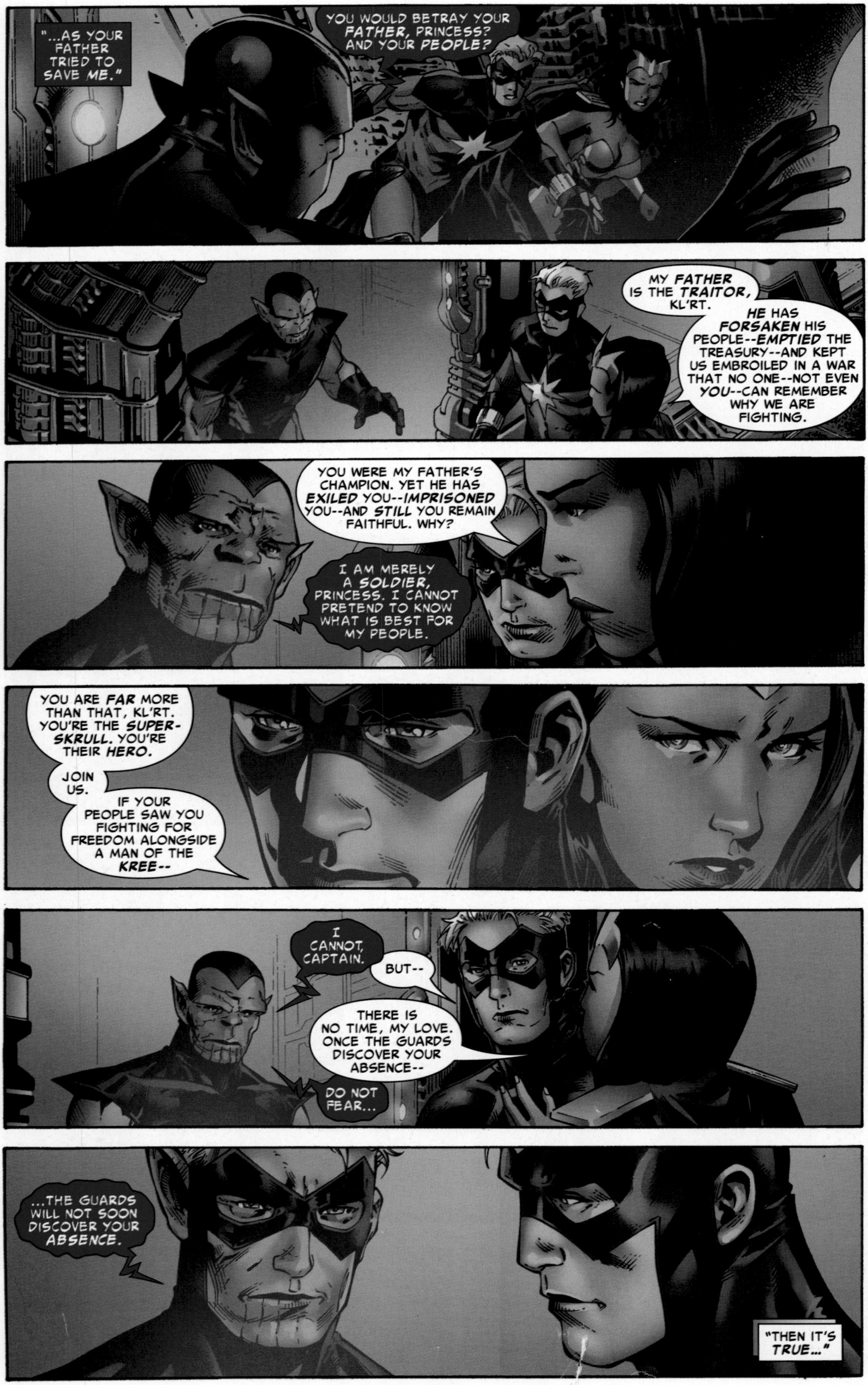
"...AS YOUR FATHER TRIED TO SAVE ME."
YOU WOULD BETRAY YOUR FATHER, PRINCESS? AND YOUR PEOPLE?
MY FATHER IS THE TRAITOR, KL'RT.
HE HAS FORSAKEN HIS PEOPLE--EMPTIED THE TREASURY--AND KEPT US EMBROILED IN A WAR THAT NO ONE--NOT EVEN YOU--CAN REMEMBER WHY WE ARE FIGHTING.
YOU WERE MY FATHER'S CHAMPION. YET HE HAS EXILED YOU--IMPRISONED YOU--AND STILL YOU REMAIN FAITHFUL. WHY?
I AM MERELY A SOLDIER, PRINCESS. I CANNOT PRETEND TO KNOW WHAT IS BEST FOR MY PEOPLE.
YOU ARE FAR MORE THAN THAT, KL'RT. YOU'RE THE SUPER-SKRULL. YOU'RE THEIR HERO.
JOIN US.
IF YOUR PEOPLE SAW YOU FIGHTING FOR FREEDOM ALONGSIDE A MAN OF THE KREE--
I CANNOT, CAPTAIN.
BUT--
THERE IS NO TIME, MY LOVE. ONCE THE GUARDS DISCOVER YOUR ABSENCE--
DO NOT FEAR...
...THE GUARDS WILL NOT SOON DISCOVER YOUR ABSENCE.
"THEN IT'S TRUE..."

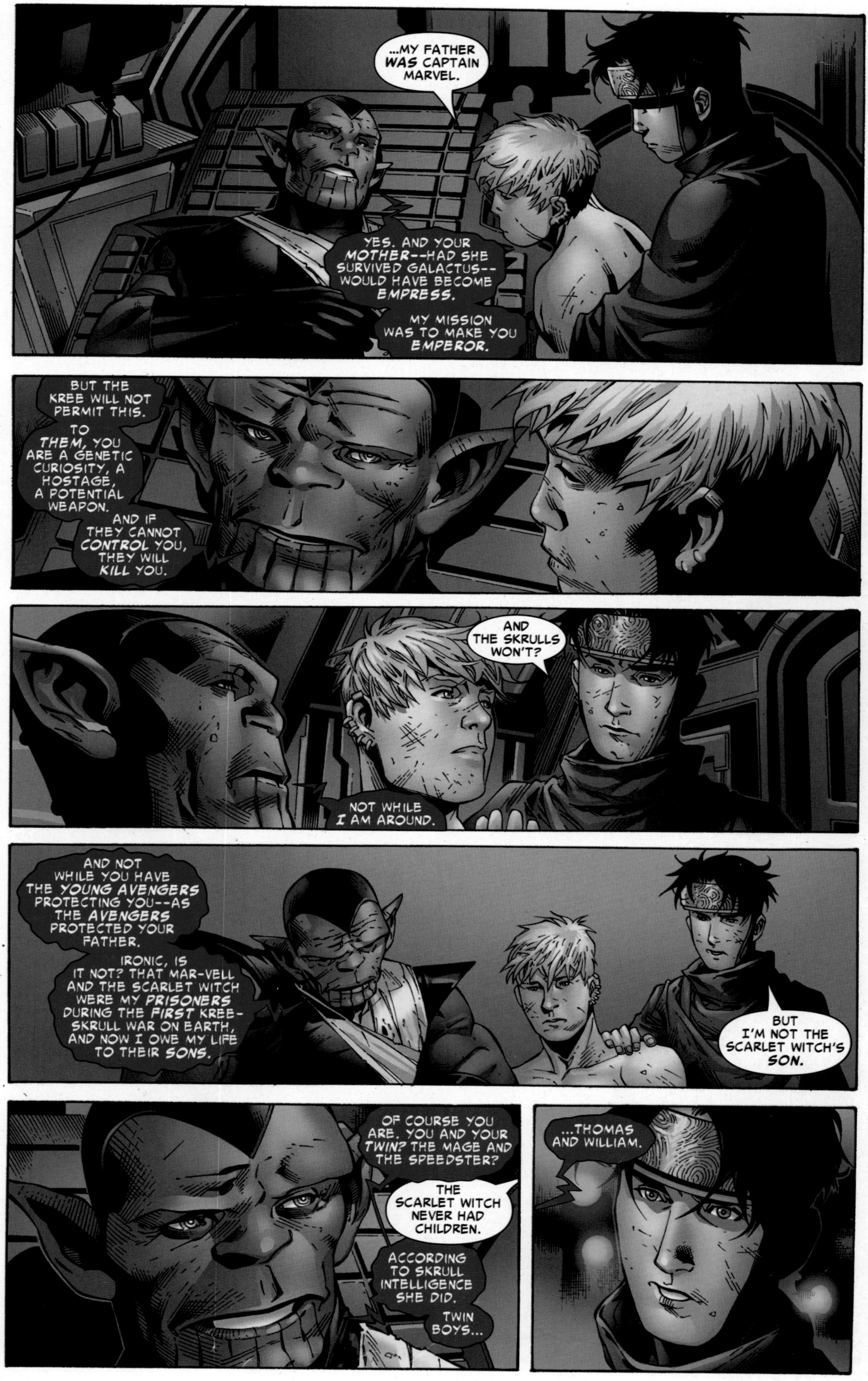
...MY FATHER WAS CAPTAIN MARVEL.
YES. AND YOUR MOTHER--HAD SHE SURVIVED GALACTUS--WOULD HAVE BECOME EMPRESS.
MY MISSION WAS TO MAKE YOU EMPEROR.
BUT THE KREE WILL NOT PERMIT THIS.
TO THEM, YOU ARE A GENETIC CURIOSITY, A HOSTAGE, A POTENTIAL WEAPON.
AND IF THEY CANNOT CONTROL YOU, THEY WILL KILL YOU.
AND THE SKRULLS WON'T?
NOT WHILE I AM AROUND.
AND NOT WHILE YOU HAVE THE YOUNG AVENGERS PROTECTING YOU--AS THE AVENGERS PROTECTED YOUR FATHER.
IRONIC, IS IT NOT? THAT MAR-VELL AND THE SCARLET WITCH WERE MY PRISONERS DURING THE FIRST KREE-SKRULL WAR ON EARTH, AND NOW I OWE MY LIFE TO THEIR SONS.
BUT I'M NOT THE SCARLET WITCH'S SON.
OF COURSE YOU ARE. YOU AND YOUR TWIN? THE MAGE AND THE SPEEDSTER?
THE SCARLET WITCH NEVER HAD CHILDREN.
ACCORDING TO SKRULL INTELLIGENCE SHE DID.
TWIN BOYS...
...THOMAS AND WILLIAM.

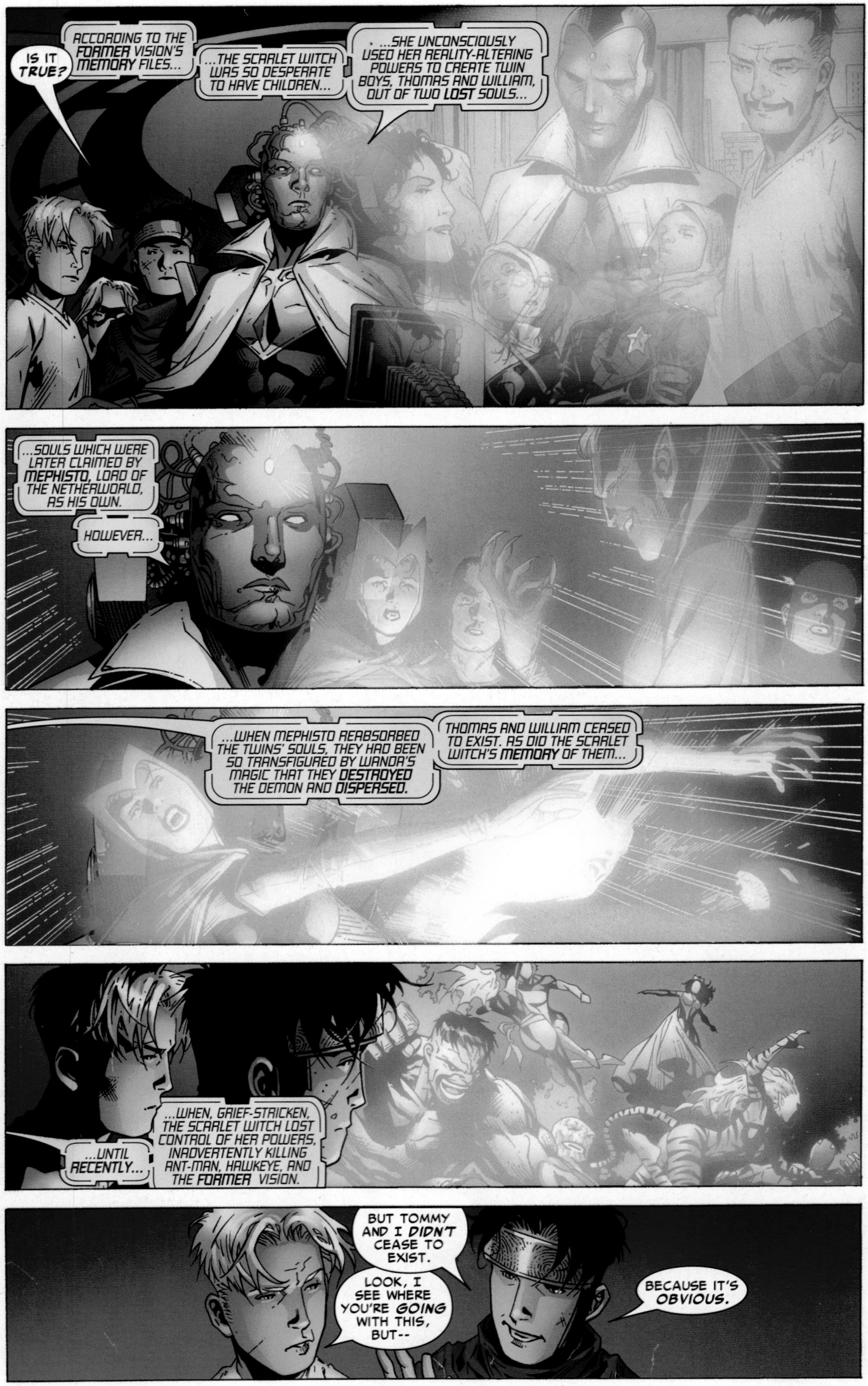
IS IT TRUE?
ACCORDING TO THE FORMER VISION'S MEMORY FILES...
...THE SCARLET WITCH WAS SO DESPERATE TO HAVE CHILDREN...
...SHE UNCONSCIOUSLY USED HER REALITY-ALTERING POWERS TO CREATE TWIN BOYS, THOMAS AND WILLIAM, OUT OF TWO LOST SOULS...
...SOULS WHICH WERE LATER CLAIMED BY MEPHISTO, LORD OF THE NETHERWORLD, AS HIS OWN.
HOWEVER...
...WHEN MEPHISTO REABSORBED THE TWINS' SOULS, THEY HAD BEEN SO TRANSFIGURED BY WANDA'S MAGIC THAT THEY DESTROYED THE DEMON AND DISPERSED.
THOMAS AND WILLIAM CEASED TO EXIST. AS DID THE SCARLET WITCH'S MEMORY OF THEM...
...UNTIL RECENTLY...
...WHEN, GRIEF-STRICKEN, THE SCARLET WITCH LOST CONTROL OF HER POWERS, INADVERTENTLY KILLING ANT-MAN, HAWKEYE, AND THE FORMER VISION.
BUT TOMMY AND I DIDN'T CEASE TO EXIST.
LOOK, I SEE WHERE YOU'RE GOING WITH THIS, BUT--
BECAUSE IT'S OBVIOUS.

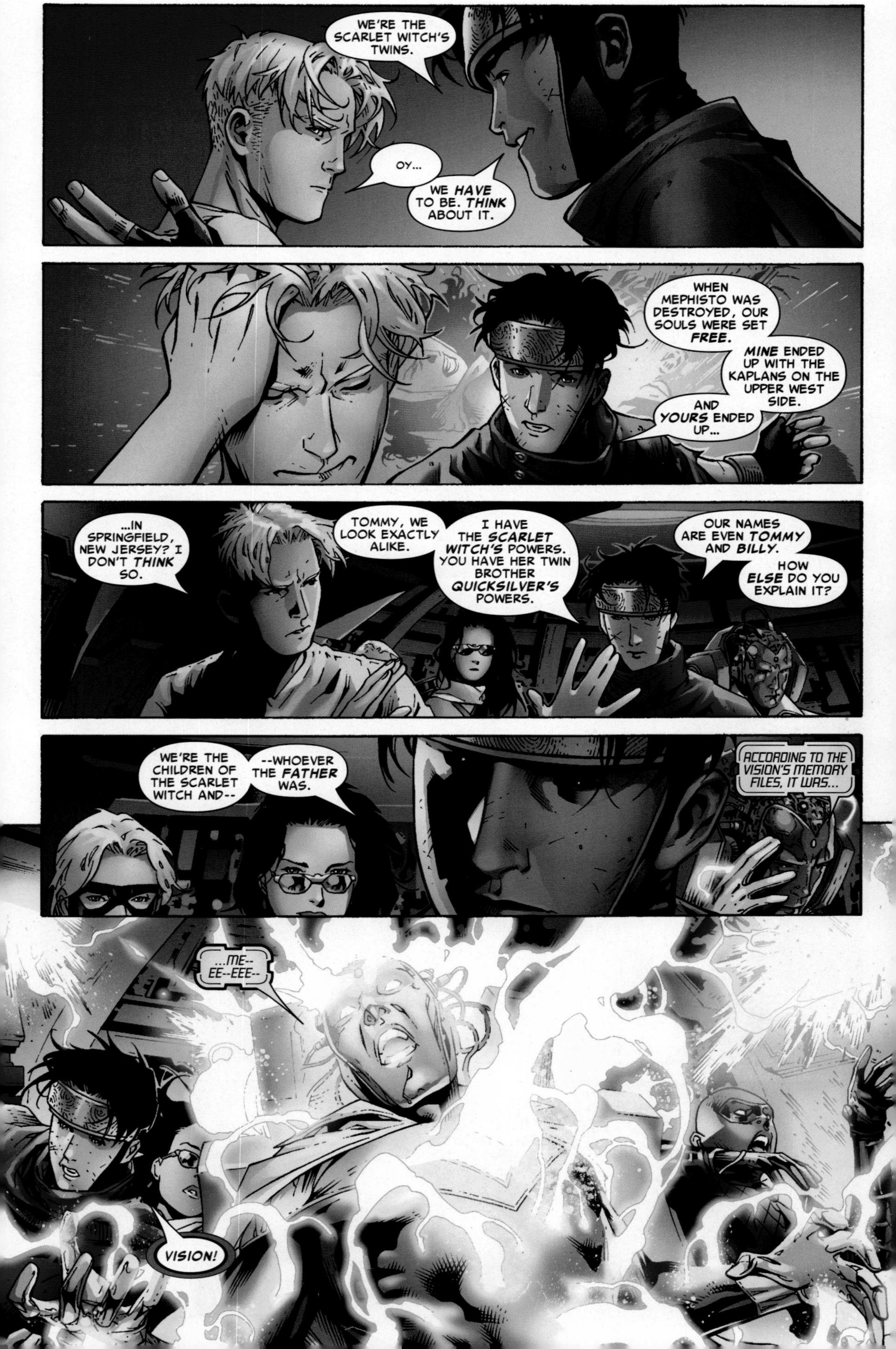

WE'RE THE SCARLET WITCH'S TWINS.
OY...
WE HAVE TO BE. THINK ABOUT IT.
WHEN MEPHISTO WAS DESTROYED, OUR SOULS WERE SET FREE.
MINE ENDED UP WITH THE KAPLANS ON THE UPPER WEST SIDE.
AND YOURS ENDED UP...
...IN SPRINGFIELD, NEW JERSEY? I DON'T THINK SO.
TOMMY, WE LOOK EXACTLY ALIKE.
I HAVE THE SCARLET WITCH'S POWERS. YOU HAVE HER TWIN BROTHER QUICKSILVER'S POWERS.
OUR NAMES ARE EVEN TOMMY AND BILLY.
HOW ELSE DO YOU EXPLAIN IT?
WE'RE THE CHILDREN OF THE SCARLET WITCH AND--
--WHOEVER THE FATHER WAS.
ACCORDING TO THE VISION'S MEMORY FILES, IT WAS...
...ME--EE--EEE--
VISION!

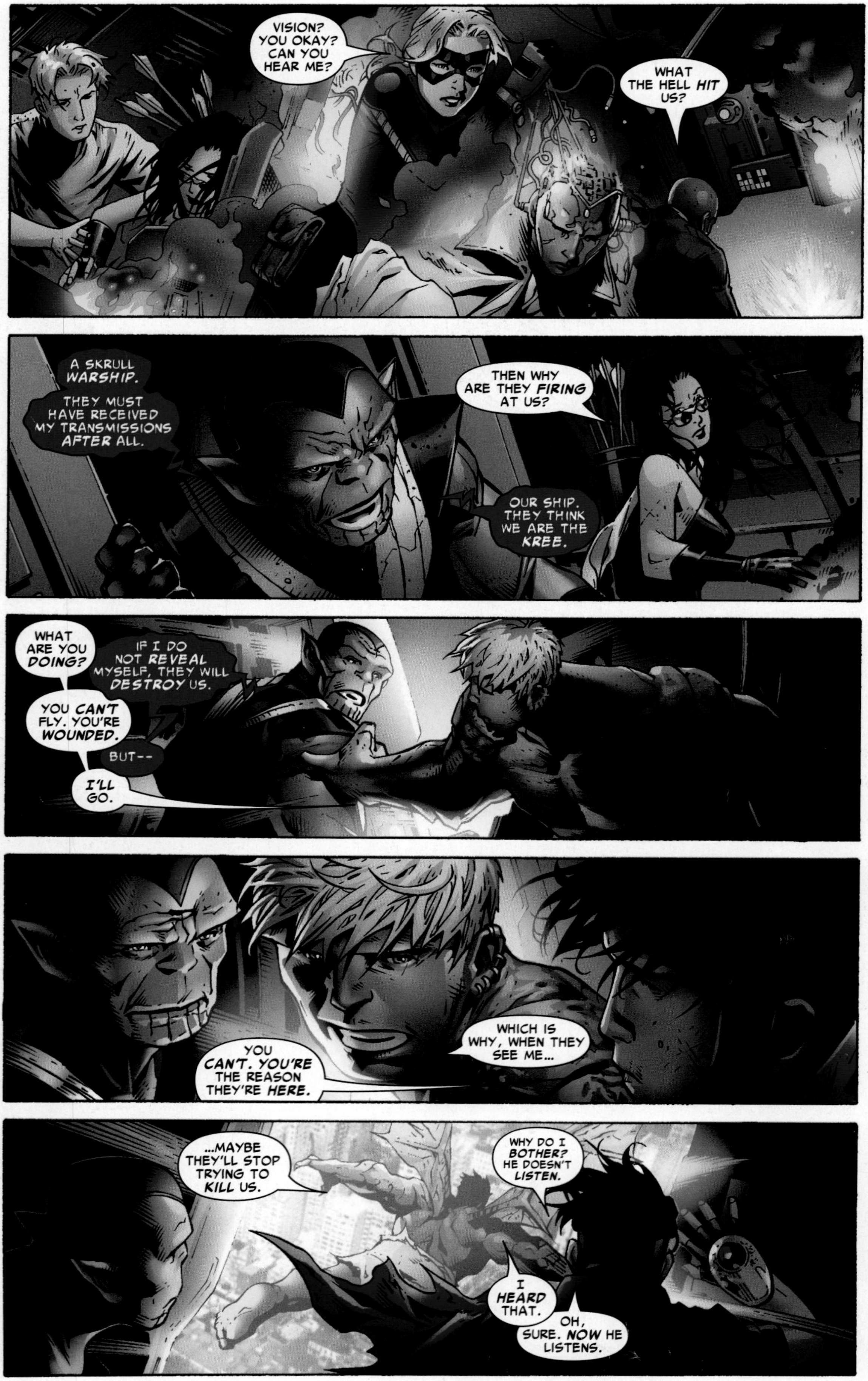
VISION? YOU OKAY? CAN YOU HEAR ME?
WHAT THE HELL HIT US?
A SKRULL WARSHIP.
THEY MUST HAVE RECEIVED MY TRANSMISSIONS AFTER ALL.
THEN WHY ARE THEY FIRING AT US?
OUR SHIP. THEY THINK WE ARE THE KREE.
WHAT ARE YOU DOING?
IF I DO NOT REVEAL MYSELF, THEY WILL DESTROY US.
YOU CAN'T FLY. YOU'RE WOUNDED.
BUT--
I'LL GO.
YOU CAN'T. YOU'RE THE REASON THEY'RE HERE.
WHICH IS WHY, WHEN THEY SEE ME...
...MAYBE THEY'LL STOP TRYING TO KILL US.
WHY DO I BOTHER? HE DOESN'T LISTEN.
I HEARD THAT.
OH, SURE. NOW HE LISTENS.

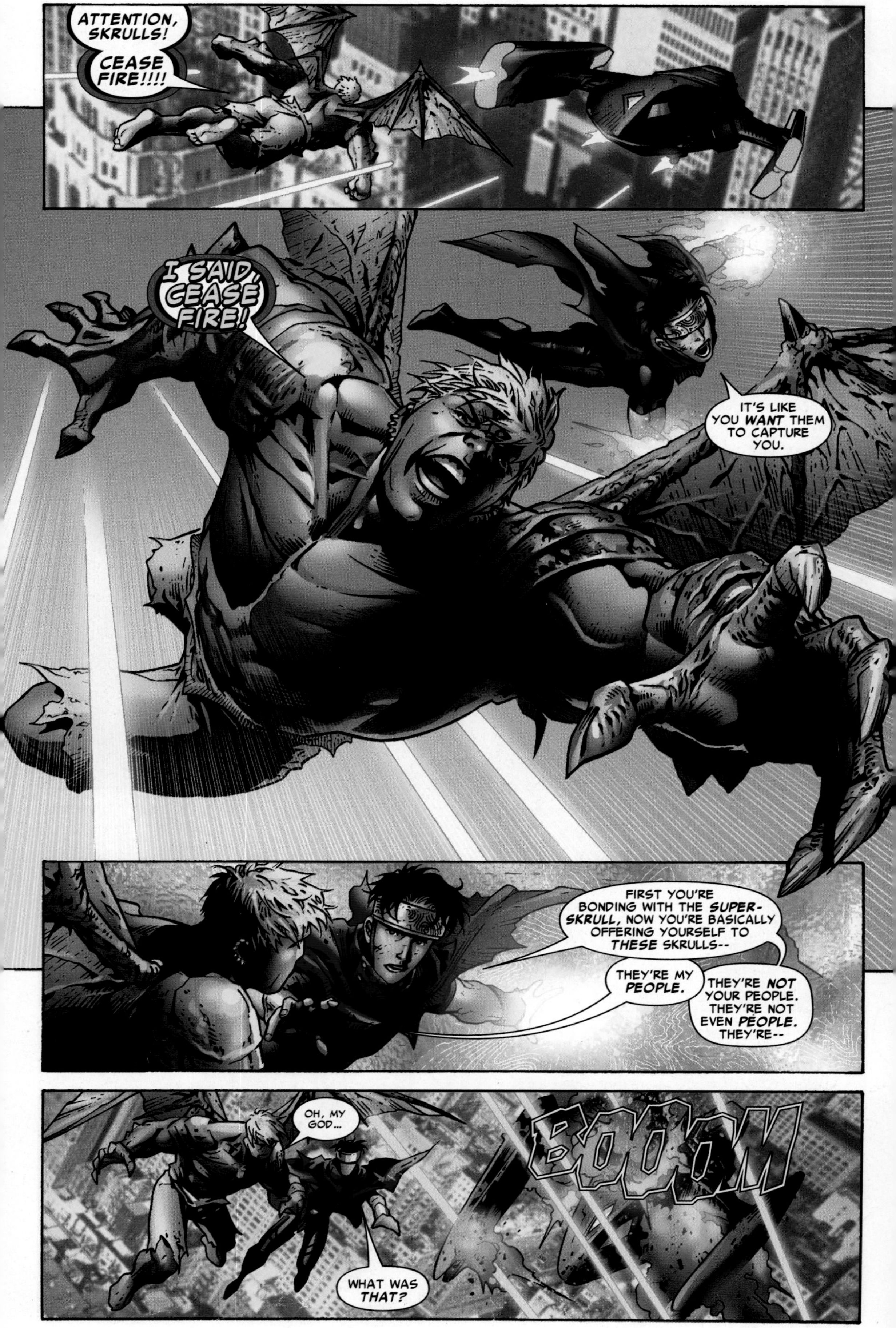
ATTENTION, SKRULLS!
CEASE FIRE!!!!
I SAID, CEASE FIRE!
IT'S LIKE YOU WANT THEM TO CAPTURE YOU.
FIRST YOU'RE BONDING WITH THE SUPER-SKRULL, NOW YOU'RE BASICALLY OFFERING YOURSELF TO THESE SKRULLS--
THEY'RE MY PEOPLE.
THEY'RE NOT YOUR PEOPLE. THEY'RE NOT EVEN PEOPLE. THEY'RE--
OH, MY GOD...
BOOOM
WHAT WAS THAT?

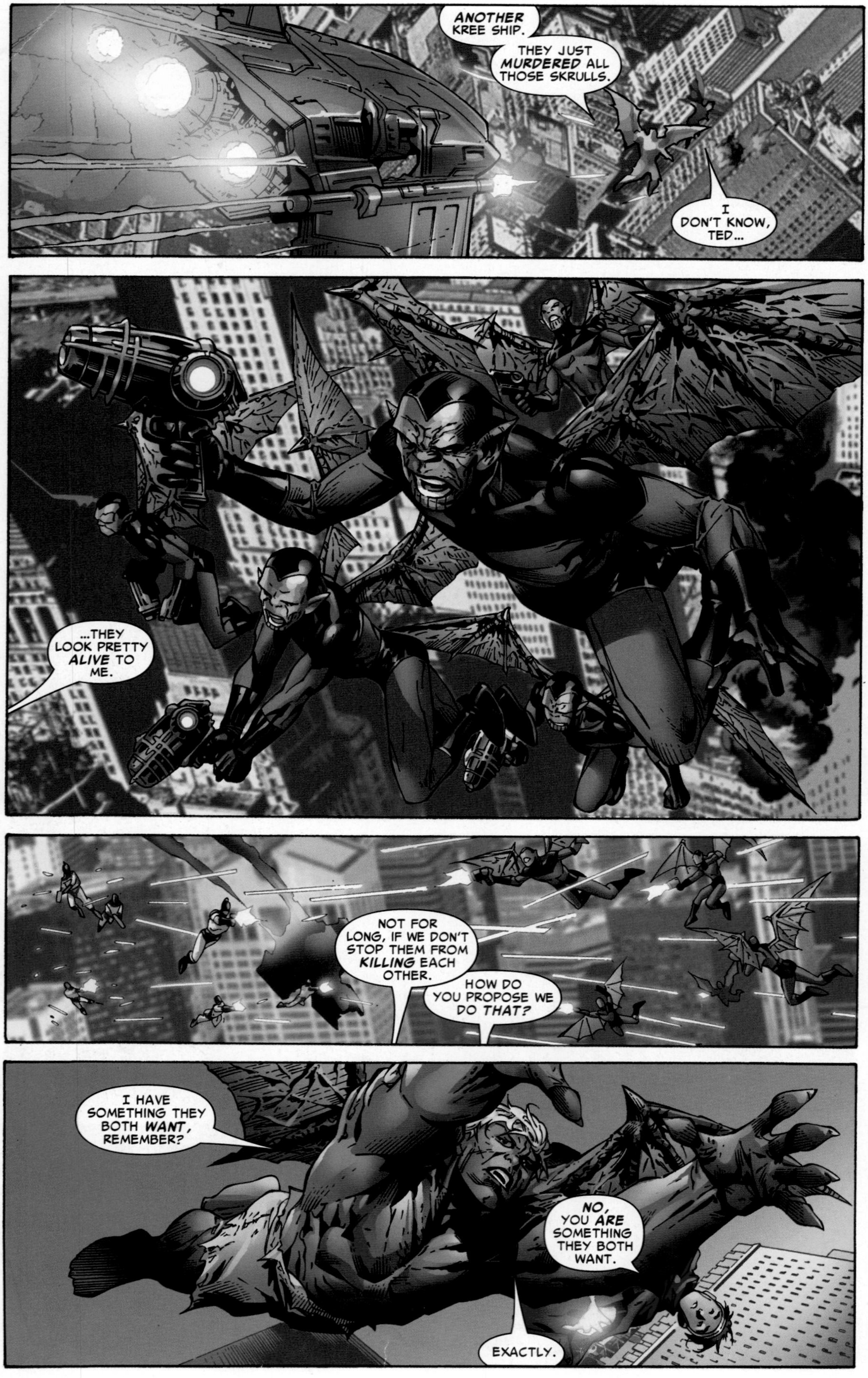
ANOTHER KREE SHIP.
THEY JUST MURDERED ALL THOSE SKRULLS.
I DON'T KNOW, TED...
...THEY LOOK PRETTY ALIVE TO ME.
NOT FOR LONG, IF WE DON'T STOP THEM FROM KILLING EACH OTHER.
HOW DO YOU PROPOSE WE DO THAT?
I HAVE SOMETHING THEY BOTH WANT, REMEMBER?
NO, YOU ARE SOMETHING THEY BOTH WANT.
EXACTLY.

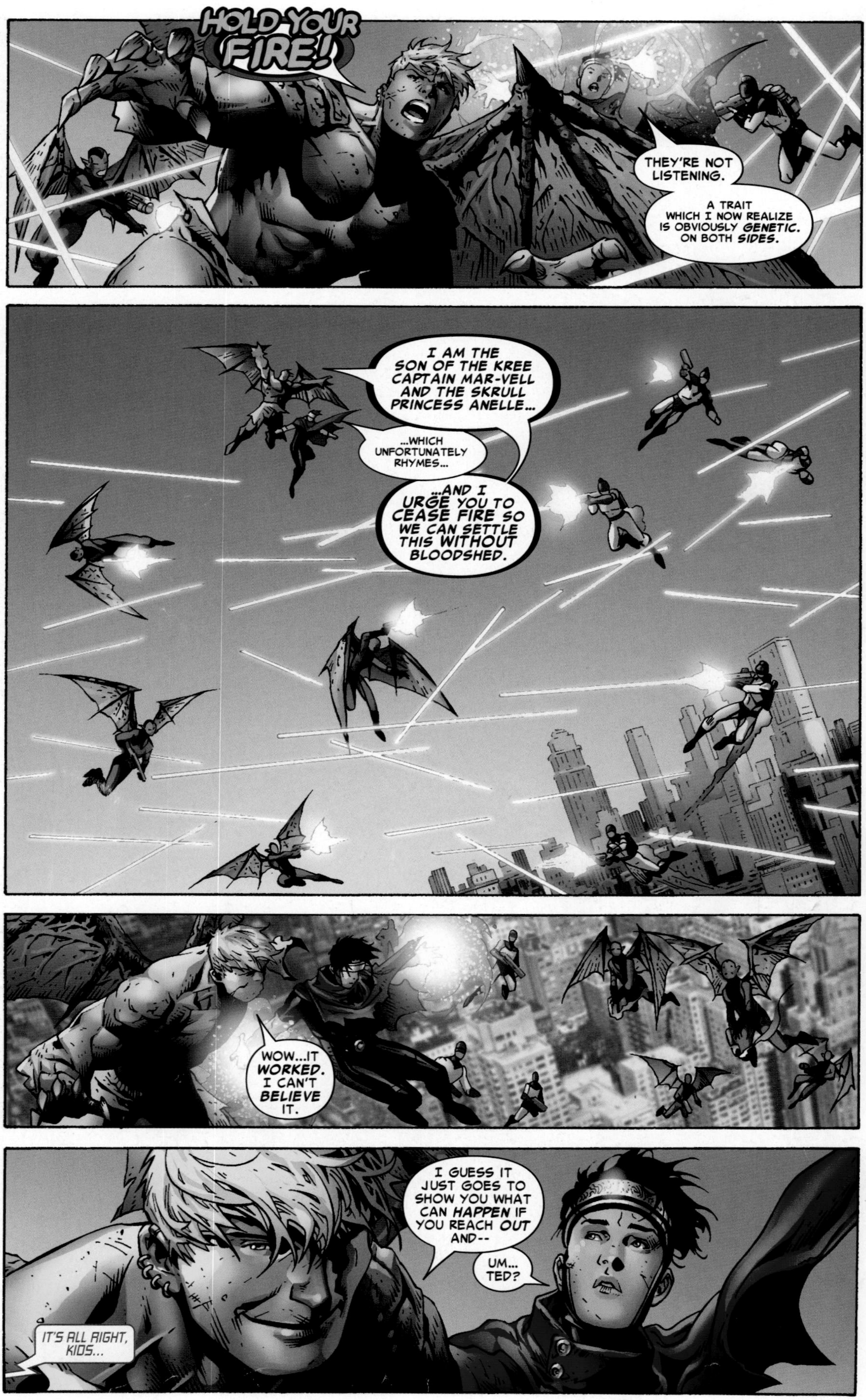
HOLD YOUR FIRE!
THEY'RE NOT LISTENING.
A TRAIT WHICH I NOW REALIZE IS OBVIOUSLY GENETIC. ON BOTH SIDES.
I AM THE SON OF THE KREE CAPTAIN MAR-VELL AND THE SKRULL PRINCESS ANELLE...
...WHICH UNFORTUNATELY RHYMES...
...AND I URGE YOU TO CEASE FIRE SO WE CAN SETTLE THIS WITHOUT BLOODSHED.
WOW...IT WORKED. I CAN'T BELIEVE IT.
I GUESS IT JUST GOES TO SHOW YOU WHAT CAN HAPPEN IF YOU REACH OUT AND--
UM... TED?
IT'S ALL RIGHT, KIDS...

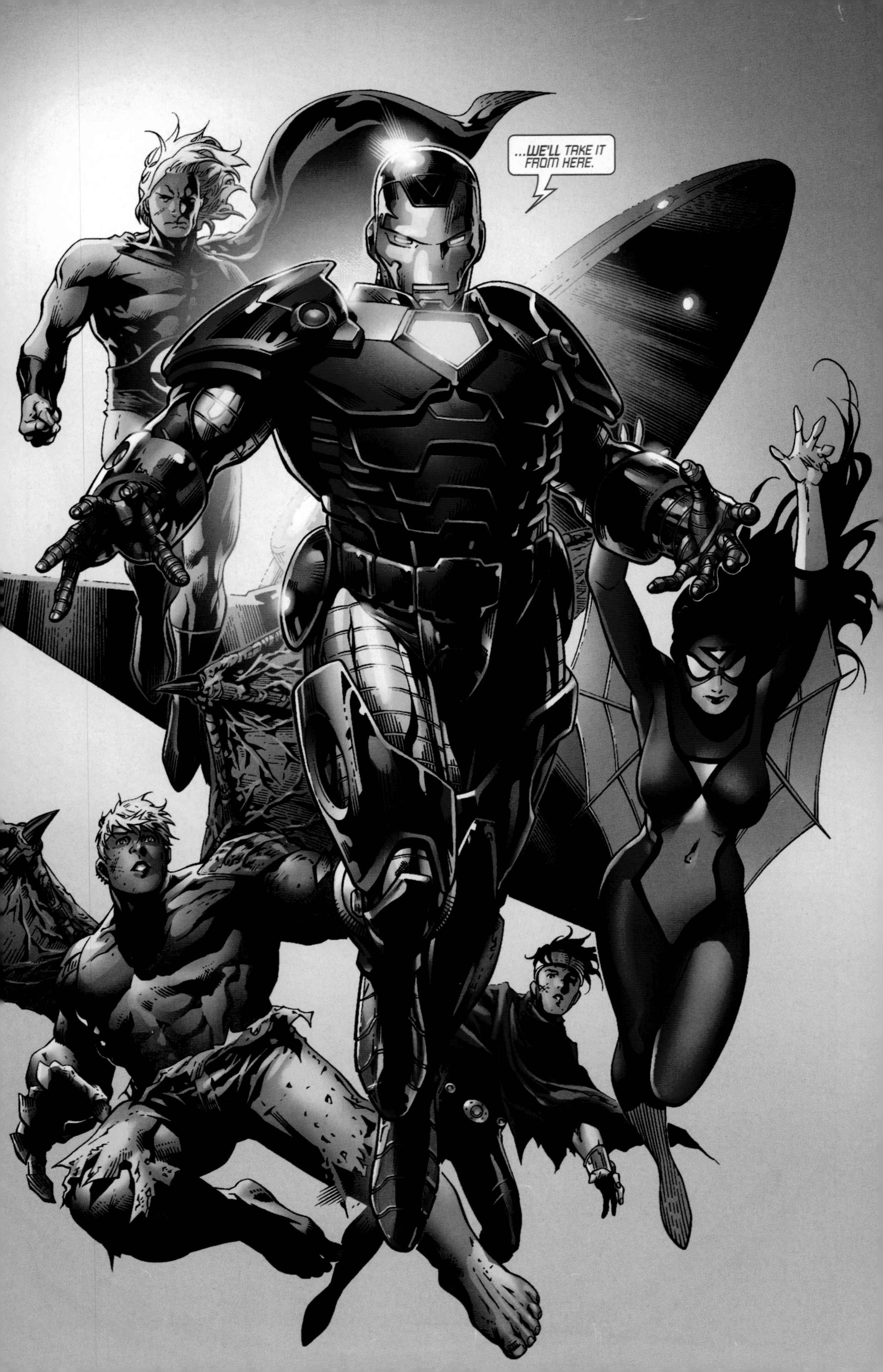
...WE'LL TAKE IT FROM HERE.

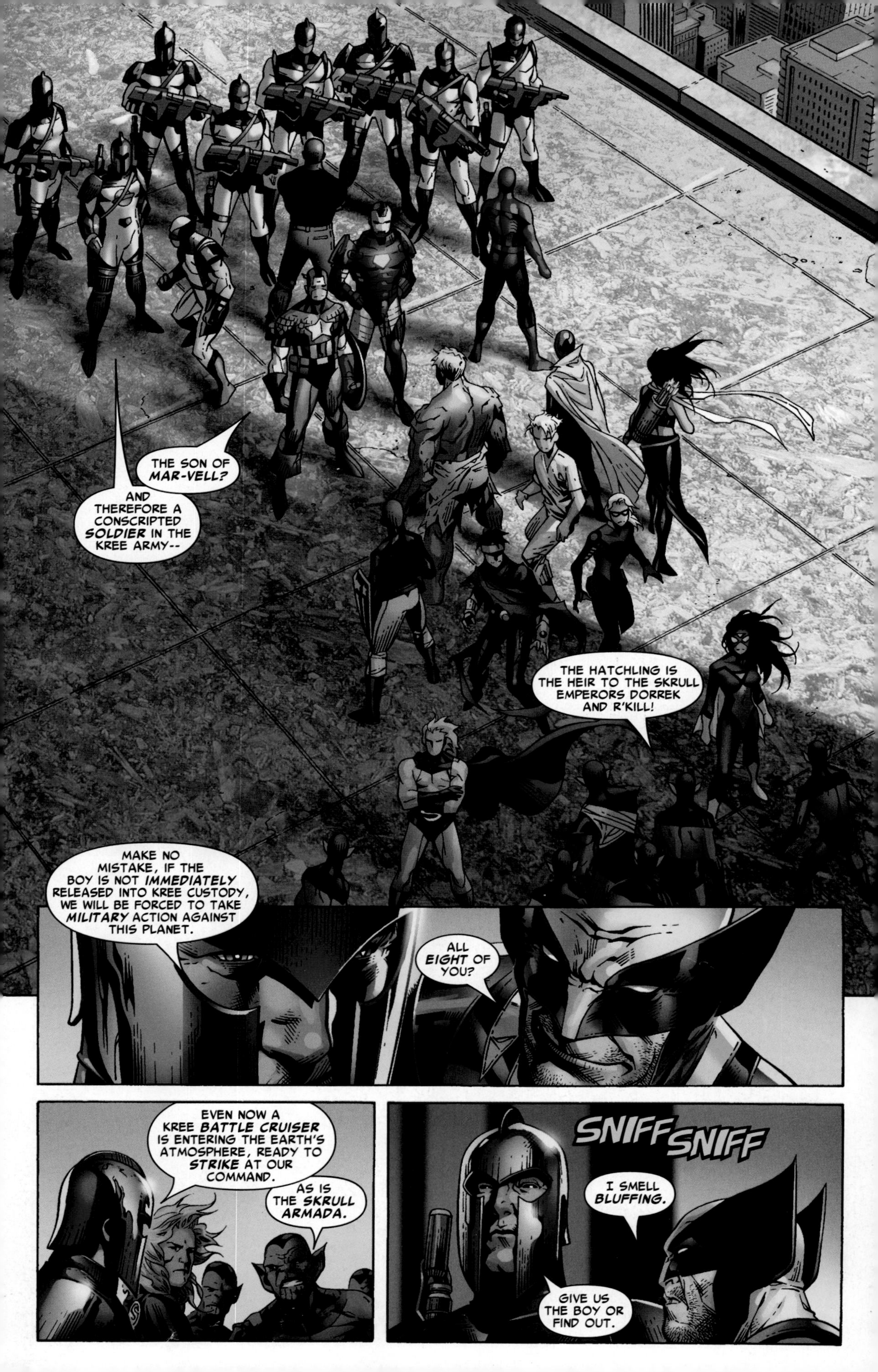

THE SON OF MAR-VELL?
AND THEREFORE A CONSCRIPTED SOLDIER IN THE KREE ARMY--
THE HATCHLING IS THE HEIR TO THE SKRULL EMPERORS DORREK AND R'KILL!
MAKE NO MISTAKE, IF THE BOY IS NOT IMMEDIATELY RELEASED INTO KREE CUSTODY, WE WILL BE FORCED TO TAKE MILITARY ACTION AGAINST THIS PLANET.
ALL EIGHT OF YOU?
EVEN NOW A KREE BATTLE CRUISER IS ENTERING THE EARTH'S ATMOSPHERE, READY TO STRIKE AT OUR COMMAND.
AS IS THE SKRULL ARMADA.
SNIFF SNIFF
I SMELL BLUFFING.
GIVE US THE BOY OR FIND OUT.

IT'S *YOUR MOVE,* HULKLING.

HE'S NOT GOING *ANYWHERE.*

CAP, *PLEASE...*

...DON'T MAKE ME GO WITH THEM.

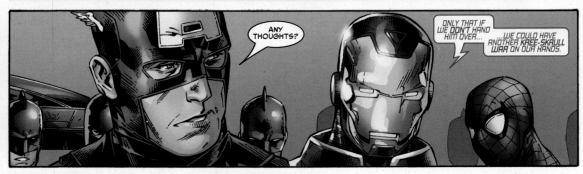

ANY THOUGHTS?

ONLY THAT IF WE DON'T HAND HIM OVER... ...WE COULD HAVE ANOTHER KREE-SKRULL *WAR* ON OUR HANDS.

WHAT IS YOUR DECISION, CAPTAIN?

CAP, *PLEASE*--TEDDY DOESN'T *BELONG* WITH THEM.

WE'RE THE ONLY *FAMILY* HE'S GOT NOW. YOU *CAN'T*--

I'VE MADE MY DECISION, ELI...

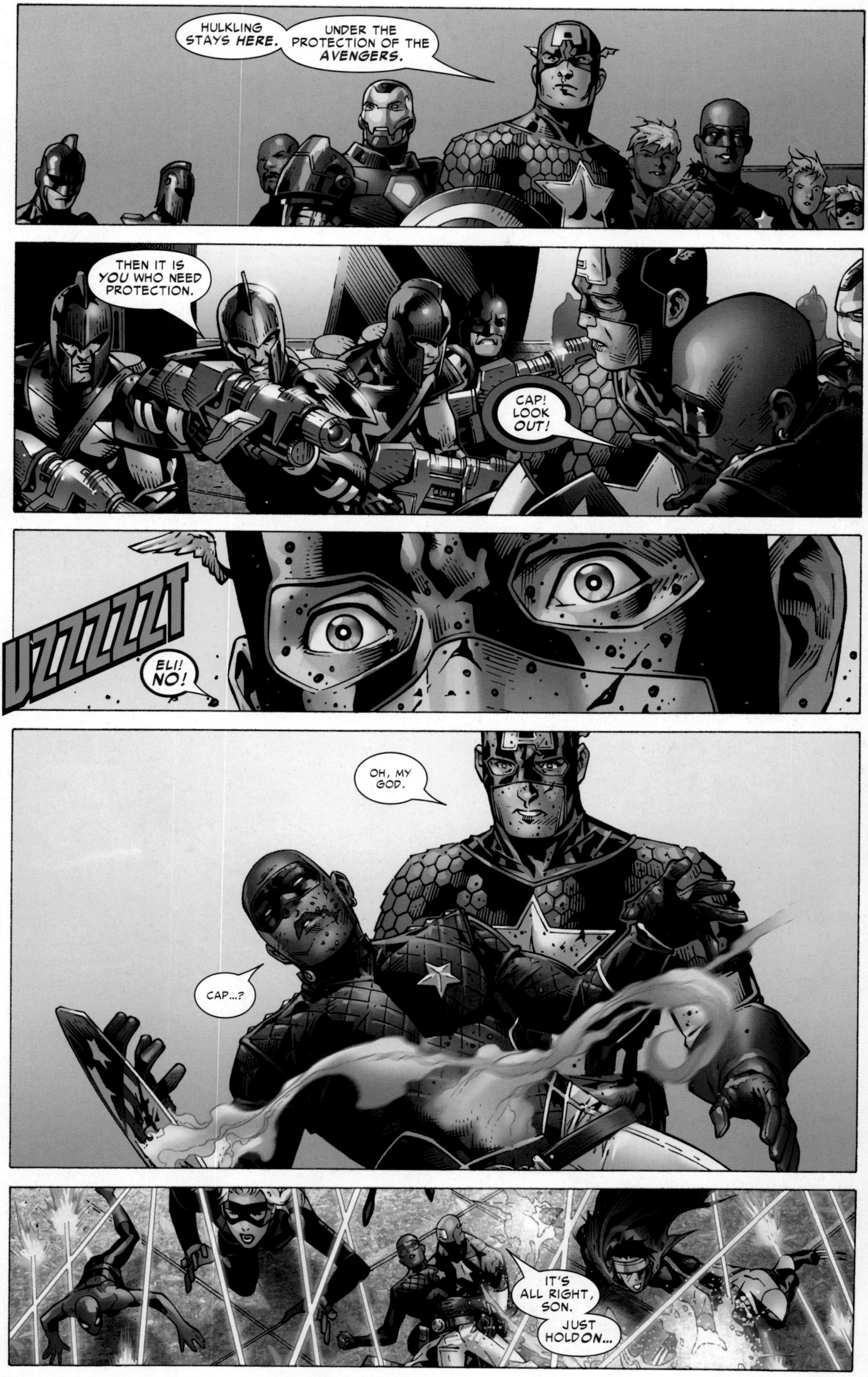
HULKLING STAYS HERE.
UNDER THE PROTECTION OF THE AVENGERS.
THEN IT IS YOU WHO NEED PROTECTION.
CAP! LOOK OUT!
UZZZZZT
ELI! NO!
OH, MY GOD.
CAP...?
IT'S ALL RIGHT, SON.
JUST HOLD ON...

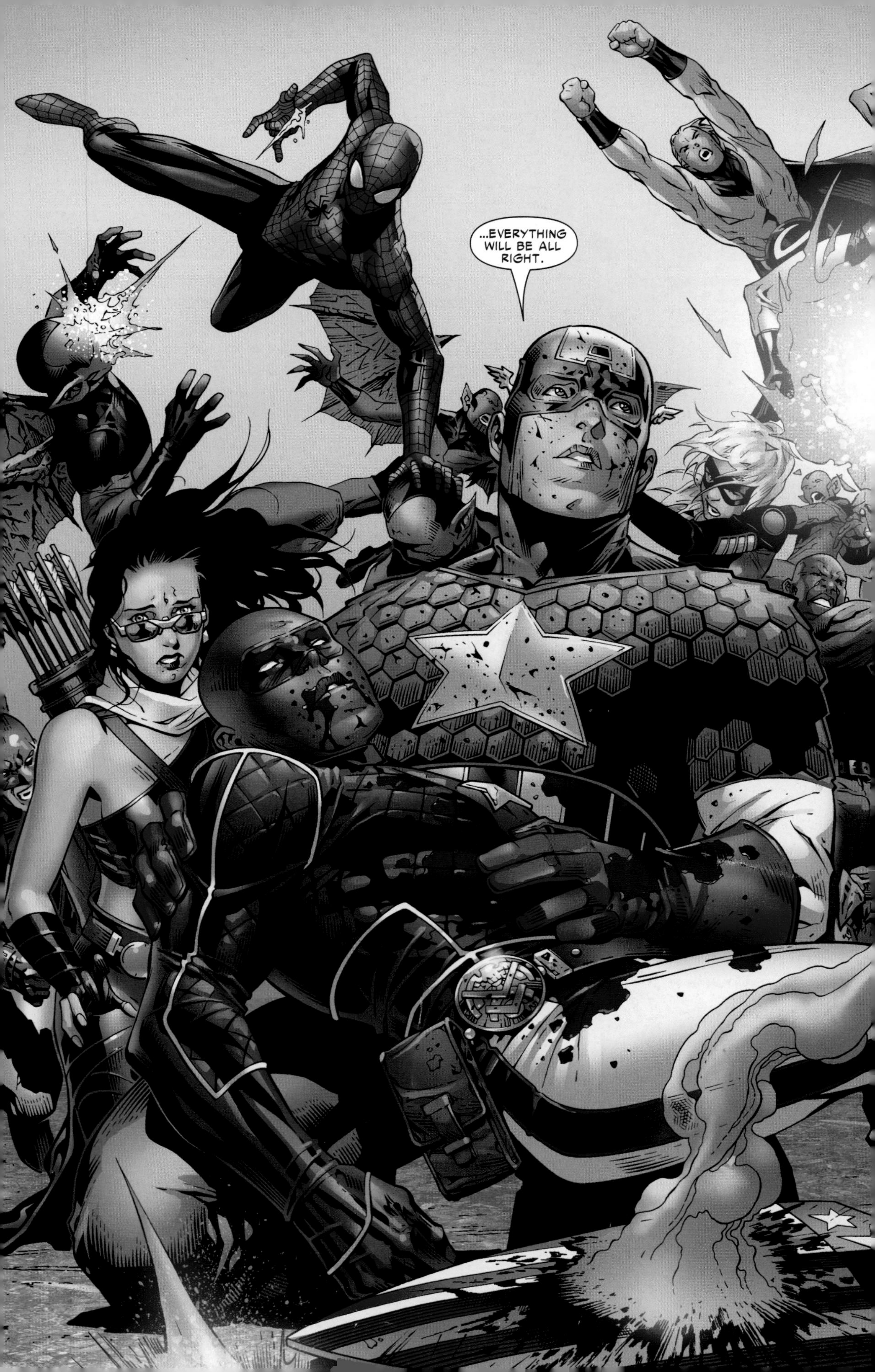
...EVERYTHING WILL BE ALL RIGHT.

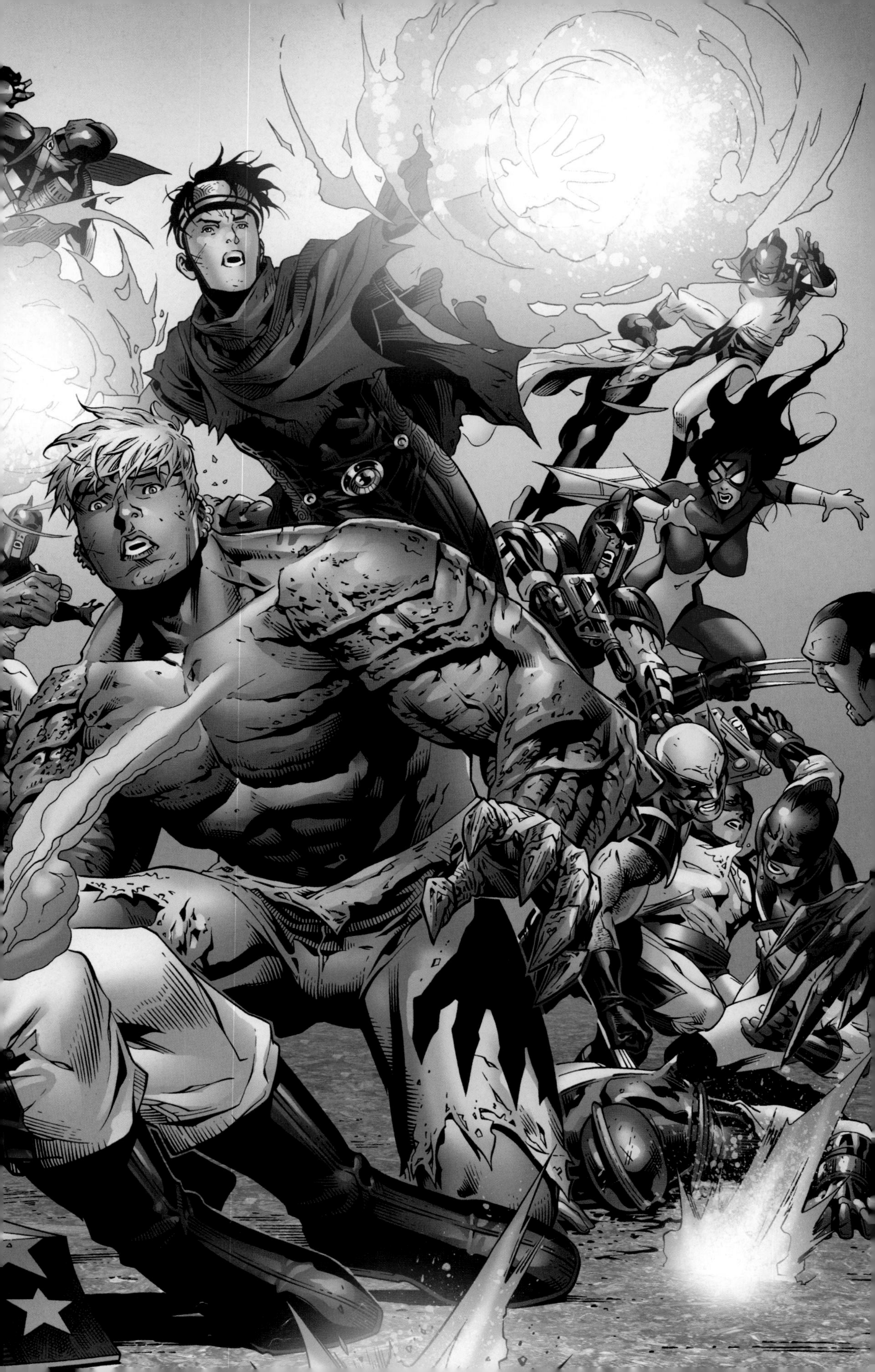

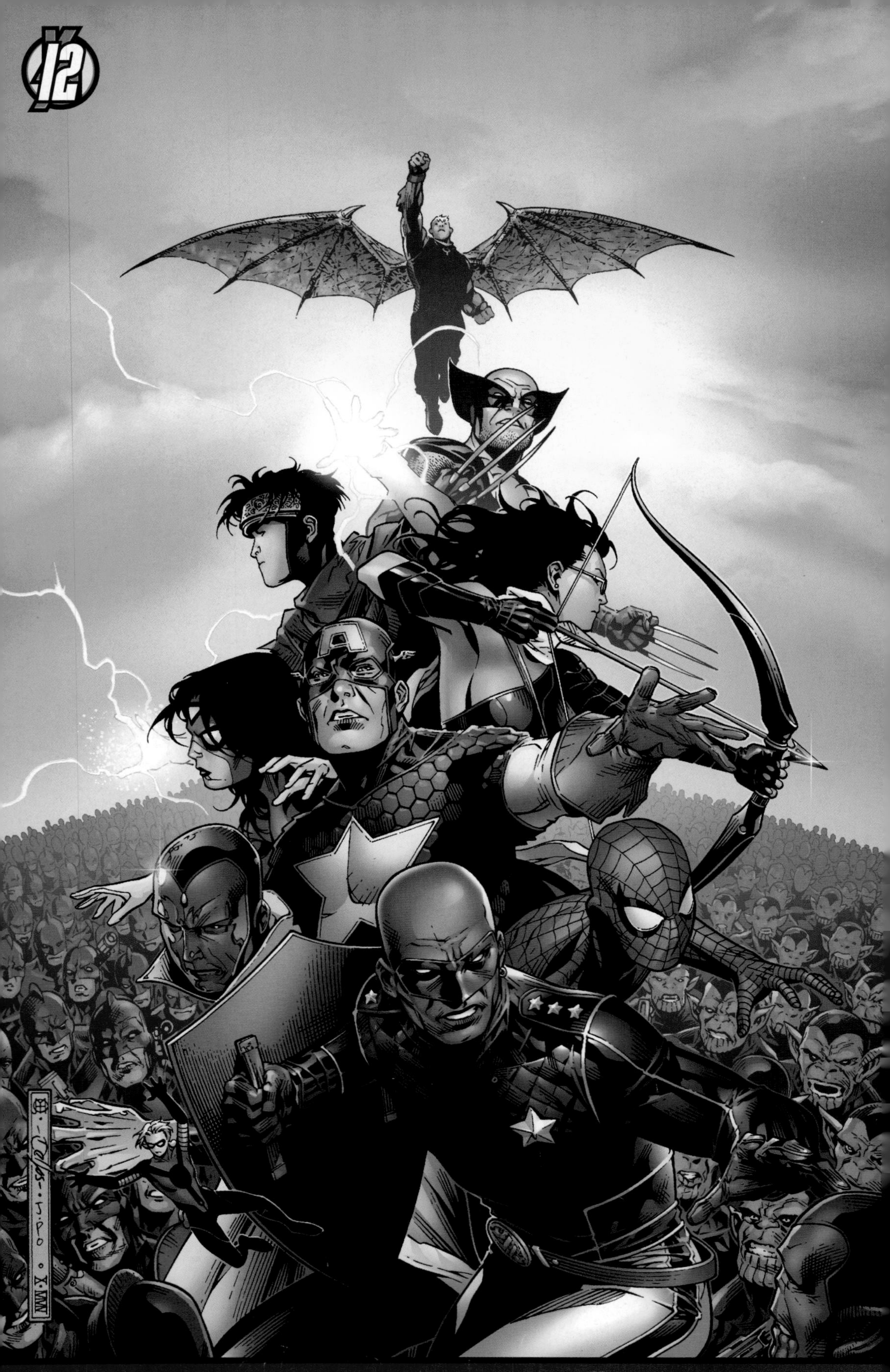

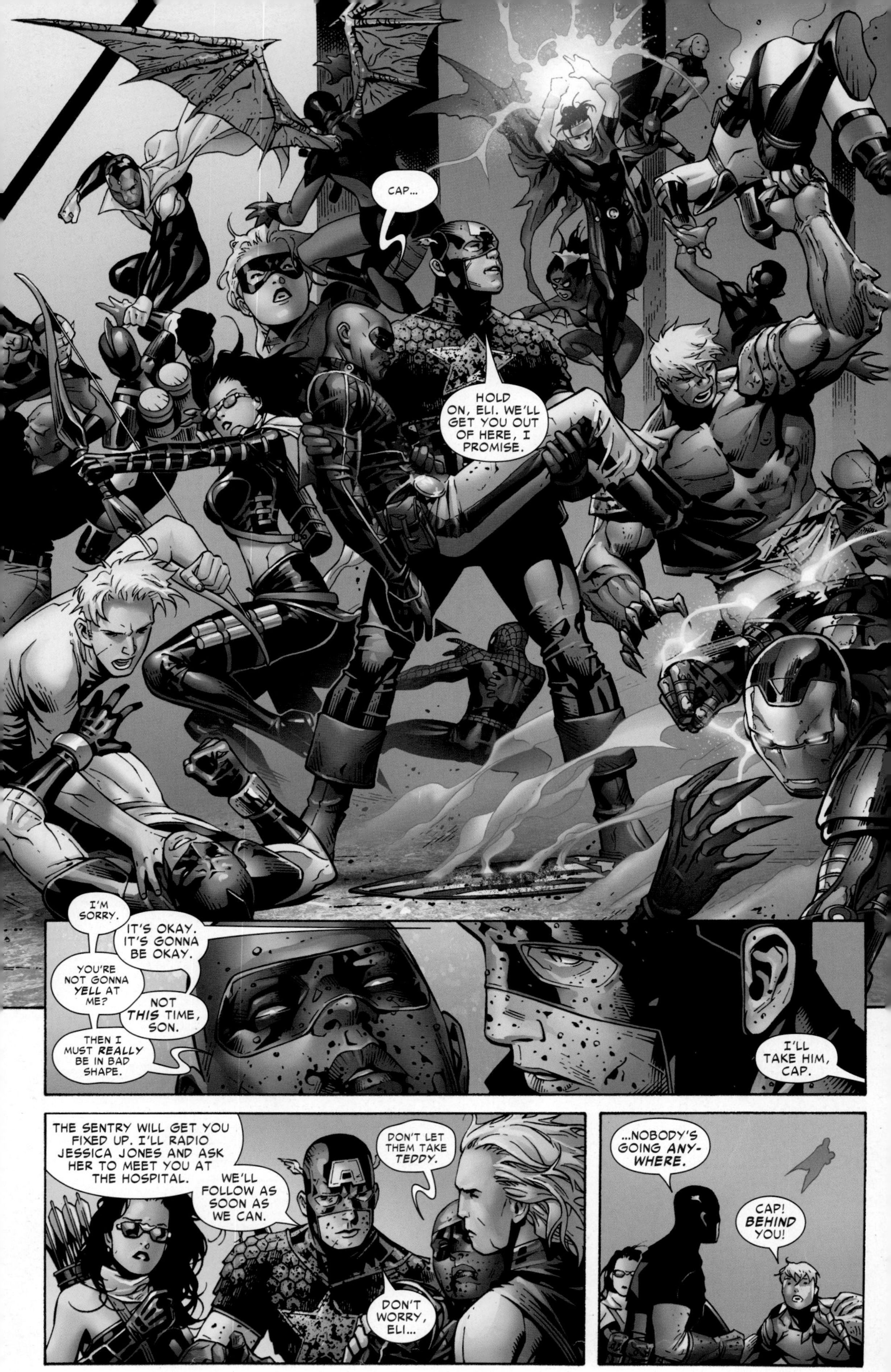
CAP...
HOLD ON, ELI. WE'LL GET YOU OUT OF HERE, I PROMISE.
I'M SORRY.
IT'S OKAY. IT'S GONNA BE OKAY.
YOU'RE NOT GONNA YELL AT ME?
NOT THIS TIME, SON.
THEN I MUST REALLY BE IN BAD SHAPE.
I'LL TAKE HIM, CAP.
THE SENTRY WILL GET YOU FIXED UP. I'LL RADIO JESSICA JONES AND ASK HER TO MEET YOU AT THE HOSPITAL.
WE'LL FOLLOW AS SOON AS WE CAN.
DON'T LET THEM TAKE TEDDY.
DON'T WORRY, ELI...
...NOBODY'S GOING ANYWHERE.
CAP! BEHIND YOU!

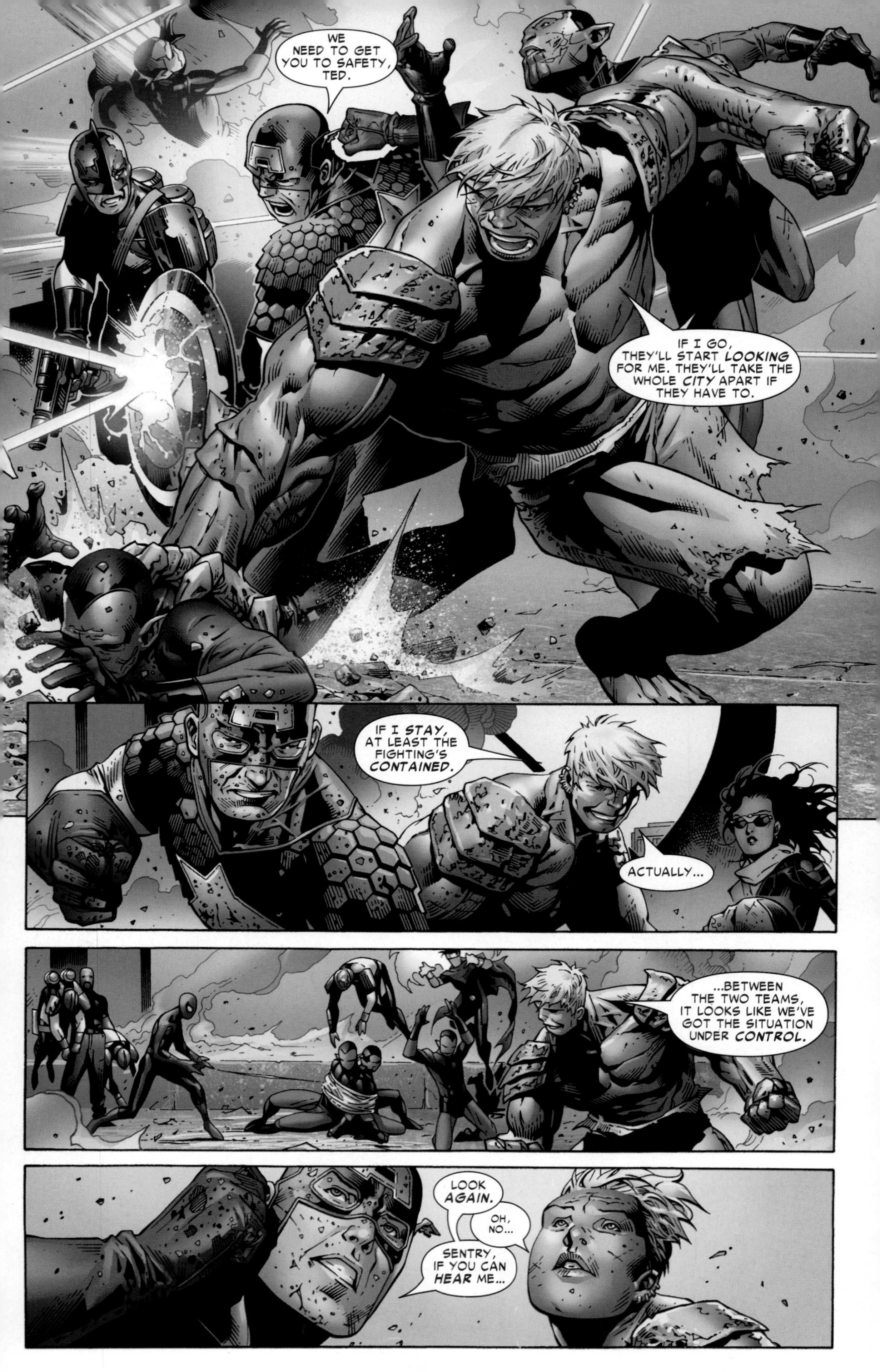
WE NEED TO GET YOU TO SAFETY, TED.
IF I GO, THEY'LL START LOOKING FOR ME. THEY'LL TAKE THE WHOLE CITY APART IF THEY HAVE TO.
IF I STAY, AT LEAST THE FIGHTING'S CONTAINED.
ACTUALLY...
...BETWEEN THE TWO TEAMS, IT LOOKS LIKE WE'VE GOT THE SITUATION UNDER CONTROL.
LOOK AGAIN.
OH, NO...
SENTRY, IF YOU CAN HEAR ME...

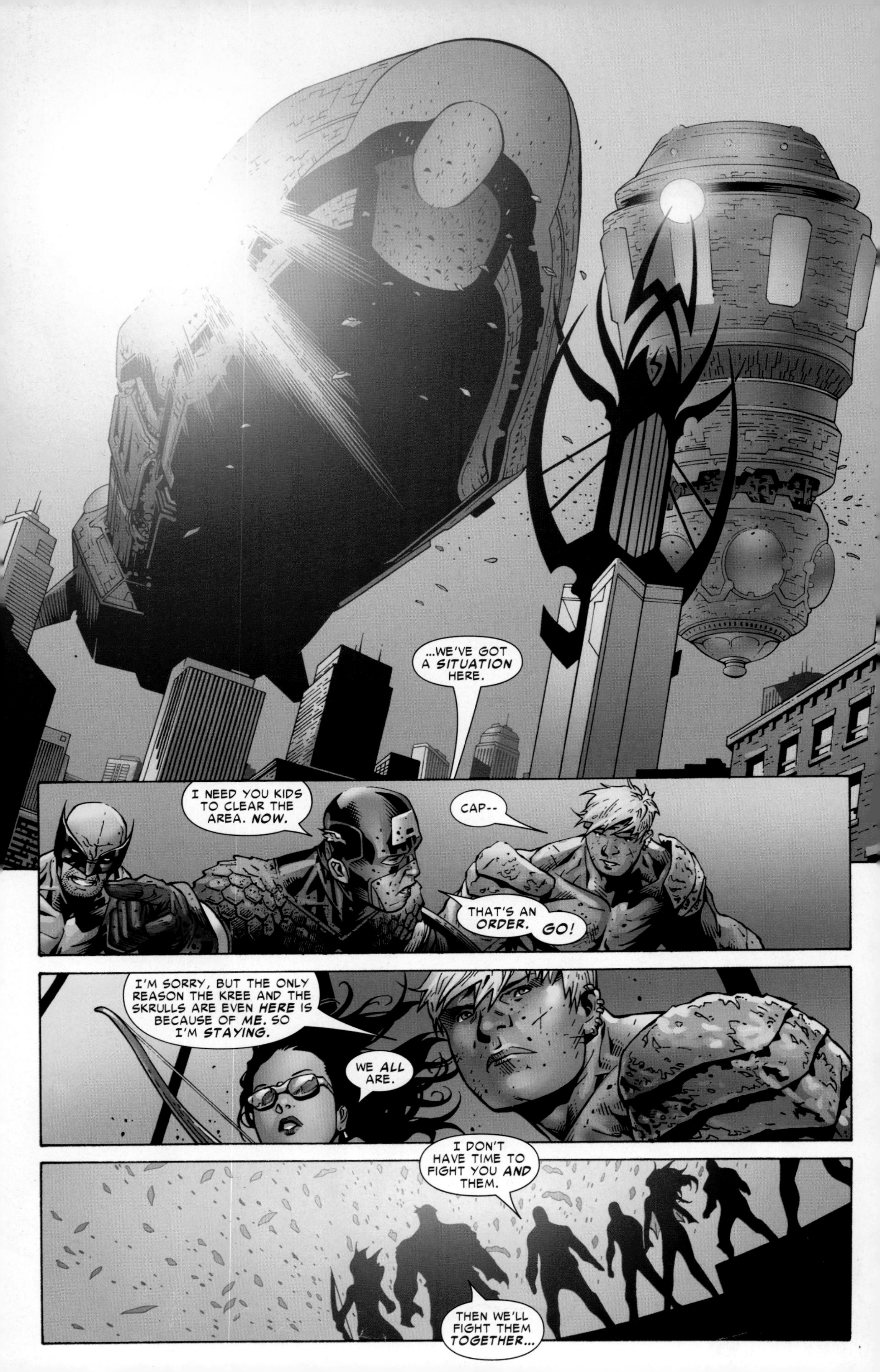
...WE'VE GOT A SITUATION HERE.
I NEED YOU KIDS TO CLEAR THE AREA. NOW.
CAP--
THAT'S AN ORDER.
GO!
I'M SORRY, BUT THE ONLY REASON THE KREE AND THE SKRULLS ARE EVEN HERE IS BECAUSE OF ME. SO I'M STAYING.
WE ALL ARE.
I DON'T HAVE TIME TO FIGHT YOU AND THEM.
THEN WE'LL FIGHT THEM TOGETHER...

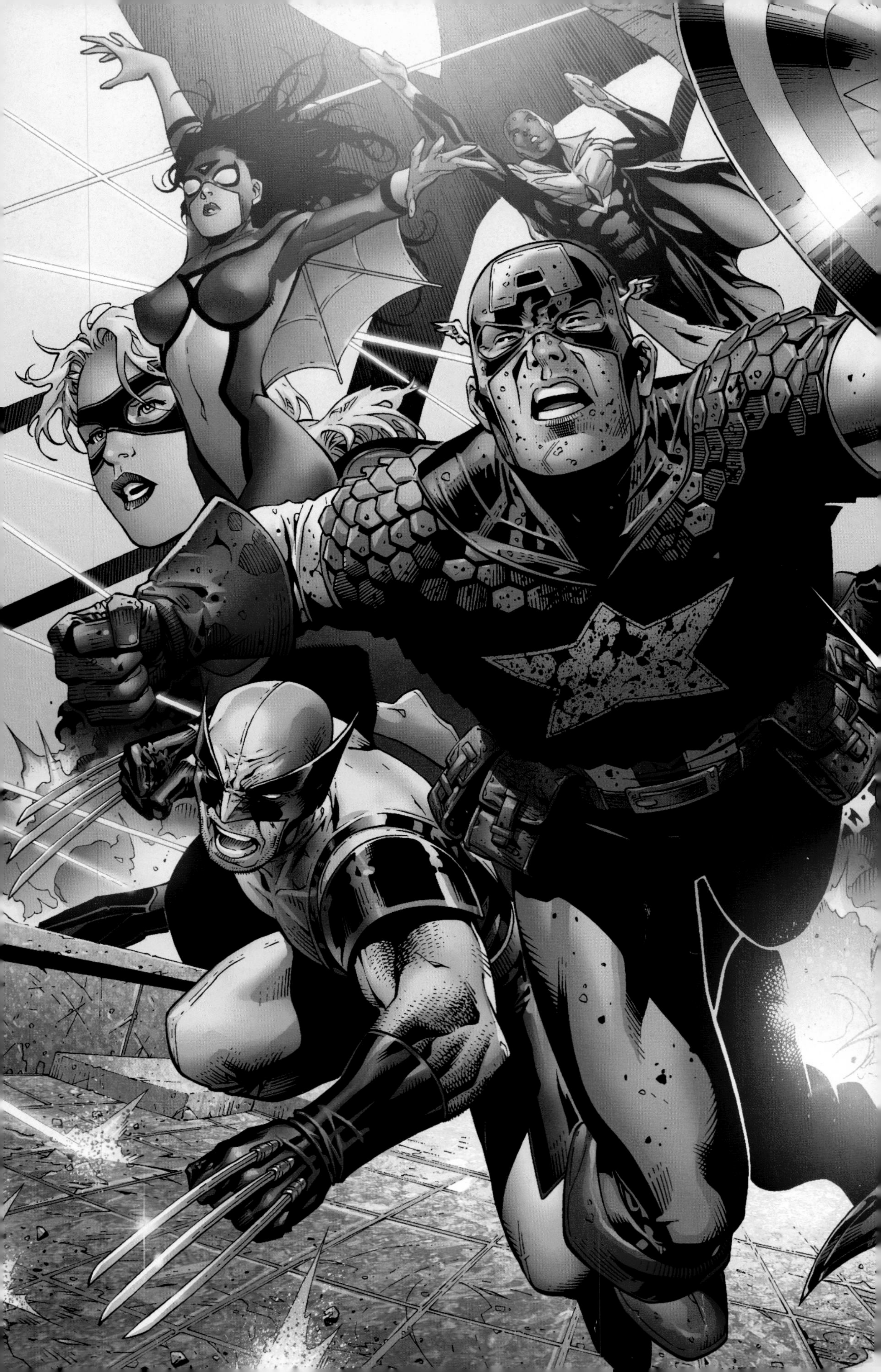

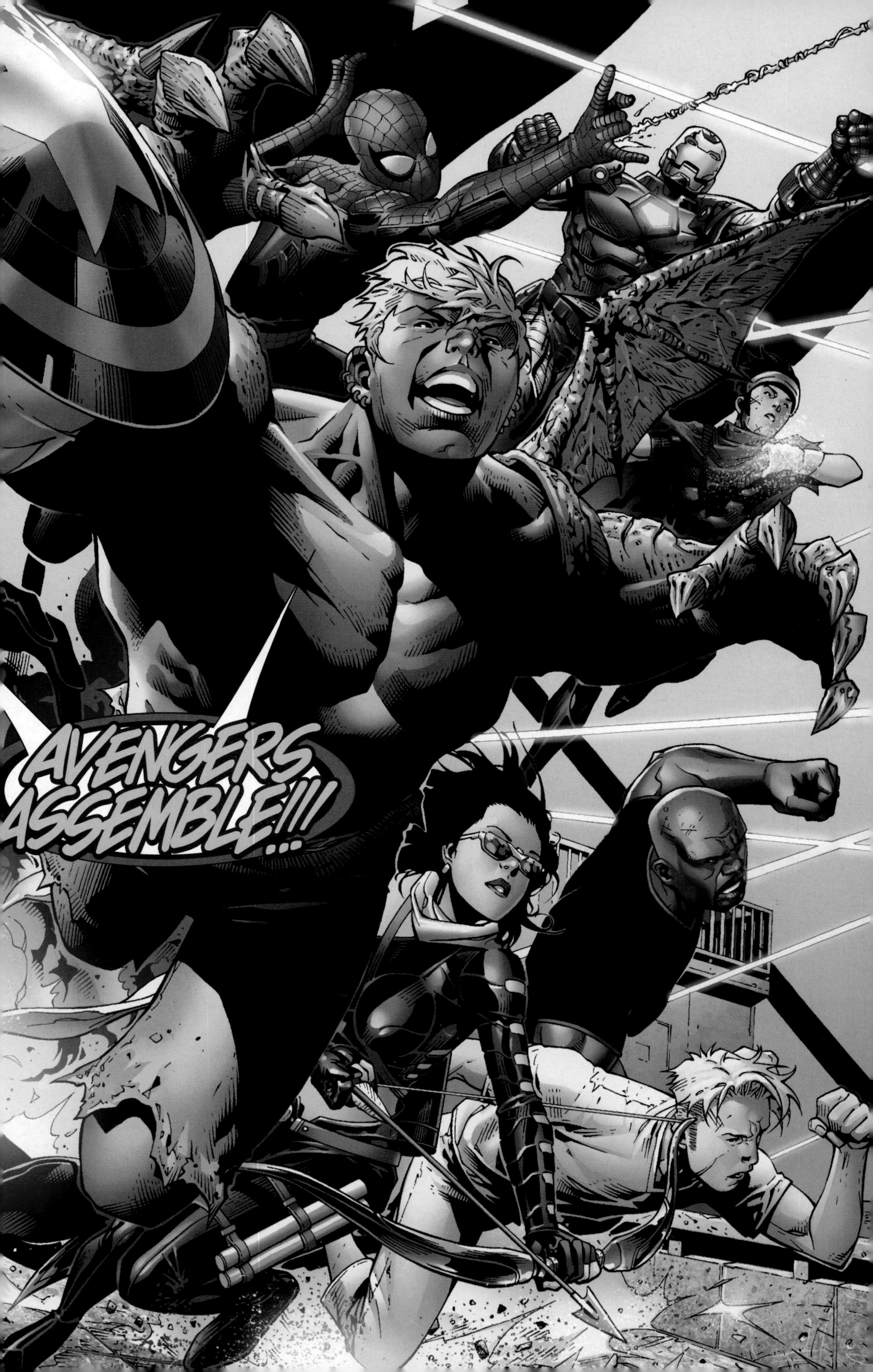
AVENGERS ASSEMBLE!!!

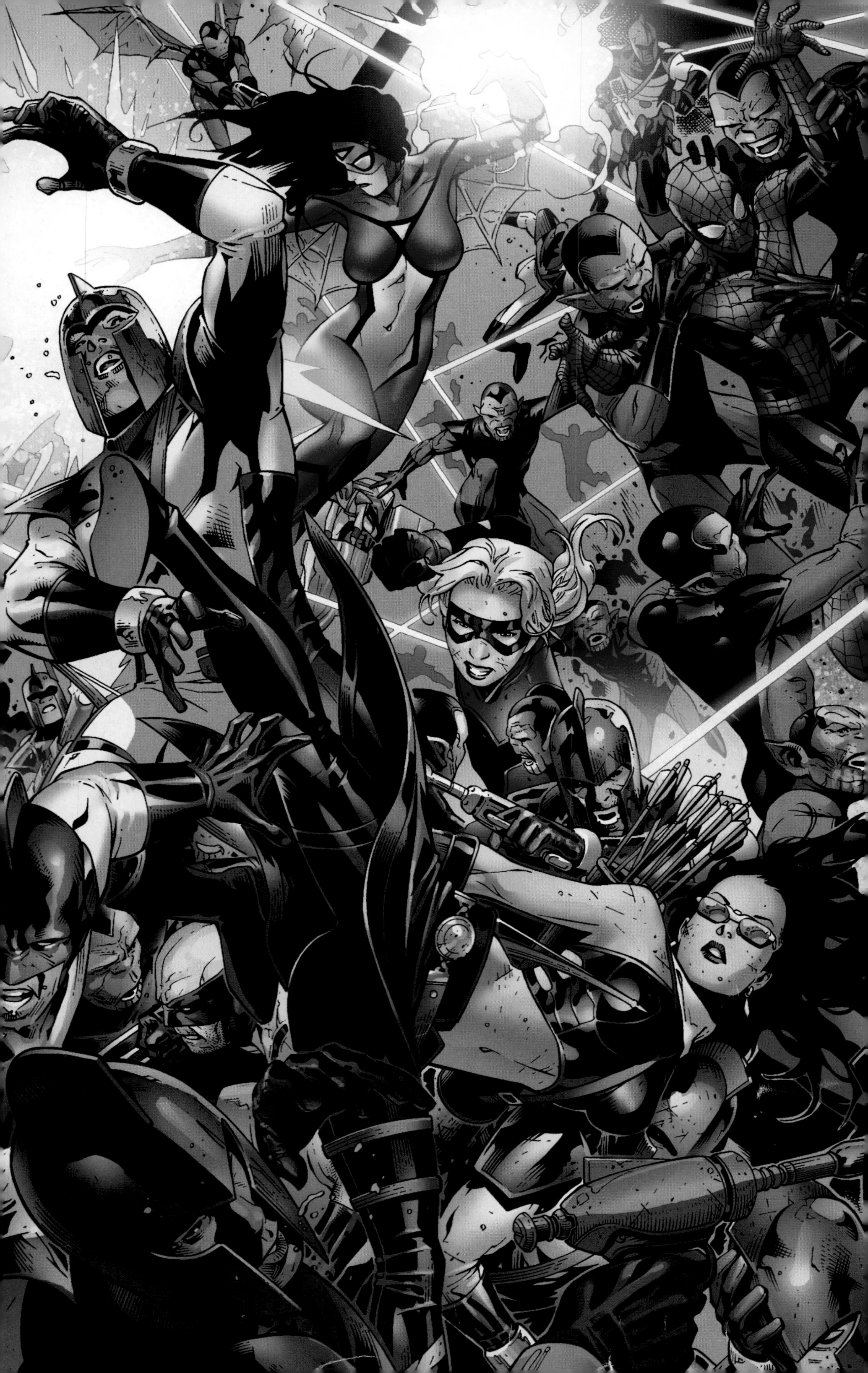

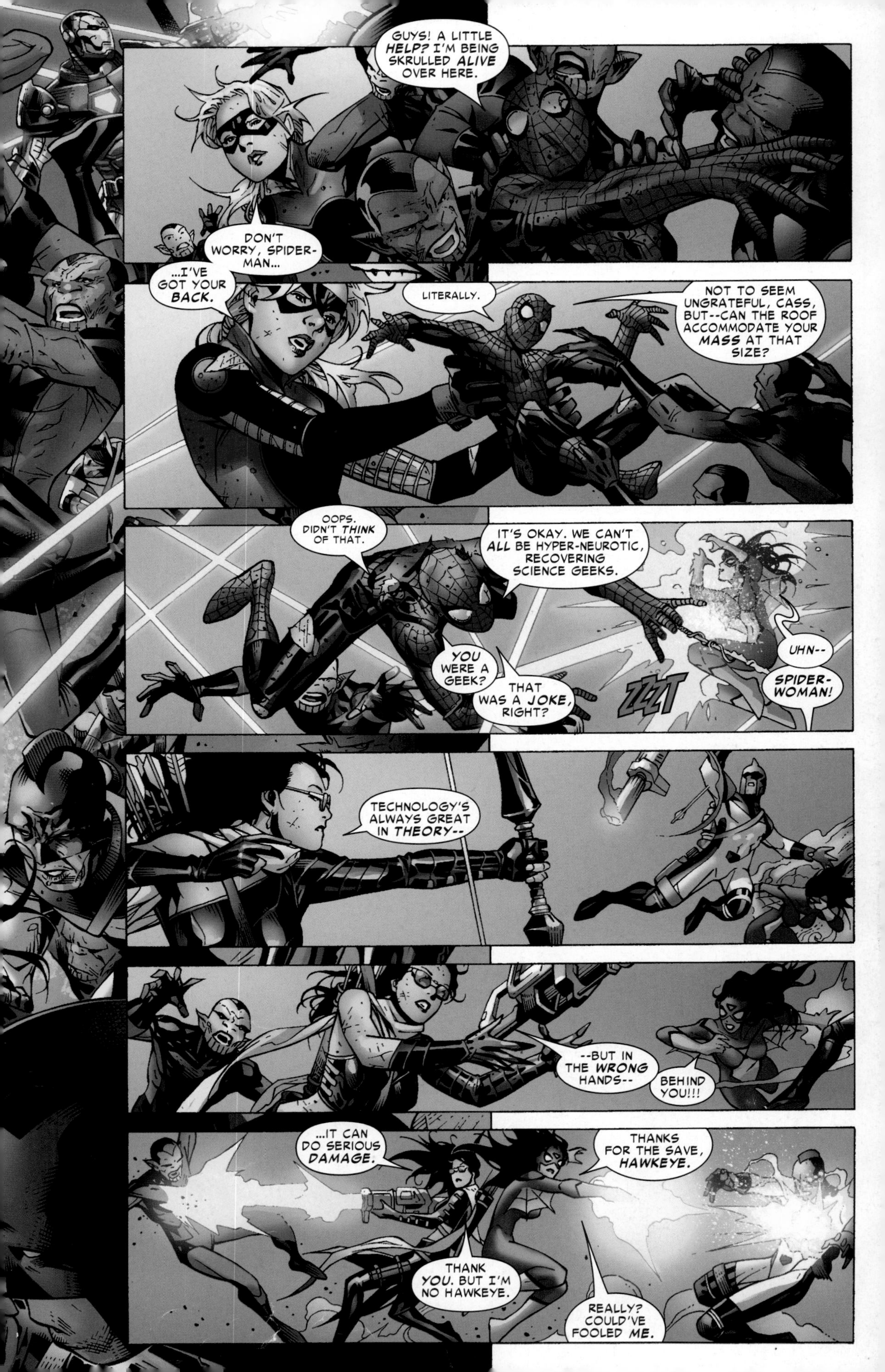
GUYS! A LITTLE HELP? I'M BEING SKRULLED ALIVE OVER HERE.
DON'T WORRY, SPIDER-MAN...
...I'VE GOT YOUR BACK.
LITERALLY.
NOT TO SEEM UNGRATEFUL, CASS, BUT--CAN THE ROOF ACCOMMODATE YOUR MASS AT THAT SIZE?
OOPS. DIDN'T THINK OF THAT.
IT'S OKAY. WE CAN'T ALL BE HYPER-NEUROTIC, RECOVERING SCIENCE GEEKS.
YOU WERE A GEEK?
THAT WAS A JOKE, RIGHT?
ZZZT
UHN--
SPIDER-WOMAN!
TECHNOLOGY'S ALWAYS GREAT IN THEORY--
--BUT IN THE WRONG HANDS--
BEHIND YOU!!!
...IT CAN DO SERIOUS DAMAGE.
THANKS FOR THE SAVE, HAWKEYE.
THANK YOU. BUT I'M NO HAWKEYE.
REALLY? COULD'VE FOOLED ME.

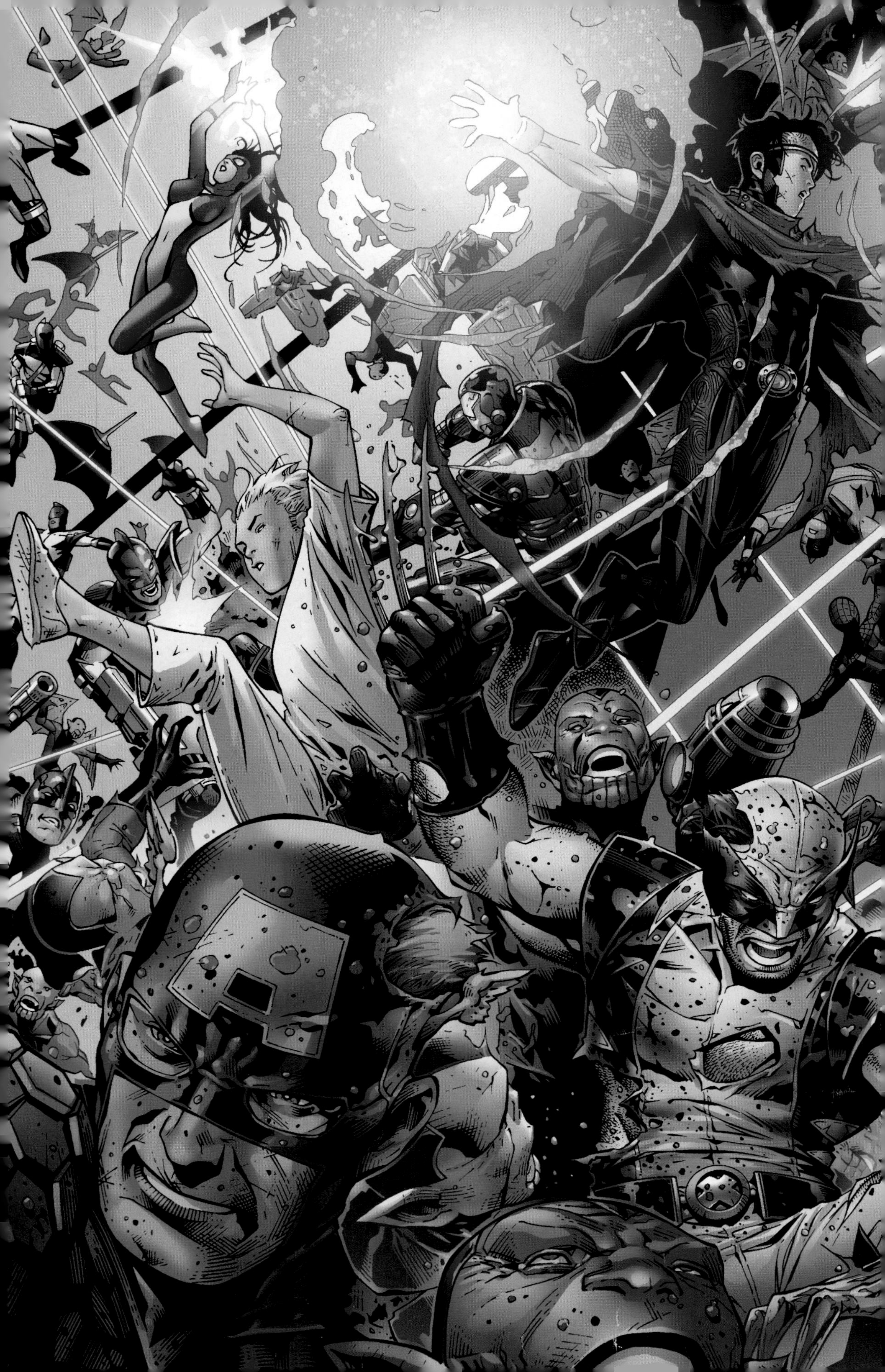

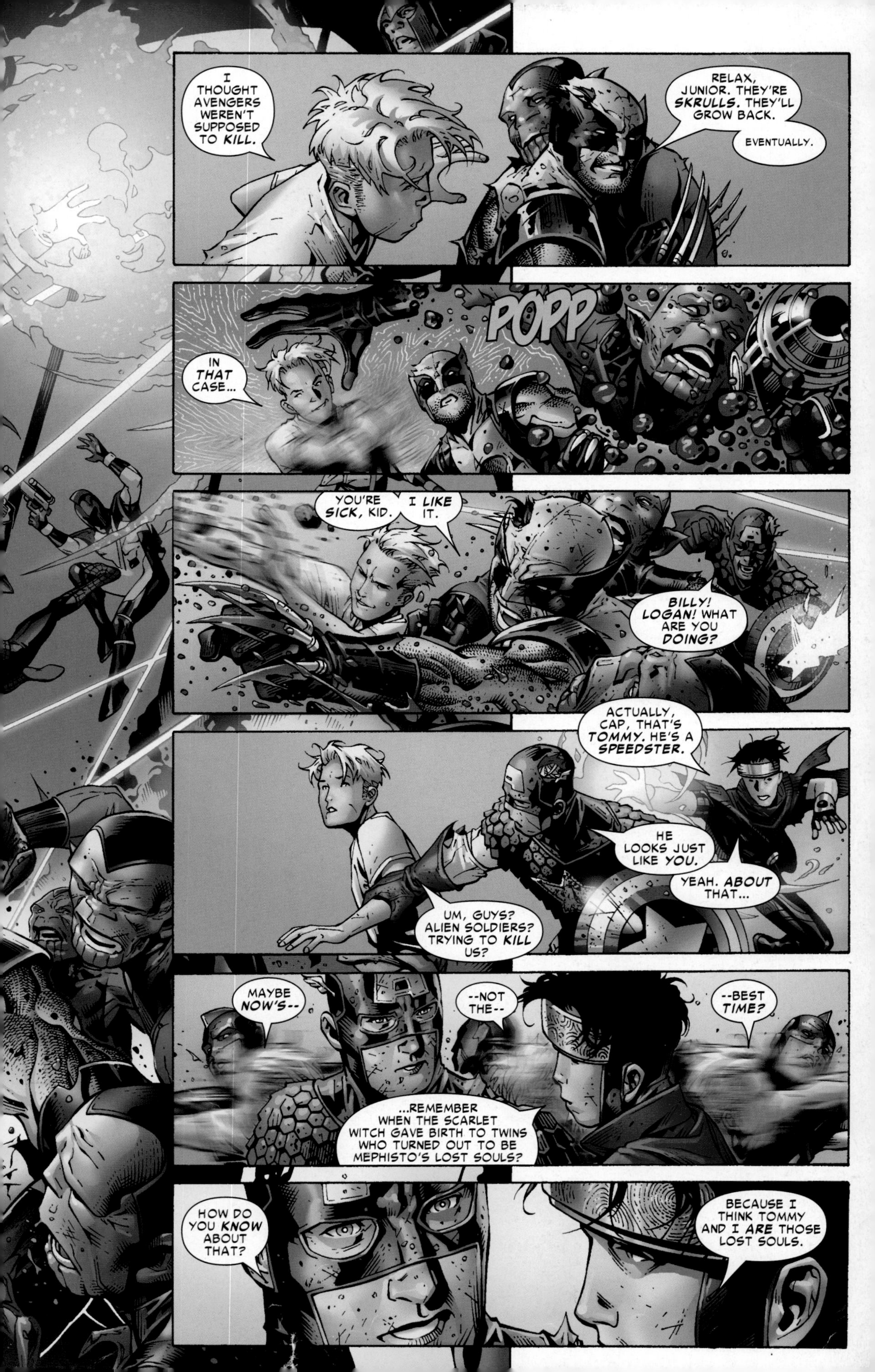
I THOUGHT AVENGERS WEREN'T SUPPOSED TO KILL.
RELAX, JUNIOR. THEY'RE SKRULLS. THEY'LL GROW BACK.
EVENTUALLY.
POPP
IN THAT CASE...
YOU'RE SICK, KID.
I LIKE IT.
BILLY! LOGAN! WHAT ARE YOU DOING?
ACTUALLY, CAP, THAT'S TOMMY. HE'S A SPEEDSTER.
HE LOOKS JUST LIKE YOU.
YEAH. ABOUT THAT...
UM, GUYS? ALIEN SOLDIERS? TRYING TO KILL US?
MAYBE NOW'S--
--NOT THE--
--BEST TIME?
...REMEMBER WHEN THE SCARLET WITCH GAVE BIRTH TO TWINS WHO TURNED OUT TO BE MEPHISTO'S LOST SOULS?
HOW DO YOU KNOW ABOUT THAT?
BECAUSE I THINK TOMMY AND I ARE THOSE LOST SOULS.

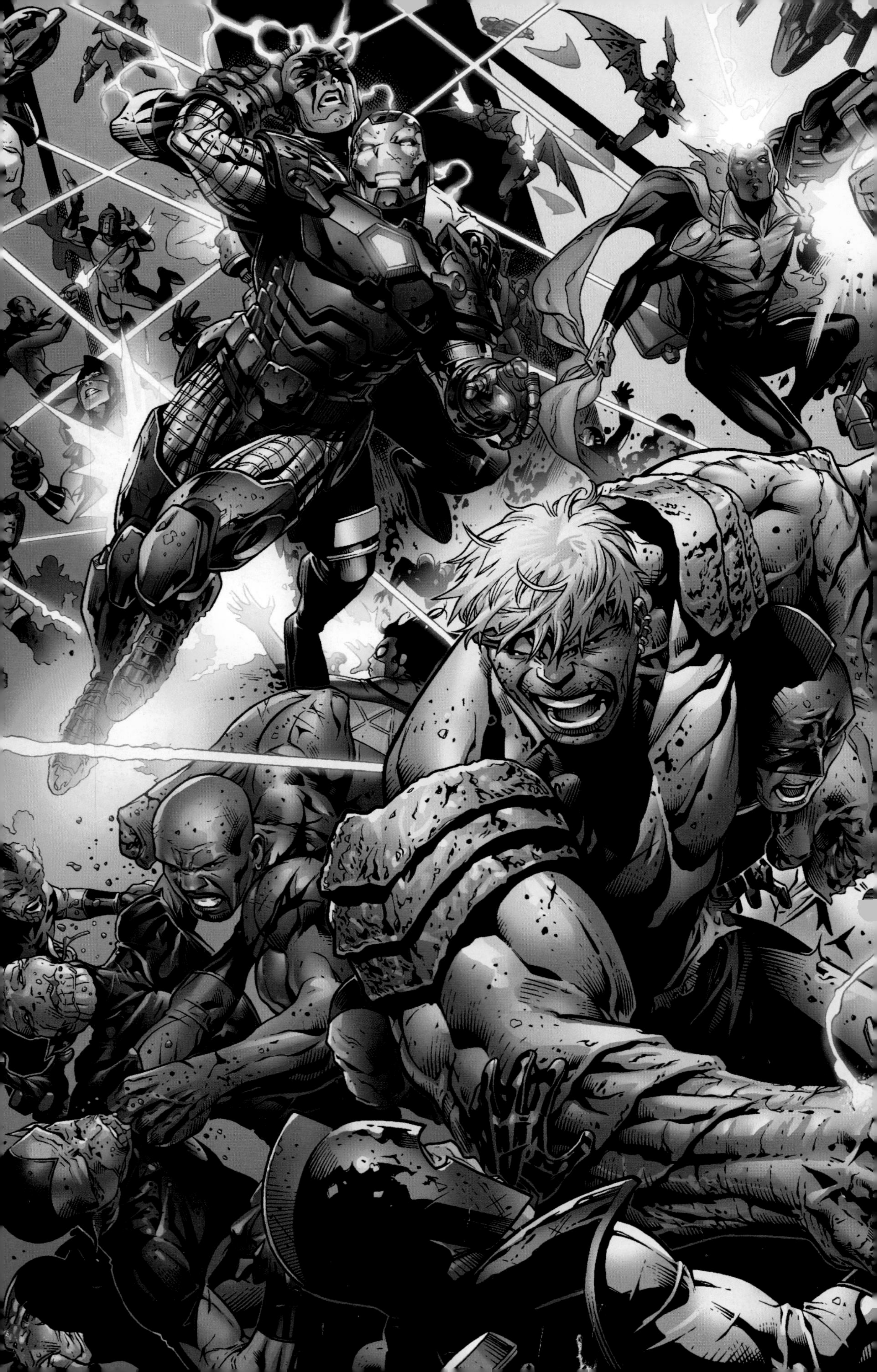

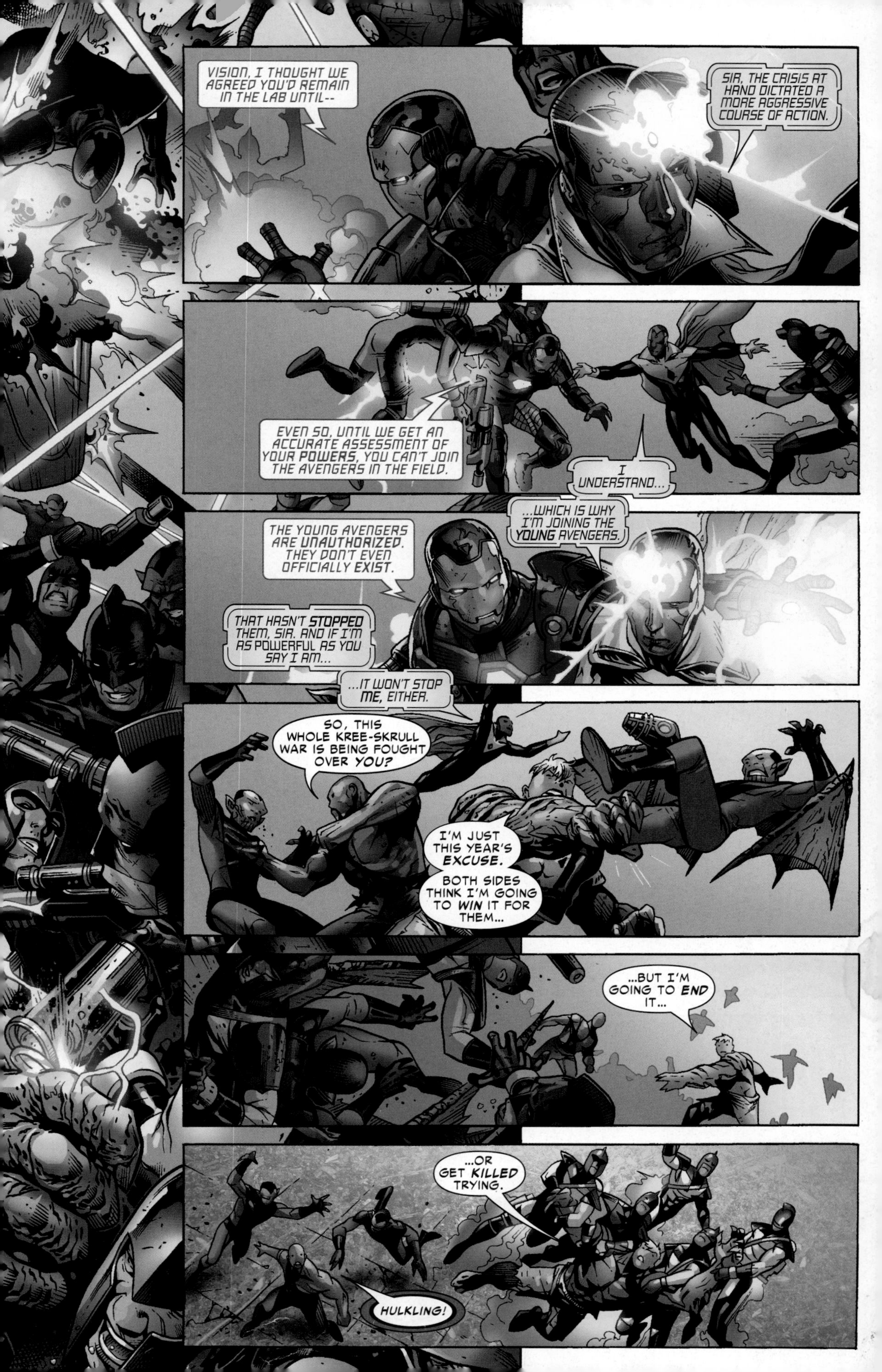
VISION, I THOUGHT WE AGREED YOU'D REMAIN IN THE LAB UNTIL--
SIR, THE CRISIS AT HAND DICTATED A MORE AGGRESSIVE COURSE OF ACTION.
EVEN SO, UNTIL WE GET AN ACCURATE ASSESSMENT OF YOUR POWERS, YOU CAN'T JOIN THE AVENGERS IN THE FIELD.
I UNDERSTAND...
...WHICH IS WHY I'M JOINING THE YOUNG AVENGERS.
THE YOUNG AVENGERS ARE UNAUTHORIZED. THEY DON'T EVEN OFFICIALLY EXIST.
THAT HASN'T STOPPED THEM, SIR. AND IF I'M AS POWERFUL AS YOU SAY I AM...
...IT WON'T STOP ME, EITHER.
SO, THIS WHOLE KREE-SKRULL WAR IS BEING FOUGHT OVER YOU?
I'M JUST THIS YEAR'S EXCUSE.
BOTH SIDES THINK I'M GOING TO WIN IT FOR THEM...
...BUT I'M GOING TO END IT...
...OR GET KILLED TRYING.
HULKLING!

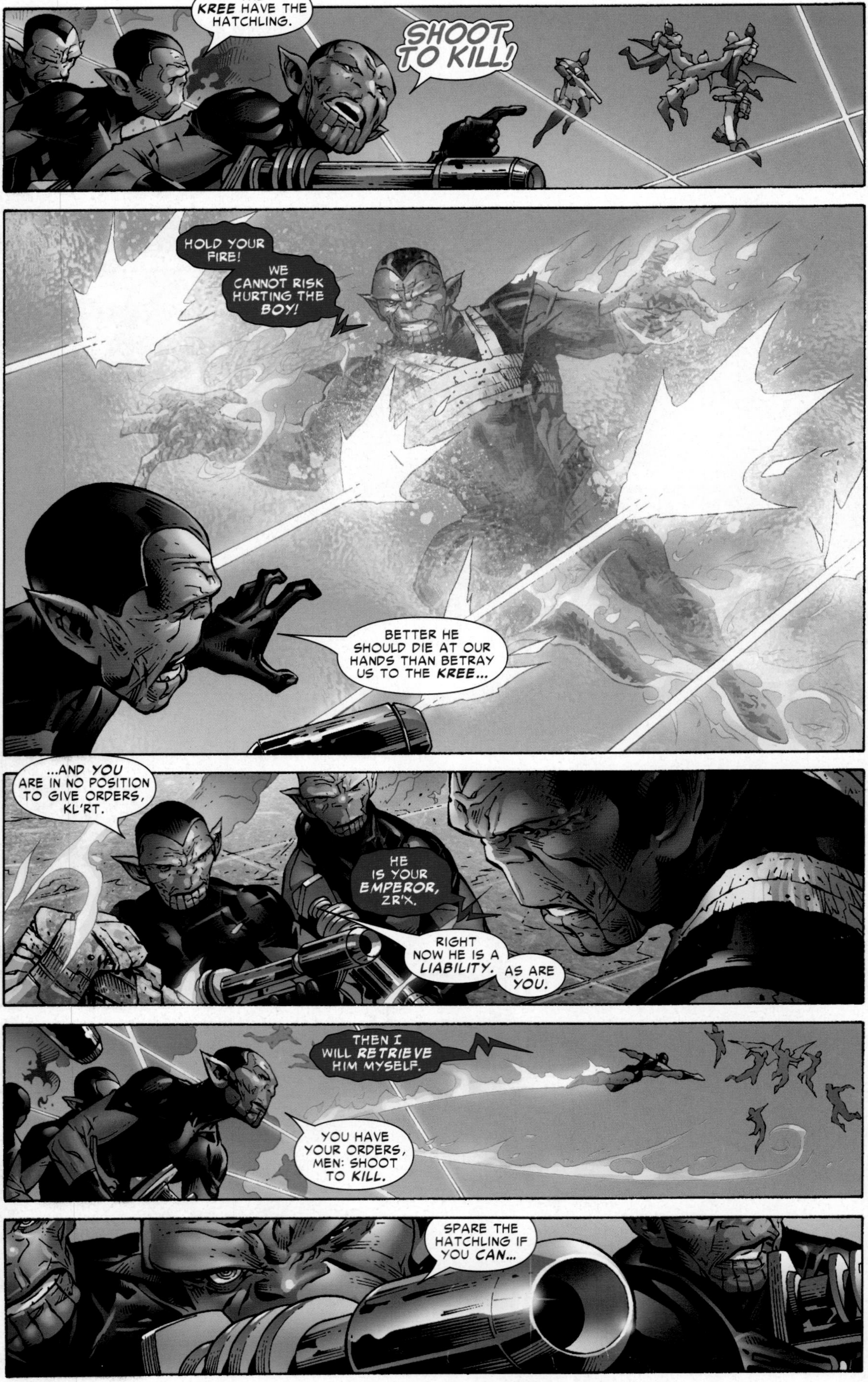
THE KREE HAVE THE HATCHLING.
SHOOT TO KILL!
HOLD YOUR FIRE! WE CANNOT RISK HURTING THE BOY!
BETTER HE SHOULD DIE AT OUR HANDS THAN BETRAY US TO THE KREE...
...AND YOU ARE IN NO POSITION TO GIVE ORDERS, KL'RT.
HE IS YOUR EMPEROR, ZR'X.
RIGHT NOW HE IS A LIABILITY. AS ARE YOU.
THEN I WILL RETRIEVE HIM MYSELF.
YOU HAVE YOUR ORDERS, MEN: SHOOT TO KILL.
SPARE THE HATCHLING IF YOU CAN...

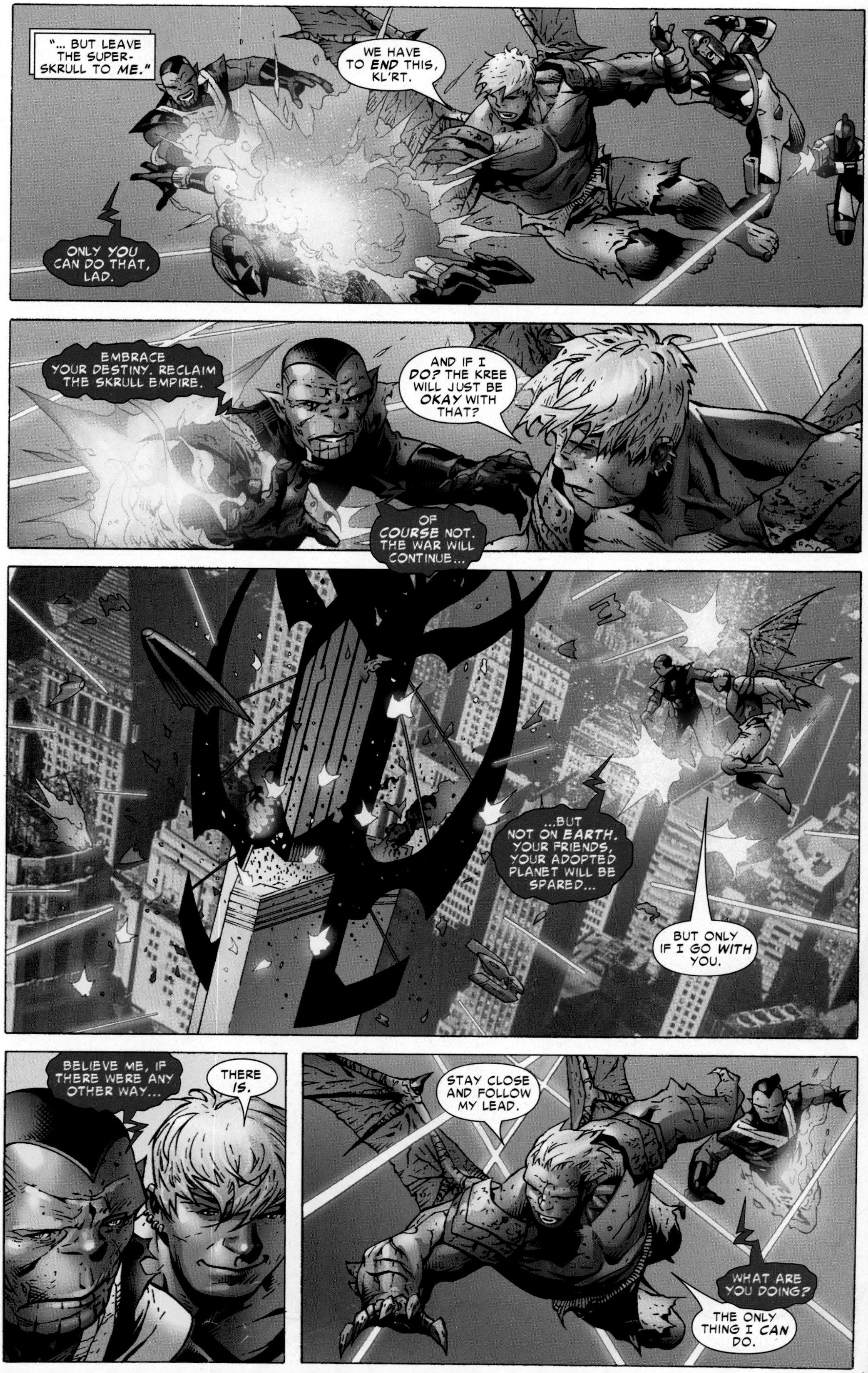
"... BUT LEAVE THE SUPER-SKRULL TO ME."
WE HAVE TO END THIS, KL'RT.
ONLY YOU CAN DO THAT, LAD.
EMBRACE YOUR DESTINY. RECLAIM THE SKRULL EMPIRE.
AND IF I DO? THE KREE WILL JUST BE OKAY WITH THAT?
OF COURSE NOT. THE WAR WILL CONTINUE...
...BUT NOT ON EARTH. YOUR FRIENDS, YOUR ADOPTED PLANET WILL BE SPARED...
BUT ONLY IF I GO WITH YOU.
BELIEVE ME, IF THERE WERE ANY OTHER WAY...
THERE IS.
STAY CLOSE AND FOLLOW MY LEAD.
WHAT ARE YOU DOING?
THE ONLY THING I CAN DO.

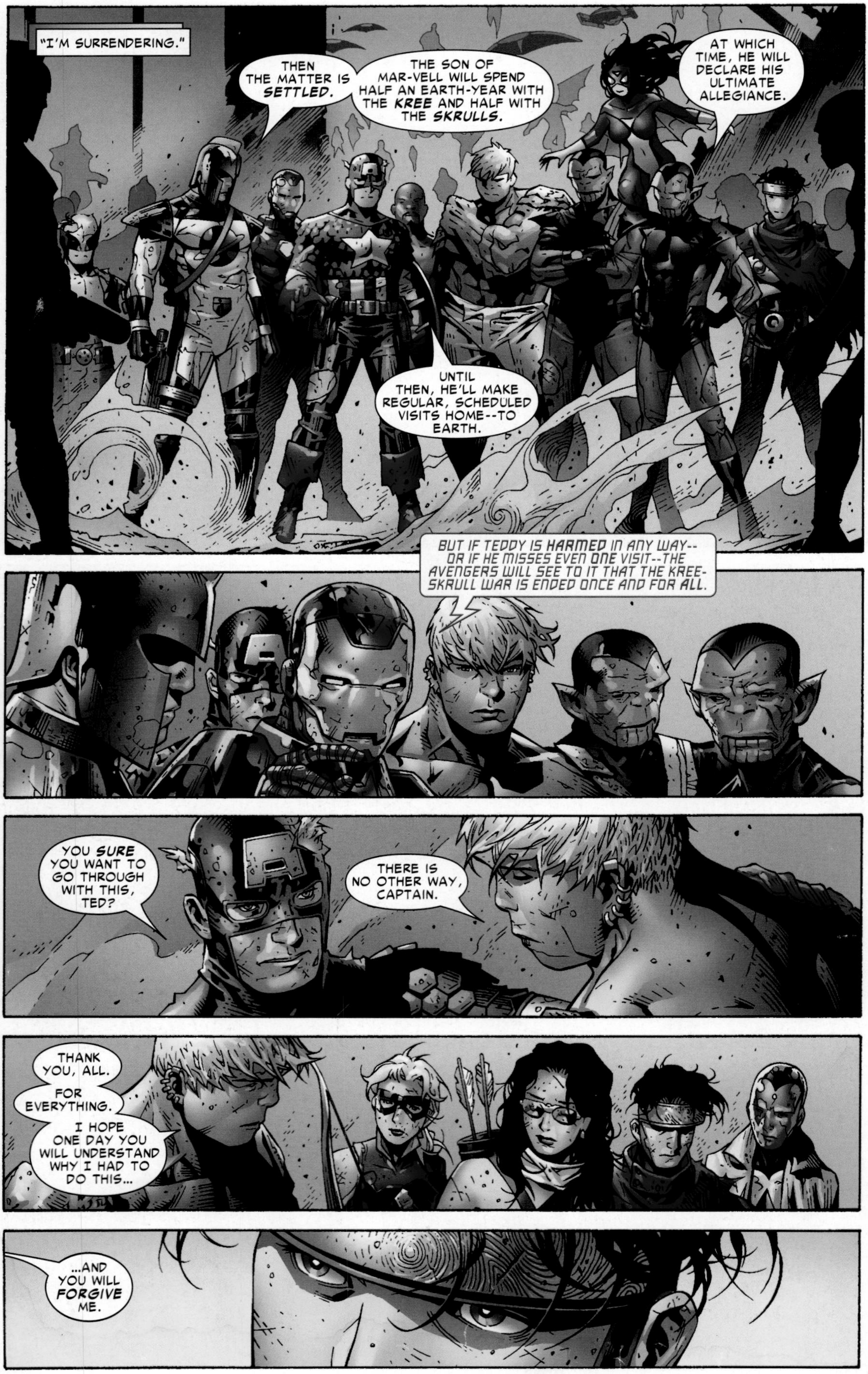
"I'M SURRENDERING."
THEN THE MATTER IS SETTLED.
THE SON OF MAR-VELL WILL SPEND HALF AN EARTH-YEAR WITH THE KREE AND HALF WITH THE SKRULLS.
AT WHICH TIME, HE WILL DECLARE HIS ULTIMATE ALLEGIANCE.
UNTIL THEN, HE'LL MAKE REGULAR, SCHEDULED VISITS HOME--TO EARTH.
BUT IF TEDDY IS HARMED IN ANY WAY--OR IF HE MISSES EVEN ONE VISIT--THE AVENGERS WILL SEE TO IT THAT THE KREE-SKRULL WAR IS ENDED ONCE AND FOR ALL.
YOU SURE YOU WANT TO GO THROUGH WITH THIS, TED?
THERE IS NO OTHER WAY, CAPTAIN.
THANK YOU, ALL.
FOR EVERYTHING.
I HOPE ONE DAY YOU WILL UNDERSTAND WHY I HAD TO DO THIS...
...AND YOU WILL FORGIVE ME.

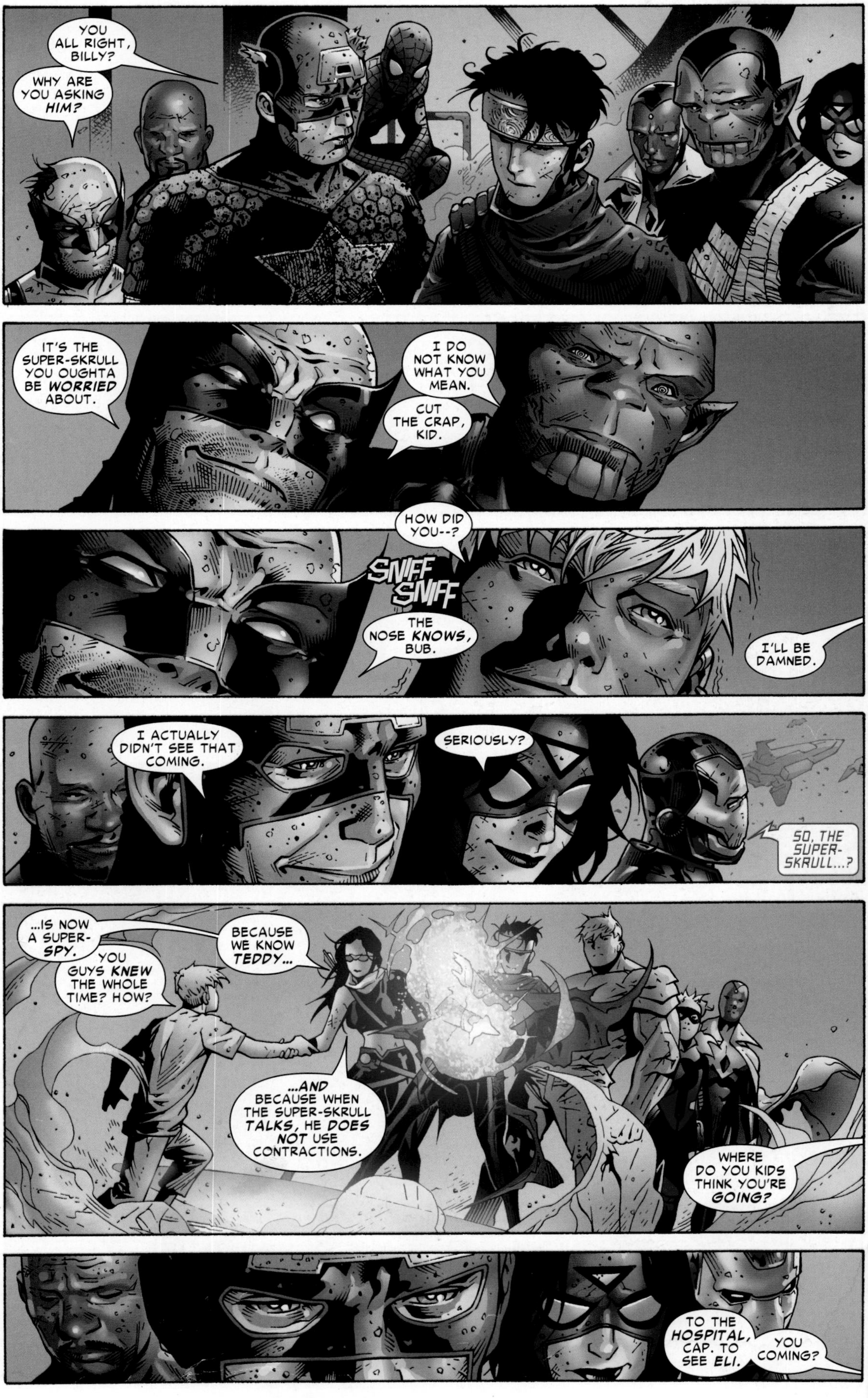
YOU ALL RIGHT, BILLY?
WHY ARE YOU ASKING *HIM?*
IT'S THE SUPER-SKRULL YOU OUGHTA BE ***WORRIED*** ABOUT.
I DO NOT KNOW WHAT YOU MEAN.
CUT THE CRAP, KID.
HOW DID YOU--?
SNIFF SNIFF
THE NOSE ***KNOWS,*** BUB.
I'LL BE DAMNED.
I ACTUALLY DIDN'T SEE THAT COMING.
SERIOUSLY?
SO, THE SUPER-SKRULL...?
...IS NOW A SUPER-*SPY.*
BECAUSE WE KNOW *TEDDY...*
YOU GUYS ***KNEW*** THE WHOLE TIME? HOW?
...AND BECAUSE WHEN THE SUPER-SKRULL *TALKS,* HE ***DOES NOT*** USE CONTRACTIONS.
WHERE DO YOU KIDS THINK YOU'RE *GOING?*
TO THE *HOSPITAL,* CAP. TO SEE *ELI.*
YOU COMING?

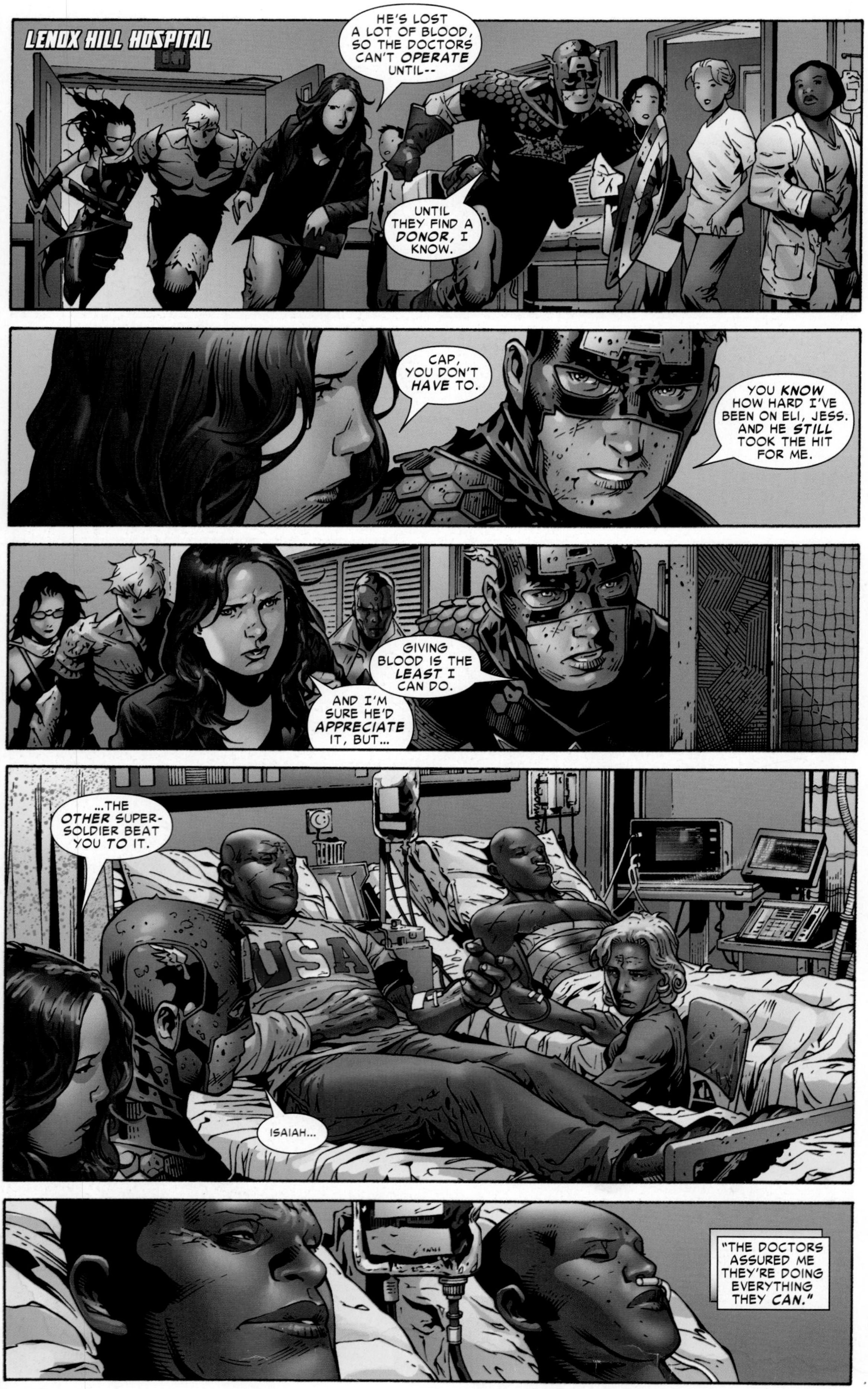
LENOX HILL HOSPITAL
HE'S LOST A LOT OF BLOOD, SO THE DOCTORS CAN'T OPERATE UNTIL--
UNTIL THEY FIND A DONOR, I KNOW.
CAP, YOU DON'T HAVE TO.
YOU KNOW HOW HARD I'VE BEEN ON ELI, JESS. AND HE STILL TOOK THE HIT FOR ME.
GIVING BLOOD IS THE LEAST I CAN DO.
AND I'M SURE HE'D APPRECIATE IT, BUT...
...THE OTHER SUPER-SOLDIER BEAT YOU TO IT.
USA
ISAIAH...
"THE DOCTORS ASSURED ME THEY'RE DOING EVERYTHING THEY CAN."

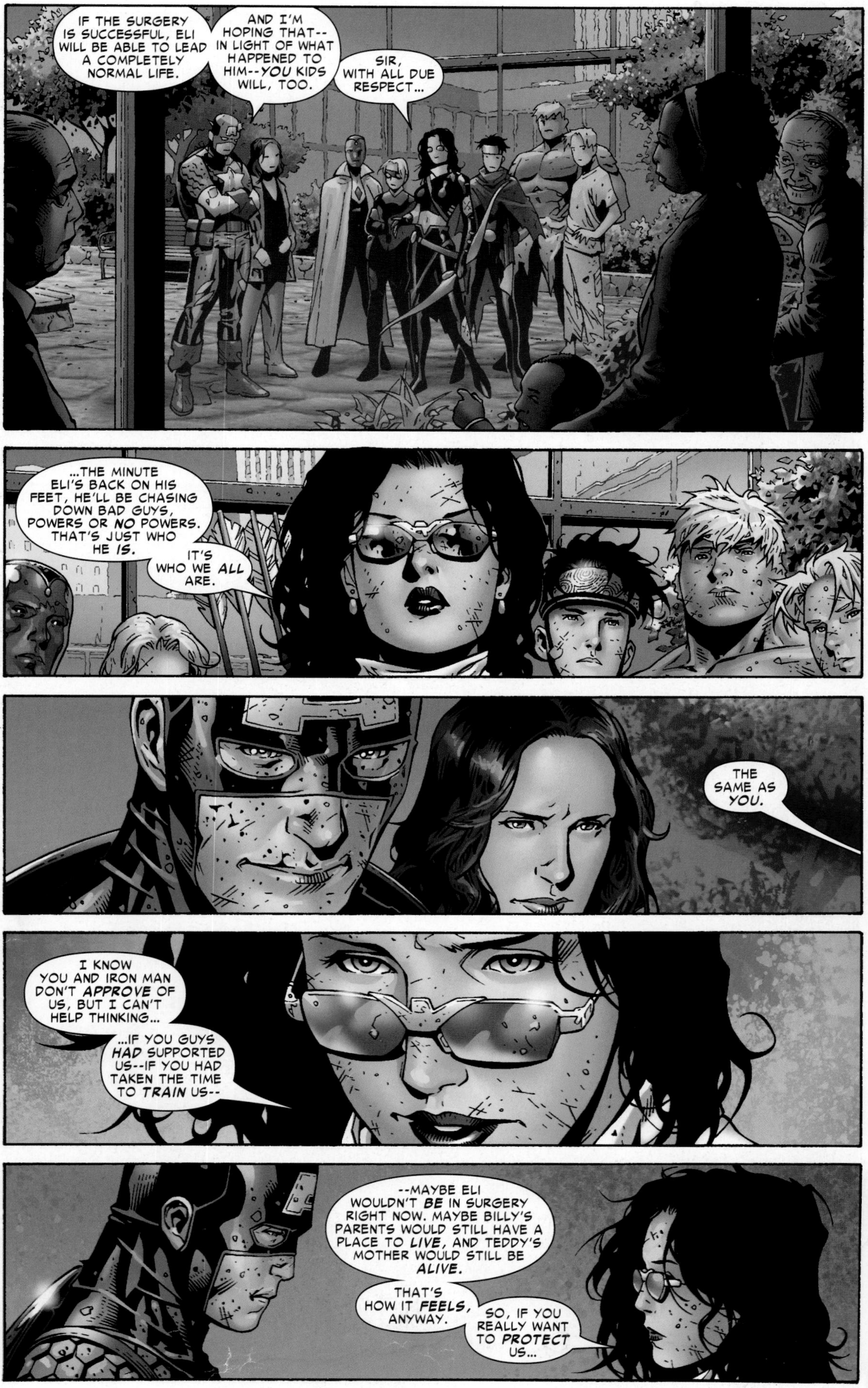
IF THE SURGERY IS SUCCESSFUL, ELI WILL BE ABLE TO LEAD A COMPLETELY NORMAL LIFE.
AND I'M HOPING THAT-- IN LIGHT OF WHAT HAPPENED TO HIM--YOU KIDS WILL, TOO.
SIR, WITH ALL DUE RESPECT...
...THE MINUTE ELI'S BACK ON HIS FEET, HE'LL BE CHASING DOWN BAD GUYS, POWERS OR NO POWERS. THAT'S JUST WHO HE IS.
IT'S WHO WE ALL ARE.
THE SAME AS YOU.
I KNOW YOU AND IRON MAN DON'T APPROVE OF US, BUT I CAN'T HELP THINKING...
...IF YOU GUYS HAD SUPPORTED US--IF YOU HAD TAKEN THE TIME TO TRAIN US--
--MAYBE ELI WOULDN'T BE IN SURGERY RIGHT NOW. MAYBE BILLY'S PARENTS WOULD STILL HAVE A PLACE TO LIVE, AND TEDDY'S MOTHER WOULD STILL BE ALIVE.
THAT'S HOW IT FEELS, ANYWAY.
SO, IF YOU REALLY WANT TO PROTECT US...

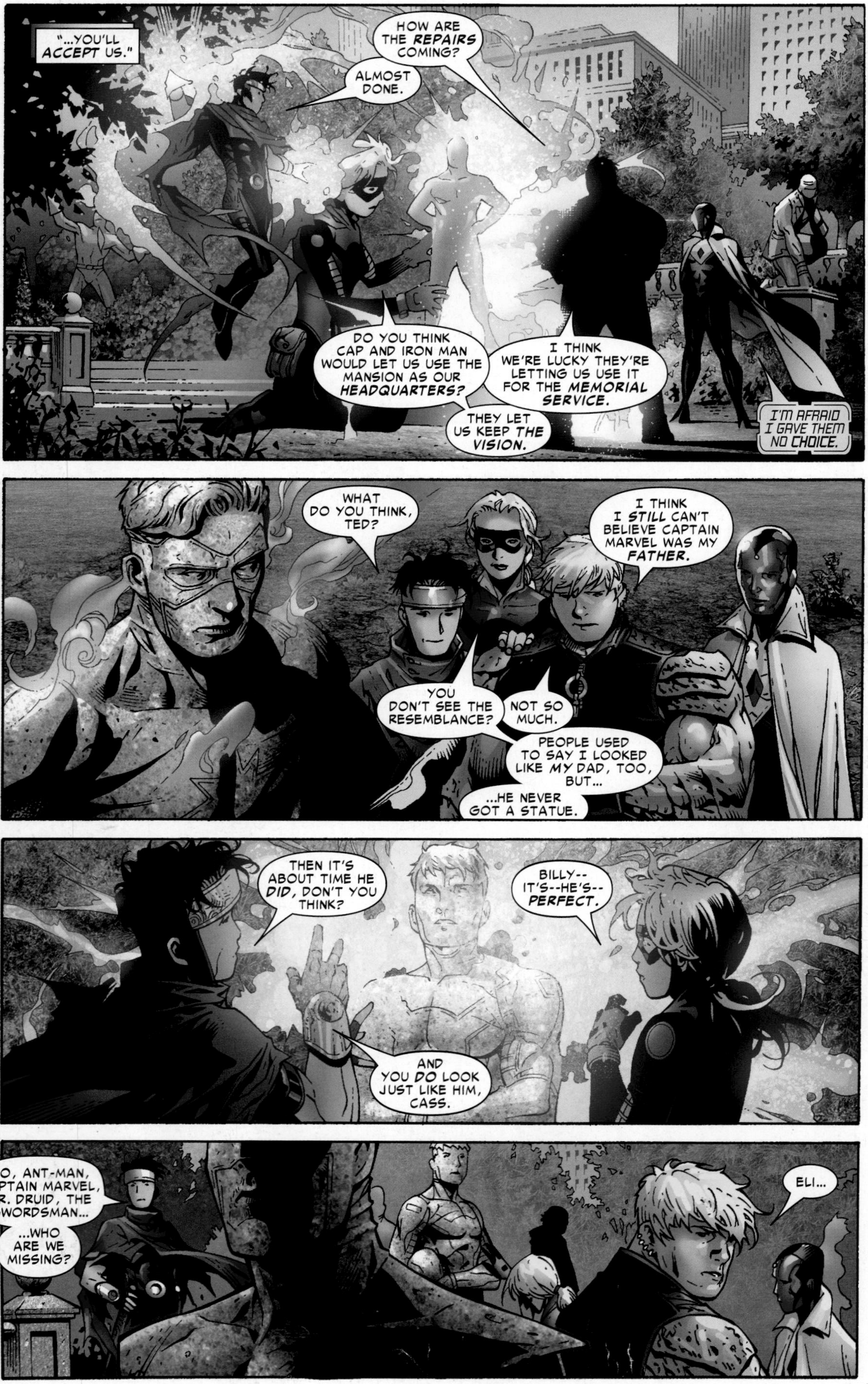

"...YOU'LL ACCEPT US."
HOW ARE THE REPAIRS COMING?
ALMOST DONE.
DO YOU THINK CAP AND IRON MAN WOULD LET US USE THE MANSION AS OUR HEADQUARTERS?
I THINK WE'RE LUCKY THEY'RE LETTING US USE IT FOR THE MEMORIAL SERVICE.
THEY LET US KEEP THE VISION.
I'M AFRAID I GAVE THEM NO CHOICE.
WHAT DO YOU THINK, TED?
I THINK I STILL CAN'T BELIEVE CAPTAIN MARVEL WAS MY FATHER.
YOU DON'T SEE THE RESEMBLANCE?
NOT SO MUCH.
PEOPLE USED TO SAY I LOOKED LIKE MY DAD, TOO, BUT...
...HE NEVER GOT A STATUE.
THEN IT'S ABOUT TIME HE DID, DON'T YOU THINK?
BILLY-- IT'S--HE'S-- PERFECT.
AND YOU DO LOOK JUST LIKE HIM, CASS.
SO, ANT-MAN, CAPTAIN MARVEL, DR. DRUID, THE SWORDSMAN...
...WHO ARE WE MISSING?
ELI...

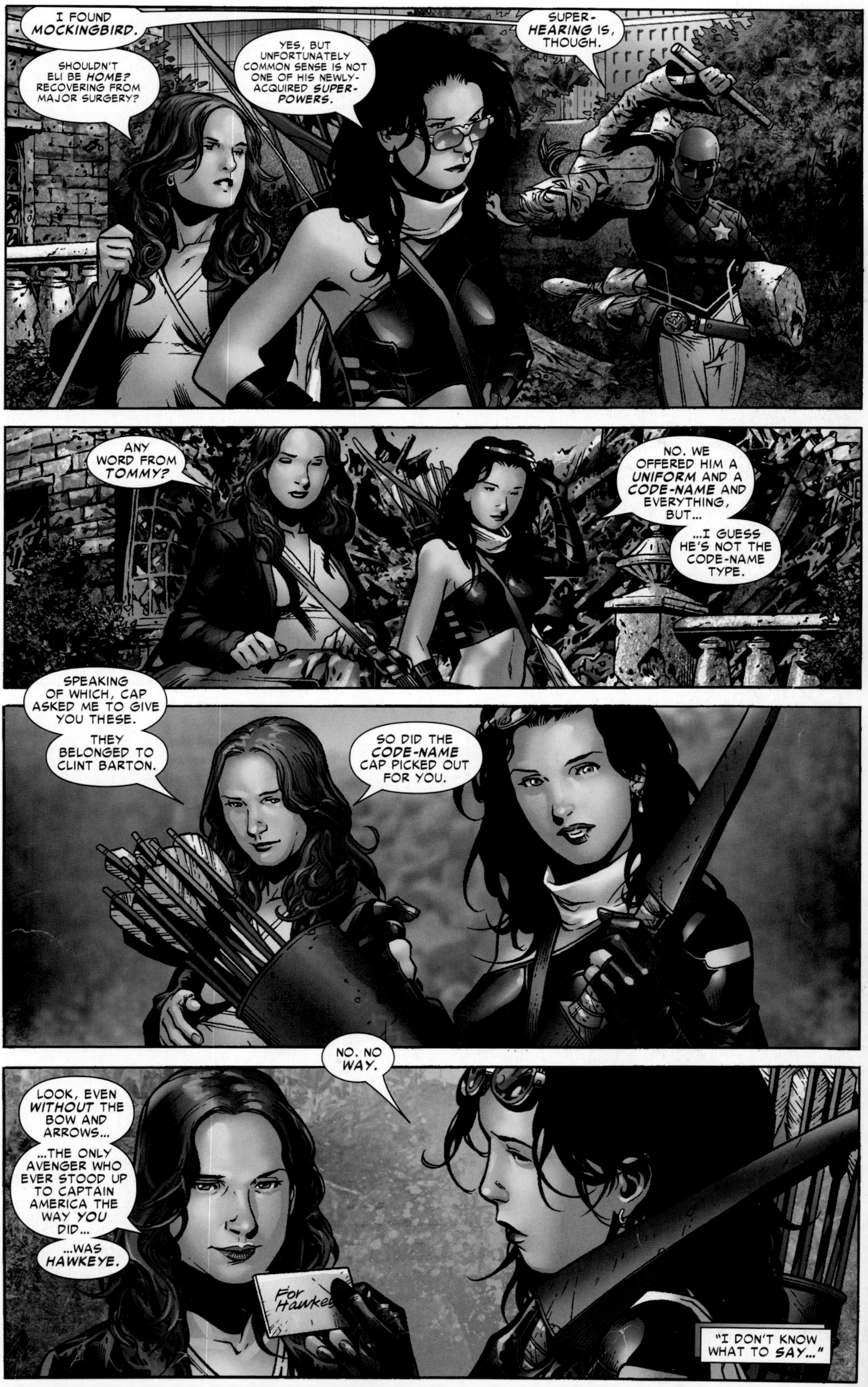
I FOUND MOCKINGBIRD.
SHOULDN'T ELI BE HOME? RECOVERING FROM MAJOR SURGERY?
YES, BUT UNFORTUNATELY COMMON SENSE IS NOT ONE OF HIS NEWLY-ACQUIRED SUPER-POWERS.
SUPER-HEARING IS, THOUGH.
ANY WORD FROM TOMMY?
NO. WE OFFERED HIM A UNIFORM AND A CODE-NAME AND EVERYTHING, BUT...
...I GUESS HE'S NOT THE CODE-NAME TYPE.
SPEAKING OF WHICH, CAP ASKED ME TO GIVE YOU THESE.
THEY BELONGED TO CLINT BARTON.
SO DID THE CODE-NAME CAP PICKED OUT FOR YOU.
NO. NO WAY.
LOOK, EVEN WITHOUT THE BOW AND ARROWS...
...THE ONLY AVENGER WHO EVER STOOD UP TO CAPTAIN AMERICA THE WAY YOU DID...
...WAS HAWKEYE.
"I DON'T KNOW WHAT TO SAY..."

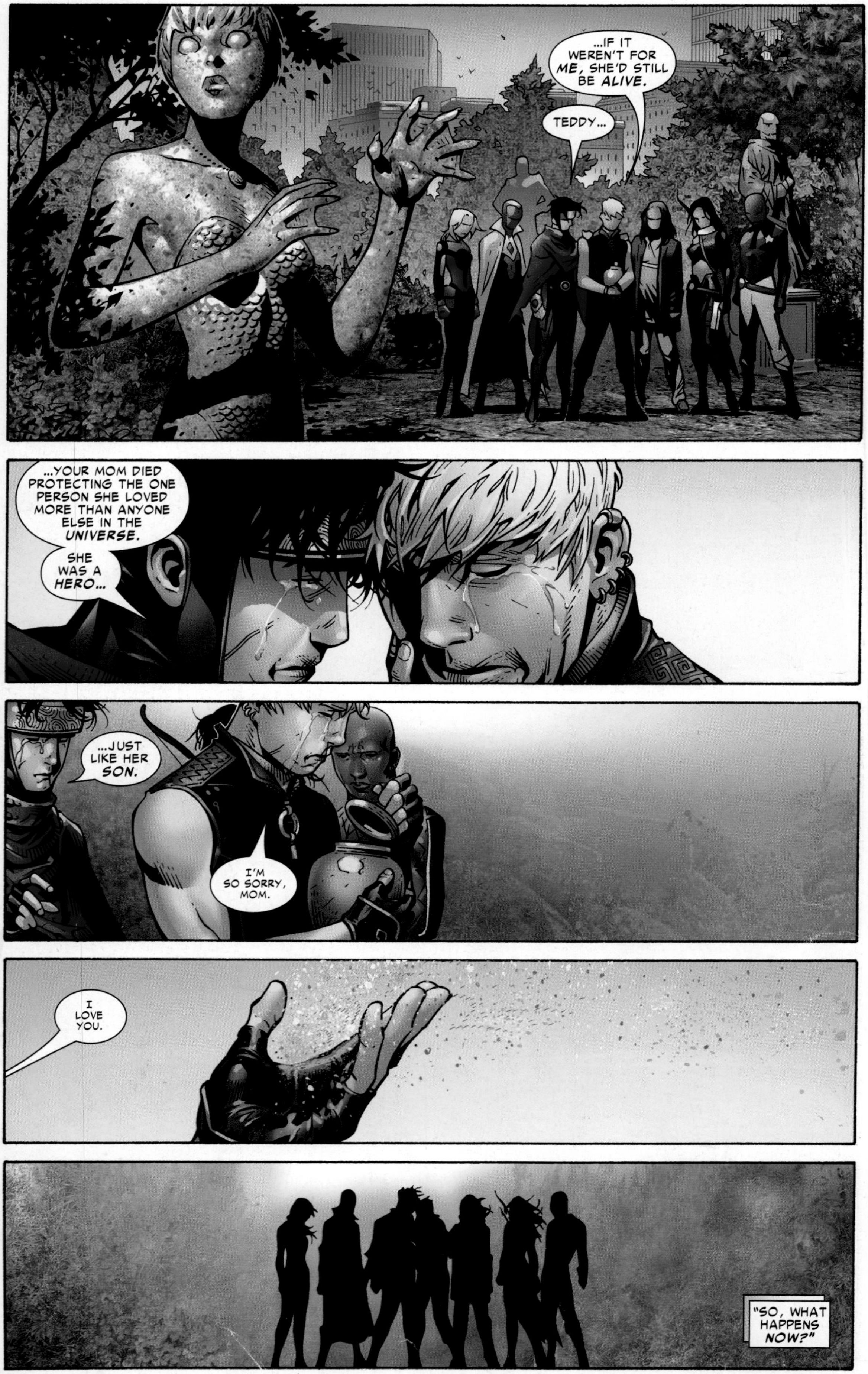

...IF IT WEREN'T FOR ME, SHE'D STILL BE ALIVE.
TEDDY...
...YOUR MOM DIED PROTECTING THE ONE PERSON SHE LOVED MORE THAN ANYONE ELSE IN THE UNIVERSE.
SHE WAS A HERO...
...JUST LIKE HER SON.
I'M SO SORRY, MOM.
I LOVE YOU.
"SO, WHAT HAPPENS NOW?"

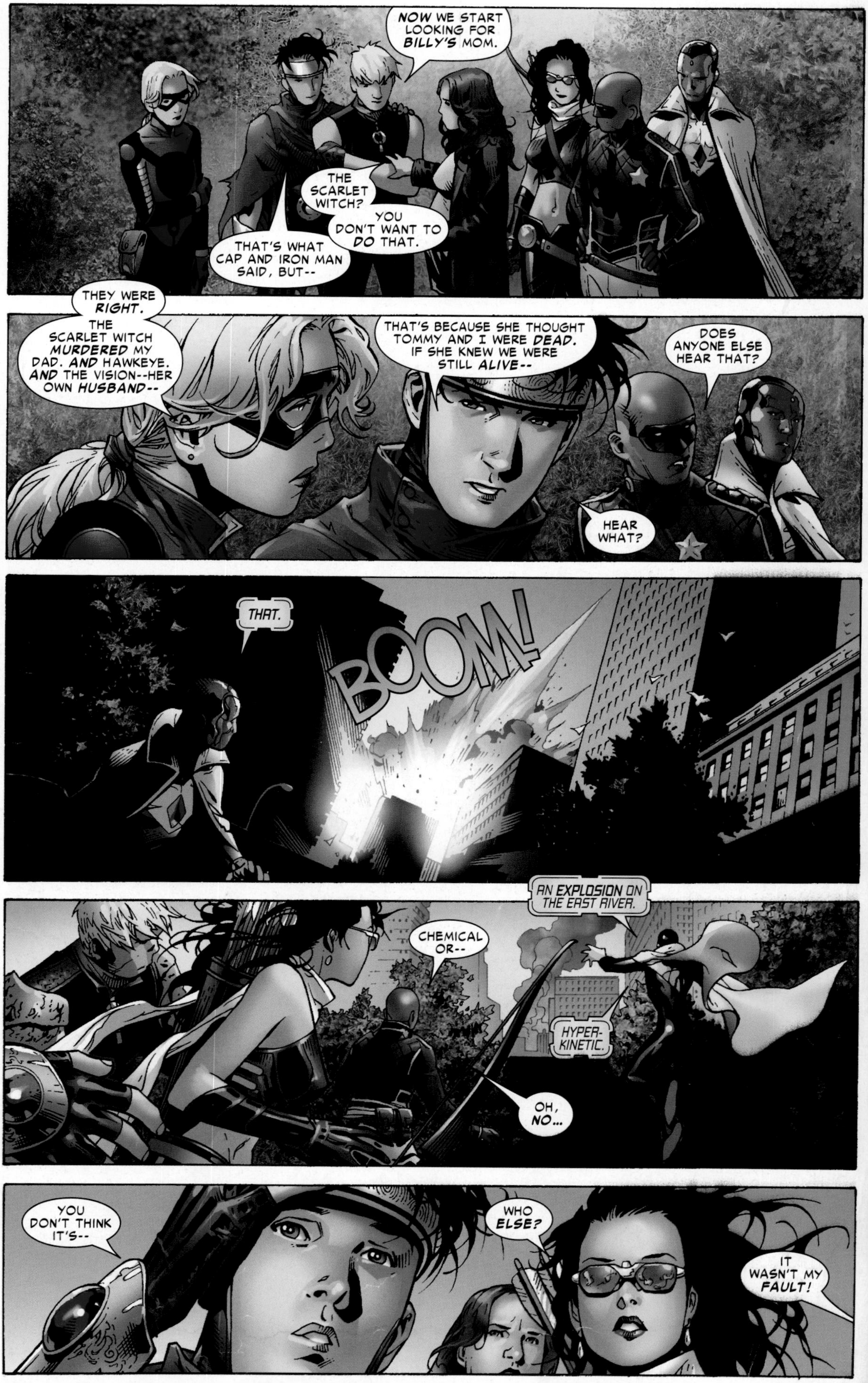
NOW WE START LOOKING FOR BILLY'S MOM.
THE SCARLET WITCH?
YOU DON'T WANT TO DO THAT.
THAT'S WHAT CAP AND IRON MAN SAID, BUT--
THEY WERE RIGHT. THE SCARLET WITCH MURDERED MY DAD. AND HAWKEYE. AND THE VISION--HER OWN HUSBAND--
THAT'S BECAUSE SHE THOUGHT TOMMY AND I WERE DEAD. IF SHE KNEW WE WERE STILL ALIVE--
DOES ANYONE ELSE HEAR THAT?
HEAR WHAT?
THAT.
BOOM!
AN EXPLOSION ON THE EAST RIVER.
CHEMICAL OR--
HYPER-KINETIC.
OH, NO...
YOU DON'T THINK IT'S--
WHO ELSE?
IT WASN'T MY FAULT!

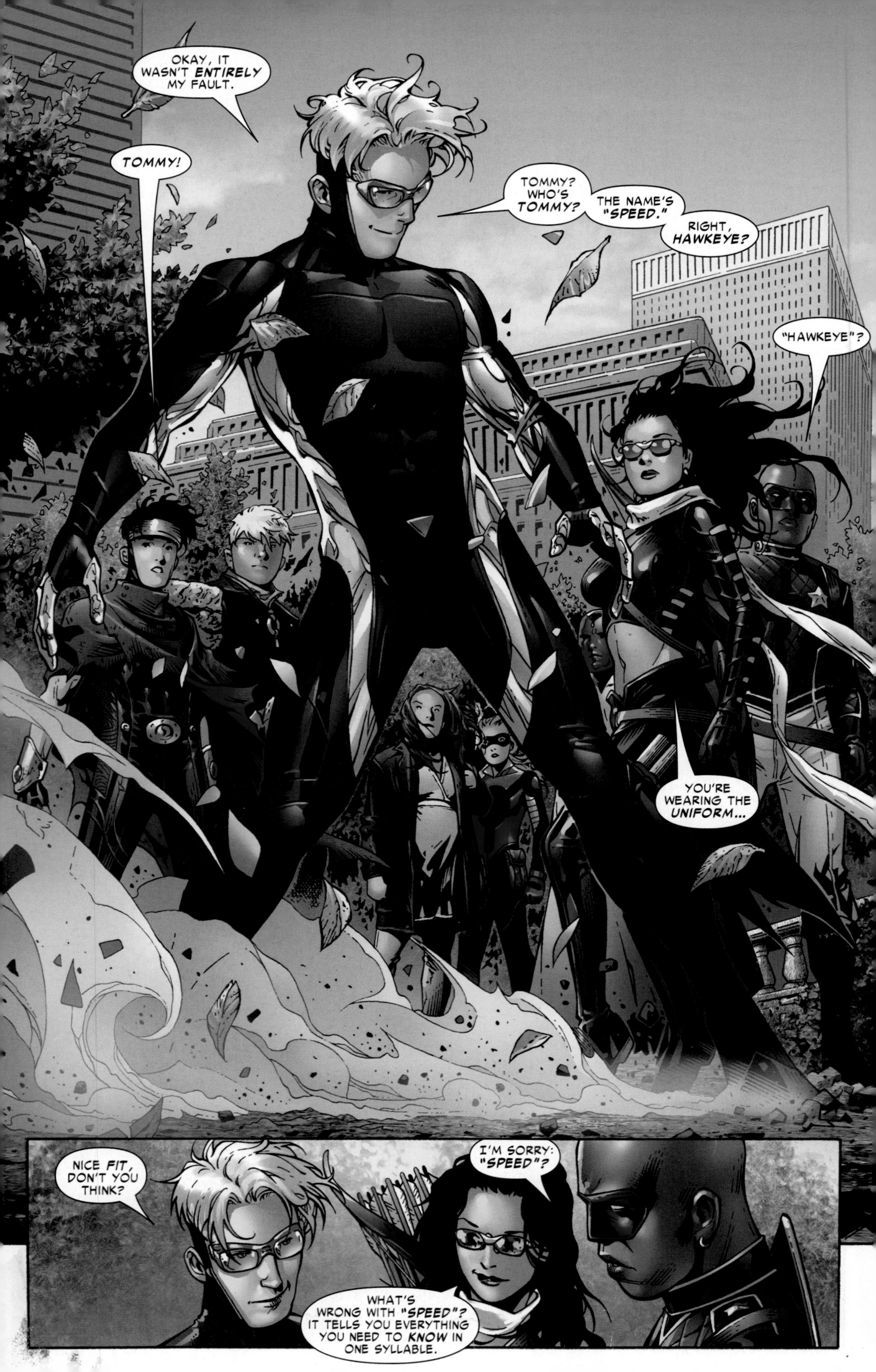

OKAY, IT WASN'T ENTIRELY MY FAULT.
TOMMY!
TOMMY? WHO'S TOMMY?
THE NAME'S "SPEED."
RIGHT, HAWKEYE?
"HAWKEYE"?
YOU'RE WEARING THE UNIFORM...
NICE FIT, DON'T YOU THINK?
I'M SORRY: "SPEED"?
WHAT'S WRONG WITH "SPEED"? IT TELLS YOU EVERYTHING YOU NEED TO KNOW IN ONE SYLLABLE.

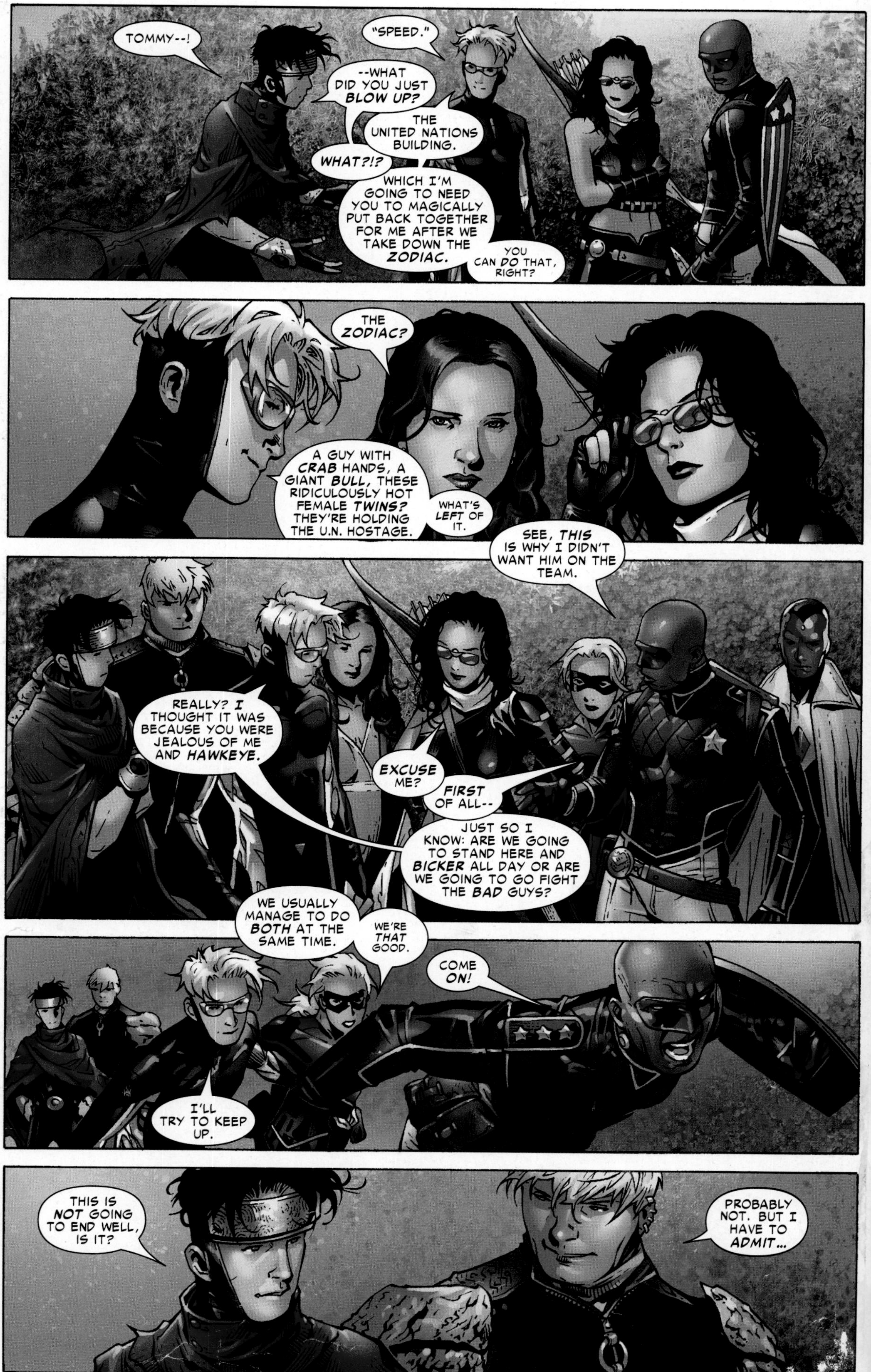
TOMMY--!
"SPEED."
--WHAT DID YOU JUST BLOW UP?
THE UNITED NATIONS BUILDING.
WHAT?!?
WHICH I'M GOING TO NEED YOU TO MAGICALLY PUT BACK TOGETHER FOR ME AFTER WE TAKE DOWN THE ZODIAC.
YOU CAN DO THAT, RIGHT?
THE ZODIAC?
A GUY WITH CRAB HANDS, A GIANT BULL, THESE RIDICULOUSLY HOT FEMALE TWINS? THEY'RE HOLDING THE U.N. HOSTAGE.
WHAT'S LEFT OF IT.
SEE, THIS IS WHY I DIDN'T WANT HIM ON THE TEAM.
REALLY? I THOUGHT IT WAS BECAUSE YOU WERE JEALOUS OF ME AND HAWKEYE.
EXCUSE ME?
FIRST OF ALL--
JUST SO I KNOW: ARE WE GOING TO STAND HERE AND BICKER ALL DAY OR ARE WE GOING TO GO FIGHT THE BAD GUYS?
WE USUALLY MANAGE TO DO BOTH AT THE SAME TIME.
WE'RE THAT GOOD.
COME ON!
I'LL TRY TO KEEP UP.
THIS IS NOT GOING TO END WELL, IS IT?
PROBABLY NOT. BUT I HAVE TO ADMIT...

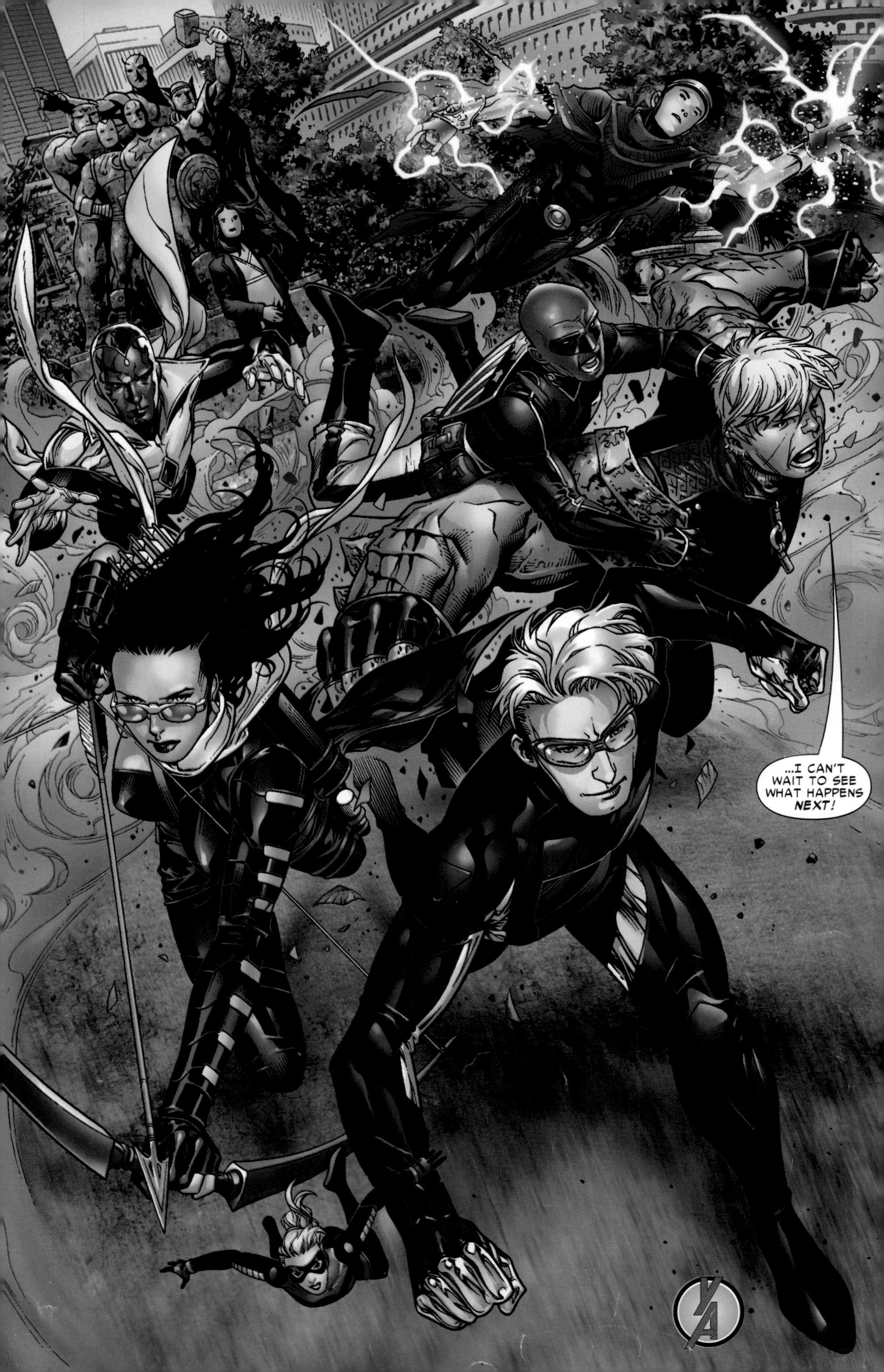
...I CAN'T WAIT TO SEE WHAT HAPPENS NEXT!

SPEED DESIGNS BY JIM CHEUNG

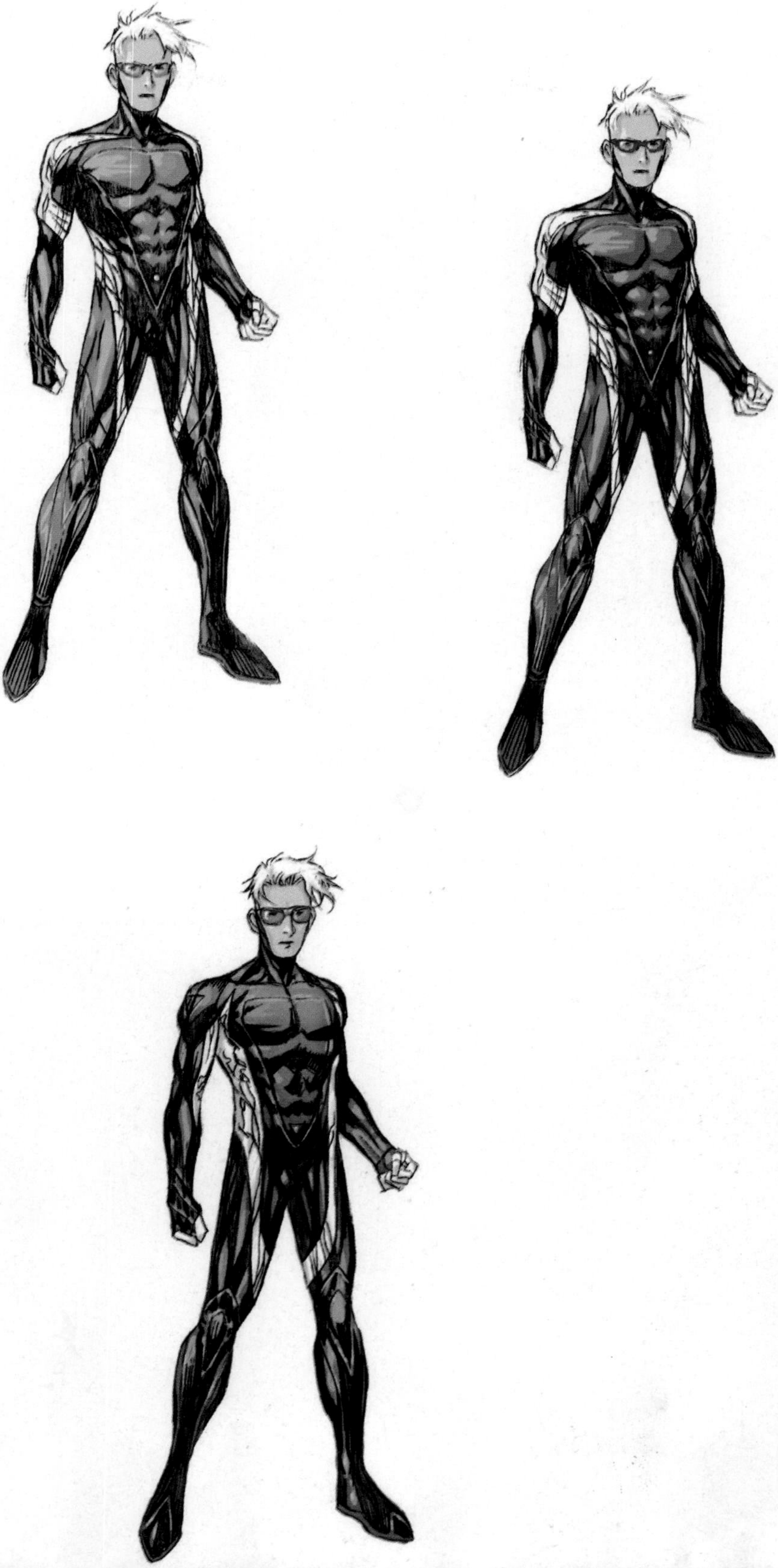

ISSUE #11 COVER SKETCHES BY JIM CHEUNG

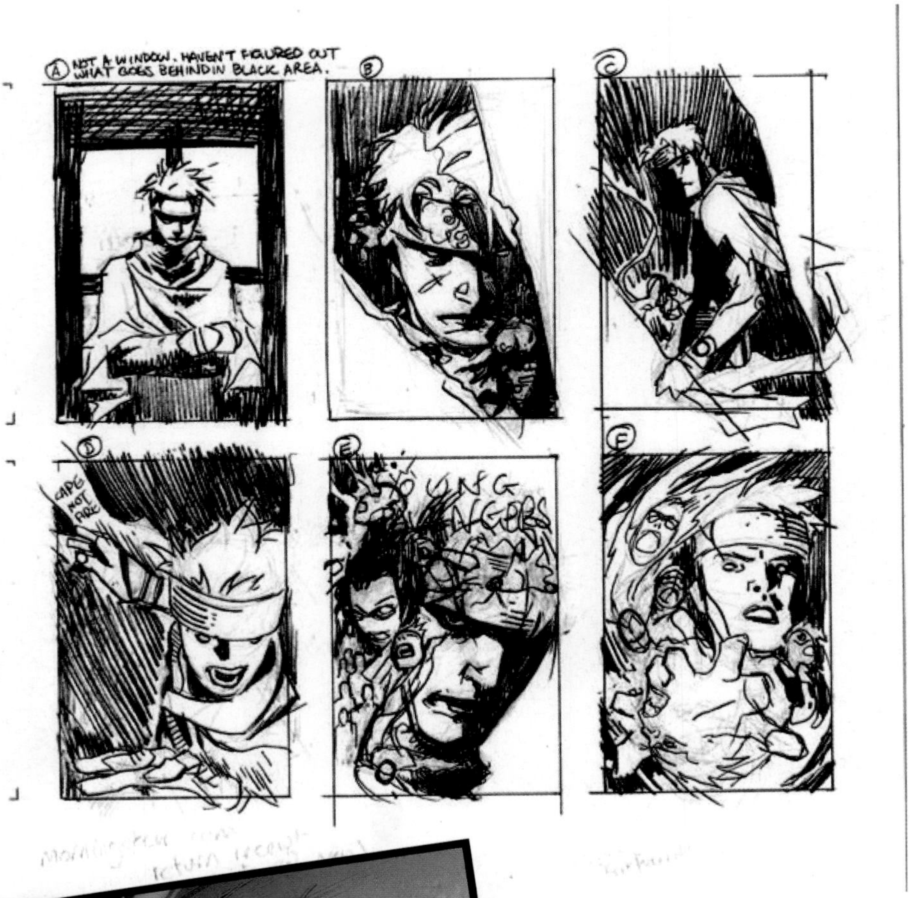
A
NOT A WINDOW. HAVEN'T FIGURED OUT WHAT GOES BEHIND IN BLACK AREA.
B
C
D
CAPE NOT FIRE
E
YOUNG AVENGERS
F

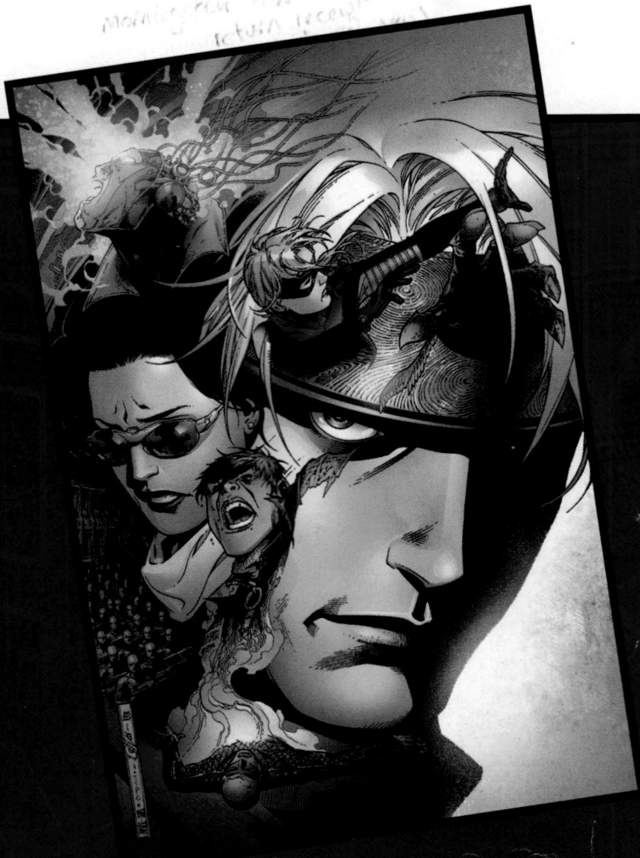

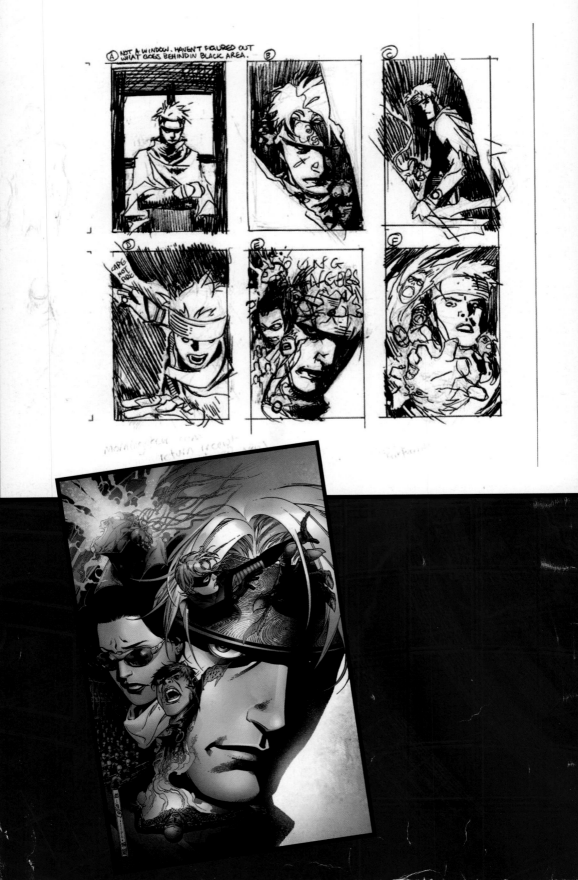

ISSUE #12 COVER SKETCHES BY JIM CHEUNG

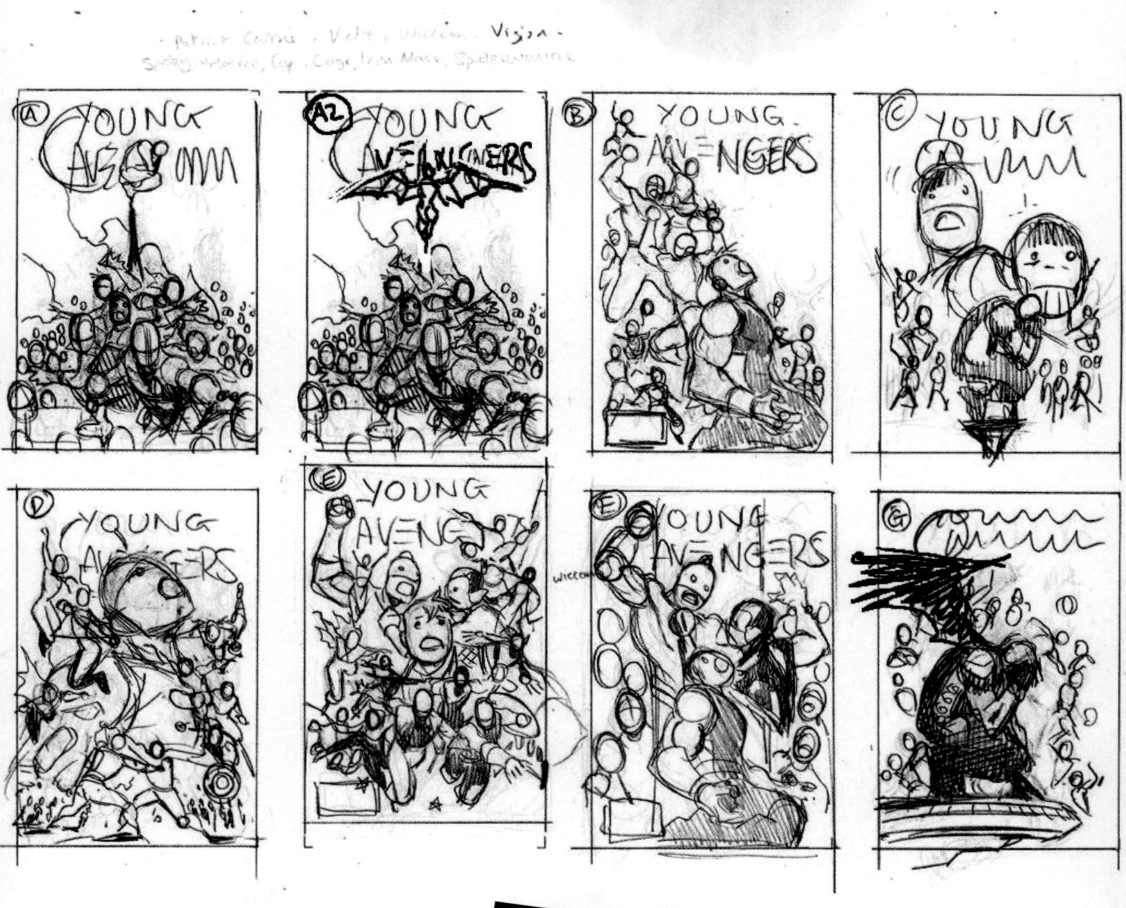
YOUNG AVENGERS

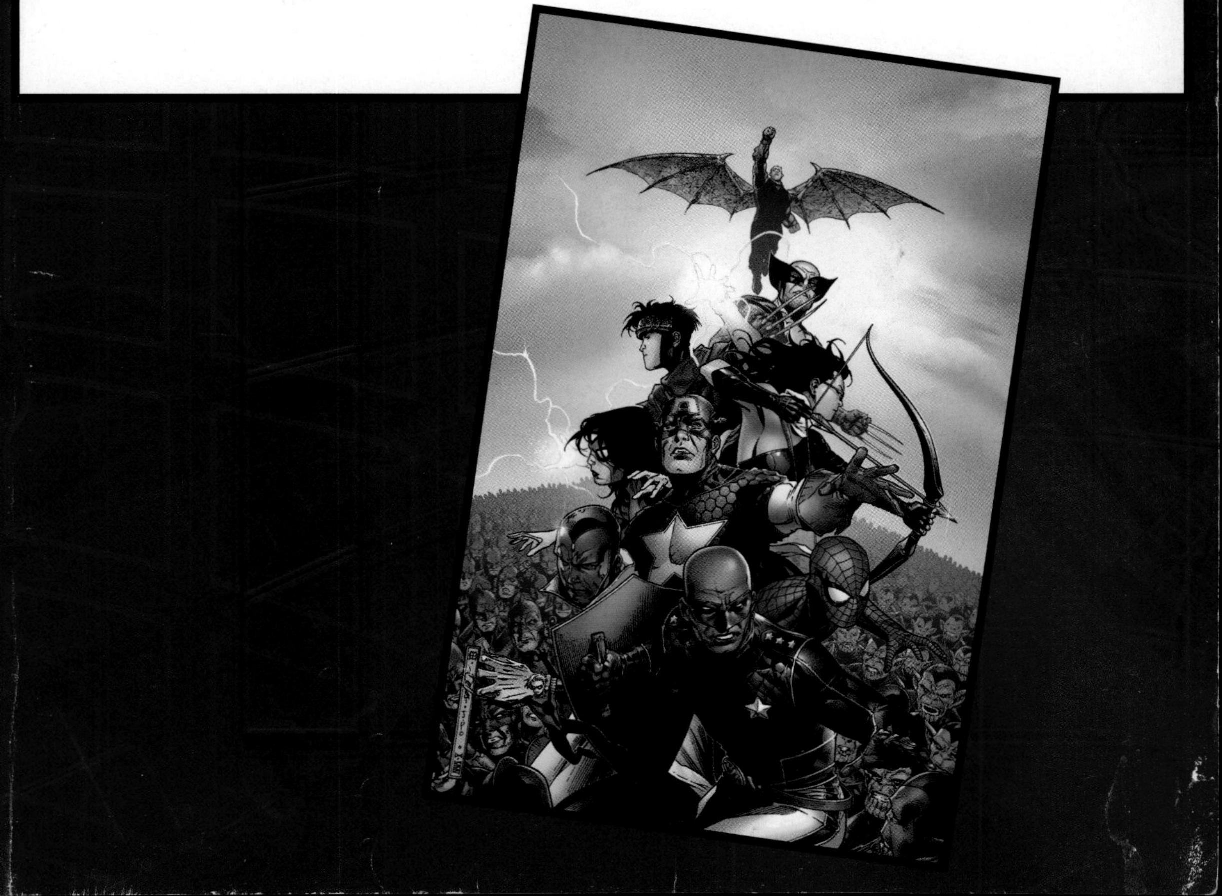